The Rise of African Slavery in the Americas

Why were the countries with the most developed institutions of individual freedom also the leaders in establishing the most exploitative system of slavery that the world has ever seen? In seeking to provide new answers to this question, *The Rise of African Slavery in the Americas* examines the development of the English Atlantic slave system in the context of European exchange with Africa and the Americas between 1650 and 1800. The book outlines a major African role in the evolution of the Atlantic societies before the nineteenth century and argues that the transatlantic slave trade was a result of African strength rather than African weakness. It also addresses changing patterns of group identity to account for the racial basis of slavery in the early modern Atlantic world. Exploring the paradox of the concurrent development of slavery (for peoples of African descent) and freedom (for peoples of European descent) in the European domains, *The Rise of African Slavery in the Americas* provides a fresh interpretation of this difficult historical problem.

D1231285

The Rise of African Slavery in the Americas

DAVID ELTIS

Queen's University

CAMBRIDGE
UNIVERSITY PRESS

PUBLISHED BY THE PRESS SYNDICATE OF THE UNIVERSITY OF CAMBRIDGE
The Pitt Building, Trumpington Street, Cambridge, United Kingdom

CAMBRIDGE UNIVERSITY PRESS
The Edinburgh Building, Cambridge CB2 2RU, UK   http://www.cup.cam.ac.uk
40 West 20th Street, New York, NY 10011-4211, USA   http://www.cup.org
10 Stamford Road, Oakleigh, Melbourne 3166, Australia
Ruiz de Alarcón 13, 28014 Madrid, Spain

First published 2000

Printed in the United States of America

Typeface Sabon 10/12 pt.   *System* LATEX2$_\varepsilon$ [TB]

A catalog record for this book is available from the British Library.

Library of Congress Cataloging-in-Publication Data
Eltis, David, 1950–
    Europeans and the rise of African slavery in the Americas / David
Eltis.
        p.   cm.
    Includes bibliographical references.
        1. Slavery – America – History.   2. Slave trade – America – History.
    3. Colonies – America – History.   4. Great Britain – Colonies – America –
    History.   I. Title.
    HT1048.E47   2000
    306.3′62′097 – dc21   99-13352
                                                                                CIP

ISBN 0 521 65231 6 hardback
ISBN 0 521 65548 X paperback

To Suzan

Contents

List of Tables

List of Maps

Preface

Slavery was an accepted element in human society for so long and reached its high point as an economic system so recently that the strong and continuing interest in the subject seems only proper. While the wrongs of slavery are among the few certainties in a postmodern world, in this, as in other areas of social activity, human behaviour and contradiction are inseparable. The aim of this work is to highlight the tensions that emerge as people pursue goals, moral or material, that cannot all be achieved at once or are at odds with some aspect of their individual and shared systems of belief. Chapter 1 begins with the puzzle of slavery and freedom emerging from the same roots in western society, and the volume ends with the morally ambiguous consequences of the abolition of coerced labor and the transportation system that supplied it. Historians should attempt to put some distance between scholarship and the values of the society in which he or she functions. We have more than enough evidence to condemn what happened in the past. No one who is aware of the below-deck conditions on a slave ship, how little these changed over three centuries, and how Europeans never subjected other Europeans to such an experience can fail to appreciate this point. Yet if condemn on the basis of modern values is all we do, then we are never likely to understand the past. At the very least, condemnation of wrong thinking in earlier societies should emerge from circumspect reflection on how present attitudes will appear to posterity. Nor will this dilemma disappear in the future. It is only human to identify with those who suffered. However, the people who inflicted the suffering, in this case owners of slaves, were perhaps less different from ourselves than late-twentieth-century sensibilities would have us believe. Not only have almost all peoples been both slaves *and* slaveholders at some point in their histories, but there are also many historical examples of individuals having been both slave and slaveholder at different points in their lives.

The attempt here to write Atlantic history rather than the history of a particular nation or group has greatly increased the author's debt to others. The community of scholars interested in the slave trade undoubtedly share information and expertise to a greater degree than those who labor in other parts of the discipline – which helps explain why collective knowledge of the subject has increased so rapidly in recent years. Scholars have made available their archival data to each other and provided tips on new sources in a way which should be a model for all historians. I am neither an Africanist nor a Caribbean specialist and have drawn heavily on the knowledge of those who are entitled to these labels.

Robin Blackburn, John Coatsworth, Peter Coclanis, Seymour Drescher, Farley Grubb, David Howard, Wim Klooster, Robin Law, Joseph C. Miller, Ugo Nwokeji, Kwabena Opare-Akurang, Stuart Schwartz, John Thornton, and Michael Turner have provided aid at critical points in the preparation of this work. Herbert S. Klein and Pieter Emmer capped many exchanges of ideas over the past decade with several pages of commentary on an earlier version of the manuscript. Within my department Don Akenson read Chapter 9 with great care and provided extensive commentary. Robert Malcolmson, James Pritchard, and Robert Shenton have read draft chapters or shared ideas and sources over the years. Discussions with Mary Turner have provided a base for many of the arguments presented here. With two colleagues I have worked closely indeed over the past five years, to the point where I am no longer sure which idea or source is mine and which is theirs. David Richardson and Stephen D. Behrendt have toiled with me on the slave trade in Hull, England, Cambridge, Massachusetts, and indeed several other locations on both sides of the Atlantic. Their knowledge of the primary sources of the slave trade, their good sense, and their friendship are deeply appreciated.

As with countless other manuscripts in this and related fields, Stanley L. Engerman provided a never-ending stream of questions to be asked, references to be pursued, obscurities in the text to be eliminated, and constant support. Counterfactual exercises usually conclude that no single innovation or individual has much impact. Yet the historiography of slavery, and, more generally labor and migration in the pre-twentieth-century Atlantic world, would not have been the same without the combination of Stan's own work and his tireless help to other scholars. This book would have been very different.

Earlier versions of some chapters were presented at seminars held at the Institute of Historical Studies and the Institute of Commonwealth Studies, both of the University of London; at the University of Pennsylvania; W. E. B. Du Bois Institute, Harvard University; the Department of Economic and Social History, University of Hull, England; the Netherlands Institute for Advanced Study, Wassenar; the Center for the Study of Freedom, University of Washington; Tulane University, New Orleans; and at Queen's

University. Parts of Chapter 1 have appeared in Stanley L. Engerman (ed.), *The Terms of Labour* (Stanford, Calif., 1999), pp. 25–49; parts of Chapter 2 in Jan Lucassen and Leo Lucassen (eds.), *Migration, Migration History, History: Old Paradigms and New Perspectives* (Bern, 1997), pp. 87–109; earlier versions of Chapter 3 in *American Historical Review*, 98(1993):1399–1423; of Chapter 5 in *Explorations in Economic History*, 32(1995):465–84 (co-authored with David Richardson); and of Chapter 8 in *Journal of Economic History*, 55(1995):321–38. I would like to thank the publishers of these volumes for permission to reproduce the relevant excerpts. Finally, I gratefully acknowledge the financial support of the Social Sciences and Humanities Research Council of Canada in the form of two standard research grants during the years 1989 to 1995, as well as several travel and research awards from the Du Bois Institute, Harvard University, the University of Hull, the United Kingdom, and my own university, Queen's, at Kingston.

Abbreviations

Add ms	Additional manuscripts, British Library.
CSPCS	Sainsbury, W. Noel, ed. *Calendar of State Papers, Colonial Series.* Vols. 1–10. London, 1860–78.
CSPDS	*Calendar of State Papers, Domestic Series.* Vols. 1–10. London, 1860–78.
Custom Books	"A Coppie Journal of Entries made In the Custome House of Barbados," Beginning August 11, 1664 to August 10, 1665; and "A Coppie Journal of Entries made In the Custome House of Barbados," Beginning August 11, 1665 to April 22, 1667.
TSTD	David Eltis, Stephen D. Behrendt, David Richardson, and Herbert S. Klein, *The Trans-Atlantic Slave Trade: A Database on CD-ROM* (Cambridge, 1999)
Voyage id	Unique number of voyage to be found in David Eltis, Stephen D. Behrendt, David Richardson, and Herbert S. Klein, *The Trans-Atlantic Slave Trade: A Database on CD-ROM* (Cambridge, 1999).

1

Slavery and Freedom in the Early Modern World

BY 1700, the two European nations generally regarded as having the most advanced capitalist culture, England and the Netherlands, had moved further away than any country in Europe from subjecting their citizens to overtly forced labor.[1] Slave ships brought the occasional slave back to England and advertisements offering slaves for sale were seen in Liverpool and Bristol newspapers.[2] It is nevertheless inconceivable that London, Liverpool, Nantes, or Amsterdam could have received complete cargoes of Africans on slave ships to be sold in public markets, as Lisbon and Cadiz did throughout the eighteenth century.[3] Yet these northern European cities were in countries with the harshest and most closed systems of exploiting enslaved non-Europeans in the Americas. Further, England and the Netherlands came to

[1] For the Dutch case see Herbert H. Rowen, "The Dutch Republic and the Idea of Freedom," in David Wootton, *Republicanism, Liberty and Commercial Society, 1649–1776* (Stanford, 1994), pp. 310–40, esp. 336–7.

[2] F. O. Shyllon, *Black Slaves in Britain* (London, 1974), pp. 3–16.

[3] The largest example of slaves consigned to England, significantly in the mid-seventeenth century, is an instruction from London merchants to a slave ship captain to bring fifteen or twenty 15-year-old Gambian slaves to London after a slaving voyage to Barbados (Letter dated Dec. 9, 1651, in Historical Manuscripts Commission, Thirteenth Report, *The Manuscripts of the Duke of Portland*, 2 vols. (London, 1893), 2:29.) TSTD contains six voyages beginning in England and carrying (or intending to carry) complete cargoes of slaves into Lisbon in the mideighteenth century. For French attitudes, much closer to the Anglo-Dutch than the Iberian model, see Sue Peabody, *'There are no slaves in France': The Political Culture of Race and Slavery in the Ancien Regime* (New York, 1996), pp. 3–22. It should be noted, however, that slave ships from Africa supplied French galleys with slaves throughout the seventeenth century, some arriving at Marseilles and some in Northern France. On this see Clarence J. Munford, *The Black Ordeal of Slavery and Slave Trading in the French West Indies, 1625–1715*, 3 vols. (Lewiston, NY, 1991), 1:144, 165–6, 170.

dominate Europe's relations with the rest of the world: the Dutch specializing in Asia, and the English in the Americas.

The contrast between Europe's social institutions and values at home and their counterparts in European-controlled overseas territories became acute in the seventeenth century and forms the focus of the present work. The major issues are simply stated. First, why would Europeans revive slavery at the time of Columbian contact, when the institution had disappeared from large parts of Europe, and then, three centuries later, begin to suppress it? Second, why would that slavery be located almost exclusively in the Americas? Third, why would the slaves in this system be exclusively of non-European descent? The search for answers amounts to nothing less than an attempt to explain the shaping of the Atlantic world in the seventeenth and eighteenth centuries and beyond. The starting point, as we have seen, is the differences between western and non-western social institutions and value systems – especially as these relate to slavery.

The argument in this and succeeding chapters touches on large issues in western history, of which only part relate to contact among Europe, Africa, and the Americas. It was not just European power and resources that made overseas expansion possible but also the subcontinent's odd (in relative global terms) social structures and values. Chapter 2 examines the genesis of these and their implications for European expansion and migration, both European free and African coerced. Yet, as this discussion hints, European behavior in the early modern Atlantic was not that of unbridled and profit-maximizing capitalists. An inquiry into deep-seated cultural attitudes on the part of both Europeans and non-Europeans provides just as much insight into the creation of the new Atlantic world as a simple search for the quest for profits. Chapters 3 and 4 assess the manifestation of these attitudes in relation to ethnicity and gender, respectively, the former defined as the way in which peoples identify themselves. Gender constructions differed markedly in Europe and Africa and these differences had a profound effect on who went (or in the African case got taken) to the Americas. Economic impulses operated within the cultural framework. Economics is given center stage in Chapter 5 as the focus switches to an examination of English dominance of the slave trade and, through that, much of the Atlantic.

Chapters 6 through 8 explore the realities of African power or, alternatively, the limits on what Europeans could do on the African coast. Just as economic motivations were heavily circumscribed by culture, so European aspirations were subject to the countervailing forces of non-Europeans. The Atlantic world of 1800 was as much a product of African as European influences and not just in the sense of Africans providing labor or alternative cultural inputs. Initially, at least, the economic and political power of African states was more important than these tangible factors. Chapters 6 and 7 examine the African-imposed limits on European expansion and the consequences of this for the slave trade and the Americas. After the epidemiological disaster that overtook aboriginal Americans, what happened in much of the Americas was the result of compromises between Africans and Europeans. Chapter 8 examines the consequences of African-European compromise in economic terms by taking a fresh look at slavery in the early English Caribbean and how it differed from slavery elsewhere. As in Chapter 5, the focus initially is on what made it possible to increase the level of exploitation and per capita output.

Chapters 9, 10, and 11 evaluate the impact of the plantation system on the Atlantic world. How did groups of overseas Europeans and Africans come to see themselves, and what were the consequences of shifts in self-perception for the long-run viability of the system? Historians have put more stress on the economic consequences of slavery in the Americas than they have on the patterns of identity and cultural preconceptions that made it possible. The offshore Atlantic sugar complex notwithstanding, plantation slavery in the Americas and the slave trade that supported it had no precedents in Africa or Europe. Experience of the system was bound to affect more than the economic sphere. Chapter 9 returns to the identity issue taken up in Chapter 3 and charts the shifts in self-perceptions as a result of interaction among peoples of Africans and European descent around the Atlantic. Chapter 10 evaluates some impacts of European overseas expansion on Europe itself. While much of this reflects the preoccupations of the current historiography on the contributions of overseas lands to European economic development, this penultimate chapter nevertheless sees the more important impact on Europe (and of Europe on the Caribbean) as being on identity and values rather than on capital accumulation and income. Finally, a short concluding chapter draws out the longer-run implications of European expansion and establishes links with the emergence of the movement to abolish the slave trade and slavery in the late eighteenth century. The ultimate aim is to explore the slave-free paradox that suffused the early modern Atlantic world and in the process to increase our understanding of that world as it emerged in the nineteenth century.

The slave-free paradox began to emerge as Europeans reached the Atlantic islands and began to revive slavery. It strengthened in the aftermath of Columbian contact but developed fully only when the Dutch and English rose to preeminence. It was not apparent to those primarily responsible for creating and maintaining it. Indeed, if it had been, then the paradox would probably not have endured. However, some awareness was expressed in 1772 when a well-known commentator of the contemporary European scene, Arthur Young, stated that only 5 percent of the world's population lived under conditions of freedom. All Africans, all Asians, and most of those in the Americas were, if not under slavery, at least unfree. Adam Smith had a similar view.

Leaving aside for the moment questions of definition of *freedom* and *slavery*, Young's opinion is not to be dismissed as merely chauvinism or the class bias of a propertied Englishman. Similar assertions – expressed without Young's obsessive precision – were common in popular eighteenth-century literature.[4] Moreover, as late as the 1850s, newspapers in the southern United States could argue that "Slavery black or white is necessary" and that free labor was an unfortunate "little experiment made in a corner of western Europe" that "has been from the beginning, a cruel failure."[5] By the midnineteenth century, unlike in Young's day, those living in the part of the world that Young considered free saw abolition of slavery everywhere as a major issue. Indeed the ending of slavery was a quintessentially western cause. People everywhere have normally tried to avoid or reject slave status for themselves, and non-western societies, especially Islamic, extensively debated issues of which persons are eligible for slavery. But the concept of abolition – the idea that a society should be free of slavery – evolved first in western Europe and the European Americas and even there only after 1750. Even Haiti was arguably a western phenomenon – the society that emerged from the revolution having more in common with Europe than with Africa.[6] In no non-western countries did abolition emerge independently as official state policy, and no non-western intellectual tradition showed signs of questioning slavery per se, as opposed to questioning the appropriateness of slavery for specific groups.[7] There would be little basis for writing a non-western

4 Seymour Drescher, *Capitalism and Antislavery: British Mobilization in Comparative Perspective* (London, 1986), pp. 16–17.
5 Russel Blaine Nye, *Fettered Freedom: Civil Liberties and the Slavery Controversy, 1830–60* (East Lansing, Mich. 1963), pp. 304, 308, 309. Quotes are from southern newspapers, cited in Robert W. Fogel, *Without Consent or Contract: The Rise and Fall of American Slavery* (New York, 1989), p. 343.
6 Private property in land, nuclear family, absence of strong kinship structures – to mention just a few – though there is a strong tendency in the modern literature to stress the African contribution to the making of revolution as opposed to its consequences. See Carolyn E. Fick, *The Making of Haiti: The Saint Domingue Revolution from Below* (Knoxville, 1990).
7 Stanley L. Engerman, "Coerced and Free Labor: Property Rights and the Development of the Labor Force," *Explorations in Entrepreneurial History*, 29 (1992):3; Martin A. Klein, "Introduction: Modern European Expansion and Traditional Servitude in Africa and Asia," in Martin A. Klein (ed.), *Breaking the Chains: Slavery, Bondage and Emancipation in Modern Africa and Asia* (Madison, Wis., 1993), pp. 3–4. The attempt of Caliph Muhammad Bello of Sokoto to preserve Muslims from slavery in the early nineteenth century is seen as evidence of a non-western abolition tradition. See Humphrey John Fisher, "A Muslim William Wilberforce? The Sokoto *Jihad* as Anti-Slavery Crusade: An Enquiry into Historical Causes," in Serge Daget (ed.), *De la traite á l'esclavage du XVIIIe au XIXéme siècle: Actes du colloque international sur la traite des noirs, 1985* (Nantes, 1988), pp. 537–55; and Paul Lovejoy, "Partial Perspectives and Abolition: The Sokoto *Jihad* and the Transatlantic Slave Trade, 1804–37," (Unpublished paper, 1998). The latter argues that "concern over the rights of Muslims was comparable to the European preoccupation with 'the rights of man,'" but there can be no doubt the Islamic debates were over who should be slaves, not

counterpart to David Brion Davis' 1966 book, *The Problem of Slavery in Western Culture.*[8]

But if slavery did not exist in the England of Young's time, how long was it since it had disappeared and how extensive was the freedom that Young counterposed? Both slavery and serfdom had been part of the social fabric of early medieval England, with just over 10 percent of the population classified as slaves in 1086.[9] Even as these institutions died, new forms of compulsion evolved. The Statute of Laborers (1350–1) forced all persons not in a recognised occupation to serve in husbandry and the only change before its repeal in the nineteenth century was the addition of a lower age limit of twelve in the Elizabethan Statute of Artificers.[10] A servant was normally bound to the master for a year, and indeed the transatlantic indentured servitude arrangement was a modification of this English institution. Like slave owners, masters habitually complained of servant insubordination but they nevertheless held large powers. Physical punishment was unexceptional and, more important, the law required that servants carry testimonials with them to new masters as evidence of good behaviour, a potential route to renewed serfdom. If we accept Gregory King's taxonomy, 40 percent of the English population lived in service to others, and those not fortunate enough to attain such status were vagrants. From 1572 the definition of a vagabond was simply "anyone refusing to work for reasonable wages."[11] Vagrants were subject to compulsory labor on pain of whipping and imprisonment.[12]

the existence of slavery per se (Ehud R. Toledano, "Ottoman Concepts of Slavery in the Period of Reform, 1830s–1880s," in Klein, *Breaking the Chains*, 37–63; John Hunwick, "Islamic Law and Polemics over Black Slavery in Morocco and West Africa," *Princeton Papers*, 7 (1998):43–68).

[8]   (Ithaca, N.Y. 1966).

[9]   John McDonald and Graeme D. Snooks, *Domesday Economy: A New Approach to Anglo-Norman History* (Oxford, 1986), pp. 16–17. Edward J. Mitchell, 'Servitude in Early England: Alternative Economic Explanations' (unpublished manuscript, 1969) estimates 9 percent.

[10] Ann Kussmaul, *Servants in Husbandry in Early Modern England*, (Cambridge, 1981), 166–7.

[11] C. S. L. Davies, "Slavery and Protector Somerset: The Vagrancy Act of 1847," *Economic History Review*, 19 (1966):535. For a modern revision of King see Peter H. Lindert and Jeffrey G. Williamson, "Revising England's Social Tables, 1688–1913," *Explorations in Economic History*, 19 (1982):385–408.

[12] George Meriton, *A Guide for constables, churchwardens, overseers of the poor* ... (London, 1669). There is of course the issue familiar to students of slavery on the frequency with which these extreme measures were invoked. According to the widely read Josiah Child in London, vagrants could beg undisturbed for many months, and the whipping and expulsion of the poor from a parish was rarely carried out "not one justice of twenty (through pity or other cause) will do it ...." *A New Discourse of Trade* (London, 1679), Chapter 2. Those meeting the legal definition of vagrants, and therefore liable to whipping and forcible relocation, probably comprised a small fraction of the mobile poor. The definition varied

Two justices of the peace could force parish children into a household for an apprenticeship term. Men were likely to be press-ganged.[13] In 1655, seventy-two prisoners from the Salisbury rising of the previous year were sold in Barbados without due process.[14] In Scotland, colliers and collieries were sold together in the aftermath of a 1606 act generally credited with the reinstatement of serfdom. Valuations for the serfs were provided separately and with as full appreciation for the discounted present value of future labor as in sales of West Indian plantations with slaves. The system had a life-span similar to slavery in the British Americas. The first Emancipation Act passed in Westminster freed Scottish miners in 1775, not West Indian slaves, and the refusal of the masters to cooperate was such that further legislation was required in 1799.[15] These anticipated the 1833 and 1838 acts aimed at the colonies by about as much as the 1606 act had preceded the establishment of chattel slavery in Barbados.

Yet despite Scottish serfdom, the legal powers of masters, press-gangs, and vagrancy laws, in the third quarter of the eighteenth century labor relations were much closer to modern conceptions of free labor than slavery. Moreover, even in Young's time, western exceptionalism was not of recent origin and neither was it shared equally by all regions of western Europe. The observations of Smith and others would have had almost the same validity if they had been made three centuries earlier, at the time of the Columbian contact. There were certainly more slaves in southern Europe in 1492 than in 1772 – slaves even comprised one in ten of the population of Lisbon in the 1460s. However, north and northwestern Europe had been free of full chattel slavery since the Middle Ages. Indeed the incidence of chattel slavery

over time and place, not least because parish officials and justices of the peace had considerable latitude in interpreting the law (Paul A. Slack, "Vagrants and Vagrancy in England, 1598–1664," *Economic History Review*, 27 (1974):362–8). Moreover, recent research has not disturbed Dorothy Marshall's assessment that "the number of persons moved was not large enough to have much effect on the mobility of labor. The number of removal orders obtained and enforced never seems to have exceeded a few tens of thousands per year for the whole 15,000 parishes and townships involved" ["The Old Poor Law, 1662–1795," *Economic History Review*, 1 (1937):39].

13 Dorothy George, *London Life in the Eighteenth Century* (London, 1925), pp. 226, 259. Nicholas Rogers, "Vagrancy, Impressment and the Regulation of Labor in Eighteenth Century England," *Slavery & Abolition*, 15 (1994):102–13.

14 Oxenbridge Foyle and Marcellus Rivers, *England's Slavery, or Barbados Merchandize; Represented in a Petition to the High and Honourable Court of Parliament* (London, 1659), p. 3.

15 James Barrowman, 'Slavery in the Coal-Mines of Scotland,' *Transactions of the Mining Institute of Scotland*, 19 (1897–8):129. For details of abolition and a different interpretation see Alan B. Campbell, *The Lanarkshire Miners: A Social History of their Trade Unions, 1775–1874* (Edinburgh, 1979), and T. Dickson, *Scottish Capitalism: State and Nation from Before the Union to the Present* (London, 1980).

everywhere in western Europe had declined irregularly since Roman times, but the pace of the decline had been greater in northern than in southern Europe. The so-called second serfdom affected primarily eastern Europe, while the Scottish mining sector remained small. Indeed, while free labor in the modern sense scarcely existed before the nineteenth century, by 1800 the coercive element in the master-servant, employer-employee relationship had been in decline for a better part of a millennium.

From a twentieth-century global perspective, the western European case was simply anomalous. From the neolithic revolution (and perhaps before) to the Middle Ages, every society had had some slaves. Suddenly there was a culture, and the larger part of a subcontinent, that did not. Perhaps we should see the beginnings of abolition not after 1750 but in the failure to revive serfdom or even slavery during the late-fourteenth-century labor shortages following the Black Death. Such shortages were not to be seen again until Europe began to occupy the Americas.[16] By contrast, plague in the Americas less than two centuries later, this time among Amerindians, helped ensure plantation slavery for Africans.

Why did the trend in Europe away from coerced labor fail to continue when Europeans established transoceanic societies? Why was slavery not an option for the elite of northwestern Europe in the second half of the fourteenth century, yet was adopted without serious questioning in the larger Atlantic world (beginning with the Canaries) just a century later? It is striking that Young and his contemporaries appeared not fully aware of the severity of the slavery that had developed under those same western polities that countenanced shifts to freer labor. From a modern perspective, the western world had a particularly repressive form of slavery embedded in its evolution until just over a century ago (and much less than a century ago if we include the parts of Africa under colonial control). Thus, Europeans not only reaccepted slavery in the face of New World realities, they also gave the institution a new scale and intensity. Indeed, all the major slave societies in human history have been either European or under European control. Moses Finley singled out five in which slaves were sufficiently central to production and social structure to warrant the term slave society – Greek, Roman, Brazilian, Caribbean, and the Southern United States. Three of these emerged in the Americas in the aftermath of European overseas expansion, and the slavery they imposed involved exploitation more intense than had ever existed in the world. It is inconceivable that any societies in history – at least before 1800 – could have matched the output per slave of seventeenth-century Barbados or the nineteenth-century Southern United States.

---

[16] Evsey Domar, "The Causes of Slavery and Serfdom: A Hypothesis," *Journal of Economic History* (1970):18–32; Stanley L. Engerman, "Introduction," in idem (ed.), *The Terms of Labor*, (Stanford, 1999), 1–15.

European exceptionalism thus extended beyond the slave-free dichotomy noted by Young and Smith in that the slavery European migrants imposed had a large economic element that made it totally different from the slavery that had ever existed in non-European societies. But if there were no slave plantations in the pre-contact Americas and Africa, neither were there many counterparts in the European Americas to the open systems of slavery that existed in parts of Africa, the indigenous Americas, and the Middle East. Peoples of African descent (the only peoples brought across the Atlantic as slaves) had small chance of non-slave status and even smaller again of full membership in European settler societies.

In Europe, on the other hand, the entrenchment of certain individual freedoms was such that there were frequently doubts about the legal status of those few enslaved peoples brought to Europe from the slave Americas. The slavery that evolved in the Americas in the three centuries between Columbus and Arthur Young was imposed by the countries that occupied the "free" global enclave to which the latter drew attention. It evolved during the Renaissance, Reformation, and Enlightenment – shifts in European thought that helped the rights of the individual against group or state to evolve into recognizably modern form.[17] In summary, at the end of the fifteenth century slavery did not exist on most western European soil. At the end of the eighteenth century it still did not exist in western Europe but it had greatly intensified and expanded in those parts of the non-European world that Europeans had come to dominate. Europe was exceptional in the individual rights that it accorded its citizens and in the intensity of its slavery, which, of course, it reserved for non-citizens.[18]

In the early years after Columbian contact it was by no means clear that a paradox of this scale and type would develop. Tables 1-1 and 1-2 chart the growing differences between Europeans in Europe and Europeans overseas. In Table 1-1 the African arrivals in column 1 and the European departures in column 3 provide a rough sum of migration into each national jurisdiction in the Americas, whereas the sum of columns 2 and 3 gives the numbers carried on board the ships of each major national carrier.[19] Table 1-2 reduces some of the raw estimates in Table 1-1 – specifically the number of slaves

---

[17] Davis, *The Problem of Slavery in Western Culture*; M.I. Finley, *The Ancient Economy* (Berkeley, 1973), pp. 70–83; William Bouwsma, "Liberty in the Renaissance and Reformation," in Richard W. Davis (ed.), *The Origins of Modern Freedom in the West* (Stanford, Co., 1995), pp. 203–34.

[18] For the drawing of a similar contrast focussing particularly on Britain, see Drescher, *Capitalism and Antislavery*, pp. 12–24.

[19] Column 1 shows African arrivals in the Americas, column 3 shows European departures. Almost all European migrants went to the areas of the Americas where their country held sovereignty. If column 3 is adjusted for deaths in transit – probably no more than 5 percent of those embarking in Europe at this time on average – then the sum of columns 1 and 3 yields total immigration into each national jurisdiction in the Americas.

Table　1-1. *European-Directed Transatlantic Migration, 1500–1760, by European Nation and Continent of Origin (in thousands)*

	Africans arriving in American regions claimed by each nation	Africans leaving Africa on ships of each nation	Europeans leaving each nation for Americas (net)	Africans and Europeans leaving for Americas (Col. 2 + Col. 3)
(a) Before 1580				
Spain	45	10	139	149
Portugal	13	63	93	156
Britain	0	1	0	1
Total	58	74	232	306
(b) 1580–1640				
Spain*	289	100	188	288
Portugal*	204	590	110	700
France	2	0	4	4
Netherlands	8	20	2	22
Britain	4	4	126	130
Total	507	714	430	1144
(c) 1640–1700				
Spain	141	10	158	168
Portugal	180	226	50	276
France	75	50	45	95
Netherlands	49	160	13	173
Britain	277	371	248	619
Total	722	817	514	1331
(d) 1700–1760				
Spain	271	0	193	193
Portugal	730	812	270	1082
France	388	456	51	507
Netherlands	123	221	5	226
Britain***	971	1286	372	1658
Total	2483	2775	891	3666
(e) 1500–1760				
Spain*	746	120	678	798
Portugal*	1127	1691	523	2214
France	465	506	100	606
Netherlands**	180	401	20	421
Britain***	1252	1662	746	2408
Total	3770	4380	2067	6447

Notes to Table 1-1: *Spain and Portugal are treated as separate countries despite the crowns of the two countries being united between 1580 and 1640. **Includes Dutch Brazil. ***Includes migrants from Germany and Africans carried on British American vessels.

Sources for Table 1-1 (number refers to row, letter refers to column):
1A, 2A: Philip D. Curtin, *The Atlantic Slave Trade: A Census* (Madison, Wis., 1969), p. 116.

5A: *Ibid*, for 1581–94; Enriqueta Vila Vilar, *Hispanoamerica y el Comercio de Esclavos* (Sevilla, 1977), pp. 206–9 for 1595–1640.

6A, 10A: David Eltis, Stephen D. Behrendt, and David Richardson, "The Volume of the Transatlantic Slave Trade: A Reassessment with Particular Reference to the Portuguese Contribution" (Unpublished paper, 1998).

7A: Curtin, *Census*, 119.

8A: Johannes Menne Postma, *The Dutch in the Atlantic Slave Trade, 1600–1815* (Cambridge, 1990), p. 21.

9A, 15A: David Eltis, "The British Transatlantic Slave Trade Before 1714: Annual Estimates of Volume and Direction," in Robert L. Paquette and Stanley L. Engerman (eds.), *The Lesser Antilles in the Age of European Expansion* (Gainesville, 1996), pp. 182–205.

12A, 13A: David Eltis, "The Volume and American Distribution of the Transatlantic Slave Trade in the Seventeenth Century" (Unpublished paper, 1995).

14A: Postma, *Dutch in the Atlantic Slave Trade*, 21, 300.

17A, 18A, 19A, 20A, 21A: Eltis, Behrendt, and Richardson, "Volume of the Transatlantic Slave Trade."

1B, 2B: Curtin, *Census*, 116 plus 20% voyage mortality. Spain/Portugal breakdown is a guess.

3B: Hawkins' voyages in Richard Hakluyt, *The Principal Navigations, Voyages, Traffiques & Discoveries of the English Nation*, 10 vols. (London, 1927), 10:7–66.

5B, 6B: 5A+6A plus 20 percent voyage mortality. Spain/Portugal breakdown is a guess.

7B: Hakluyt, *Principal Navigations*, 7:95–6 indicates some early French slaving activity in Africa, but the French Americas contained few slaves and no record of French slave trading to the Iberian Americas has surfaced.

8B: Postma, *Dutch in the Atlantic Slave Trade*, 21.

9B, 12B through 21B: Eltis, Behrendt, and Richardson, "Volume of the Transatlantic Slave Trade."

11B: Spanish were reported buying slaves in Cacheo, 1678–83 (T70/10, 1: T70/16, 50), though this may have been for Spanish markets. No records of Spanish ships selling in the Americas at this time has survived. An allowance of 150 a year is assigned to allow for such activity.

1C, 5C: Magnus Morner, "Spanish Migration to the New World prior to 1810: A Report on the State of Research," in Fredi Chiapelli et al. (eds.), *First Images of America: The Impact of the New World on the Old* (Berkeley, 1976), p. 771 less 20 percent for return migration.

2C, 6C, 12C: Vitorino Magalhaes-Godinho, "L'émigration portuguaise du XVéme siècle á nos jours: Histoire d'une constante structurale," in *Conjoncture économique-structures sociale: Hommage á Ernest Labrousse* (Paris, 1974), pp. 254–5 estimates gross emigration. This is divided by three to allow for movements to Atlantic Islands, Goa, and returns.

7C, 13C, 19C: Leslie Choquette, *Frenchmen into Peasants: Modernity and Tradition in the Peopling of French Canada* (Cambridge, Mass., 1997), pp. 20–22, 162, multiplied by 5 (Gabriel Debien, "Les engagés pour les Antilles," *Revue d'histoire des colonies*, 38 (1951): 9–13, 141–2 found a ratio of 4:1 for the Caribbean and Canada).

8C, 14C, 20C: Lucassen, *Dutch Long Distance Migration*, 22–3 less 20 percent returns.

9C: Gemery, "Emigration from the British Isles," multiplied by 2 to allow for pre-1630 emigration.

11C: 5C multiplied by ratio of Americas silver production, 1640–1700/1580–1640. For the latter see Arthur Attman, *American Bullion in the European World Trade, 1600–1800* (Goteborg, 1986), p. 20.

15C: Gemery, "Emigration from the British Isles," for 1640–50, and Galenson, *White Servitude*, 216–18 plus 5 percent voyage mortality for 1650–1700.

17C: 5C multiplied by ratio of Americas silver production, 1700–1760/1580–1640. For latter see Attman, *American Bullion*, 20.

18C: Magalhaes-Godinho, "L'émigration portuguaise," 255 estimates gross emigration. These estimates are divided by two to allow for net movements to Atlantic Islands and Goa.

21C: Galenson, *White Servitude*, 216–18 plus 5 percent voyage mortality.

Table 1-2. *Slaves Carried to the*
Americas as Percentage of All
Transatlantic Migrants, 1500–1760

	Slaves as % of all migrants
All carriers combined	
Before 1580	24.2
1580–1640	62.4
1640–1700	61.3
1700–1760	75.7

Source: Calculated from Table 1-1.

carried – to percentages. Europeans took African slaves to the Americas and enslaved the Amerindians whom they found there from the beginning. But initially, northwestern Europeans were little involved in transoceanic migration, and the proportion of slaves that the Spanish and Portuguese carried to the Americas before 1530 was little different from the proportion of slaves in their domestic societies. Moreover, the institution of indentured labor – seen by many scholars as temporary slavery and under which most English made their transatlantic passage between 1650 and 1780 – was virtually unknown to Spanish and Portuguese migrants of the early modern period. Elaborate systems of dependency bound the majority of Iberian migrants to their social superiors, but these ties were not well suited to extracting intensive labor in mines and plantations. After 1540 the transatlantic slave trade increased markedly with the result that between 1492 and 1580 (covered by panel (a) of Table 1-1) almost one-quarter of the migrants to the New World were African slaves.

Panels (b), (c), and (d) of Table 1-1 show that after 1580, as more of the Americas came under European control and as the direction of transatlantic migration passed steadily from southern to northwestern European hands, the slave element in the migrant flow increased. Table 1-2 shows that the slave component increased from less than one-quarter between 1492 and 1580 to more than three-quarters between 1700 and 1780. With few exceptions it would seem that within three generations of Columbian contact Europeans imposed or at least accepted slavery wherever they settled outside Europe. Of the 23 percent of transatlantic migrants who were not slaves in the 1700–60 period, most crossed the ocean under indenture or carrying a labor debt. Indentured servitude grew out of the annual master-servant contract in English agriculture.[20] However, the length of the term and the

[20] David Galenson, *White Servitude in Colonial America: An Economic Analysis* (Cambridge, 1981), pp. 1–15.

master's power that evolved in the Americas would not have been tolerated within Britain. The position of the servant was inconsistent with modern conceptions of free labor and at odds with concepts of full membership of the community that held in early modern Britain.

The trend toward a large African component in transatlantic migration continued after 1780. In the 1820s, just prior to a movement from Europe that saw over fifty million Europeans relocate in the Americas in less than a century, 90 percent of those coming across the Atlantic were African, not European. The peak years of the transatlantic slave trade, from 1680 to 1830, were sandwiched between early Iberian, then English emigration on the one side, and the later mass migration emanating from first northern and then southern Europe on the other. The forced, African component was much larger than the European component before the nineteenth century and this occurred, in part, because of the voluntary nature of the latter. Much of the later European migration came about because abolition denied employers in the Americas access to slaves.

The shift north in the magnitude of migration was pronounced. Before 1580 the Iberian nations accounted for almost all transatlantic movements of peoples. By 1700 to 1760, on the other hand, Britain, France, and the Netherlands were carrying nearly twice as many people across the Atlantic as were the Iberians, with the British alone carrying nearly half of everyone shipped. Northwestern Europeans carried almost three-quarters of slaves and indentured servants to the Americas in the same period.[21] Except for the Spanish, all European nations carried more Africans than Europeans to the Americas in the first three centuries after the Columbian contact, but the nations of northwestern Europe carried the most African slaves and the most bound Europeans. Despite the great size and amount of attention the migration from Britain receives, the British actually carried three Africans to the New World for every European until the beginning of the nineteenth century, and almost nine out of ten people on British ships before 1800 were there under some obligation to labor for others upon their arrival in the Americas. It was the northwestern Europeans in particular who were likely to impose slavery or employ indentured labor whenever they found themselves in transoceanic lands. Yet over the preceding three centuries it was these nations that had developed concepts of the modern liberal state (and notions of personal freedom) that have become central parts of the western cultural domination of the late-twentieth-century world.

Both the nature of the labor regime and the nationality of the leading shipper were heavily influenced by exports from the Americas. Coerced and

---

[21]   This estimate is calculated on the assumption that two-thirds of those leaving Europe on British ships before 1700 and one-half after 1700 were indentured servants. For French and Dutch ships the assumed proportion of servants for all periods is one half.

non-coerced migrant streams alike gravitated toward export-producing regions. Plunder and trade may have dominated the early decades of European expansion, but the main focus quickly became production; between 1500 and 1760 the peak decades for migration within each national group coincided broadly with the peak years of exports produced by coerced and free migrants and their descendants. Despite much scholarly attention, trade with indigenous peoples in the Americas was trivial. In Africa, while African-produced gold predominated before 1700, the raison d'être of the slave trade, which thereafter became many times more valuable than gold, was for the production of commodities in the European-dominated Americas. Long-distance migration in the pre-contact Americas and within Africa and Asia as well had never been as closely associated with commerce, production, and the intensive use of forced labor of other peoples. The terms of the charter for the Virginia Company of 1612 and the Royal African Company sixty years later are similar in the sense that the companies expected to profit from the overseas production of goods.[22] If transatlantic migration was an extension of migration within Europe, then productive enterprises located across the Atlantic, whether they used slave or non-slave labor, were initially replicas of Old World organizations. They drew upon the same pools of capital, management expertise, and, in the non-slave sector, markets for European labor. The success or failure of a transatlantic enterprise hinged on the same factors as did domestic enterprise.

Thus it is not difficult to see why slaves formed an increasing proportion of transatlantic migration until the nineteenth century and but for abolition might have done so until the twentieth. From the standpoint of New World users of labor, slavery was an institutional arrangement particularly well suited to both transoceanic transportation and the kinds of tasks necessary to produce most New World exports. The best data we have concern British directed migration. After an early period without a dominant crop during which English settlement hung in the balance, tobacco and sugar exports correlated well with the movement of both Europeans and Africans to the English Americas. Similarly, the early Portuguese slave trade was tied to bullion exports from Spanish America and Brazilian sugar production.

After 1700, further sugar expansion and gold production were associated with new peaks in both slave and free migration to Brazil.[23] Much of the literature on French migration has attempted to link emigration with economic

---

[22] W. R. Scott, *The Constitution and Finance of English, Scottish and Irish Joint-Stock Companies to 1720*, 3 vols. (Cambridge, 1910), 2:20, 246.

[23] For gold and silver production in Spanish and Portuguese America see Artur Attman, *American Bullion in the European World Trade, 1600–1800*, trans. by Eva and Allan Green (Goteborg, 1986), pp. 18–26. For a survey of the key role of Africans in the export sectors of the Americas see John Thornton, *Africa and Africans in the Making of the Atlantic World, 1400–1680* (Cambridge, 1992), pp. 129–51.

trends in France whereas, in fact, even this relatively small migrant flow seems better explained by the volume of tobacco, sugar, and fur from the French Americas.[24] Preoccupied, perhaps, with Asia, the Dutch were the only exceptions in that (leaving aside the temporary Dutch occupation of northeastern Brazil) production in the Dutch Americas was trivial until the development of Surinam in the last quarter of the seventeenth century. Yet, as with the Portuguese, prior to the English Navigation Acts and Colbert's reforms of the 1660s, the Dutch organised, fetched, and carried for other nations.

The advantages of slave labor over free were not confined to relative physical productivity in the plantation Americas. Potentially, at least, slave labor was cheap to obtain in the Old World and cheap to transport relative to free. Societies in all parts of the world have always had criminals and prisoners of war, the conversion of whom into full chattel slaves could have occurred with few costs beyond those normally involved in keeping order and waging war. In addition, as millions of Africans found out, the preferences of involuntary migrants could be ignored during the transatlantic voyage. The crowding, feeding, selection, and organization of people into barracoons and ships that followed from the voicelessness of slaves translated into large savings based on the number of migrants carried per ton of the vessel. On the American side, because a buyer of a slave obtained the balance of a life of labor instead of a fixed term of years (and would be prepared to pay more for the former), transatlantic slave merchants could afford to organize longer and more costly voyages and thus draw on a wider range of provenance zones. Early modern European migrants went to the New World under labor regimes that were close adaptations of those under which they had worked or with which they would have been familiar at home. These involved varying degrees of dependence on the employer and a legal imbalance in the latter's favor. Migrants from Spain and Portugal had the closest non-market ties with their subsequent employers in the Americas; those from England had the least in the sense that participation in an impersonal market for indentured labor was normal for most migrants.[25] But

---

[24] For a review of the literature see Choquette, *Frenchmen into Peasants*, 151–78; and Henry A. Gemery and James Horn, "British and French Indentured Servant Migration to the Caribbean: A Comparative Study of Seventeenth Century Emigration and Labor Markets," *The Peopling of the Americas: Proceedings of an IUSSP Conference at Vera Cruz* (Liege, 1992), pp. 289–94. French Canada is the one example of an American colony where long-term viability hinged on trading with an indigenous population rather than production organised and carried out by immigrants. It was also an area that received almost no African slaves, though enslavement of Amerindians was of significance. On the other hand, the fur trade was of trivial significance compared to other branches of transatlantic trade.

[25] For the dominance of royal officials, members of religious orders and their servants, soldiers and seamen in the early seventeenth century, see Auke Pieter Jacobs, "Legal and Illegal Emigration from Seville, 1550–1650," in Ida Altman and James Horn (eds.), *"To Make America": European Emigration in the Early Modern Period* (Berkeley, 1991), pp. 64–5, 75–9. Ida Altman finds tradespeople

in no case were Europeans brought as slaves and, apart from occasional members of an African elite on a business, diplomatic, or educational visit to Europe, Africans were never carried over as anything other than slaves. The switch from European to African migration thus also implied a switch from non-slave to slave labor for use in the dominant export sector. If the traffic in people from Africa to the Americas had been restricted to shorter terms and voluntary recruitment, it would have no doubt started later than the slave trade (if at all) and carried fewer people.

But why use Africans instead of Europeans? And, to pose a related question, why do so without any apparent self-questioning of this decision, particularly given the long absence of slavery from northwestern Europe? The divergence of slave and non-slave regions within the European world, from the revival of slavery and its imposition on the Americas, is extraordinary. On the continent of Europe, Bartolomé de las Casas and, later, Jean Baptiste du Tertre encouraged reflection and in the former case real change in the way aboriginal peoples were treated, but both accepted the idea that some peoples – specifically Africans – were natural slaves. Samuel Johnson's question, why "drivers of Negroes" should make "the loudest yelps for liberty" was not even posed more than a century earlier as the English Commonwealth, fresh from overcoming the tyranny of the crown, vigorously laid out the foundations of a Caribbean slave empire. In the midst of a comprehensive switch to slavery, the Barbados assembly claimed in an address to Cromwell that they were "Englishmen of as clear and pure extract as any (and should) enjoy ... liberty and freedome equal with the rest of our countrymen ...."[26] Later in the 1650s, a number of royalist sympathizers taken by the Protectorate and sold in Barbados described their situation to Parliament as slavery (and therefore, because they were English, unjust) without betraying any awareness of the condition of the Africans with whom they must have worked.[27] Some English Levellers advocated slavery as a punishment

and professionals significant in her sample, but even here familial, patronage, and other non-market ties were critical in the decision to emigrate ("A New World in the Old: Local Society and Spanish Emigration to the Indies," *ibid.*, 30–58). For the literature on the social composition of Spanish emigrants see Magnus Morner, "Spanish Migration to the New World prior to 1810: A Report on the State of Research," in Fredi Chiappelli et al. (eds.), *First Images in America: The Impact of the New World on the Old*, 2 vols. (Berkeley, 1976), 2:747–9. For institutional arrangements for most English migrants see David Galenson, *White Servitude*, pp. 3–15.

[26] "Address of the Assembly of Barbados to Oliver Cromwell," Sept. 1653, Add ms, 2395, f. 175.

[27] The petitions of the prisoners and the parliamentary debate they occasioned are in Thomas Burton, *Diary of Thomas Burton, esq. Member in the Parliaments of Oliver and Richard Cromwell, From 1656 to 1659*, 4 volumes (London, 1828), 4:253–73. A careful reading of this discussion shows that the main concern of the house was the lack of due process in the dispatch of the prisoners to Barbados, not the fact that they had been sold and were working on plantations.

for Englishmen, though unlike African slavery in the Americas this never became a reality.[28] In the late sixteenth and early seventeenth centuries, it was the remnants of villiage in England rather than the emergence of chattel slavery in the Americas that provoked comment from English observers.[29] As their slave empire approached its zenith, the British could sing "Rule Britannia" (written in 1714, set to music in midcentury), including the line "Britons never, never, never shall be slaves" with no hint of irony. As late as 1780, press-ganged sailors could be described as "the only class of beings in our famed Country of Liberty really Slaves."[30] Clearly, the British viewed black slaves, including the few who lived in England, as British chattels rather than British citizens, if they saw them at all.

A parallel situation existed with respect to European gender roles. The scope for individual action that evolved in northwestern Europe in the early modern period was greater for males than for females. Women may have had slightly better occupational opportunities than they were to have during and after the Industrial Revolution, but they were hugely underrepresented in all skilled occupations and professions in seventeenth-century England and the Netherlands.[31] Likewise their legal rights were greater than nineteenth-century marriage property acts allowed. Primogeniture practices throughout the West – to take just one example – denied them anything approaching a legal status that matched that of males. Women were clearly not slaves in the sense that non-Europeans became. In addition, women in northwest Europe had significant reproductive rights compared to non-European women, particularly with respect to whether to marry and the choice of mate if they elected marriage. Yet the fact remains that the substance as well as the discourse on marriage that emerged in the pre-nineteenth-century West simply bypassed the question of equal status for women. The argument is not that European marriage and European imposed slavery were similar, but that Europeans thought inequality between the sexes no more worthy of comment than the exclusively non-European quality of slavery. As with the slavery issue, no radical groups called mainstream attitudes regarding women into question.[32]

---

[28] Gerard Winstanley, *The law of freedom in a platform ... Wherein is declared, what is kingly government and what is commonwealth's government* (London, 1652).

[29] J. H. Baker, "Personal Liberty Under the Common Law of England, 1200–1600," in Davis (ed.), *Origins of Modern Freedom*, 187–91.

[30] R. M. S. Pasley (ed.), *Private Sea Journals, 1778–1782* (London, 1931), p. 61, cited in Daniel A. Baugh, *British Naval Administration in the Age of Walpole* (Princeton, N.J., 1965), p. 147.

[31] For a fuller discussion of these issues see Chapter 4.

[32] For a review of the literature on the parallels between marriage and slavery in the early modern period, including examples of the sale of wives, see Carole Pateman, *The Sexual Contract* (Stanford, 1988), pp. 116–53.

Just as European conceptions of ethnicity ensured that most transatlantic migrants before 1800 would be of African origin, so gender roles ensured that European migration that did occur was overwhelmingly male. Because European women were systemically prevented from acquiring non-domestic skills and were regarded as unsuited for field labor on plantations, they formed a tiny fraction of the indentured servants who left Europe. In sharp contrast to African women, European females travelled across the Atlantic primarily as family members (in their reproductive role) rather than as providers of labor. More important for the argument advanced here, contemporaries, while aware of the facts, considered gender imbalances unworthy of comment, much less debate. The relationship between ethnicity and gender – more specifically, the contribution of attitudes toward gender to the "unthinking decision" to use Africans as slaves on New World plantations – is examined later. As with enslaved Africans, females in the early modern Atlantic world were not perceived as having the potential for full membership in the community and ironically, equality between the sexes was greater under slavery than in societies in both Europe and Africa from which the plantation Americas were created.[33]

Blindness to differences in the treatment of ethnic and gender groupings is of central importance in understanding the slave-free dichotomy in the western world and forms a central point in the reassessment of the relationship between slavery and freedom offered here. The slavery that Europeans revived and refined was for non-Europeans. Indeed the absolute line of ethnicity would have been hard to enforce in a waged labor market. "Every negro is a slave wherever he happen to be," agreed the British and French military commands, somewhat inaccurately, during negotiations in New York in 1747, and was to be confiscated, like merchandise, not exchanged, like a prisoner.[34] Even under apartheid or in the post-Reconstruction South in the United States, occupation and ethnic divisions never coincided with the exactness that existed in American slave societies. Productivity of slaves was probably much higher in the nineteenth century than earlier; as slave values increased, the capacity of slaves to resist ill-treatment and the "space" allowed slaves all likely improved.[35] Yet the exclusively non-European nature of the institution remained absolute, and so did the barrier against using European women in whip-driven gangs in the fields. The power of the owner remained overwhelming through nearly four centuries. But it was the ethnic

[33] For the "patriarchal construction of civil society" in the early modern era and the implication that possessive individualism was premised on the conception of women as non-persons see, inter alia Pateman, *Sexual Contract*. The quote is from p. 143.
[34] E. B. O'Callaghan (ed.), *Documents Relative to the Colonial History of New York*, 15 vols. (New York, 1853–57), 10:210.
[35] J. R. Ward, *British West Indian Slavery, 1750–1834* (Oxford, 1988).

divide that provided Europeans with the blinkers necessary to come to terms with an institution that was so different from the labor regimes that they saw as appropriate for each other.

Non-European (more particularly African) exclusivity of slavery in the Americas is the first key point in reassessing the slave-free paradox; the second is the increasing reliance of Europeans and their descendants in the early modern era on the peculiar institution (in global terms) of waged labor. It is widely recognized that there were no equivalents to full plantation-based chattel slavery among Amerindian or African cultures at the time of the Columbian contact.[36] But what receives less attention is that there were few counterparts in the non-European world to seventeenth-century concepts of free labor and its associated labor market. More exceptional again was the emergence of a labor force where employer and employed were equal before the law. All European and early American societies were hierarchical and contained vestiges of the medieval concept of labor as a common community resource subject to community allocation and prescription. The master's authority over the servant was in part a jurisdiction defined and delegated by society and in part a proprietal right over persons exercised temporarily during servitude.[37] There are interesting parallels between the relationship of an individual to society that this potent mix of freedom and authority implies and its counterpart in the kin-group-based societies of Africa and many Amerindian peoples. But a global perspective suggests that European wage and free labor systems and the social structures that supported them shared far more with each other than either did with labor regimes that lay outside the European orbit.

Waged and free labor systems alike provided the basis for economic growth greater in the west than in the non-European areas of the world. Slave societies around the Atlantic likely had a capital/output ratio comparable to any industrializing society prior to the mid-nineteenth century. While they did not experience industrialization directly, they probably at least kept pace with their non-slave counterparts in output per capita. The nineteenth-century evidence suggests that the productivity advantage lay with the coerced rather than the free labor regions of the Atlantic.[38] The evidence for the seventeenth

[36] Paul Lovejoy, *Transformations in Slavery: A History of Slavery in Africa* (Cambridge, 1983), 1–22; Suzanne Miers and Igor Kopytoff (eds.), *Slavery in Africa: Historical and Anthropological Perspectives* (Madison, Wis., 1977), pp. 3–77; Thornton, *Africa and Africans*, pp. 72–97.

[37] Robert J. Steinfeld, *The Invention of Free Labor: The Employment Relation in English and American Law and Culture, 1350–1870* (Chapel Hill, N.C., 1991), pp. 55–93; Kussmaul, *Servants in Husbandry*, 5–9, 31–4.

[38] Fogel, *Without Consent or Contract*, pp. 60–80; Elizabeth Fox-Genovese and Eugene D. Genovese, *The Fruits of Merchant Capital: Slavery and Bourgeois Property in the Rise of and Expansion of Capitalism* (New York, 1983), pp. 34–60; David Eltis, *Economic Growth and the Ending of the Transatlantic Slave Trade* (New York, 1987), pp. 185–204.

century, some of it reviewed in Chapter 8, is less systematic, but the important point here is that in the post-Columbian Atlantic world, Europeans and their descendants owned and used slaves for the same reason that masters hired servants in the non-slave sector, which was to produce goods for sale to others. Indeed, in the Atlantic world as a whole, the share of slave labor involved in such activities, especially goods destined for export, was no doubt greater than the share of non-slave labor similarly employed. A corollary also holds: the proportion of non-slave labor providing personal services and involved in "non-productive" activities was greater than its slave counterpart.[39] Just as important, masters in both labor sectors obtained the labor they needed from well-organised markets in which buyers and sellers responded to price changes. In short, employers of both free and slave labor bought their labor and set it to work to produce goods and services. The focus on production, particularly on production for sale in transoceanic markets, as well as the reliance on markets to obtain the necessary labor, separated European- from non-European–dominated slavery and European from non-European non-slave regimes.

Despite parallels between the communal ties of pre-Columbian European societies and counterparts in Africa and the Americas, the balance between individual and group rights had, in relative global terms, shifted toward the former in Europe before the era of European expansion and well before the emergence of possessive individualism in the seventeenth century.[40] Europe was characterized by the absence of a single dominating structure of government for the subcontinent as a whole. Individual states exercised great powers and influence at different times, but none equivalent to, say, the imperial governments of China. And within these European states, the curbs on the arbitrary acts of government were such as to give powers to individuals against surplus-extracting elites that did not exist in the non-European world. In the economic sphere, capital and labor could move within and beyond the subcontinent with considerable ease relative to any other part of the world in 1500. It was an environment particularly well suited to the "technological drift," in Eric Jones' words, that provided Europeans with the means to establish transoceanic trading and imperial links. Traditional

---

[39] Compare the occupational distributions of the slave labor force in the British West Indies of 1834 in Barry Higman, *Slave Populations of the British Caribbean* (Baltimore, Md., 1984), pp. 47–8 with those in Britain in 1841 in B.R. Mitchell, *British Historical Statistics*, 2nd ed., (Cambridge, 1988), p. 104.

[40] This paragraph is based on E.L. Jones, *The European Miracle: Environments, Economies and Geopolitics in History of Europe and Asia* (Cambridge, 1981), especially pp. 85–149; and David S. Landes, *The Wealth and Poverty of Nations: Why Some Are So Rich and Some Are So Poor* (New York, 1998), pp. 3–44. The major criticisms of Jones, at least, which the latter has attempted to address in subsequent publications, hinge on questions of individual motivation and the universality of "economic man" rather than his description of how Europe differed from the rest of the world.

ties still bound workers to masters in early modern Europe. Free labor in the modern sense did not exist even in England, the North American colonies, and the early American Republic. A master-servant relationship gave masters a proprietal right so that non-performance by the servant was theft, punishable by incarceration. Yet choice of masters was increasingly possible even if the option of avoiding the labor market and working for oneself became less available over time.[41]

Nor, from a global perspective, was the ability to choose between masters regularly circumscribed by the threat of starvation after 1650, not, at least, in northwest Europe. The last life-threatening food shortage in England occurred in 1623, later than in Holland and perhaps a century earlier than in France; famines on an African or Asiatic scale had disappeared centuries before, if indeed they ever occurred. State action in times of crisis was a palliative, but this supplemented rather than replaced individual responsibility.[42] For most social historians it is the harshness of the English Poor Laws and their counterparts in other European countries as well as their place in securing the position of elite classes that calls for analysis. Yet however miserable the support provided, there appear to have been few systems of poor relief in the non-European world of four centuries ago that attempted to offset deprivation as inclusively as, say, English parish relief, and none at all that left the realm of individual action so uncircumscribed. Relief in England by the early modern period was based on place of residence of the individual rather than membership in a group such as kin or family and was not conditional on the surrender of long-term "rights in people," including labor.[43]

---

[41] Steinfeld, *The Invention of Free Labor*, pp. 15–54; idem, "Changing Legal Conceptions of Free Labor," in Engerman, *The Terms of Labor*, pp. 137–67.

[42] Keith Wrightson, *English Society, 1580–1680* (London, 1982), p. 145; John D. Post, "Famine, Mortality, and Epidemic Disease in the Process of Modernization," *Economic History Review*, 29 (1976):14–37.

[43] John Iliffe, *The African Poor: A History* (Cambridge, 1987), pp. 1–94, and especially the comparative introduction on pp. 1–8, concludes that the poor in England and Africa had in common the fact they could rely only on their own resources. This may have been the case in Africa where the poor (and we might add the potentially enslavable) were generally the kinless but not in England. Iliffe argues for a different type of poverty in Africa and that such poverty changed over time, but his evidence for widespread poverty in precolonial Africa is incontrovertible. Taken together with the evidence of famine into twentieth-century Africa, it suggests that the mesh of the kin-based safety net was larger and the net itself set – of necessity – considerably lower than in Europe, though he does not himself make this point. For a different view from Iliffe's of precolonial Africa as less stratified socially than Europe and colonial Africa see Jack Goody, *Cooking, Cuisine and Class* (Cambridge, 1982). Poverty in most parts of Asia was of a different order of severity to that in Europe, and I have been able to find no one who argues to the contrary or can point to a non-European, state-based palliative system.

Relative to Africans, Asians, and precontact aboriginal Americans, early modern Europeans were more nutritionally secure and less subject to natural or man-made catastrophe. Life expectancy in western Europe in 1500 was much lower than it was to become, but it was higher than elsewhere on the globe.[44]

The key distinction is not that individuals in sixteenth-century Europe had more rights in relation to society than those in Africa and the precontact Americas, though this was probably true and certainly came to be the case. Rather it is that property rights in particular, especially those in human labor, one's own and others, were vested in the individual in Europe rather than the group.[45] Kinship structures in the non-European world, especially in Africa, varied, but generally, status and rights in much of Africa and the pre-Columbian Americas derived not from autonomy and independence but from full membership of a kin-group or some other corporate body.[46] Such a group would make collective decisions and hold, again collectively, at least some of the property rights in persons which in the European Atlantic world would be held by individuals. Europeans might purchase property rights in others (slaves) outright, or they might enter the labor market themselves and temporarily trade some of their rights in persons in return for wages but in either case there was an individual owner of the rights in persons and a market transaction. To be a full citizen in much of the non-European world meant

---

[44] J. Hajnal, "European Marriage Patterns in Perspective," in David Glass and D. E. C. Eversley (eds.), *Population in History* (London, 1965), p. 31; Jones, *European Miracle*, 22–41; Joseph C. Miller, "The Significance of Drought, Disease and Famine in the Agriculturally Marginal Zones of West-Central Africa," *Journal of African History*, 23 (1982):17–61; Robert McCaa, "Paradise, Hells, and Purgatories: Population, Health and Nutrition in Mexican History and Prehistory," paper presented to a Conference on History and Physical Anthropology held at Ohio State University, Sept. 1993.

[45] Interpretations of the evolution of western economic dominance that stress the critical role of private property rights usually set up a polarity between private property rights on the one hand and common property resources on the other with the former being classed as western. For a well-known example see Douglass C. North and Robert Paul Thomas, *The Rise of the Western World: A New Economic History* (Cambridge, 1973). In fact, group or corporate rights – a hybrid in terms of the polarity cited here – have been the global norm, a norm to which the western world has returned in a sense since the advent of widespread business incorporation in the nineteenth century. Most post-neolithic societies – western or not – must have drawn a very small share of their total income from common property resources.

[46] Philip Curtin, Steven Feierman, Leonard Thompson, and Jan Vansina *African History* (Boston, 1978), pp. 156–71; Suzanne Miers and Igor Kopytoff, "African Slavery as an Institution in Marginality," in Miers and Kopytoff (eds.), *Slavery in Africa* (Madison, Wis., 1977), pp. 3–77. For some interesting parallels in one context in the Americas see William A. Starna and Ralph Watkins, "Northern Iroquoian Slavery," *Ethnohistory*, 38 (January 1991):34–57.

having more social bonds and less autonomy than would a marginal person without kinship ties. Freedom meant a belonging, not a separateness.[47] By contrast, in Europe and the European Americas full citizenship meant freedom from such bonds, full ownership of property rights in oneself, and, before the eighteenth century at least, the ability to avoid hiring out these rights to others in return for wages. The basic unit of the expansionist societies of Europe in the early modern period was, or became, the individual; the basic unit of the societies with which they came into contact in the extra-European Atlantic world was some corporate entity comprising groups of individuals.

If, in the Western world, possessive individualism meant a recognition that one owns full rights in oneself and that one has the right in a market society to bargain away such rights, it might also mean the accumulation of rights in others in the hands of a few, as indeed happened in the slave societies of the European Atlantic. A market system per se and the vesting of property rights in persons with an individual instead of the group were perfectly consistent with both waged and slave systems. It was the concept of rights, including rights to the labor of oneself and others, being vested in the individual that deserves the title "the peculiar institution" to a much greater degree than did slavery.[48] Indeed, the idea that holding such rights should qualify one for full membership in society was exceptional in global terms. The dual slave-free implications of vesting rights in the individual rather than the group played out along an ethnic divide. Servants, laborers, and women were not full citizens in the early modern West but eventually became so, though there seems to be nothing inevitable in this shift in status. Non-Europeans falling under European control risked becoming the most thoroughgoing chattel slaves in human history.[49]

Western systems of slavery and free labor thus had the same roots – the relative latitude allowed for individual action in Europe in the era of expansion. It is likely that the capacity of Europeans to sail beyond oceans and establish and maintain trading systems and empires hinged on a relationship between the citizen and the state, between elite and non-elite, and between employer and employed that was without precedent in non-western societies

---

[47] Orlando Patterson, *Freedom* 3 vols. (New York, 1991–), 1: *Freedom in the Making of Western Culture*, 20–44.

[48] If slavery is defined more restrictively in terms of a "slave society" in Moses Finley's sense, then the description "peculiar" remains apt, because, as noted earlier, there have been only five such societies. See his "A Peculiar Institution," *Times Literary Supplement*, July 2, 1976, p. 819. But Finley also notes how unusual was the Greek practice of incorporating "peasantry and urban craftsmen into the community . . . as full members" (p. 821).

[49] From present-day perspectives, of course, it was the new concept of freedom or more precisely, the new relationship between the individual and society, rather than the new concept of slavery that had and is having by far the larger impact on the non-European world.

in the scope it allowed for the individual. European overseas expansion could not have occurred without such a scope, which implied the freedom to enslave others. If neither Africa nor the Americas expanded overseas, it was, perhaps, because of their social structures rather than any limited wealth and technology. A corollary is that the impact of European values and social relationships on the non-European world may have been more important than the impact of European wealth and technology.

The export of European concepts of the individual and the slave and waged labor systems that these supported had uneven effects on the peoples and environments that Europeans found across the oceans. In Asia there was little initial impact. In many land-abundant areas of the globe, by contrast, Europeans were able to establish chattel slavery quickly; in areas with plantation potential they reserved waged labor mainly for themselves. Yet in the most land-abundant area of all, the Americas, native peoples were able to resist or quickly came to be classed as unsuitable for plantation slavery. While Amerindian social structures were destroyed or adapted to European purposes, in the Spanish Americas, the encomienda, mita, and repartimiento systems of labor allocation nevertheless had more affinity to preconquest structures than to either end of the European slave-free polarity. After 1650 Amerindians played little role in the export economies of the Americas.[50] Even within Africa, some societies such as the kingdom of Benin remained largely untouched by European contact; in Africa as a whole, it could be argued that societies were sufficiently resilient and self-sufficient that fundamental change in relations between the individual and the larger group began only with the colonial period.[51]

To summarize, early modern Europeans shifted property rights in labor toward the individual and away from the community. This trend was consistent with either free or slave labor. With respect to Europeans it led eventually to the former. As applied to non-Europeans (at least in the eyes of Europeans) it led to the latter. Europeans who had initially worked in the plantation fields as non-slaves gradually withdrew from such activities from the mid-sixteenth to the late seventeenth centuries, though in the absence of Africans and Amerindians (and after the attendant rise in wages) some would no doubt have continued to work under such conditions. The geographic pattern of African slave use in Europe in the sixteenth century was similar to what it was to become in the Americas in that regions closest to Africa were most likely to use slave labor.[52] Moreover, if Africans had been

[50] Juan A. and Judith E. Villamarin, *Indian Labor in Mainland Colonial Spanish America* (Newark, N.J., 1975), pp. 3–48.

[51] See most recently Thornton, *Africa and Africans*, 13–151.

[52] William D. Phillips, *Slavery from Roman Times to the Early Atlantic Slave Trade* (Minneapolis, Minn., 1984), pp. 66–88; David Brion Davis, *Slavery and Human Progress*, (New York, 1984), pp. 51–82.

provided with the shipping conditions enjoyed by European migrants, the resultant higher shipping costs would have slowed down the evolution of the African slave trade (and the trade in plantation produce) even further.[53]

The slave-free dialectic became more intricate and the associated paradoxes starker during the first two centuries after Colombus. Initially, as Table 1-1 indicates, the transatlantic slave trade to the Spanish Americas was small by later standards. The rapid expansion of silver production in both New Spain and Peru came after 1573 with the widespread adoption of the amalgamation method of refining.[54] Though African slaves were not used extensively in the silver mines, for reasons given later, this was also the era of the strongest growth of slave arrivals from Africa to the Spanish Americas prior to the nineteenth century. Despite this, Table 1-1 indicates that the Spanish Americas took about as many slaves in years 1580 to 1640 as the British Caribbean did between 1640 and 1700, when the British plantation system was only just developing and was still centered on the tiny island of Barbados. To make another comparison, the single island of Cuba took nearly twice as many slaves in the first sixty years of sugar expansion in the nineteenth century as the Spanish Americas did during the peak sixty years of its gold and silver production. In terms of Atlantic trade – either commodity exports or slave imports – specie production and its ancillary activities were insignificant compared to output levels in the plantation Americas. It was not until plantation produce began to cross the Atlantic in large quantities that the transatlantic slave-free paradox blossomed.

As already noted, the Spanish forced relatively few African slaves to labor in the mines and the Amerindians they used instead were not slaves. The reluctance of the Spanish to enslave Amerindians meant that the line separating European from non-European labor was not as sharp in the sixteenth as in the seventeenth century and later. The paternalism and head tax features of encomienda to which the Spanish subjected the conquered Central American aboriginals were not unimaginable in a European setting, and even in Potosí under the mita, or corvée labor system, "the tasks performed by the Indians ... were not unlike those performed by vassals of the Hapsburgs elsewhere, including Iberia and Austria."[55] Some Amerindian enslavement

[53] For the servant trade see Galenson, *White Servitude*, pp. 141–68; Hilary McD. Beckles, *White Servitude and Black Slavery in Barbados* (Knoxville, Tenn., 1989), pp. 46–59. For the importance of shipping costs in the slave trade, see H. A. Gemery and J. S. Hogendorn, "The Atlantic Slave Trade: A Tentative Economic Model," *Journal of African History*, 15 (1974):223–46; Stuart B. Schwartz, *Sugar Plantations in the Formation of Brazilian Society* (Cambridge, 1985), pp. 15–27, 51–72.

[54] Peter J. Bakewell, *Silver Mining and Society in Colonial Mexico, Zacatecas 1546–1700* (Cambridge, 1971), pp. 138–49.

[55] Jeffrey A. Cole, *The Potosí Mita, 1573–1700: Compulsory Indian Labor in the Andes* (Stanford, Calif., 1985), p. 18.

occurred even after such slavery was banned in 1542, but the great bulk of the labor force in the silver mines of both New Spain and Peru was Indian and received remuneration. Just over half the workers – called mingas in Potosí – got market rates and most of the rest were mitayos, basically corvée labor paid at below-market rates. In New Spain, where free labor Indians (naborías) have usually been thought to have been more important than in Peru, the ratio of free labor was higher, but not markedly so.[56]

But while coerced Indian labor was the mainstay of the silver mines, the number of free and mita laborers employed in the production of silver in New Spain and Peru even at peak export periods was small compared to the number of slaves that were to be found later on sugar plantations. Indeed, this broader perspective suggests that the question of the relative size of the export sector in the Spanish Americas is poorly understood. The work force in the mines of New Spain in the late sixteenth and early seventeenth centuries was below ten thousand, and its counterpart in Potosí was perhaps double this in 1603, though a larger mita draft sustained this number.[57] The combined work force of say twenty-nine thousand was equal to the number of slaves producing sugar on a single island in the early eighteenth-century Caribbean – perhaps Barbados or a little later Martinique or Guadeloupe.[58] Even after population declines, specie did not call directly on the labor of a large share of the population of the Spanish Americas. Specie did create prosperity and a demand for slaves. The large numbers brought into New Spain, and especially Peru, worked in a wide range of activities, many of them urban. Their presence is explained by the fact that the Spanish Americas were, together with Brazil, the richest part of the Americas before 1650. Thus, even though slaves were not vital to exports, the export sector created the prosperity that allowed society to buy

---

[56]   Peter J. H. Bakewell, *Miners of the Red Mountain: Indian Labor in Potosí, 1545–1650* (Albuquerque, N.M., 1984), pp. 81–135, 179–86, especially, 120–35 for the mingas.

[57]   *Ibid.*, 182; Cole, *Potosí Mita*, 15–17, 29. The mita labor was divided into three shifts, each of which in the original formulation of Viceroy Francisco de Toledo worked one week in three.

[58]   The slave population of Barbados is estimated at 65,000 in 1710 (John J. McCusker, *Rum and the American Revolution: The Rum Trade and the Balance of Payments of the Thirteen Continental Colonies, 1650–1775* (New York, 1989), 699). About half would have been employed on sugar estates and about half again would have been women and children. The slave work force had a high participation rate so that almost all could be included in the work force, though such workers were probably equivalent to only two-thirds full-time prime males. The Barbados sugar work force in 1710 may have amounted to 27,500 prime male equivalents. Spanish mines had almost no women and child workers, but the annual number of hours worked by a prime age mitayo or minga would on average be fewer than that of a slave. Precise comparisons are thus difficult, but the basic point stands.

slaves. Slave use declined in the Spanish Americas between the late seventeenth and late eighteenth century not because of fluctuations in silver output but rather because the colonial Spanish could no longer afford to buy slaves at the high prices generated by booming sugar plantations in the non-Spanish Caribbean.[59]

The difference between Spanish exploitation of labor in the Americas and its Dutch, English, and French counterpart is often explained, at least partly, in terms of the different European backgrounds of the exploiters. Given the small size of the export sector, would the Dutch or English have behaved differently with respect to obtaining labor if they, instead of the Spanish, had taken over Mexico and Peru? Much of this volume argues for important differences between the Iberians and the north-western Europeans. One implication of the more rapid evolution of possessive individualism in northwest Europe was that the English government exercised far less control than its Spanish counterpart over the way colonists treated non-Europeans. Perhaps modern historians would reconsider Tannenbaum's emphasis on the legal and religious heritage of European migrants determining different attitudes to race in the Americas if it were recast in terms of national differences in the latitude allowed for individual action.[60]

Yet the records of the Dutch and English in Brazil and Asia suggest that the colonial environment was of some importance and northwestern Europeans would not have acted differently if they had preceded, instead of followed, the Iberians. The Spanish sent large numbers of the free "olive coloured" Guanches into slavery in Madeira, an island without a preconquest native population, when alternative labor appeared scarce, though to produce sugar in the Canarian archipelago they used mainland Africans.[61] In both Central America and Asia, by contrast, the native population was sufficiently numerous relative to the potential export sector that exports – silver and hides in the Spanish case – could be produced without slavery, either Indian or African.[62] Production of such goods did not require the factory-like

[59]   In the eighteenth century silver exports from New Spain began to grow once more but the Indian population grew even more rapidly and the demand for slaves as indicated by number of sales continued to decline (Dennis Nodin Valdés, "The Decline of the Sociedad de Castas in Mexico City" [Unpublished PhD thesis, University of Michigan, 1978], pp. 139–74).

[60]   Frank Tannenbaum, *Slave and Citizen, the Negro in the Americas* (New York, 1947); Herbert S. Klein, *Slavery in the Americas: A Comparative Study of Virginia and Cuba* (Chicago, Ill., 1967), especially, pp. 1–126.

[61]   Felipe Fernández-Armesto, *The Canary Islands After the Conquest, The Making of a Colonial Society in the Early Sixteenth Century* (Oxford, 1982), pp. 39–40, 70.

[62]   Gold in lowland Peru was an exception. African slave labor was introduced into the silver mines of New Spain in the second half of the sixteenth century, but it was never central. See Colin Palmer, *Slaves of the White God: Blacks in Mexico, 1579–1650* (Cambridge, Mass., 1976), pp. 74–82.

gang-labor system that characterised work on a sugar plantation and which free labor (whether European, Amerindian, or African) assiduously avoided.[63] There were no sugar plantations producing for transoceanic markets in the sixteenth-century Central Americas and western Caribbean for simple reasons of geographic distance. Not until the late seventeenth century would transportation technology bring Jamaica and St. Domingue within range of European commodity and African slave markets. Thus, the slave-free paradox emerged later rather than earlier because, in the sixteenth century, when Amerindians were numerous enough to supply free labor in large quantities, only specie would bear the cost of transportation. By the time the western Caribbean came on stream as a potential location for a plantation complex exporting to Europe the demographic disaster meant there was no alternative to Africans.

The history of the other Iberians in the Americas reinforces the argument. Unlike the Spanish in Central America, the Portuguese had difficulty in producing an export commodity on the basis of waged labor, in part because they occupied areas with smaller aboriginal populations and weaker state structures. Morever, some of the Brazilian captaincies of the mid-sixteenth century were close enough to Europe and Africa to make competition with the sugar producers of São Tomé in the Old World possible. Under these circumstances they had no inhibitions about enslaving Amerindians, as well as switching to African slaves when Amerindians declined in numbers and African slaves became cheaper in response to a more efficient slave trade. The Spanish debate over the enslavement of Amerindians before 1550 could not have taken place in contemporary Portugal and would not have taken place in Spain either if silver production had hinged on the enslavement of aboriginals. Bartolomé de las Casas may have had regrets late in life about advocating the enslavement of Africans while defending the Indian but no one then, or for the next 250 years, seriously contemplated an America without the enslavement of non-Europeans. The Spanish did not need to enslave Indians on a large scale and, as we have seen from Table 1-1, the numbers of enslaved Africans crossing the Atlantic before the north-western Europeans took up the business were modest compared to what came later. It was only after 1650 that the slave systems of the Americas expanded drastically and intensified in the sense that the basis of slavery was now the plantation complex, not the highly varied types of slave employment to be found in the early Spanish Americas. Spanish slavery was in any event in decline after 1650 until Cuba embraced the plantation complex in the late eighteenth century.

From a modern perspective then, it was not the Iberian contact with Amerindians but the Dutch-English interaction with Africans that ultimately

---

[63] For descriptions of work routines see Bakewell, *Miners of the Red Mountain*, 137–78.

reshaped conceptions of freedom and race into forms recognisable in the early twenty-first century. Accordingly, we first take a closer look at trends within Dutch and English society, particularly the latter, before turning to Africa and then the Americas. It was the Americas claimed by the northwestern Europeans that provided the setting for the sharpest paradoxes between freedom and slavery.

2

The English, the Dutch, and Transoceanic Migration

THE IBERIANS BEGAN THE PROCESS of imposing a European view of the world on Atlantic regions (specifically of labor) before Columbus, when they began to enslave the Guanches, natives of the Canary Islands. Yet, as argued in Chapter 1, the full development of that view, along with the ability to impose it, occurred in northwest Europe after 1650. The concepts of slavery and freedom, the linking of these concepts with non-Europeans and Europeans, respectively, and the apogee of European power in the prenineteenth-century world awaited the rise to dominance of the Dutch in Asia and English in the Atlantic. Both the nature of the European world-view as well as the power of its proponents to project it across oceans stemmed ultimately from Europe's view of the relationship of the individual to society. Chapter 1 has argued for important differences between Europe and the rest of the world on this issue, and, within Europe, between England and the Netherlands together and other countries. Chapter 2 examines some of the social structures associated with this Anglo-Dutch view of the world and how these structures affected economic performance in general and transatlantic migration, both free and coerced, in particular.

Thirty years ago Carl Bridenbaugh attributed "the first swarming of the English" to poor social conditions within England. A large social history literature has supported this position or at least testified to a rising incidence of poverty until the mid-seventeenth century.[1] But large-scale free migration, like its coerced counterpart, is more likely associated with imbalances between donor and recipient areas than with outright economic destitution at either point of origin or point of arrival. More specifically, free transatlantic emigration was not necessarily a sign of desperate economic circumstances in early

---

[1] *Vexed and Troubled Englishmen* (Oxford, 1968), pp. 394–433. For a more recent similar view by economic historians see Gemery and Horn, "British and French Indentured Servant Migration to the Caribbean," pp. 285–93.

modern Europe. The decline of the Spanish economy and the "seventeenth-century crisis" did not generate a mass movement to the Americas despite the abundance of land in Meso and South America. Indeed migration from Spain was greater in the century before 1600 than in the century after. Similarly German migration was far more important in the eighteenth century than during and after the Thirty Years War. Before the cheap passages of the nineteenth century, transoceanic population shifts were apparently associated with economic expansion and a rising potential for ocean-going trade rather than with economic contraction.

This was not just a question of accumulating enough to pay for the transatlantic fare. Economic motives, albeit shaped by less overt and slowly changing cultural values, have usually provided the basic reason for migration. But given the absence of a durable "peace beyond the line" before the eighteenth century, individuals usually made the transatlantic move without stepping outside the political boundaries within which they had been born. Persecuted minorities such as the Jews and Huguenots are exceptions to this rule rather than the norm. In broad terms the ability to establish and hold transatlantic territory and provide a market for its exports implied both economic strength on the part of the coloniser and the flexibility to ship resources, particularly people, across the oceans. Thus prosperity at the end of the voyage, or point of attraction, was normally associated with a measure of material well-being, and the availability of a pool of labor and capital at the beginning.

The English and Dutch cases demonstrate the point. Overseas expansion was preceded and accompanied by profound social changes at home. While the changes themselves are well known, their implications for transoceanic expansion and migration in particular have received much less attention. Indeed, despite the clear chronology, scholars have generally searched harder for the effects of overseas expansion on European economic performance than vice versa. Three interrelated characteristics of English and Dutch agriculture and family life, each of which were less common elsewhere, are pertinent. One was the early emergence of the nuclear family. A second was the non-feudal nature of land ownership together with, in the English case, the early move to enclose common lands. A third was the related productivity advancements in food production that permitted a larger non-agricultural population. Indeed, the Dutch and English had smaller agricultural work forces and greater commercialization than other countries even in the late medieval era.[2]

---

[2] See the discussion in Fernand Braudel, *The Identity of France*, 2 vols. (1988–), 1:103–9. R. H. Britnell, *The Commercialisation of English Society, 1000–1500* (Cambridge, 1993), pp. 155–78; Alan Macfarlane, *Origins of English Individualism* (London, 1978), pp. 135–40, 174–5; Ann Kussmaul, *A General View of the Rural Economy of England, 1538–1840* (Cambridge, 1990), pp. 103–25;

The first of these is not an indicator of economic well-being so much as a prerequisite of enhanced responsiveness to economic opportunities or at least an ability to absorb changes in the socioeconomic system. Variations in age at marriage linked fertility and real income in pre-industrial England. In a regime of nuclear families, marriage is a crucial economic decision: The incentive to search for economic alternatives, one of which might be emigration, is altogether greater than in a system of extended families.[3]

On the land-tenure issue, heritable peasant tenure in parts of both England and the Netherlands was already lost by the end of the Middle Ages and customary dues payable to the lord had evolved into variable rents. The replacement of copyhold by leasehold between the fifteenth and seventeenth centuries was more complicated than the simple landowner-initiated conversion at the death of a tenant. Courts could interpret copyhold as carrying with it rights of inheritance. However, outright purchase of freeholds by either tenant or owner was at least as common as conversion to leasehold, and larger assemblies of land by even sub-tenants of copyholders were not unknown.[4] In the Dutch case land tenure patterns varied markedly among provinces, but consolidation of holdings and improved productivity occurred across several different regimes. The point for the present argument is that both the average size and the market orientation of English and Dutch farming operations increased in the early modern period. Attachment to the land was simply weaker and less widespread in England and the Low countries than elsewhere, and the dependence on wages greater. But the major link between agriculture and migration is not landholding tenure but rather agricultural productivity. English and Dutch agriculture proved capable of supporting a steadily increasing nonagricultural population after 1600 with little diminution in general living standards in the long run.[5] The non-agricultural pool of

Jan de Vries, *The First Modern Economy: Success, Failure and Perseverance of Dutch Economy, 1500–1815* (Cambridge, 1997), 159–234; idem, *European Urbanization, 1500–1800* (Cambridge, Mass., 1984), 116–18, 210–12.

3   E. A. Wrigley, *People, Cities and Wealth: The Transformation of Traditional Society* (Oxford, 1987), pp. 215–41; de Vries, *First Modern Economy*, 687–93; J. Rogers (ed.), *Family Building and Family Planning in Pre-Industrial Society* (Uppsala, 1980), pp. 1–15.

4   Robert Brenner, "Agrarian Class Structure and Economic Development in Pre-Industrial Europe," *Past & Present*, 70(1976):45–53, 61–8; R. W. Hoyle, "Tenure and the Land Market in Early Modern England: Or a Late Contribution to the Brenner Debate," *Economic History Review*, 43(1990):1–20.

5   There is still considerable debate on when yields per acre began to increase, but probate studies and a new approach using labor inputs suggest 1600 as a likely starting point in England. P. Glennie, "Measuring Crop Yields in Early Modern England," in B. M. S. Campbell and M. Overton, *Land, Labour, and Livestock: Historical Studies in European Agricultural Productivity* (Manchester, 1991), pp. 255–83; Gregory Clark, "Yields per Acre in English Agriculture, 1250–1860: Evidence from Labour Inputs," *Economic History Review*, 44(1991):445–60. For

people (especially in the Netherlands) was not bound to migrate, but young adults were likely to prove responsive to opportunities that might include internal or overseas migration. If English ties to the land had been as secure and widespread as those in France and Portugal (prior to the eighteenth century), the English might well have been much less willing to migrate. Most of those who did migrate from France came from the non-traditional sectors of society.[6]

Improved productivity was not confined to the agricultural sector. The advances in manufacturing and services, particularly transportation, are well known in the case of the early modern Netherlands.[7] For England, the vagrancy issue and subsistence crises between 1500 and 1660 have spawned a large literature and have tended to obscure the fact that in the nonagricultural sphere too the English position improved over this period relative to all Continental states except for the Dutch. Between the mid-fourteenth and the early sixteenth centuries the basic English export, which throughout the Middle Ages had comprised raw wool, became woollen cloth.[8] In the first half of the seventeenth century new woollen fabrics supplemented and eventually overtook the traditional English shortcloths among exports from London. Major developments in the substitution of coal for wood occurred, as well as new processes in metallurgy. The relative position of English technology in Europe improved markedly in the two centuries before 1700.[9] Import substitution policies, aggressively pursued by the English but not by the Dutch, may have been significant from the late seventeenth century.[10]

a less optimistic assessment, at least before 1700, see Mark Overton, *Agricultural Revolution in England: The Transformation of the Agrarian Economy, 1500–1850* (Cambridge, 1996), pp. 63–132. For a detailed survey and analysis of the Dutch case, see de Vries, *First Modern Economy*, 198–223, 543–561.

6   Choquette, *Frenchmen into Peasants*, 1–76.

7   de Vries, *First Modern Economy*, 179–92, 279–349.

8   E. M. Carus Wilson, "Trends in the Export of English Woollens in the Fourteenth Century," *Economic History Review*, 3(1950):162–79; Peter J. Bowden, *The Wool Trade in Tudor and Stuart England* (London, 1962), pp. 37–8. The same pattern of structural change is traced in Joseph Inikori, "Slavery and the Development of Industrial Capitalism in England," in Barbara Solow and Stanley L. Engerman (eds.), *British Capitalism and Caribbean Slavery: The Legacy of Eric Williams* (Cambridge, 1987), pp. 79–101. For Inikori, however, the source of structural change in the English economy is shifts in demand, in particular, export demand, and more especially demand from the Atlantic system. As suggested later, the absence of a generalised growth and industrialization process similar to the English pattern in other western European economies with large connections to the Atlantic system (France, Holland, and Portugal) would seem to question this approach.

9   J. U. Nef, *The Conquest of the Material World* (Chicago, 1964), pp. 121–328. F. J. Fisher, "London's Export Trade in the Early Seventeenth Century," *Economic History Review*, 3(1950):151–61.

10 Trevor Griffiths, Philip Hunt, and Patrick O'Brien, "Political Components of the Industrial Revolution: Parliament and the English Cotton Textile Industry,

But neither this nor simple export demand, however rapid its expansion, can explain early English growth: all European governments attempted to substitute domestic goods for imports. On the eve of the English Civil War per capita exports were £0.32 in official values – including reexports. By the 1660s this ratio had more than doubled to £0.72 and by 1700 amounted to about £1.27. There are no equivalent figures for the Netherlands before 1650, but shipping data indicate extraordinary growth in Dutch trade between 1580 and 1650, most of it with European rather than transoceanic areas.[11]

The service sector exhibited similar trends. The special case of the slave trade is taken up in Chapter 5, but the general shipping picture is relevant here. The shipping of merchandise to and from England had been dominated by non-British shippers in the Middle Ages, with the Hanse towns playing a dominant role in the woollen trade with Flanders, for example. By the seventeenth century the Dutch dominated the bulk commodity trades of northern Europe, but in the rich trades of the Atlantic and the East Indies, requiring a ship different from the Dutch fluit, the English were able to hold their own.[12] Voyages to the East from England were one-third the Dutch equivalent in 1601–10, rising to 43 percent in 1650s, but by the 1670s and 1680s the value of imports from Asia carried by the Dutch and English East India Companies were almost the same, with the price advantage for

---

1660–1774," *Economic History Review*, 44(1991):395–423. For the argument that such policies were critical before 1700 see Inikori, "Slavery and the Development of Industrial Capitalism," 79–101.

[11] The calculation of these ratios is as follows: for 1640 Fisher ("London's Export Trade in the Early Seventeenth Century," 153–4) lists values of commodities other than shortcloths exported from London by English and foreign merchants at £694,856 of which £454,914 are woollens. Shortcloths "almost equalled in value the trade in . . . the newer fabrics" and the value of these is set at £400,000. To convert London trade into English trade a ratio of 0.67 is used as the divisor. For the 1660s, actually an average of 1663 and 1669, and 1700, export data are from Ralph Davis, "English Foreign Trade, 1600–1700," *Economic History Review*, 7(1954):164–5. For population data (for 1641, 1666, and 1701, respectively) see Roger S. Schofield and Edward A. Wrigley, *The Population History of England, 1541–1871: A Reconstruction* (London, 1981), pp. 528–9. Europe in the last phase of the Thirty Years War could not be expected to provide strong markets for English exports and the 1640 figure is likely below the long-term trend. Nevertheless, this is strong growth indeed, and the growth rate in the generation before the 1660s was probably in excess of that in the last third of the century. We should also note that reexports were important in this process, but reexports drew on many regions outside the Americas. The root of its growth lay in a highly competitive English merchant fleet and a bulking credit and distribution system in London, the chief entrepot in this business, as well, of course, as the Navigation Acts. For Dutch trends see de Vries, *First Modern Economy*, 362–408, especially, 404.

[12] Violet Barbour, "Dutch and English Merchant Shipping in the Seventeenth Century," *Economic History Review*, 2(1930):261–90.

East Indian textiles lying with the English.[13] English merchant shipping tonnage increased fivefold in the century after 1582. The rate of growth was somewhat faster after 1629 than before, but there was little difference in this growth in the quarter-centuries before and after 1660.[14] Large increases in mercantile credit and insurance facilities occurred, much of it before the massive growth of reexports – the most important source of the general expansion of English trade in the second half of the seventeenth century.[15] It is also clear that London's ability to generate large pools of capital was established early. Since the beginning of the century, and certainly by the 1640s and 1650s when London merchants organised credit for Cromwell's ventures, overseas conquest, and a host of private investment activities, the capital-generating capacities of the London merchant community were unrivalled outside Amsterdam.[16]

The cumulative impact of these trends was that the relative position of the two small northwest European economies improved substantially well before industrialization, as conventionally defined, or the establishment of significant colonies.[17] The same is true of the Netherlands, though here, rapid expansion at home in the so-called Golden Age between 1580 and 1650 corresponded with the growth of international trade, the great bulk of which was with the rest of Europe. The growth of total exports from England

[13] War in the quarter-century after 1688 allowed the Amsterdam company to pull ahead once more so that the English company did not overtake its Dutch counterpart until the 1730s. See Niels Steengard, "The Growth and Composition of The Long-Distance Trade of England and the Dutch Republic Before 1750," in James D. Tracy (ed.), *The Rise of Merchant Empires: Long-Distance Trade in the Early Modern World, 1350–1750* (Cambridge, 1990), pp. 108–12. For Kristof Glamann, however, the English company was already underselling the Dutch at the end of the seventeenth century [*Dutch-Asiatic Trade, 1620–1740* (The Hague, 1958), pp. 141–8].

[14] Ralph Davis, *The Rise of the English Shipping Industry* (London, 1962), pp. 11, 15.

[15] Violet Barbour, "Marine Risks and Insurance in the Seventeenth Century," *Journal of Economic and Business History*, 1(1929):561–96; Davis, "English Foreign Trade, 1600–1700," 150–66.

[16] Theodore K. Rabb, *Enterprise & Empire: Merchant and Gentry Investment in the Expansion of England, 1575–1630* (Cambridge, Mass., 1967), pp. 52, 68, and Robert Brenner, *Merchants and Revolution: Commercial Change, Political Conflict, and London Overseas Traders, 1550–1653* (Cambridge, 1993), pp. 577–613.

[17] There is remarkable unanimity on the economic and social trends that preceded English and, indeed, European overseas expansion. Three major syntheses on European expansion in the early modern period – familiar to countless students in the English-speaking world – are by Eric Jones, Eric Wolf, and Immanuel Wallerstein. Each is written from a radically different world-view (literally). Yet the uniqueness of late-medieval and early-modern Europe and more specifically England is a theme common to all three. Each also gives the Netherlands less attention than it should.

was well established before the 1660s and therefore before the plantation Americas could have had a significant impact on reexports, most of which came from the East Indies, the Atlantic fisheries, and the northern trade.[18] Improved competitiveness and the distinguishing features of what Jan de Vries calls a "modern economy," were apparent well before industrialization and, in the English case, well before the strong expansion of foreign trade and the creation of overseas colonies.[19] Such colonies initially drew on the capital, skills, and labor of the metropolitan center to produce commodities that supplemented in a small way the dietary, recreational, and fashion needs of the well-to-do Europeans. The English economy did not come close to overtaking the Dutch in this period, at least in per capita terms. But in the first half of the seventeenth century the Dutch and the English together grew both absolutely and relative to the rest of Europe.

The discussion so far has stressed trends common to English and Dutch domestic developments. But why, with this shared domestic experience, was Dutch overseas expansion so markedly different from its English counterpart – especially in relation to settlement colonies and migration? The missing term on the Dutch side of the Dutch-English equation is emigration. "Romans, Spanish, and Dutch did and do conquer," wrote Sir Ferdinando Gorges sourly to Charles I's secretary Windebank in 1638, "not plant tobacco and Puritanism ... like fools .... If they (the English) had stayed at home they would have labored in the Commonwealth for their sustenance."[20] In the two centuries before 1800 the Dutch experienced little outmigration on a net basis. The English over the same period had a net emigration of 1.25 million, almost all of whom settled around the Atlantic basins. Perhaps a mere thirty thousand people left the Netherlands for the Americas and Africa on a net basis and many of these were not Dutch. The East Indies were more important, but even there probably less than five hundred thousand individuals left for the East Indies and did not return, most of them sailors and soldiers rather than laborers for an export sector. Overall, such net departures from the Netherlands were offset by arrivals from other sources, though the arrivals occurred disproportionately in the seventeenth century.[21]

---

[18] Davis, "English Foreign Trade, 1600–1700," 165; Fisher, "London's Export Trade in the Early Seventeenth Century," 154.

[19] de Vries, *First Modern Economy*, 693.

[20] Great Britain, Public Record Office, *Calendar of State Papers, Colonial Series: America and the West Indies*, London, 1860, Vol. 1, p. 276 (henceforth CSPCS).

[21] Over two centuries over one million people left the Netherlands for Asia, of whom about half returned. In-migration from the rest of Europe in the same period was about the same order of magnitude. See Jan Lucassen, "Dutch Long Distance Migration: A Concise History, 1600–1900" (IISG research paper, Amsterdam, 1991), 20–3, 35–42; idem, "The Netherlands, the Dutch, and Long-Distance Migration in the Late Sixteenth to Early Nineteenth Centuries," in Nicholas Canny (ed.), *Europeans on the Move. Studies on European*

The reasons for this discrepancy, so critical for explaining patterns of early modern overseas migration, are to some extent the obvious ones. The English population was two and one half times the size of the Dutch. The structural changes undergone by the English economy in the early modern period may have led to improved living standards and international competitiveness, but the Dutch economy in the same period did much better again. In 1700, per capita income was perhaps 40 percent greater in the Netherlands than in England, with an even larger differential holding for most of the preceding century.[22] Like the English, the Dutch may have lacked the ties to the land and pre-modern social structures that inhibited migration elsewhere, but more important, with relatively high incomes, they also lacked the English incentive to emigrate. In addition, the location of the Netherlands and the internal waterways that linked it with the poorer areas of Europe, especially Germany, ensured a steady flow of migrants into the country. England was much more isolated by comparison. A disproportionate share of immigrants into the Netherlands served in the army and merchant marine and indeed became emigrants. For every Dutch there was at least one non-Dutch overseas migrant between 1600 and 1800, and the earlier estimates of Dutch emigration have to be doubled to take these into account. After making all allowances for these factors, however, the difference between the English and the Dutch experiences – the net emigration of the one and the net immigration of the other – still stands out, and there may be a case to be made for less tangible factors.

Despite – or perhaps because of – the successful Dutch agricultural and manufacturing sectors, the elites of Zeeland and Holland who organised overseas endeavours appear to have placed more emphasis on exchange than the production activities stressed by London merchants. Perhaps because of the long war with Spain, investors in Amsterdam organised around large companies and sent out expeditions aimed at plunder and creating or protecting trade routes. By contrast, and at considerable risk of oversimplification, the hundreds of small overseas English ventures in the first half of the seventeenth century, most of which failed, were more willing to contemplate a plantation (in the seventeenth-century sense) in the aftermath, of course, of the search for precious metals, which preoccupied everyone at first. The Royal African Company and official plantations correspondence has abundant evidence of the search for new plants and methods, and the post-Columbian global exchange of flora acquired a modern, systematic, and purposeful form in the seventeenth century. When the English found what they were looking for – varieties of cotton, tobacco, and eventually sugar – often with Dutch help, it was usually the Dutch that carried the

Migration (Oxford, 1994), pp. 153–91; Schofield and Wrigley, *Population History of England*, 528–9.
[22] de Vries, *First Modern Economy*, 699–707.

resulting output back to Europe. Indeed between 1600 and 1650 there was some specialisation of function in Dutch and English activities in the Atlantic world. When Dutch plantations did take root as in Surinam, they had a large English component. The Dutch Americas, like the Dutch East Indies and the Dutch Gold Coast, comprised trading emporia: St. Eustatius and Curaçao in the slave trade, Nieuw Amsterdam, with half its small population non-Dutch, in the fur trade.[23] Much of what the Dutch sold in these centers they had produced in the Netherlands.

Dutch dominance of European migrant flows to Asia and probably, too, trading and ownership of slaves within Asia may have matched that of the British in the Atlantic. But given the relative demographic and cultural resilience of indigenous societies in Asia and the Americas, the Dutch impact on Asia was much less than that of the British in the Americas.[24] Moreover, while plantation labor was never extensive in Dutch Asia, the Dutch carried European perceptions of themselves as separate from non-Europeans further than did any other Europeans who established transoceanic colonies. Indeed, of all European states, England and the Netherlands had the strongest conceptions of individual rights, had moved farthest down the road toward free labor, and had become the most secure havens for political refugees from other countries by 1700. Yet they led other European nations in imposing intensive coerced labor, albeit in different global hemispheres, and in treating others with the minimum of inclusiveness.

Our main concern here is with the Atlantic. Table 1-1 not only provides an overview of early modern transatlantic migration, it also illustrates the emergence of the British as the preeminent nation in supplying both European non-slave labor and African slave labor prior to 1760, despite their trivial importance in the sixteenth century. In the second half of the seventeenth century the English began to carry more transatlantic migrants, both free and coerced, than any other nation. Panel (d) in Table 1-1 shows their closest rivals, Portugal, carrying less than two-thirds the British total by the 1700–60 period, despite dominating the slave trade before 1650. In the half century after 1760 (not shown here) it is likely that the British carried 60 percent or more of transatlantic migrants, most of them to the English-speaking

---

23 David Steven Cohen, *The Dutch-American Farm* (New York, 1992), 15–18. Seymour Drescher has pointed to a lack of "cultural and political support networks and a cadre of leaders interested in reproducing Dutch culture" in the Americas ("The Long Goodbye: The Dutch Case in the Capitalism and Anti-Slavery Debate," Robert L. Paquette and Stanley L. Engerman (eds.), *The Lesser Antilles in the Age of European Expansion* (Gainesville, Fla., 1995), n. 56).

24 J. Fox, "'For Good and Sufficient Reasons': An Examination of Early Dutch East India Company Ordinances on Slaves and Slavery," and S. Abeyasekere, "Slaves in Batavia: Insights from a Slave Register," both in Anthony Reid (ed.), *Slavery, Bondage and Dependency in South-East Asia* (St. Lucia, Queensland, 1983), pp. 246–62, 286–314.

Americas. Most of the non-slave migrants were British. Between 1600 and 1700 over seven hundred thousand people left England – about 17 percent of the English population in 1600. Over half of these went to the Americas, with Ireland absorbing much of the rest. Indeed, without Ireland, the English influx into the Americas, as well as the contrast with the Dutch, would have been even greater than it was. Just as the American West diverted U.S. interests away from overseas imperialism in the nineteenth century, so Ireland restrained English activity in the seventeenth-century Americas.[25] English predominance in the European transatlantic migrant stream contributed to a thirty-year decline in the population of England at the end of the seventeenth century. Over the same period, the English carried more than 370,000 people from Africa. Thus about equal numbers of British and African people went to the English Americas, but three-quarters of the former arrived before 1675 and almost all the latter after 1625. In the second half of the century between ten thousand and twenty thousand people a year were leaving for the English colonies – the most concentrated migration to any jurisdiction within the Americas up to that time.

After 1700, the pace of departures from Britain slackened, but British shipments of Germans to the mid-Atlantic colonies became significant. At the same time the British slave trade tripled in size compared to the four decades before 1700. The French, Spanish, and Dutch, even counting Brazil as Dutch in the second quarter of the seventeenth century, brought a third or less of the English total. Overall, from 1500 to 1760, the Portuguese flow approached the total of the English directed stream, but it was spread over the whole period whereas the British flow occurred mainly after 1630. The English contribution was thus exceptional in its intensity, if not in its mix of peoples from Africa and Europe.

In the mid-seventeenth century, there were probably just under one hundred thousand English settlers, evenly split between mainland North America and the Caribbean. Among them they owned a few thousand slaves. Coerced African labor was largely confined to Brazil and Spanish America. Fifty years later about 150,000 African slaves labored under English masters, most of them in the Caribbean. There were probably more African slaves under English control in 1700 than in the rest of the European Americas combined, with the possible exception of Spanish America.[26] The shift in the

[25] Stanley L. Engerman, "British Imperialism in a Mercantilist Age, 1492–1849: Conceptual Issues and Empirical Problems," *Revista de História Econômica*, 15 (1998):195–234.

[26] Calculated from McCusker, *Rum Trade*, 584, 692–708; Christian Schnaken-bourg, "Statistiques pour l 'histoire de l'économie de plantation en Guadeloupe et Martinique (1635–1835)," *Bulletin de la Société de la Guadaloupe*, 31(1977):41, 44. Cf. David Watts, *The West Indies: Patterns of Development, Culture and Environmental Change since 1492* (Cambridge, 1987), pp. 311–20, although Watts does not appear to have incorporated either the Schnakenbourg or McCusker archival data in his estimates. Population data for seventeenth-century Brazil are

center of gravity of plantation produce – for plantations colonies were the major target of both groups – was just as sharp. The English Caribbean had overtaken Brazil as the leading sugar-producing region in the world before the end of the seventeenth century and by 1700 the value of English plantation produce – sugar, rum, tobacco, ginger, and indigo – probably rivalled that produced in the rest of the Americas combined.[27] But the growth of the white population from both migration and natural population increase was also rapid. By 1700 there were 260,000 people of British descent in the Americas, more than those of Portuguese origin and not far behind the number of Hispanic peoples, whom they would soon overtake.[28] They had, moreover, crossed the ocean with the least government regulation and support of all European migrants.[29] Despite the disproportionate power in the hands of employers and the leading role of London merchants in

limited. Roberto C. Simonsen, *História Econômica do Brasil (1500/1820)*, 6th ed. (São Paulo, 1969), p. 271 suggests 110,000 slaves in Brazil in 1660. For my own assessment I have taken the relatively solid data for the Captaincy of Bahia in 1724 from Schwartz, *Sugar Plantations in the Formation of Brazilian Society*, 88, and adjusted them downward in proportion to changes in sugar exports between 1698–1702 and 1721–26 (*ibid*; 502–3). I have further assumed that the slave population of Brazil was double that of the Captaincy of Bahia in 1700. This suggests a slave population of about 55,000 in that year. The great unknown is Spanish America.

[27] Data taken from Stuart B. Schwartz, "Colonial Brazil, c. 1580–c. 1750: Plantations and Peripheries," in Leslie Bethell (ed.), *The Cambridge History of Latin America*, II (Cambridge, 1985):430–1; McCusker, *The Rum Trade*, 896. If gold is included then the value of Brazil probably regained its preeminence during the first half of the seventeenth century. For data see Vitorino Magalhaes Godinho, "Le Portugal, les flottes du sucre et les flottes de l'or, 1670–1770," *Annales: économies, sociétiés*, civilisations, 5(1950):192–3.

[28] Gemery, "Emigration from the British Isles," 212, estimates 257,000 in English America in 1700. McCusker, *The Rum Trade*, pp. 584, 586, 712, whom Gemery did not use, indicates 262,000 but includes non-British residents. For Brazil, Oliver Onody has 300,000 non-indigenous residents at the end of the seventeenth century, with about one-third slaves—consistent with the comments in n. 26 ["Quelques traits caracteristiques de l évolution historiques de la population de Brésil," in Paul Deprez (ed.), *Population and Economics: Proceedings of the Fourth Congress of the International Economic History Association, 1968* (Winnipeg, 1970), pp. 335–7]. For Spanish America there are estimates of 575,000 in 1650 in Angel Rosenblat, *La Poblacion Indigena Y el Mestizaje en America*, 2 vols. (Buenos Aires, 1950), 1:59. Immigration into Spanish America was at very low levels in the second half of the seventeenth century and comparison with data for 1825 (*ibid*, 36) indicates an average annual growth between 1650 and 1825 of about 1 percent, though this growth was probably less at the beginning and greater at the end of this period. On the basis of Rosenblat's figures we might hazard 800,000 to 900,000 people in 1700.

[29] For the small significance of government intervention in English migration relative to its Spanish counterpart see Mary M. Kritz, "The British and Spanish Migration Systems in the Colonial Era: A Policy Framework," *The Peopling of the Americas: Proceedings*, 3 vols. (Vera Cruz, 1992), 1:263–82.

establishing the early plantations, English migrants were probably more representative of the society they left behind than any other national group.[30] The attitudes toward coerced labor that they carried with them derived as much from English society as from the new environment.

From an even longer perspective, the English experience is just as striking. The English who accounted for less than 5 percent of western Europe's population in 1550 made up nearly 7 percent in 1680 and 15 percent in 1900. If we include the neo-Europes, then the English at home and abroad constituted 7.5 percent of Europeans in the world of 1680. Thus, well before the eighteenth century began, the English had already become 50 percent more numerous in relative European terms in a century or so and, as argued later, with no obvious loss of material well-being.[31] In the process of shipping people from two continents to the Americas and eventually establishing the most sophisticated form of labor exploitation developed anywhere to that point, the English created a network of "communication and community" across the Atlantic unrivalled in its depth, complexity, and reliability of contact and unprecedented in the history of long-distance migration up to that time.[32]

All Europeans faced land-abundant Americas and aspired to the same mercantilistic goals of a large self-sufficient empire and a favorable balance of trade. Spain, Portugal, and France could extract profits and plunder from the Americas and stood to gain from rising Atlantic demand as well as England. Yet the benefits apparently accrued to the latter in particular, despite the fact that English competitors had had a head start. Nor was the expansion of the English Atlantic system driven by an efficient manufacturing sector. Apart from lacking diverse and well-established overseas links in the early seventeenth century, the English could not even produce most of the goods they traded in overseas markets. English manufacturing competitiveness may have improved in European terms, but as late as the 1680s – and

---

[30] Mildred Campbell, "Social Origins of Some Early Americans" in James Morton Smith (ed.), *Seventeenth Century America* (Chapel Hill, N.C., 1959), pp. 63–89; David Galenson, "'Middling People' or 'Common Sort'? The Social Origins of Early Americans Reexamined," and Mildred Campbell, "Response" *William and Mary Quarterly*, 39(1978):499–540; idem, "The Social Origins of Some Early Americans: A Rejoinder," *ibid*, 36(1979):264–86. Ida Altman points to heavy representation of hidalgos, artisans, and professionals from two cities in southwestern Spain (Altman, "A New World in the Old," 39–40, 43–7).

[31] Wrigley, *People, Cities and Wealth*, 216, calculates English ratios for western Europe alone. For the English share of the neo-Europes, I have used population data for the English Americas from Gemery, "Emigration from the British Isles to the New World," 211–12, and have assumed that the English living in Ireland in 1680 were as numerous as those living in the Americas (certainly an underestimate).

[32] Ian K. Steele, *The English Atlantic, 1675–1740: An Exploration of Communication and Community* (Oxford, 1986).

into the nineteenth century for some items – the English obtained iron bars, spirits, a wide range of textiles, and hardware that they traded in Africa and the Americas from foreign suppliers, not from their own manufacturers.[33] When pressing for rights to supply Spanish-American slave markets in 1675, an English official argued that the Spanish need not fear the smuggling of goods along with an English slave trade because the English, like the Spanish themselves, obtained these goods from the Dutch.[34] Thus smuggling would not increase, merely the nationality of the smugglers.

The source of this sudden and unprecedented English activity, as suggested earlier, was sophisticated London credit facilities, the availability of English labor for migration, and either the lower cost of English services or the impact of the English Navigation Acts on Dutch competition – probably the former. These made possible the establishment of the English plantation system using white indentured rather than slave labor initially.[35] As Table 1-1 implies, the British Americas, and indeed all the European Americas, were settled and carried firmly into the plantation export sector of the Atlantic economy with the aid of a mainly European, rather than African or Amerindian, labor force. Only one or two thousand Africans a year arrived in Barbados in the 1640s, rising to perhaps two to three thousand a year in the 1650s. By 1660 white and black populations were in rough balance in that island though whites were still more numerous elsewhere in the English Caribbean.[36] Throughout this period more whites than blacks arrived in the Caribbean, however, and

[33] Kenneth G. Davies, *The Royal African Company* (London, 1957), pp. 165–79; 350–7; Julia de Lacy Mann and Alfred P. Wadsworth, *The Cotton Trade and Industrial Lancashire* (New York, 1968), pp. 124–7, 148–58.

[34] Anon, "Considerations about the Spaniards buying negro's of the English Ro'll Company . . .," Jamaica, Feb. 2, 1675, Add ms, 2395, f. 501.

[35] Morgan, "The Labor Problem at Jamestown, 1607–18," 595–611; Hilary McD. Beckles, *White Servitude and Black Slavery in Barbados, 1627–1715* (Knoxville, Tenn., 1989); David Eltis, "Labor and Coercion in the English Atlantic World from the Seventeenth Century to the Early Twentieth Centuries," *Slavery & Abolition*, 14(1993):207–26.

[36] Population data form an important part of any assessment of arrivals prior to 1660. The best review of the evidence on the white population of Barbados is Gemery, "Emigration from the British Isles," 219–20. John J. McCusker has also done the basic archival work on this and in addition presents the evidence on the black population in the Caribbean in McCusker and Menard, *Economy of British America*, 153–4. Few Africans could have arrived in the English Americas outside Barbados before 1660. As late as 1672 there were less than 2,600 Africans in the whole of the English Leewards with nearly three-quarters in Nevis ("A particular of the Leeward Islands," Add ms, 2395, f. 530). For direct evidence of slave arrivals in the mid-seventeenth century see Gary Puckrein, *Little England: Plantation Society and Anglo-Barbadian Politics, 1627–1700* (New York, 1984), pp. 67–72; Eltis, "The British Transatlantic Slave Trade Before 1714," and Russell R. Menard, "'The Sweet Negotiation of Sugar:' 1640–1660" (Unpublished paper, January 1995).

far more white people went to the Caribbean than to the North American mainland before 1660. The fact that Africans became more numerous than Europeans in Barbados is because white people, particularly servants and prisoners at the end of their term, could leave and search for land elsewhere.

Before the mid-seventeenth century, the colonies appeared to complement the mother country not just in product types and natural resources but in labor. Labor was more productive in the colonies and therefore more highly valued than at home, and there appeared to be a surplus of labor within England. The first major shipments of poor children from London went to Virginia shortly after its foundation, and the first official discussion of convict migrants dates from 1607.[37] Most social commentators before 1650 saw the colonies as a desirable outlet for England's surplus population and, before the Barbadian tobacco era, the best prospects for settlement were seen as temperate regions such as Newfoundland. Colonies in warmer climes were initially targets for trade rather than settlement.[38]

Mid-seventeenth-century commentators always assumed that the metropolitan center was more important than the colonial fringe. They were preoccupied with manufactured exports, mainly cloth, and the related issue of ensuring a cheap domestic labor supply. Europe was by far the largest market for English exports, and woollen cloths by far the most important category of merchandise exported. In 1640, 80 to 90 percent of London's exports comprised woollen cloth.[39] Europe was also a highly competitive market, not least because of tariffs on finished goods; for these, the level of wages was a critical cost factor. When continental markets for English cloth periodically collapsed, the distress in England was widespread, especially before 1650. Mercantilistic attitudes to labor are well known. No seventeenth-century commentator believed that labor could be fully mobilised by wages alone. Richard Haines' 1678 evocation of the backward bending supply curve for labor is typical: "Is it not true," he asked,

"that the Poor rarely endeavour to lay up anything for Sickness and Old age, and will work by their good wills only for Necessity? Which is the reason that our Manufactures are generally more plenty, and as cheap, when provisions are dearest. Most of them, if they can but get Victuals, will play away half their time;"[40]

---

[37] R. C. Johnson, "The Transportation of Vagrant Children from London to Virginia, 1618–22," in H. S. Reinmuth (ed.), *Early Stuart Studies in Honor of D. G. Willson* (Minneapolis, Minn., 1970), pp. 137–51; CSPCS, 1:28, January 28, 1620.

[38] See for example Richard Eburne, *Plaine pathway to plantations: that is, A discourse in generall concerning the plantation of our English People in other countries . . .*, London, 1624.

[39] Fisher, "London's Export Trade," 151–61; Davis, "English Foreign Trade, 1660–1700," 163–6.

[40] *Provision for the Poor: or Reasons for the erecting of a working-hospital in every county . . . Linnen Manufactory*, London, 1678, p. 3. "Typical" does not mean

A surplus population, coercive social legislation, and low wages would guarantee competitive prices of cloth in export markets.

Beginning in the mid-seventeenth century, however, mercantilist attitudes faced dramatic new demographic and colonial developments as well, perhaps resulting from new conceptions of work among sections of the English labor force. The first of these is the most fundamental. Population decline threatened to end the continued expansion of the English economy, both domestic and colonial.[41] There were actually more people living in England in the mid-1650s than at any time thereafter until the 1720s. For the three decades, 1651 to 1680, the population declined. In the 1680s there were perhaps 8 percent fewer people in England than a quarter of a century earlier. Estimated age and sex distributions suggest that the impact on the domestic labor force was not as immediate as for the population as a whole. Nevertheless this was the only occasion between the sixteenth and twentieth centuries that the English population fell, and it happened just as overseas settlement colonies had become obviously viable.

But colonies were more than viable. They grew in number and the crops grown in them became more labor intensive. The English acquired their plantation colonies in two major steps. Ireland, Barbados, Jamaica, and the base of the North American possessions became English in the 1600 to 1655 period, with most of the balance in the Western Hemisphere coming as a consequence of the Napoleonic Wars. More specifically, English control of Ireland was limited to Derry and Dublin in 1649. Two years later, it extended to most of the island, and the overriding English concern was how to people it and at the same time make it secure. In the subtropics, the new lands meant not only an increase in settlement opportunities but also new labor-intensive crops. The major expansion of English plantation agriculture came between 1650 and 1700. Sugar imports into London from the English West Indies rose from negligible amounts in the early 1640s to 7,500 tons a year in the mid-1660s (though tobacco and sugar together still amounted to less than East India Company imports) and nearly 20,000 tons by 1700.[42] At the end of the century tobacco and sugar comprised 15 percent of English imports.[43] It is striking that these developments coincided with the most enduring check to English population growth in four centuries.

---

that many writers did not dissent from this view even in the late seventeenth century. See Joyce Oldham Appleby, *Economic Thought and Ideology in Seventeenth Century England* (Princeton, N.J., 1978), pp. 129–57.

[41] This paragraph and part of the next are based on Schofield and Wrigley, *The Population History of England*, pp. 207–9, 227, 441–9.

[42] This is a mean of London imports for 1663 and 1669 taken from CO 388/2, fols. 7–11, 13–17. For a discussion of the reliability of these data see McCusker, *Rum Trade*, 991–2.

[43] Davis, "English Foreign Trade, 1660–1700," 150–66; McCusker, *Rum Trade*, 891.

The domestic response to a tightening supply of labor was rising real wages. This coincided with increasing mercantilist restrictions on English goods in Europe – France in particular. Manufactured goods, chiefly textiles, dominated English exports and wages accounted for a much larger part of manufacturing costs than was the case in the later, more capital-intensive, industrial age. Higher wages and higher duties should have meant lost European markets for English cloth.[44] The fact that the English economy and international trade in particular continued to grow at this period suggests an alternative scenario, one that involved new trade-offs of work for leisure for some of the labor force.

Attitudes to work are at the center of the concept of modernization, which is increasingly viewed by labor and economic historians as cultural rather than economic.[45] Seventeenth-century England may not have had slavery but it did give masters large powers to enforce contracts. Those who would not enter such contracts and who did not own sufficient land to support themselves faced severe laws against vagrancy and idleness, the aim of which was the extraction of labor from those unwilling to volunteer it for wages. Waged labor had low status among the non-elite, and migration – perhaps within England, but increasingly overseas – may be viewed as an attempt to avoid this status and achieve the premodern ideal of a piece of land and independence from the labor market. The fact that such smallholdings might mean less income than reliance on the labor market did not matter. Freedom dues in the form of land disappeared early for servants moving to the Americas, especially for those sailing to Barbados. But the prospects of land were as enticing for migrants as for the Levellers who chose not to migrate, and some Chartists nearly two hundred years later who attempted to set up a land-bank scheme. From this perspective indentured servitude was something to be entered into voluntarily and endured temporarily by young people as an escape route from waged labor. The Republican working class of the mid-nineteenth-century urban United States apparently had a parallel view of waged labor, seeing it as a necessary prerequisite to land-holding in the West.[46]

---

[44] Schofield and Wrigley, *Population History of England*, pp. 420, 638–44; Galenson, *White Servitude*, 151–5; Russell Menard, "From Servants to Slaves: The Transformation of the Chesapeake Labor System," *Southern Studies*, 16 (1971):355–90; William A. Green, "Race and Slavery: Consideration of the Williams Thesis," in Solow and Engerman, *British Capitalism and Caribbean Slavery*, 35–42.

[45] Engerman, "Coerced and Free Labor," 1–29; idem, "Cultural Values, Ideological Beliefs, and Changing Labor Institutions: Notes on their Interactions," in John N. Droback and John Nye (eds.), *The Frontiers of the New Institutional Economics* (San Diego, 1997), pp. 95–119. See also the several essays in John Brewer and Roy Porter (eds.), *Consumption and the World of Goods* (London, 1993).

[46] Christopher Hill, "Pottage for Freeborn Englishmen: Attitudes to Wage Labor in the Sixteenth and Seventeenth Centuries," in H. Feinstein (ed.), *Socialism, Capitalism and Economic Growth: Essays Presented to Maurice Dobb* (Cambridge, 1967), pp. 338–50; Eric Foner, *Free Soil, Free Labor, Free Men: The Ideology of*

In Jamaica in the late 1650s when whites still outnumbered blacks by ten to one and most blacks were not slaves, the soldiers of the Cromwellian army worked as field laborers for the officers. The disbandment of the force posed an enormous labor problem. The Council of Foreign Plantations was told that "soldiers are at libertie whither they will work or noe. Hunger and necessitie only compelling them. Not above a sixth part or 8th part doe work, by reason they have ordinarie provisions sufficient ...."[47] Spanish Jamaica had been the same according to another observer; it had "had very little dependence on Trade & but lived in a Sedantary way on the product of a fertile Country wch furnished them wth most of the necessarys they wanted."[48] For the English elite, this made colonies pointless. In a fascinating anticipation of Colonial Office discussions of emancipation nearly two centuries later, an internal memo on the army of occupation argued that disbandment would mean "plantations will quickly fall and be ruined, for the soldier will be meditating how he may escape ...."[49] In both the seventeenth and nineteenth centuries the English shipping industry came to the rescue, though for Jamaican planters the African slave trade proved a more successful solution than was Asian contract-labor for labor shortages in the aftermath of emancipation.

At some point in the centuries touched on here, however, worker aspirations in, first, England, and then Europe, shifted. Perhaps the essential meaning of modernization is worker acceptance of waged labor and a stress on consumption of goods and services – for which pecuniary income is necessary – over non-pecuniary rewards in the form of leisure or independence. As James Steuart said on the eve of industrialization, people must be slaves to others or slaves to want. Such a shift in attitudes to work and consumption is usually associated with the mid-eighteenth century but was perhaps already under way in the late seventeenth. It was never enough to bring forth a supply of waged labor for New World plantations. However, if some workers were prepared to substitute goods for leisure then higher wages would elicit an increase in the quantity of labor and higher labor productivity at home. This may have been sufficient to protect and even increase exports to Europe. We know that the wages of building craftsmen rose much faster in the second half of the seventeenth century than in the first. If this is indicative of general

---

the Republican Party Before the Civil War (New York, 1970), pp. 11–29; Eltis, *Economic Growth*, 17–28.

[47] "At the Committee of ye Council of forreigne plantations," Jan. 10, 1660, Add ms, 2395, f. 289.

[48] Papers Relating to the Island of Jamaica, n.d., but c. 1694, Add ms, 22,676, f. 6.

[49] "Overtures for the better providing for Jamaica before the Lord Windsor's going away Governor of that place," n.d., but c. 1660, Add ms, 2395, f. 301; For the pre-slave plantation structure of Jamaica see CO1/14, pp. 84–6. For a parallel interpretation of English labor in the early days of Virginia, see Edmund S. Morgan, "The Labor Problem at Jamestown, 1607–18," *American Historical Review*, 76 (1971):595–611.

wage levels, then perhaps labor was more productive and willing to work in response. Higher wages would certainly have helped close off emigration. Indeed, rising English wages have an important role in recent explanations of changing sources of labor flows into the English Americas at this time. But a few thousand less English going to the Americas inevitably meant much less to the relatively large domestic labor market than to the colonies.

Yet increased worker responsiveness to rising wages could have been only part of the story. In the eyes of many of the propertied classes, higher wages would induce less rather than more work, especially among those considered vagrant, idle, and poor.[50] For this segment of the labor market, force – not persuasion – was called for. The pamphlet literature of the second half of the seventeenth century suggests an increased interest in coercing those who would not offer more work in response to rising wages. Scottish mine owners managed to reinstitute, then intensify, serfdom. The English revised their poor laws in 1662, 1683, and 1697 to encourage local authorities to establish permanent physical facilities for the poor and facilitate a shift from the concept of the poorhouse to that of the workhouse. Children and the old were to be set to work at as early and as late an age as possible, respectively, in the former case in the hope of encouraging "habits of industry" in later life.[51] Several pamphleteers advocated the use of machines in special workhouses to increase the pace of work in a striking parallel to the gang-labor system on Caribbean sugar plantations. Others advocated schools for the poor aimed at increasing hours of work as well as work intensity.[52] Such plans assumed a bureaucracy that did not then exist. Local government in England, as the Shakespearean comedies testify, was not very efficient. The capital requirements of work centers appear hopelessly large in the light of the effective tax base. Serfdom in England never revived. Edward

50 One of the best discussions of the increasing attempts to extract work from the poor is still R. H. Tawney, *Religion and the Rise of Capitalism* (London, 1961), pp. 251–70. Richard C. Wiles, "The Theory of Wages in Later English Mercantilism," *Economic History Review*, 21(1968):113–26 provides a balanced view of the high- versus low-wage positions in the pamphlet literature of the early eighteenth century.

51 Spinning flax was widely advocated for this group "who cannot see to wind Silk, nor yet stitch bodies, or work with a needle." T. Firmin, *Some Proposals for the imploying of the poor especially in and about the city of London* (London, 1678), p. 8. See also Appleby, *Economic Thought and Ideology*, 129–57; Edgar Furniss, *The Position of the Laborer in a System of Nationalism* (New York, 1921).

52 The question of how much exploitation of the poor actually increased after 1650 has yet to be addressed systematically. There are relatively few known cases of the grandiose plans for extracting labor progressing beyond planning (e.g., the odd linen-producing workhouse in London). In the end, the high population densities and the threat of starvation meant that for domestic employers of labor such centers of coercion were unnecessary. For a fuller discussion see Eltis, "Labour and Coercion in the English Atlantic World," 207–26.

Chamberlayne could comment by the midseventeenth century that testimonials (the avenue to collier serfdom in Scotland) were rarely used.[53] Labor was clearly not free, but increased coercion of labor was more likely to be discussed than implemented. Whatever the combination of worker response and compulsion, success from the employers' standpoint is suggested by rising per capita export ratios and the growth of exports to continental Europe, despite additional protective duties in some countries. These point to continued improvement in productivity within the English economy compared to its European counterparts.

For the colonies, rising real wages reinforced the impact of a declining English population. The labor crisis was more severe for the plantation Americas, especially the sugar colonies, than for the domestic economy.[54] More than one hundred thousand people departed from England in the 1640s – the second highest decadal level of departures before the nineteenth century. With Ireland in rebellion, Jamaica yet to be acquired, the population of Virginia about the same size as that of Barbados at the beginning of the decade, and a new demand for labor triggered by sugar, it seems likely that many of them went to Barbados.[55] Emigration is estimated to have increased nearly 20 percent from the early 1640s to the early 1650s before beginning its long post-1655 slide. But by now there was much stronger competition for migrants from elsewhere in the English Empire, noticeably Ireland. Here and, increasingly as the century wore on, in the Chesapeake, mortality rates for migrants were less severe than in the West Indies and lower, too, than in the earliest days of settlement. It is also likely that the availability of land in North America drew people away from Barbados. By the end of the seventeenth century, departures from England declined until they approached the lowest levels estimated in the modern era, presumably in response to rising domestic wages. For the English Caribbean, the pressure on the supply of labor from England must have begun shortly after 1650 and, in the Chesapeake, the same pressures began to be felt after 1660.

---

[53] Edward Chamberlayne, *Angliae Notitia or the Present State of England: Together with Divers Reflections on the Antient State thereof*, London, 1672, 6th ed., p. 383.

[54] The importance of British demographic trends for immigration into Maryland is stressed in Lois Green Carr and Russell R. Menard, "Immigration and Opportunity: The Freedman in Early Colonial Maryland," in Thad W. Tate and David L. Ammerman (eds.), *The Chesapeake in the Seventeenth Century: Essays on Anglo-American Society* (Chapel Hill, N.C., 1979), pp. 206–42.

[55] Richard S. Dunn, *Sugar and Slaves: The Rise of the Planter Class in the English West Indies, 1624–1713* (New York, 1972), p. 55. The widely cited compilation of London passenger registers for 1635 predated the sugar boom in Barbados whereas data on destinations of indentured servants begin only in the 1650s, *after* the switch to African labor began.

Table 2-1. *Number of Migrants Arriving in the Chesapeake and the English Sugar Islands by Origin, Slave and non-Slave Status, and Decade, 1661–1710 (in thousands)**

Destination	1661–70	1671–80	1681–90	1691–1700	1701–10
Virginia/Maryland/Carolinas					
Total migration	19.7	20.8	16.4	6.6	38.6
Africa	0	3.1	3.5	3.4	13.2
British Isles	19.7	17.7	12.8	3.2	25.4
Row 3/Row 1	1.00	0.85	0.78	0.49	0.66
Sugar Islands**					
Total migration	58.5	62.9	90.7	86.4	101.1
Africa	46.0	51.3	81.0	66.9	91.3
British Isles	12.5	11.6	10.7	19.5	9.8
Row 3/Row 1	0.21	0.18	0.12	0.23	0.10

* British arrivals are net; arrivals from Africa are gross and therefore include slaves subsequently sold to the Spanish Americas.   ** Includes Jamaica, Barbados, and Nevis to 1680; Jamaica, Barbados, and Leeward Islands, 1681–1710.
Source: Britain, Galenson, *White Servitude,* 216–18; Africa, Eltis, "British Transatlantic Slave Trade Before 1714," 196–200.

Table 2-1 provides a decadal series of transatlantic arrivals in the sugar islands and the plantation regions of the mainland by the categories slave and non-slave or African and European. The table supports propositions that have become familiar in recent research on indentured servants and overall migrant flows. First, migrants were powerfully attracted to regions that had established export sectors. Second, the total number of migrants to all destinations declined steadily after 1660. Third, within the overall decline, the data here show the swing from the Caribbean to the North American mainland that has emerged from studies of both indentured servants and overall migrant flows. The Caribbean received more English emigrants until 1660, after which the mainland plantation area became the dominant destination.

Slaves became more numerous than servants on Barbadian sugar estates in the mid-1640s.[56] The English Civil War may have had an initial effect "[f]or that sorte of people that did use to go the Plantations go now into the armyes,"[57] but the boom in sugar was such that servants continued to

---

[56] Menard, "The Sweet Negotiation of Sugar," Table 3; Dunn, *Sugar and Slaves,* 54, 68; Hilary McD. Beckles and Andrew Downes, "The Economics of Transition to the Black Labor System in Barbados, 1630–1680," *Journal of Interdisciplinary History,* 18(1987):235. The broad outlines of the explanation of the switch to slaves followed here is that of Menard.

[57] The comment is actually from the 1690s, but it was no doubt valid at any point in the seventeenth century (Edward Littleton and William Bridges, Barbados, to

arrive in increasing numbers throughout the 1650s.[58] Slave prices fell from mid-century to 1680s and then began to rise. Servant prices in Barbados increased strongly in the twenty years to 1660 and after 1650 diverged from the trend in the Chesapeake where servant prices actually declined.[59] In the sugar islands, the decline in arrivals from Britain had already taken place when the complete migrant series begins in 1661, and the temporary increase in the 1690s probably has more to do with wartime troop movements than permanent migration. In the Chesapeake, Africans did not replace British migrants immediately. There was, as Menard suggested, a gap of two decades, especially pronounced in the 1690s when immigration from all sources remained very low compared to the 1660s and the early eighteenth century. In the sugar islands, the British share of arrivals decreased continuously, except for the 1690s, but in absolute terms the total number of arrivals from Europe and Africa combined doubled between the 1660s and early 1700s. Even after allowing for slaves reshipped to the Spanish Americas from the English Caribbean, the sugar islands still received between two and three times more people in the early 1700s than the Carolinas and the Chesapeake combined. At least three times more migrants (free and coerced) went to the English Caribbean than to the English plantation mainland between 1661 and 1710. Most important, whereas only one in three migrants to the English Americas was an African slave in the 1650s, fifty years later three out of every four arrivals were African.[60] The white population of the Chesapeake was increasing naturally from the 1660s and was more important than migration as a source for additional labor by the end of this period. Nevertheless, sugar was much more important than tobacco, and exports from the English Americas at this period hinged on the African connection.

The driving force in this growth and transition in migration was, first, rising demand for both servants and slaves associated with a boom in plantation produce, especially sugar, and second, the fact that the supply of slaves from Africa proved to be more responsive to the rising price of labor than did the supply of servants from England, Ireland, and Scotland. Greater supplies

Lords of the Committee of plantations, Sept. 27, 1692, CO28/1, f. 174). Farley Grubb and Tony Stitt make the same point for Liverpool servants during the War of the Spanish Succession ("The Liverpool Emigrant Servant Trade and the Transition to Slave Labor in the Chesapeake, 1697–1707," *Explorations in Economic History*, 31(1994):376–405).

58 Russell R. Menard, "British Migration to the Chesapeake Colonies in the Seventeenth Century," in Lois Green Carr, Philip D. Morgan, and Jean B. Russo (eds.), *Colonial Chesapeake Society* (Chapel Hill, N.C., 1988), 105.

59 Menard, "The Sweet Negotiation of Sugar"; David Galenson, *Traders, Planters and Slaves: Market Behavior in Early English America* (Cambridge, 1986), pp. 64–9.

60 White migration calculated from Galenson, *White Servitude*, 216–18; slave arrivals in the 1650s estimated at 2,000 a year (see Eltis, "British Transatlantic Slave Trade Before 1714," 183).

Table 2-2. *Prisoner Status and Destination of Migrants Leaving England*
for the Americas by Decade, 1651–99

Destination	1651–60	1661–70	1671–80	1681–90	1691–99
Virginia/Maryland					
Total migration	3,115	2,547	1,898	2,156	839
Prisoners	2,110	43	232	992	299
Row 2/Row 1	0.68	0.02	0.12	0.46	0.36
Other North American Mainland					
Total migration	7	103	214	104	59
Prisoners	1	1	0	15	0
Row 2/Row 1	0.14	0.01	0	0.14	0
Caribbean					
Total migration	6,805	2,787	1,504	3,123	826
Prisoners	82	1,144	841	1,733	789
Row 2/Row 1	0.01	0.41	0.56	0.55	0.96
All destinations					
Total migration	9,927	5,437	3,616	5,383	1,724
Prisoners	2,193	1,188	1,073	2,740	1,088
Row 2/Row 1	0.22	0.22	0.30	0.51	0.63

Source: David Eltis and Ingrid Stott, "Coldham's Emigrants from England, 1640–1699: A Database."

of slaves stemmed from improved productivity in slave trading, discussed at length in Chapter 5, and a resultant fall in slave prices. Initially the decline in slave prices had its major impact on the sugar colonies, bringing about a relatively smooth substitution of slaves for free. At first, these developments left the Chesapeake unaffected because slave prices still remained too high for tobacco planters. Both the sugar and tobacco growing sectors experienced a downturn in the 1680s, but tobacco experienced the longer and more severe decline. The continued fall in the servant/slave price ratio eventually brought slaves into contention in the Chesapeake in the 1690s, the upturn in slave prices at the end of the 1680s having been more than matched by increasing values for servants. Even in the early eighteenth century, however, the Chesapeake constituted a minor market for slaves compared to the Caribbean.

But an examination of Table 2-2 indicates that coercion was not limited to slaves. Analysis of lists of emigrants published by Peter Wilson Coldham allows us a glimpse of prisoners, of particular interest because, like African slaves, they were forced to leave the Old World against their will and enter, in the words of one group, an "insupportable Captivity ... now generally grinding at the Mills attending the Fornaces, or digging in this scorching land (Barbados)."[61] They were the only European emigrants who lacked choice over destination as a matter of course. Table 2-2 shows the destinations and prisoner status, broken down by decade, of 20,704 emigrants from England in the years 1651 to 1699. The data comprise perhaps a tenth of total emigration from England in these years.[62] To facilitate analysis the destinations are grouped into three major geographic categories: the Caribbean, the Chesapeake, and the rest of the mainland plus Newfoundland. The final row in each panel shows prisoners as a proportion of total migrants. Although the sample size is relatively large, there is no doubt that prisoners are overrepresented. As a general rule, prisoner migrants were more likely to leave documentary evidence of their departure than were non-prisoners, even if the latter were indentured servants. The ratios in the last row of each panel should not therefore be taken as representative of the population of migrants.

The prisoner category actually combines two distinct groups of prisoners of war and convicted felons. The former account almost entirely for the large exodus of prisoners in two batches to Virginia in 1651 and 1653, comprising Scots and Irish in the main. These were almost the only kind of prisoners that the Chesapeake colonies received at this time. Not shown in Table 2-2, however, is the fact that Barbados received several times more of this group than the Chesapeake. A petition from the island's planters in 1655 claimed that the latter had "received 12,000 prisoners of warr . . . who were noxious whilest they remained here." The planters had "rendred" them "beneficiall to this Commonwealth."[63] Convicts, the product of the English

---

[61] Foyle and Rivers, *England's Slavery, or Barbados Merchandize*, 5.

[62] More precisely, 11 percent of total departures for the Americas from England as estimated by Gemery, "Emigration from the British Isles to the New World," 216. The database is David Eltis and Ingrid Stott, "Coldham's Emigrants from England, 1640–1699: A Database." The major source of Coldham's data is the record of registrations of indentured servants at Bristol on which historians have already drawn, but other sources containing data on non-servant migrants contribute over half the Coldham sample. The investigation thus goes beyond previously published work. See Peter Wilson Coldham, *The Complete Book of Emigrants, 1607–1660* (Baltimore, 1988), and *The Complete Book of Emigrants, 1661–1699* (Baltimore, Md., 1990). For discussion of the data, particularly their representativeness in the light of various published estimates of transatlantic migration in seventeenth-century English Atlantic, see Ingrid Stott, "Emigration from England, 1640–1680," MA thesis, Dept. of History, Queen's University, 1993. Migrants listed as shippers or merchants have been excluded from the data because many of these individuals appear more than once either for the same voyage or different voyages. In addition, Coldham's sources seem particularly thin for the 1642 to 1650 period for which there are records of only 491 migrants, with only single entries for some years. Analysis here is thus confined to the post-1650 period.

[63] Thomas Povey, Book of Entrie of Forreigne Letters, Add ms, 11,411, f. 9.

judicial system rather than war, account for almost all the rest of the prisoner group in Table 2-2.

The sugar islands received over three-quarters of the prisoners leaving England after 1660. A similar ratio would hold if we extended the comparison back to the mid-1640s and included the twelve thousand "noxious" prisoners in Barbados not listed in Table 2-2. This ratio is almost as high as the proportion of the total English slave trade that Jamaica, Nevis, and Barbados absorbed in the 1662–1700 period. Antigua sought prisoners in 1655, and in the mid-1670s the Lords of the Committee of Trade agreed to subsidize the transportation of prisoners to the Leeward Islands.[64] It is not surprising then that Table 2-2 shows prisoners making up a steadily rising share of all English emigrants leaving for the sugar islands after 1650, even though the size of that share, as explained earlier, is biased upward. Virginia and Maryland did attempt to ban convict migrants in 1670 and 1676, respectively,[65] but the determining factor in the direction of the convict flow was more likely to have been crop type. The unpleasant nature of sugar cultivation put a premium on coercion. Although the numbers of European prisoners of war and convicts never approached those from Africa and never compensated for the fall in servant and free migration, it is clear that the slave trade was not the only coerced migration that accelerated after 1650.[66]

Prisoners were never more than a supplementary source of labor, and Table 2-1 shows the dominant migrant stream to the English Americas was the one from Africa by the 1660s. A trade in coerced labor, including supply networks and well-organised markets, already existed, thanks to the Portuguese and Dutch.[67] But the activities of the English slave merchant nevertheless had a major role in accounting for the successful English response to the colonial labor supply problem. The competitiveness of the early English slave trader is addressed more fully in Chapter 5, but whatever the relative performance of the general Dutch and English shipping

---

[64] "A Report to His Majesty from the Lords Committee of Trade touching the Leeward islands," Rawlinson manuscripts Bodleian, Oxford. (Henceforth, Rawlinson), A295, fols. 45–59.

[65] Convict labor and political prisoners are discussed in Beckles, *White Servitude and Black Slavery*, pp. 52–8. The slave ratio is calculated from Eltis, "The British Transatlantic Slave Trade Before 1714."

[66] For early transportation see John M. Beattie, *Crime and the Courts in England, 1660–1800* (Princeton, N.J., 1986), 470–83; Peter Wilson Coldham, *Emigrants in Chains: A Social History of Forced Emigration to the Americas of Felons, Destitute Children, Political and Religious Non-Conformists, Vagabonds and Other Undesirables, 1606–1776* (Baltimore, Md., 1992), pp. 3–43. Lyle Koehler, *A Search for Power: The 'Weaker Sex' in Seventeenth Century New England* (Chicago, 1980), p. 113, cites the case of Massachusetts refusing a consignment of fifty Newgate women in this period.

[67] Thornton, *Africa and Africans*, 13–42.

industries at this time, it is clear that the English quickly displaced or at least outstripped the Dutch in the slave trade after the mid-seventeenth century.

English merchants who had first created the plantation complex with indentured labor were able to fashion an unprecedented response to the post-1660 colonial labor crisis. In the subtropical colonies the master-slave relationship became the norm because labor was even more scarce there than in post-1650 England. Without coercion there would have been little production for export in a land-abundant environment. Fewer indentured servants meant more slave labor, but the ethnic exclusivity of the latter ensured that the slave labor would be African, not European. The English plantation complex assumed characteristics not seen before in the Americas. Technology carried from Brazil by the Dutch and perhaps Dutch supplies of slaves may have been important in both these processes, but it was English Barbados, not Dutch St. Eustatius or Surinam that dominated the plantation world of the second half of the seventeenth century.

For supplies of slaves the English could increasingly rely on their own merchants. Between 1660 and 1713, for every slave shipped by the Dutch, the English shipped between three and four. The two nations competed on equal terms in the Spanish market, and the Dutch had as great an access to the English Caribbean islands as did the English interloper traders (those English who were separate from the Royal African Company).[68] Curaçao, exclusively supplied by the Dutch themselves, was the major slave entrepot in the Caribbean. Yet despite the Dutch role in selling slaves to all-comers in the Americas, gold remained their chief concern in Africa throughout this period. "The natives," wrote James Blaney from Cape Coast Castle in 1706, "by Custom are used to carry their slaves to the English & Gold to the Dutch."[69] This pattern evolved, moreover, during the forty years after 1645 or so when the price of Africans newly arrived in the Americas decreased. Indeed, by the 1680s, slave prices in Barbados had probably reached an all-time low for any market in the Caribbean.[70] Given declining prices for

---

[68] Johannes Menne Postma, *The Dutch in the Atlantic Slave Trade, 1600–1815* (Cambridge, 1990), p. 110. For Dutch sales to English islands see Henry Carpenter and Thomas Belchamber, Nevis, June 3, 1686, T70/12, p. 128 and Edward Parsons, Sept. 7, 1688, Montserrat, *ibid*, p. 101.

[69] James Blaney to RAC, August 3, 1706, T70/5, f. 38. A swing to slaves by the Dutch had been noted two years earlier by Dalby Thomas, the RAC's chief agent on the coast, but even then the Dutch aim was to supply the English competitors to the RAC rather than Dutch slave ships: "Dutch buy little else but gold, but of late have struck into ye Negro trade to supply the Ten percent men" (November 16, 1704, T70/14, f. 82). For a more formal assessment of the relative importance of the slave and gold trades, see David Eltis, "The Relative Importance of Slaves in the Atlantic Trade of Seventeenth Century Africa," *Journal of African History*, 35(1994):237–49.

[70] Patrick Manning, *Slavery and African Life: Occidental, Oriental and African Slave Trades* (Cambridge, 1990), p. 178; Beckles, *White Servitude and Black*

slaves, the rise of English slave trading after 1650 was even more spectacular than the rise of the English slave system as a whole.

In summary, expansion at home and abroad coincided with a tightening supply of white labor in both England and the Americas. In the colonies the productivity of the English slave fleet allowed the expansion to proceed. Given an export market, oceangoing and plantation technologies, a sophisticated structure of financial intermediation, and a refusal of either English or Africans to work in plantation agriculture voluntarily, land abundance dictated slavery. English, and more generally, European, refusal to impose slavery or slave-like conditions on other Europeans ensured the African and Amerindian nature of slavery in the Americas. At home there was a combination of higher wages and increasingly draconian social legislation, underpinned by relatively high population densities. But if the solutions to the labor crisis within the English Atlantic system varied, the end result was from one perspective remarkably similar. Exports from both England (woollen textiles) and the colonies (sugar and tobacco) increased strongly in the face of declining prices for these commodities.[71] The English system was strikingly flexible. Perhaps historians should look at what the colonies had in common with the English domestic economy at the outset of the plantation system and then trace the differing transatlantic responses to pressures that were fundamentally the same, rather than focussing on the large differences that eventually developed in labor regimes across the Atlantic. More specifically, English exports retained and expanded traditional markets on the European mainland in the face of increasing domestic wages and rising protective measures on the continent. Likewise, English advances in the slave-shipping sector allowed a successful response to tightening labor supplies in the colonies, and Chapter 8 provides some evidence of parallel developments in the sugar islands. Domestic and colonial labor regimes, which already had begun to diverge with the conversion of the English master-servant contract into indentured servitude, now went in different directions, but the driving forces – a pursuit of higher productivity and consumer demand for cheaper goods – were the same for both.

Finally, we should note that much of the English success was encouraged by a decentralised imperial power structure, itself a manifestation of evolving English conceptions of individualism. The faltering progress of early Virginia

---

Slavery, 117; Galenson, *Traders, Planters and Slaves*, 64–9; Richard N. Bean, *The British Trans-Atlantic Slave Trade*, (New York, 1975), p. 211.

[71]   James Thorold Rogers, *A History of Agriculture and Prices in England* (Oxford, 1887), vol 5:462–3; N. W. Posthumus, *Inquiry into the History of Prices in Holland* 2 vols. (Leiden, 1946–64), 1:503, 507, 515–16. The volume of English cloth exported to major markets in continental Europe for selected years is in Margaret Priestley, "Anglo-French Trade and the 'Unfavorable Balance' Controversy, 1660–1685," *Economic History Review*, 4(1951):46–7.

and the ultimate disaster at Providence Island in the early seventeenth century may be attributed in part to a decision-making process concentrated in the hands of investors at home, in this case London.[72] This was a characteristic of all early European settlement ventures but a different strategy quickly emerged in the English Atlantic; it is almost impossible to imagine the Spanish allowing as much latitude to their transatlantic settlements as the English did to theirs. The opening statement of a petition presented to the Lord Protector in 1655 noted that:

[M]any Englishmen that have by their own Industry settled themselves in Remote parts . . . had little or no Encouragement or proteccon from ye Supremacy of England. Nor hath there been any Councill or Corporacon appointed by ye State to take care and provide for them as all other States have done . . .[73]

This willingness to allow (or inability to prevent) the emergence of the degree of local autonomy that successful colonization required was as much a product of northwest Europe as was the separation of the peasant from the land.

Slave regimes existed not just because of European economic growth but also on account of the related phenomenon of European freedom. As explained in Chapter 1, in contrast to other peoples, Europeans conceived freedom as an individual owning his or her own person without obligation to others, and such freedom seemed equally compatible with waged and slave labor in the seventeenth century in the sense that if one owned oneself, one could presumably sell oneself.[74] The movement within Europe and its overseas settlements toward a modern labor force where employers no longer held property rights in the employed began to evolve just as Europeans revived chattel slavery for others. One consequence of possessive individualism was a freedom for Europeans, more particularly, English, to move and enslave others without much reference to the metropolitan authorities. Another was an accelerated, if unequal rise in incomes within Europe – economic growth for one side of the ideological divide and separation of labor from the means of production for the other. "Modernisation" meant a greater responsiveness to incentives and acceptance of a labor market but, given the awfulness of gang labor, the labor market in the sugar islands was for slaves. Until the free-labor markets of the North Atlantic became

---

[72] For this argument in relation to Providence Island see Karen Ordahl Kupperman, *Providence Island, 1630–1641: The Other Puritan Colony* (Cambridge, 1993), especially 320–48.

[73] Thomas Povey, "Book of Entrie of Forreigne Letters," Add Ms, 11, 411, 3v.

[74] The Levellers did deny the right of the individual to alienate all the property in his/her person. See C. B. Macpherson, *The Political Theory of Possessive Individualism: Hobbes to Locke* (Oxford, 1962), p. 266. For a fuller definition of possessive individualism, see pp. 263–4.

larger and more integrated, fewer English emigrants meant more pressure on Africa.

Some of the English work force who did not accept "modernisation" or had transgressed social norms became convicts, vagrants, and inmates of workhouses. In some cases, as Table 2-2 shows, they were sent to the colonies. Given mercantilist convictions about the determination of people to avoid work and the weakness of the central government beyond the line, we might have expected the draconian measures explored in the pamphlet literature to have become a reality for white workers on the sugar islands. Did not serfdom thrive in contemporary Scotland? Compared to the master-servant contract in England, indentured servitude was draconian, but enslavement of Europeans was never an option. Why? Chapters 3 and 4 address the issue.

3

Europeans and African Slavery
in the Americas

SUB-SAHARAN REGIONS were not the only parts of Africa for which European ships laden with goods set out to obtain people. In the seventeenth and eighteenth centuries, the Dutch and English, in particular, periodically sought slaves from the Mediterranean ports of North Africa. Here, however, the slaves were invariably white, and their fate, after their African owners had received the appropriate amount of goods, was not hard labor in the Americas but rather reentry into the nascent West European free labor market. In striking contrast to their attitudes toward non-Europeans a little to the south, European governments extended "Compassion to the Poor Slaves" and negotiated the redemption of their compatriots after the Barbary Powers had enslaved the latter. Down to the 1640s there were more English slaves in North Africa than there were African slaves under English control in the Caribbean. Release of the former became feasible when the "Emperor of Fez and Morocco ... [sent] word what English Comodities he will have in Exchange for them ...."[1] Clearly by the seventeenth century there was a slave-free dichotomy within Europe that followed the divide between Africans and Europeans. Why did a century or more have to pass before significant numbers of Europeans found similar compassion for Africans carried across the Atlantic? Indeed, why, from a broader perspective, should Europeans feel it necessary to seek the release of their fellows held in captivity? This last concern appeared first on a significant scale in sixteenth-century Spain and Portugal when religious orders dedicated to the redemption of

[1] See for example William Meade, Theodore Eccleston, William Ingram, and Joseph Wastey, "Concerning the English Slaves at Macqueness ... & Elsewhere in South Barbary." n.d., but c. 1690, Co388/3 f. 172, and the follow-up letter, *ibid.*, f. 174, both of which refer to Dutch as well as English negotiations. A proclamation of the English Parliament in 1624 estimated 1,500 English held in slavery in all the Barbary states combined (cited in Stephen Clissold, *The Barbary Slaves* (London, 1977), p. 137).

Spanish and Portuguese captives in North Africa raised huge sums privately for that purpose. The state was heavily involved by the end of the century. Redemptions and the funds behind them were far more significant than in the Middle Ages when the only beneficiaries were high-ranking members of society. They were far greater too than equivalent efforts in North Africa to redeem Muslim captives in Iberia. Muslim exchanges for Christians did not begin on a large scale until after 1750.[2]

For most scholars there is perhaps little need to explore the manifestation of this issue in the Americas, namely racial slavery. That Europeans used only non-Europeans as slaves after the Middle Ages for primarily economic reasons has wide support in the literature. All we know about the early modern European commercial elites and planters or the plantation system would seem to vindicate this position. Whatever the definition of capitalism, elites would surely use the cheapest option possible within the limits of mercantilist policies.[3] Moreover, Chapters 1 and 2 have shown that Europeans went to the New World to take advantage of economic opportunities. Yet such motives operated under the aegis of fundamental non-economic values, in part socially constructed in the modern terminology, which created the Atlantic slave system and the slave trade that sustained it, just as much as the drive to consume and produce plantation produce. One central issue here is perception of race, ethnicity, or, less controversially, who is to be considered an outsider and is therefore enslavable and who is an insider and thus unenslavable. A second, addressed in the next chapter, is gender. Anyone who has opened an academic journal in the 1990s will find race and gender a familiar duo, one that is used yet again below to question the consensus on the unqualified link between economic motivation and slavery in the Americas. Few scholars now rely heavily on economic paradigms to explain the ending of slavery. The number of slaveholders who voluntarily converted their slaves into wage-earning laborers in order to increase profits was not large, nor were the numbers of non-slaveholders who benefited directly from abolition. Recent studies of abolition draw heavily on the cultural and ideological spheres of human activity. Perhaps the origins of the system are in need of a similar reassessment.

The truly interesting question is not why slavery (or abolition) per se but rather which groups are considered eligible for enslavement and why this eligibility changes over time. As noted in Chapter 1, most settled societies

---

[2] Ellen G. Friedman, *Spanish Captives in North Africa in the Early Modern Age* (Madison, Wis., 1983), pp. 105–28, 157.

[3] Even George Frederickson, the historian who has perhaps looked furthest beyond class and economics for the sources of racism, has written that if white slavery had appeared profitable it would have been introduced. See George M. Frederickson, *The Arrogance of Race: Historical Perspectives on Slavery, Racism and Social Inequality* (Middletown, Conn., 1988), p. 194.

incorporated slavery into their social structures. Moreover, few peoples in the world have not been a major source of slaves at one time or another. The African component may dominate interpretations of slavery in the Atlantic world and, from somewhat earlier, in the Islamic world, but the more fundamental question from a longer and wider view is what separates outsiders – those who are eligible for enslavement – from insiders, who are not. Nathan Huggins has answered the often-asked question of how Africans could enslave other Africans and sell them into the slave trade with the astute response that the enslavers did not see themselves or their victims as Africans. Seventeenth-century Europeans understood this very well when they ensured that the castle slaves who staffed the forts on the Gold Coast were drawn from the distant Gambia or Slave Coast regions. Richard Hellie has made the same point differently in writing of the efforts of slave owners in sixteenth-century Russia to claim spurious foreign origins for themselves so that the enslaved could be held at a distance.[4] In the Americas, the names Indian bands gave themselves translate as original people (e.g., Iroquois) but the names they gave to others meant raw meat eaters (Eskimos) or rattlesnakes (Nottoway).[5] The questions of why certain groups are deemed more appropriate than others for enslavement and the degree to which their status can be changed are of interest to anthropologists studying non-Western societies more often than historians and economists.[6] However, posing such questions in the European rather than the Asian, African, and indigenous American contexts promises some new insights.

If almost all societies in Europe, Africa, and the Americas and, indeed, in the rest of the world, accepted slavery at the time of the Columbian contact, they had different definitions of outsider status. In Africa and the Americas, such status might include anyone who was not part of the immediate lineage, but, more frequently, it was restricted to those not belonging to the nation or tribe – implying a somewhat wider definition of insider. For example, in 1682 two groups of people – the Abora and the Coromantines – both members of the Fante Confederacy on the Gold Coast, had a dispute that resulted in the former raiding the latter and taking prisoners. At Anomabu, an English factor saw in this event an opportunity to obtain slaves for Royal African Company ships. Regrettably, he reported, "although the Abbraers panyarred the Cormanteen people, yet they dare not sell them for they are all

---

[4] Nathan Irvin Huggins, *Black Odyssey: The Afro-American Ordeal in Slavery* (New York, 1977), p. 20; Richard Hellie, *Slavery in Russia, 1450–1725* (Chicago, 1982), pp. 393–4.

[5] James Axtell, *Beyond 1492: Encounters in Colonial North America* (New York, 1992), p. 33.

[6] James L. Watson, "Slavery as an Institution, Open and Closed Systems," James L. Watson (ed.), *Asian and African Systems of Slavery* (Berkeley, 1980), pp. 1–15, and other essays in this volume for an introduction to the literature.

of one country."[7] This was roughly the situation in Europe during and immediately after Roman times. However, by the fifteenth century the concept of insider had come to include all natives of the subcontinent, among whom there were some who were non-white, although few were non-Christian.[8] Slavery in Europe was not extensive but where it existed it was confined to non-Christians or natives of Africa and their immediate descendants. A similar pattern was established in the Islamic world. The more extreme the circumstances, the clearer the dividing line. The counterpart of an African kin group disposing of its most marginal members during famine has a parallel in the behavior of storm-tossed European mariners discussing the killing of non-Europeans in their midst to save the larger group.[9]

The line dividing insider from outsider in the European case had some flexibility even in the short term. The Spanish, though not the Portuguese or English, had banned the enslavement of American Indians by the 1540s. Despite this move to include non-Europeans, it was religious rather than ethnic barriers against outsiders that fell first. Jews and Muslims (or at least North African and European Muslims) were accorded insider status well before Africans. But the line was never drawn strictly in terms of skin color or race, however defined. The Spanish in America may have reserved full chattel slavery for sub-Saharan Africans but slaves in Sicily as late as 1812 were Arab or at least North African Muslims.[10] Among insiders, the Portuguese-speaking

---

[7] Richard Thelwall, Aug. 9, 1682, Rawlinson manuscript, c. 746.

[8] A full evaluation of the amalgam of the cultural norms, behavior patterns, physical appearance, circumstances of birth, class, and economic status that determined insider-outsider status would require much more space than is available here, and precision is not in any event essential to the argument. Winthrop Jordan's *White Over Black: American Attitudes Toward the Negro, 1550–1812* (Chapel Hill, N.C., 1968), especially, pp. 3–11 focusses on the English and Africans and puts more emphasis on the ethnic component in the insider-outsider divide than the present chapter, but the early chapters still provide useful insights into European perceptions of non-Europeans in the early modern era. See more recently Alden T. Vaughan and Virginia Mason Vaughan, "Before Othello: Elizabethan Representations of Sub-Saharan Africans," *William and Mary Quarterly*, 54(1997):19–44.

[9] When provisions ran short on the return of Columbus from his second transatlantic voyage, Amerindian slaves being carried back to Spain were at risk of being eaten (Alfred W. Crosby, *Ecological Imperialism: The Biological Expansion of Europe, 900–1900* (Cambridge, 1986), p. 117). When the English ship *Luxborough Galley* (voyage id 75,795) foundered mid-Atlantic on its return from the West Indies, survivors in an overloaded open boat proposed throwing overboard the two African boys among them. The debate was ended by the expiration of one of the Africans and one European (Nigel Tattersfield, *The Forgotten Trade: Comprising the Log of the Daniel and Henry of 1700 and Accounts of the Slave Trade from the Minor Ports of England, 1698–1725* (London, 1991), pp. 209–11).

[10] Charles Verlinden, *The Beginnings of Modern Colonization: Eleven Essays with an Introduction* (Ithaca, N.Y., 1970), pp. 27, 40.

community that ran the slave traffic to Bahia had an African component.[11] More striking – at least if we think of the issue from the European perspective – one of the "marchants" of an English slaving venture in 1657 was "a Christian Negroe" and a slave-ship captain of the Royal African Company in 1702 was black.[12] Moreover, as noted later, the widening process was neither inevitable nor irreversible.[13] The process may have stopped short of or avoided slavery but, as recently as 1802, the French had no difficulty in reinstating full chattel slavery in their colonies a decade after they had eliminated it. The key issue is not why slavery died out in western Europe by the early modern period or even why it had become confined to groups from other continents by 1500, but rather why it was not reintroduced on its old (and less exclusionary) basis when the potential of American mines and plantations became apparent.

In the English Americas, especially the North American mainland, there is a widely held perception that the association between blacks and slavery was less strong before 1670 than it was to become, or in terms of the argument presented here, that blacks were not considered outsiders initially. Yet for the English state, at least, the dividing line was both absolute and clear from the moment the English slave trade became significant. "Servants," stated a report of a committee of the English Council of Foreign Plantations before 1660, "are either Blacks or whites: Blacks are brought by ... Trade ... and are ... per[pet]uall servants." As for whites, there were three categories. The first "are such as are in diverse waies gathered upp here in England" to serve various terms. Not only were these not perpetual servants but the report also recommended legislation to protect them against "the many evills wch doe happen in the forceing tempting and seduceing" of them. A second category of whites were "felons and such as are condemned to death unless for murther or treason," who "should bee repreived and designed to Forreigne Plantations to serve twice seven yeares." The third category was "all sturdy beggars as Gipsies and other incorigeible Rogues and wander[er]s,"

---

[11] Verger, *Trade Relations*, 392–427.
[12] SP 18/158, f. 276 cited in John C. Appleby, "A Guinea Venture, c. 1657: A Note on the Early English Slave Trade," *Mariner's Mirror*, 79(1993):86; RAC to Benjamin Alford, March 10, 1702, T70/58, ff. 16–17.
[13] Twentieth-century Europe (Nazi Germany, Stalinist Russia, the Balkans) might be taken as providing examples of inward shifts in perceptions of insider status. On the other hand none of these cases have resulted in the institution of the systematic degradation of another (and all that others' progeny) into full chattel slavery for the purpose of maximising profits. Europeans can still apparently hang, torture, mutilate, and burn other Europeans, but they cannot bring themselves to convert their fellows (or anyone else) into forced laborers (or forced skilled workers or forced professionals, etc.) for life. Much less are they able to use the offspring of such a group for similar purposes. Above all, they have not sold such individuals on open markets in which the price is competitively determined by the interaction of many potential buyers and sellers.

who were to be "taken up by Constables and imprisond until the next Assizes" and, after due process, "sent to the Plantations for five years undere the condition of servants." According to the preamble, it was "universally agreed that People are the foundation and Improvement of all Plantations and ... are encreased principally by sending servants thither," but blacks were slaves, whereas whites, of any status, served for a limited term and had either freedom of choice or access to due process.[14]

If the existence of the line between insiders and outsiders is apparent in the sources, the reasons for changes in perceptions of which groups were suitable for enslavement are less clear, but it is at least possible to chart the process. We begin with a cursory assessment of the existing literature before exploring one crucial area that this literature has tended to bypass. Comparisons between Europe and the rest of the Atlantic world and between one European country and another form the basis of an alternative view of the issues presented in the final section.

In the last two decades, a short description of the dividing line between insiders and outsiders has been power relationships. Analyses along class and interest lines have dominated literatures on both the rise and fall of American slavery. Elites in Europe and Africa cooperated to ensure a supply of labor for the American plantations, and the shifting perceptions of a European elite – driven by protest from below in either the dominant or the slave society according to some – brought the system to an end. Myths about slaves and other underclasses emanated from associations that at root and at first had a large economic component.[15]

This approach fits well with the more narrowly focussed literature on the transition to slavery in the Atlantic world. It is frequently argued that the substitution of African slaves for the various forms of coerced native labor and European indentured servants in the plantation regions of the Americas was driven by relative costs and was thus in essence an economic decision. Debate over the mechanics of this process continues. For British North America, a combination of an elastic supply of slave labor, falling slave transportation costs, and rising servant prices governed the transition, as discussed by David Galenson, Russell Menard, and others.[16] For Brazil, Stuart Schwartz

---

[14] "Certaine Propositions for the better accomodating the Forreigne Plantations with Servants ... " CO1/18, ff. 224–6, n.d., but c. late 1650s.

[15] William McKee Evans, "From the Land of Canaan to the Land of Guinea: The Strange Odyssey of the 'Sons of Ham,'" *American Historical Review*, 85 (February 1980):15–43 and for the more recent literature Barbara Jeanne Fields, "Slavery, Race and Ideology in the United States of America," *New Left Review*, 181(May–June 1990):95–118. For a historiographical survey and a dissenting view see William A. Green, "Race and Slavery: Considerations on the Williams Thesis," Barbara L. Solow and Stanley L. Engerman (eds.), *British Capitalism and Caribbean Slavery: The Legacy of Eric Williams* (Cambridge, 1987), 25–49.

[16] Russell R. Menard, "From Servants to Slaves: The Transformation of the Chesapeake Labor System," *Southern Studies*, 16(Winter 1977):355–90; Galenson,

has shown how more expensive and productive African slaves came to replace their Brazilian Indian counterparts in the first seventy years of sugar
production in the Reconçavo. Similar switches from indigenous to African
labor occurred in sixteenth-century Caribbean and later in South Carolina.
In 1708, nearly one in four of the slave population in South Carolina was
Indian, and the colony exported captives to the West Indies. Farther north,
French Canadians could not afford African slaves, and their slaves remained
overwhelmingly Amerindian.[17] By contrast, the southern temperate zones,
closer to Africa and yielding exportable agricultural commodities of coffee
and hides, had an entirely African slave labor force. Much remains unex-
plored, but future research will not undermine the role played by economic
factors in these transitions. From a broad perspective, the large-scale traffic
in slaves for plantation use focussed first on northeastern Brazil, the region
closest to Africa, moved next to the easternmost of the Antilles, Barbados,
and had an impact on the Americas farthest away from Africa only later. If
we leave aside the issue of alternative forms of labor, this process is consistent
with trends in slave prices and transatlantic shipping costs.

But were costs as central as the extensive literature on the labor transition assumes? If coerced-native, indentured, or free-waged European slave
labor or African slave labor were the only options open to planters, then the
answer must be yes. But why should these combinations of ethnic groups
and labor regimes be the only possibilities for the early plantation Americas?
The extent to which other alternatives were attempted or even considered is
ignored in the literature, despite the fact that widening the question provides
insights into more than just substitution of one form of labor for another. As
Eric Williams realised half a century ago, what is at stake here is not just the
economics and morality of early European expansion but the foundation
of relations between European and African peoples in the Americas. The
current literature cannot deal easily with the questions, why no European
slaves, or why no African indentured servants, even though Winthrop Jordan
posed the former a quarter-century ago.[18] Scholars are now less likely to

White Servitude. For a recent discussion of trends in contract lengths (a proxy
for servant prices), which seem not to have increased in the 1654–1775 period,
see Farley Grubb, "The Long-run Trend in the Value of European Immigrant Servants, 1654–1831: New Measurements and Interpretations," *Research in Economic History,* 14(1992):167–240.

[17] Schwartz, *Sugar Plantations in the Formation of Brazilian Society,* 15–27, 51–72;
Peter H. Wood, "Indian Servitude in the Southeast," Wilcomb E. Washburn (ed.),
Handbook of North American Indians, Vol. 4, *History of Indian White Relations*
(Washington, 1988), pp. 407–9; Theda Perdue, *Slavery and the Evolution of
Cherokee Society, 1540–1866* (Knoxville, Tenn., 1979), pp. 19–35; Robin Winks,
Blacks in Canada: A History (New Haven, 1971), pp. 1–19. Sanford Winston
commented "the relationship between the number of Indian and Negro slaves
was ... inverse," in "Indian Slavery in the Carolina Region," *Journal of Negro
History,* 19(October 1934):436.

[18] Jordan, *White Over Black,* 66.

counterpose slavery and freedom or coercion and consent, especially in studying the beginning and ending of slavery in the Americas.[19] There can be no doubt that major groups subjected to slavery, such as Canaanites, Slavs, and Africans, were quickly assumed fit subjects for such status even if they were not so regarded initially. But the creation of later stereotypes does not explain why Europeans went thousands of miles to Africa for slaves in the first place. Nor does it explain why at some point between the eighteenth and nineteenth centuries, in the face of three centuries of stereotyping, the majority of Europeans and their descendants decided that Africans were no longer suitable subjects for enslavement.

If we wish to understand the origins of African slavery in the New World or indeed in the pre-Columbian Old World, we must first explore the labor options of early modern Europeans – both those that were tried and those that were not. Second, we need to assess how close Europeans came to imposing slavery or slavelike conditions on other Europeans and finally what for them set slavery apart as a status for others. These steps will help clarify the cultural and ideological parameters that at once shaped the evolution of African New World slavery and kept Europeans as non-slaves. Various forms of European forced labor were in fact tried. A comparison of these options across national boundaries reveals differences in what major European colonial powers considered feasible as labor regimes. Yet no West European power after the late Middle Ages crossed the basic divide separating European workers from full chattel slavery. And while serfdom fell and rose in different parts of early modern Europe and shared characteristics with slavery, serfs were not outsiders either before or after enserfment. The phrase long-distance serf trade is an oxymoron. Even in the twentieth century, totalitarian states have used slave labor primarily as a punitive strategy against perceived enemies of the state, and while they have extracted labor from their victims, they have never instituted full chattel slavery primarily as an economic device.

Although there is no evidence that Europeans ever considered instituting full chattel slavery of Europeans in their overseas settlements, the striking paradox is that no sound economic reasons spoke against it. By the

---

[19] Rebecca Scott, "Comparing Emancipations: A Review Essay," *Journal of Social History*, 20(Spring 1987):565. Most recently see the special issue of *Slavery & Abolition*, 14 (April 1993), edited by Michael Twaddle, entitled *The Wages of Slavery in Africa, the Caribbean and England*, and Mary Turner (ed.), *From Chattel Slaves to Wage Slaves: The Dynamics of Labor Bargaining in the Americas* (London, 1995). For a similar orientation, this time at the inception of the system and centred on the study of white labor in Barbados, see Beckles, *White Servitude and Black Slavery*, especially pp. 5–10. Orlando Patterson's distinction between slave and non-slave centered on the absolute power of the slave's master and the origin of enslavement as an alternative to death is a useful corrective to this tendency to roll together slave and non-slave status [*Slavery and Social Death: A Comparative Study* (Cambridge, Mass., 1982), pp. 21–7].

seventeenth century, the most cursory examination of relative costs suggests that European slaves should have been preferred to either European indentured labor or African slaves. And while native Americans were cheap to enslave, their life expectancy and productivity in post-Columbian plantation conditions hardly compared with that of pre-industrial or, indeed, post-industrial Europeans.

Before pursuing the issue of costs it is worth noting that social devices used in African and Indian societies to deprive people of their liberty were incorporated fully into European societies. Judicial process sent English, French, Portuguese, and, to a lesser extent, Spanish men and women to the plantations. It also condemned the French, Spaniards, Germans, Italians, and Poles to the galleys. England, the Netherlands, and France used houses of correction to exact labor from the poor beginning in the sixteenth century and, from the late seventeenth century, from criminals as well. Impressment into service was also prevalent in Europe. The early literature on indentured servitude and engagés stressed the role of force in the acquisition of servants. If, in the Americas and Africa, informal raids or more organized military actions were major ways to obtain slaves, then in Europe wars appear to have been frequent enough both within and between nations – setting aside the incentive to acquire and sell slaves – to ensure a healthy supply of captives. In Europe, war provided a justification for impressing one's own people into service, for example, into the British navy.[20] The holding of captives and the infliction of death and torture in war and as punishment were common to European, African, and Native American societies at the time of the founding of transatlantic slave colonies. By the seventeenth century, Europeans might not enslave other Europeans, but enslavement does not appear brutal or unlikely in view of the hanging, torturing, mutilation, and burning that they inflicted on each other. European prisoners, political as well as criminal, were frequently sent to the plantations instead of to execution, and the substitution of slavery for death, explicitly recognised by John Locke, legitimated slavery throughout history. The similarity of the mechanisms for depriving people of their liberty on all four continents is striking.[21]

Moreover, as noted in earlier chapters, there were elements in the master-servant relationship in all European states in the late medieval period that could, and in several cases did, provide the basis for a revival of serfdom. And, if serfdom, why not slavery? Serfdom had disappeared in Sweden, Scotland, and the Low Countries no later than the early fourteenth century. But the institution not so much reappeared as appeared for the first time in Eastern

---

[20] For the social context of impressment as a forced labor device see Rogers, "Vagrancy, Impressment and the Regulation of Labor," 102–13.

[21] For discussion of these in an African context see Kopytoff and Miers, "African Slavery as an Institution in Marginality." For the same phenomena in one important North American context see Starna and Watkins, "Northern Iroquoian Slavery," 34–57.

Europe after these dates – and on a large scale. As already noted, marginal elements of European societies – convicts and vagrants – might have been candidates for forced labor in the Americas, but not only these. As late as the immediate antebellum period, there were ideologues in the southern United States who advocated slavery for poor whites as well as blacks.

From the strictly economic standpoint there were strong arguments in support of using European rather than African slave labor. The crux of the matter was shipping costs, which comprised by far the greater part of the price of imported bonded labor in the Americas. First, although the wind system of the Atlantic reduced the differential somewhat, it was normally quicker to sail directly to the Americas from Europe than to sail via Africa. In addition mortality and morbidity among both crews and passengers (or slaves) were lower in the north Atlantic than in the south. If we take into account the time spent collecting a slave cargo on the African coast as well, then the case for sailing directly from Europe with a cargo of Europeans appears stronger again. In the 1680s the Royal African Company (RAC) would often hire ships to carry slaves on its behalf. The hire rate was typically between £5 and £6 per slave landed alive in the Americas – a price that was understood to cover the full cost of sailing to Africa, acquiring slaves, and carrying them to the RAC's agents in the West Indies. The return cargo from the Americas was a separate speculation.[22] The cost of shipping convicts to Barbados and the Leeward Islands at this time was similar.[23] As noted later, however, ships carrying convicts, indentured servants, and fare-paying passengers always carried far fewer people per ton than did slave ships. There is little doubt that if ships carrying Europeans had been as closely packed as those carrying Africans, costs per person would have been much lower for Europeans than for Africans.

A further reason for using European rather than African slave labor derives from relative prices of African slaves and convict English labor – the nearest the English came to using Europeans as chattel slaves. Unskilled male convicts from England and Ireland sold for £16 each in Maryland in the years 1767–75 at a time when newly arrived African male slaves in the prime age group were selling for about triple this amount in Virginia and Maryland.[24] The British males worked for ten years or less, the Africans for life. If convicts and their descendants had been sold into a lifetime of service, it is

[22]   Davies, *Royal African Company*, 198. For sample rates see T70/943, ff. 12 and 13.
[23]   John C. Jeaffreson, *A Young Squire of the Seventeenth Century: Papers of Christopher Jeaffreson*, 2 vols. (London, 1878), I:159; II, 206–7. For information on costs of freighting indentured servants cf. Beckles and Downes, "The Economics of Transition," 235.
[24]   Calculated from Bean, *British Trans-Atlantic Slave Trade*, 206–8. A. Roger Ekirch, *Bound for America: The Transportation of British Convicts to the Colonies, 1718–1775* (Oxford, 1987), pp. 71, 124–5.

reasonable to suppose that planters would have been ready to pay a higher price for them. At this higher price, the British government and merchants might have found ways to provide more convicts. Shipping costs alone would not have interfered with the process. From this standpoint, convicts could have been sold into lifelong servitude for a price little more than that for seven or ten years of labor. Thus in the absence of an improbably rapid decline in slave prices as buyers switched from Africans to Europeans, we might suppose that there were no shipping cost barriers to European slaves forming the basis of the plantation labor forces of the Americas.

The other major cost categories in shipping Africans to the New World were enslavement, factoring (the costs of assembling a cargo prior to shipment), and distribution (the costs of selling a slave in the Americas).[25] Together, they made up about half the cost of a new slave in the Americas. According to Philip Curtin, enslavement costs in Africa were trivial. Most of the price of a slave sold to a factor on the African coast was made up of transportation costs.[26] Could this low cost at the point of enslavement explain the apparent preference for Africans? Given the opportunities in Europe for enslavement discussed earlier it seems unlikely. From an economic standpoint, adapting these opportunities to produce slaves instead of merely prisoners would have been neither difficult nor costly.

Indeed enslavement in Europe might have been less costly than its African counterpart. First, transportation costs, which loomed so large within Africa, were bound to be lower in a subcontinent where major population centers were located near navigable waters. Established routes for "chains" existed for French convicts heading to Marseilles, Toulon, and later Brest, for Spanish convicts to Cartagena, and for Portuguese to Lisbon, some incorporating travel on canals. In England, the barges carrying parish children from London to northern textile mills could have just as easily carried people to major ports. Second, population growth in western Europe in general, and England in particular, was considerable during the era of the slave trade. Despite a net migration of 2.7 million from the mid-sixteenth to mid-nineteenth century, England's population rose sevenfold. Scholars debate the impact on the African population of the loss of twelve million people to the Americas.[27] It is certain that this number of additional emigrants from

---

[25] These categories are taken from David Turnbull's work. Turnbull had extensive experience of the nineteenth-century slave trade. See his *Travels in the West. Cuba: with Notices of Porto Rico and the Slave Trade* (London, 1840), pp. 403–6.

[26] Philip D. Curtin, *Economic Change in Precolonial Africa: Senegambia in the Era of the Slave Trade*, 2 vols. (Madison, Wis., 1975), 1:156–7, 168–9, 173–7; 2: 45–53; and "The Abolition of the Slave Trade from Senegambia," David Eltis and James Walvin (eds.), *The Abolition of the Atlantic Slave Trade* (Madison, Wis., 1981), pp. 89–91.

[27] For different assessments see Manning, *Slavery and African Life*, 38–85, and Eltis, *Economic Growth and the Ending of the Transatlantic Slave Trade*, 64–71.

a more heavily populated Europe over the same period would have had a negligible effect.

Arguments that Africans could stand up to the epidemiology of the Caribbean are irrelevant here. Whatever the European-African mortality differentials, a hostile disease environment was never enough to prevent European indentured servants from working in the Caribbean sugar sector. Medical evidence would be pertinent only if Europeans had never labored in the Caribbean under any labor regime or if European slavery had been tried and found wanting because of excess mortality. In fact, peoples of Europe and Africa died prematurely for different reasons in the Caribbean, but life expectancies for the two groups were not very different. The Dutch East Indies was no less dangerous than the Caribbean, but four thousand East India Company personnel per annum went anyway. European demographic barriers to a supply of slaves were thus no greater than those for their African counterparts.

In fact, nearly one thousand convicts a year left Britain in the half-century after 1718. This may not seem like many compared to an African slave trade drawing twenty-five thousand a year from Africa in the last third of the seventeenth century and rising to an average of fifty thousand a year in the half century after 1700. Yet consider that the population of England was only 7 percent that of Europe in 1680, and, if the rest of Europe had followed the English practice in proportion, fourteen thousand convicts would have been available. A traffic in degredados from Portuguese possessions to Brazil and Angola existed from the sixteenth to the nineteenth century, and the massive fortifications at Havana and San Juan, as well as Spanish outposts in North Africa, were built in part with Iberian convicts. Germanic states that lacked maritime facilities sold convicts to Italian city states for galley service. In France about a thousand convicts a year arrived at Marseille in the later seventeenth and early eighteenth centuries, but these were all male and mostly between twenty and thirty-five years of age. The potential for a large, more demographically representative traffic in French convicts is clear.

Possible sources other than convicts were numerous. Prisoners from wars, as in Africa, could have provided many additional plantation laborers. The English were well aware of the cheap labor possibilities of the latter. Just when sugar production in Barbados was expanding most rapidly and within a year or two of their acquisition of Jamaica, the English used Scottish prisoners taken at the Battle of Dunbar and Dutch prisoners (taken from Dutch naval vessels) to help drain the fens.[28] Indeed, when in rebellion, the Irish and Scots alone could have filled the labor needs of the English colonies. Nor

---

[28]   J. Korthals Altes, *Sir Cornelius Vermuyden* (London, 1925), pp. 99-100. Henry C. Darby, *Draining the Fens*, second ed. (Cambridge, 1956), p. 76. While the labor was forced, in the case of the Dutch at least, the English paid common laborers' wages (CSPDS, 1652–3, 5:402).

does this speculation fully incorporate vagrants and the poor. A properly exploited system drawing on convicts, prisoners, and vagrants from all countries of Europe could easily have provided fifty thousand forced migrants a year without serious disruption to either international peace or existing social institutions that generated and supervised these potential European victims.[29] If such an outflow had been directed to the plantation colonies, it is also unlikely that mercantilist statesmen would have questioned either the scale or the direction of the flow.

More specifically, British convicts could have replaced African slaves in the Chesapeake, the destination of most transport ships. The first recorded shipment of convicts dates to 1615. Until 1770 the number of convict arrivals was at least two-thirds that of slaves in total, although in the 1730s and 1740s slave arrivals were between two and four times larger. If all whites and their subsequent progeny sent against their will to the colonies had been accorded the slave status of African immigrants, there is no reason why the number of white slaves in Maryland and Virginia would not have been at least as large as the actual black slave population at the end of the colonial period.[30]

---

[29] Gregory King estimated six hundred thousand adults receiving alms and thirty thousand vagrants in late-seventeenth-century England. "Natural and Political Observations and Conclusions upon the State and Condition of England, 1696," in *The Earliest Classics: John Graunt and Gregory King* (Farnborough, 1973), pp. 48, 57. For convicts leaving England see Ekirch, *Bound for America*, 27. The most recent estimate of slaves leaving Africa at this period is David Richardson, "Slave Exports from West and West-Central Africa, 1700–1810: New Estimates of Volume and Distribution," *Journal of African History*, 30 (January 1989): 1–22.

[30] Coldham, *Emigrants in Chains*, 43–4; Abbot Emerson Smith, "The Transportation of Convicts to the American Colonies in the Seventeenth Century," *American Historical Review*, 39(1933–4):233–6; Beattie, *Crime and the Courts*, 470–83. Perhaps one hundred thousand Africans arrived in the Chesapeake by 1770 (Allan Kulikoff, *Tobacco and Slaves: The Development of Southern Cultures in the Chesapeake, 1680–1800* (Chapel Hill, N.C., 1986), pp. 65–7, and Galenson, *White Servitude in Colonial America*, 216–17). No firm estimates of convict arrivals before 1718 exist, but the number was less than the fifty thousand that came to the Americas in the fifty-seven years after this date. Peter Wilson Coldham has found records of 7,500 convicts transported before 1718 from England alone [counted from *The Complete Book of Emigrants in Bondage, 1614–1775* (Baltimore, 1988); cf. Smith, "Transportation of Convicts," 238, who counted a minimum of 4,431, 1655–99], and Scotland, Wales, and particularly Ireland supplied many more. The estimate of rough equivalency between the descendants of convicts and the black slave population takes into account the earlier arrival of convicts and the fact that rates of natural population increase were a little higher for the white population than for the black. For those who would argue that such a system would have foundered on the difficulty of control, we should note that this issue never seemed to have threatened the existing systems of long-distance penal servitude, many involving private traders and employers.

A cursory examination of potential factoring and distribution costs indicates a similar pattern of benefits in Europe relative to Africa. A factoring network of sorts actually existed. French and Spanish merchants formed the link between courts and galleys. Between 1718 and 1775, the British government contracted out the collection as well as the shipping of convicts to the Americas. Companies in London came to specialize in assembling cargoes of convicts including transfers from regional jails prior to embarkation.[31] A network of other merchants in the Caribbean and mainland North America placed convicts, indentured servants, and often slaves with masters. The system could surely have functioned just as well if the bulk of this labor had been enslaved Europeans rather than enslaved African.

Given these transportation and production cost advantages European slave labor would have been no more expensive and probably substantially cheaper. Slavery in the Americas (white slavery) would have been extensive in the sixteenth and seventeenth centuries before African slaves arrived in large numbers.[32] Plantations would have developed more quickly and European consumers would have enjoyed an accelerated flow of sugar and tobacco. The fact that African slavery in the Americas took longer to evolve than any European counterpart would have done – at least in North America – is accounted for by the greater costs of moving people from Africa as opposed to Europe.

It was, of course, inconceivable that any of the labor pools mentioned earlier (convicts, prisoners of war, or vagrants) could have been converted into chattel slaves. The barrier to European slaves in the Americas lay not only beyond shipping and enslavement costs but also beyond any strictly economic sphere. The English Vagrancy Act of 1547 prescribing slavery

---

[31]   Ekirch, *Bound for America*, 17–18; Coldham, *Emigrants in Chains*, 59–87.
[32]   Robin Blackburn rejects this argument by positing a counterfactual world of the early Americas developing rapidly on the basis of exclusively free labor. He also suggests that Europe would have benefited materially (as well, presumably, as morally) from this. Free labor was, of course, tried. In 1624, William Usselinx argued for the Swedish Trading Company that "slaves were not to be introduced into the Swedish Colonies because their labor would be less profitable than that of Europeans" and Georgia prohibited slave-holding until 1749 (Mary Stoughton Locke, *Anti-Slavery in America* [Boston, 1901, reprinted 1968], pp. 9–12). The problem then, and for some historians now, is to explain how that free labor could have been persuaded to produce plantation output at prices that European consumers would pay. Blackburn does recognize the "greater expense ... of free labor" (compared to slave) but thinks that if this had been paid, there would have been massive demand for British products as free colonial workers used their wages to buy imports. It is hard to believe that prices of tobacco and sugar would have stayed the same under these circumstances or even have remained in a range where much would have been sold. It is even harder to believe that such a straightforward alternative never occurred to any early modern merchant capitalist (*The Making of New World Slavery: From the Baroque to the Modern 1492–1800* [London, 1997], pp. 360–1).

was never enforced. The seventy-two English political prisoners who were taken at Salisbury in 1654 and sent to Barbados the next year claimed to be "[f]ree-born People of this Nation, now in Slavery" and were able to petition Parliament in 1659; they occasioned an extensive discussion there not extended to Africans for another 130 years.[33] There were serfs in Scotland as we have seen but there were no slaves. Across the English Channel a 1716 law was necessary to deny slaves brought privately to France their enfranchisement when they arrived in the country.[34] In Spain, Portugal, and all Mediterranean countries by the sixteenth century, Moors and Africans could be slaves. Christians, which meant in practice Europeans, because non-Europeans who became Christian remained slaves, could not.[35] Even Jews were less likely to be enslaved in Spain by the later Middle Ages. In 1492, they were expelled, not enslaved. Some who fled to Portugal saw their children taken from them and sent to São Tomé but not as chattel slaves. Between the late fifteenth century and 1808, the Spanish Inquisition burned at the stake thirty-two thousand conversos (Jewish converts to Christianity) for false conversion. Enslavement for this group was not an issue.[36] But before addressing the aversion to slavery in the face of clear economic imperatives, we need to assess how close to chattel slavery (and the slave trade that supported it) Europeans were prepared to go within Europe and what differences existed between European nations.

As already noted, similar devices for depriving people of liberty existed in Africa, the Americas, and Europe. Yet if on the African and American continents these might result in enslavement – and often ownership by Europeans on both sides of the Atlantic[37] – in Europe the same procedures fell short of creating such a status, at least for Europeans. Throughout Europe the state could take the lives of individuals in Europe, but enslavement was no longer an alternative to death; rather it had become a fate worse than death and as such was reserved for non-Europeans. Europeans would accept lawbreakers and prisoners as slaves only if they were not fellow Europeans. Conceptions of insider had expanded to include the European subcontinent whereas for

[33] Foyle and Rivers, *England's Slavery, or Barbados Merchandize.*
[34] Davies, "Slavery and Protector Somerset" 533–49; William B. Cohen, *The French Encounter with Africans: White Response to Blacks, 1530–1880* (Bloomington, Ind., 1980), pp. 5, 44–6.
[35] Davis, *The Problem of Slavery in Western Culture*, 221–47.
[36] Idem, *Slavery and Human Progress*, 95; Haim Beinart, "The Conversos and Their Fate," Elie Kedourie (ed.), *Spain and the Jews* (London, 1992), pp. 92–122; Timothy Joel Coates, "Exiles and Orphans: Forced and State-Sponsored Colonizers in the Portuguese Empire, 1550–1720" (Unpublished PhD dissertation, University of Minnesota, 1993), p. 98.
[37] For the use of West Africans and American aboriginal slaves in the French galleys see Munford, *Black Ordeal of Slavery*, 1:169; Paul W. Bamford, *Fighting Ships and Prisons: The Mediterranean Galleys of France in the Age of Louis XIV* (Minneapolis, Minn., 1973), pp. 156, 165–6, 310–11.

Africans and American Indians a less than continent-wide definition of insider still pertained. In a profound but scarcely novel sense chattel slavery for Africans and Indians in the Americas was thus a function of the non-slave status that Europeans considered appropriate for themselves – a situation with historical parallels in many slave societies. Put differently, if Africans or Indians instead of Europeans had initiated the plantation system and had possessed the means to begin a slave trade with Europe, a trade in Europeans would not have been extensive. Slavery might have been just as prevalent in the western world but not likely confined to people from another continent. Logically, therefore, those European states least likely to countenance the coercion of their own citizens may well have been among the more likely to develop a system of chattel slavery overseas.

While the rejection of European slavery was, like the acceptance of its African counterpart, an unthinking decision, some states came closer to imposing chattel slavery on their citizens than did others. Convict labor, especially that sent beyond the domestic borders of the country, would seem to be the closest that Europeans came to enslaving other Europeans. The merging or increasing cooperation between state and church courts and the movement away from strictly physical chastisement of criminals in early modern western Europe triggered experiments with transportation and penal servitude. The French, Portuguese, Spanish, and English manned many of their early exploration voyages with convicts, and the French and Portuguese opened up their galley corps to convicted felons at about the time that the Portuguese began experimenting with transporting the same group to São Tomé, Goa, and Brazil. Exile to Siberia for Russian prisoners became significant from the end of the sixteenth century. Most West European countries, including England, contemplated or experimented with both galleys and transportation for convicts. In the end the Spanish and Italian states sent most convicts to galleys, the English favored transportation to distant colonies, the French and Portuguese promoted both, and the Dutch, except for fleeting experiments, did neither. Eventually, the French accepted felons for use in galleys and naval bases from other European states such as Savoy, Poland, and some German principalities. In Spain, France, and Portugal convicts worked alongside slaves from the Mediterranean littoral, Eastern Europe, Africa, and the Americas.[38]

[38] Coates, "Exiles and Orphans," 32–67; Emile Campion, *Etude sur la colonisation par les transportés anglais, russes et français* (Rennes, 1901), pp. 44–5; Beattie, *Crime and the Courts in England*, 450–519, esp. 470–4; John H. Langbein, *Torture and the Law of Proof: Europe and England in the Ancien Regime* (Chicago, 1977), pp. 27–44; Zysberg, "Galley and Hard Labor Convicts in France," 78–110; Pike, *Penal Servitude in Early Modern Spain*, 3–26; Alan Wood, "Siberian Exile in the Eighteenth Century," *Siberica*, 1(1990):39–63; Pieter Spierenburg, *The Prison Experience: Disciplinary Institutions and Their Inmates in Early Modern Europe* (New Brunswick, 1991), pp. 259–62.

At the lowest common denominator two critical features kept convict labor separate from chattel slavery. First, Africans went to the Americas as chattel slaves for life. In a sample of 21,254 emigrants from England between 1651 and 1680 the mean length of term for 10,011 servants was 53.1 months. Pregnancy could result in a lengthening of this term, but of course the master had no claim over the newborn child. Convicts in the same sample are much less well represented, but the mean term for seventy-six of these was 114.2 months.[39] It might be added that no sentence in an English court at this time required hard labor from a convicted felon. It was the merchant and the owner of the contract in the Americas that exacted the labor – in effect, to pay transport costs. The fact that the term was longer than for indentured servants was probably because convicts were less subject to careful selection and were more likely to escape. The term thus incorporated a risk premium. Moreover, an individual usually had to commit a crime in order to become a convict. Set laws and judicial procedures meant that potential convicts faced less arbitrary treatment than those who fell into slavery. The power of the state over the convict and the master over convict labor was more circumscribed than that of the slave owner over the slave.

Second, criminal status was not heritable, whereas the progeny of Africans were always slaves. In both French and Spanish galleys, convicts had great difficulty winning release from the galleys whatever the term of their sentence, their property was sold upon conviction, and they had no standing in law. But Europeans, except for some adherents to the Greek Orthodox faith, were not technically slaves. Unlike Turks, Muslims, Russians, and Africans who had been specially purchased to supplement the galley corps, they could not be resold, and their status was not transmitted to their progeny.

It is striking that the more strenuous work – specifically the farthest inboard position on the oars in galleys – was reserved for slaves, not convicts. And when the useful life of oarsmen came to an end and the state wished to reduce expenses, old slaves were usually returned to their state of origin on the basis of treaties, sold at European slave marts or, if African, sometimes taken to the French West Indies to be sold. Convicts who managed a discharge from the French galley corps also ended up in the French Americas, but they were always sold as indentured servants. Portuguese degredados could be paid by the state for their labor and in São Tomé and Angola had sufficiently different status from slaves that many of them were involved in

---

[39] The standard deviation for free migrants was 14.2, for convicts, 13.6 months, with the difference between the means significant at the .01 percent level. See Table 2–2 for the source. Length of term for the Monmouth rebels in 1686 was ten years. See John Camden Hotten (ed.), *The Original Lists of Persons of Quality; Emigrants; Political Rebels; Serving Men Sold for a Term of Years; Apprentices; Children Stolen; Maidens Pressed; and Others who Went from Great Britain to the American Plantations, 1600–1700* (London, 1874), pp. 315–45.

the slave trade that supplied São Tomé and Brazilian plantations.[40] The most that can be said by way of comparison is that the spread of African slavery in the Americas coincided with the spread of forced labor in punishment systems within Europe (transportation in the English case). But no one was in any doubt about the distinctions between the two and certainly not the prisoners and slaves.

Nevertheless, interesting differences among states emerge in the treatment of convicts. Penal servitude became a feature of the continental European systems – effectively for life in the case of the French and Spanish. The English imposed neither lifelong banishment nor much penal servitude; the Bridewell houses held few long-term prisoners and did not always have a labor regime.[41] In the Netherlands, penal servitude supplemented then replaced banishment, although the Dutch did hold long-term prisoners who had been incriminated, as opposed to convicted. They also used torture after that practice was discontinued in England, where in fact it had never been part of the Common Law.[42] For the English, transportation meant shipment across the Atlantic with no right of return for seven or, for those reprieved from death sentences, fourteen years. Once in the Americas the vast majority of prisoners were sold into seven-year terms of servitude, but the sentence itself did not provide for this.[43] Prisoners with resources could in fact buy their freedom at the point of disembarkation and, as long as they stayed away from England, convert their sentence to temporary banishment. The servitude that accompanied transportation was actually a device to pay its costs and, apart from a longer term, did not differ materially from that voluntarily experienced by non-convict indentured servants.[44] In Portugal, where

---

[40] Coates, "Exiles and Orphans," 57, 98–9; Bamford, *Fighting Ships and Prisons*, 139–52, 250–71; Pike, *Penal Servitude in Early Modern Spain*, 8–14. The term slavery is occasionally used loosely in the penology literature. J. Thorsten Selling in his widely read *Slavery and the Penal System* (New York, 1976) uses the term to cover any form of coerced labor. Spierenburg, *The Prison Experience*, refers ambivalently to the bondage of convicts throughout his book (see especially, 10). Such usage skates over distinctions important to the issue of slavery in the Americas.

[41] Spierenburg, *The Prison Experience*, 1–68, 259–76; Zysberg, "La société des galériens," 43–75; Bamford, *Fighting Ships and Prisons*, 173–83; Coates, "Exiles and Orphans," 71–2. In Spain sentences for forzados were limited to ten years in 1653, though as noted earlier detention beyond the formal term was common (Pike, *Penal Servitude in Early Modern Spain*, 7–8).

[42] Spierenburg, *The Prison Experience*, 41–60, 143–7; *idem*, "The Sociogenesis of Confinement and its Development in Early Modern Europe," *Centrum voor Maatschappij Geschiedenis*, 12(1984):38. For the ending of torture see Langbein, *Torture and the Law of Proof*, 10–12, 50, 134–5.

[43] Ekirch, *Bound for America*, 16–21.

[44] The longer term, equivalent to a lower price, might have reflected the greater likelihood of convicts escaping, being dishonest, a more diverse age and sex mix than was the case with regular indentures, or some combination of these factors. Formal analysis has yet to be carried out on convict labor.

the state bore the cost of transportation or imposed it on others, the sentence constituted exile with the labor required varying according to the needs of the state. The system was remarkably flexible in alternating between galleys and transportation to the colonies, with or without forced labor.[45]

Vagrants formed a larger group than convicts in every European country, and the destitute poor, dependent on state aid, a larger group again. From the mercantilist standpoint the productive potential of these groups in a slave society was enormous. With the increasing breakdown of church-sponsored charity systems from the midsixteenth century on, workhouses mushroomed in northwestern Europe, especially England, Holland, and France – three of the leading early plantation powers.[46] Penal servitude for felons was grafted onto this system in the eighteenth century.[47] Hardening attitudes toward the poor were seen throughout western Europe in the early modern period, although the exaction of labor in return for relief appeared first in protestant areas. The Dutch system of workhouses was the most efficient and became a model for the rest of Europe. It was greatly admired, though never wholly emulated by the English elite, and it was also the most generous.[48] The English subjected their vagrants to compulsory labor on pain of whipping and imprisonment, expected their poor to work, and sent indigent children, forcibly separated from their parents, to masters at home and in the colonies until the twentieth century, if we include those sent from the Dr. Barnardo homes for orphaned and destitute children. Yet the inefficiency of local government was such that the numbers caught in the system were modest.[49] Centralised administrations in Spain, however, ensured the impressment of vagrants and gypsies into arsenals (naval dockyard and armament manufactories) as late as the second half of the eighteenth century. And in France 7 percent of the galley corps at the time of its merger with the navy in 1748 were vagrants, but as the needs of the galleys declined after 1700 this group was more likely to be sent to the West Indies.[50] Overall in Europe, those sent to the Americas or put in the galleys formed a small share of the poor receiving relief; the

[45] Coates, "Exiles and Orphans," Chapter 5; Charles R. Boxer, *The Golden Age of Brazil, 1695–1750* (Berkeley, Ca., 1962), 140.

[46] Spierenburg, "The Sociogenesis of Confinement," 9–77, especially 31–2.

[47] Spierenburg, *The Prison Experience*, 12–86; Beattie, *Crime and the Courts in England*, 492–500.

[48] Spierenberg, "The Sociogenesis of Confinement," 24; Simon Schama, *The Embarrassment of Riches: An Interpretation of Dutch Culture in the Golden Age* (New York, 1987), 174–5, 570–9.

[49] Marshall, "The Old Poor Law, 1662–1795" (1937):39; Meriton, *Guide for constables*; *Statutes at Large*, 43 Eliz c. 2; Smith, "The Transportation of Convicts," 244, indicates vagrants among a group going to Virginia in the 1660s.

[50] Pike, *Penal Servitude in Early Modern Spain*, 67–9; Zysberg, "La société des galériens"; Bamford, *Fighting Ships*, 260; Christian Huetz de Lemps, "Indentured Servants Bound for the French Antilles and Canada in the Seventeenth and Eighteenth Centuries," in Altman and Horn 'To Make America,' 188–9.

fate of those sent to the Americas was invariably indentured servitude, not slavery; and the poor who could not avoid the state system were probably treated less harshly in the Netherlands and England (though for different reasons discussed later) than in France and Spain.

Prisoners taken in the course of European military action may be divided into two groups for present purposes. Those captured in the act of rebellion against established government could expect death if they were leaders or banishment if they were deemed followers, but never enslavement. The English sold many Irish in Barbados during the seventeenth century after military campaigns in Ireland but always as indentured servants with a maximum term rarely exceeding ten years. During the English Civil War there was an "etiquette of belligerence," equivalent to that between warring European states, though the English explicitly excluded the Irish from its terms when fighting in Ireland.[51] In France in 1662 nearly five hundred rebellious Boulonnais were sent to the galleys, not into slavery, despite the inability of French merchants at the time to sustain an African slave trade to the French Americas.

A second group consisted of those captured in conflicts between states. Victors commonly sold prisoners into slavery during the Dark Ages in Europe and down to the twelfth century in the case of the Celts struggling against the Anglo-Normans.[52] Ransom replaced this practice during the Middle Ages and, from the later Reformation to the French Revolutionary wars, prisoners of war were the best treated of all European groups considered here. The impact of atrocities in the Thirty Years War on the public mind is explained in part by their exceptional status. "Fair quarter" or detention followed by prisoner exchanges or ransoming became the norm. English, Dutch, and French prisoners could be consigned to the galleys in Spain, but slave status there was reserved for non-Christians. Even the latter group, however (in the case of North Africans enslaved in French and Spanish galleys), had some prospect of release in exchange for Christians held by rulers of Algiers, Tunis, and other Mediterranean Muslim powers.[53] Prisoner exchanges seem

---

[51]   Barbara Donagan, "Codes and Conduct in the English Civil War," *Past and Present*, 118(1988):65–95, especially pp. 93–5.

[52]   Matthew Strickland, *War and Chivalry: The Conduct and Perception of War in England and Normandy, 1066–1217* (Cambridge, 1996), pp. 30, 313–17.

[53]   Alfred Vagts, *A History of Militarism: Civilian and Military* (New York, 1959), pp. 113–14; Bamford, *Fighting Ships and Prisons*, 176–7, 261–4. Heinz Buhofer and Bruno S. Frey argue that the relatively good treatment of prisoners of war came from their market value and by implication that the European/North African differential arose from a relative lack of interest on the part of the North African powers in buying back at least low-status prisoners ("A Market for Men, or There is no such Thing as a Free Lynch," *Journal of Institutional and Theoretical Economics*, 142(1986):739–44). This approach can explain much, but the really interesting question is why, if neither the English nor the Algerians would buy back all their prisoners from the Spanish in the late sixteenth century and

to have been less common in Africa and the Americas, where captives were more likely to be killed, absorbed into the captor's society, or traded away. Some might see the trading of captives as the distorting impact of a European-generated market for slaves, but the key point is that this option was also open to commanders of European armies when they took European prisoners, and they rarely elected to use it.

Against outsiders, or non-Europeans, in Europe, different standards applied. In July 1596, the English Privy Council (which less than two centuries later would be organizing extensive hearings on the African slave trade sympathetic to abolition) ordered the deportation of all black slaves from England.[54] They were to be taken to Portugal and Spain and sold. In January 1601, a further royal proclamation repeated the provision, licensed a merchant to round up the "Negroes and blackamoors," and threatened owners of slaves that did not comply with the Queen's displeasure. The reason advanced for this drastic action was that the Queen's "own natural subjects" – who could clearly not be blackamoors – were "greatly distressed in these hard times of dearth."[55] Once more the image of African kin groups reacting to pressures is evoked. The English were disposing of the most recently acquired and dispensable members first in the interests of the kin group as a whole. There would first be fewer mouths to feed, second there would be revenue earned, and third, and most strikingly in the present context, the merchant charged with this task "hath somewhat deserved of this realm in respect that by his own labor and charge he hath relieved and brought from Spain divers of our English nation" – prisoners of war in fact who were obviously more central members of the English kin group than "blackamoores."[56] In 1596 the prospects of a similar transaction elicited the comment that "[H]er Majesty .... doth thincke yt a very good exchange and that those kinde of people [blacks] may be well spared in this realme."[57] More than a quarter of a century before the first settlement of Barbados it would be harder to find a clearer indication of the outsider status of Africans in the eyes of the English (and by implication, Europeans in general). In addition, while the common law might have held a different view, it is clear

---

both groups were sent to the galleys because of a zero value on the exchange market, only the Algerians were enslaved. Likewise, to take one of Buhofer and Frey's examples, the need for labor can explain fluctuations in the treatment of death-camp prisoners over the course of World War II in Germany but not the existence of the death camps themselves.

[54] *Acts of the Privy Council of England, 1452–1628*, 32 vols. (London, 1890–1907), 26:20.

[55] Paul L. Hughes and James F. Larkin (eds.), *Tudor Royal Proclamations*, 4 vols. (New Haven, 1969), 3: *The Later Tudors (1588–1603)*, 220–1. The document is entitled "Licensing Casper van Senden to Deport Negroes."

[56] *Ibid.*

[57] *Acts of the Privy Council*, 26:20.

that in the eyes of the crown, slavery continued to flourish – at least for blacks.

As we might expect, in the colonies the dividing line became even more sharply defined. The recent historiography has tended to draw strong parallels between the social and material conditions of white and black labor in the early sugar economy of Barbados.[58] Yet it is the differences rather than the similarities in legal status and treatment that stand out. Apart from the length of servitude and heritability of status, servants had first claim on skilled occupations and when they rebelled or ran away they were less likely to suffer death as punishment. But the contrast between insider and outsider status is particularly stark in the transatlantic shipping arrangements regarded as appropriate for Africans and Europeans, as well as in the demographic structure of the migrant flows from Africa and Europe, both of which Europeans controlled. The demographic makeup of transatlantic migration is taken up in more detail in Chapter 4 and the shipboard conditions in Chapter 5, but on the latter we should note that there is no evidence that any European transatlantic voyagers, whether steerage passengers, convicts, soldiers, or indentured servants, were ever subjected to conditions that were the norm on slave ships. Crowding was three or four times as severe on slave ships from the seventeenth to the nineteenth century, and only galley ships, rarely out of sight of land and never at sea in bad weather, matched the human density of a slave ship.

States, merchants, and consumers of plantation produce all stood to gain from shipping convicts, prisoners, and indeed indentured servants in slave-like conditions. The fact that they did not do so says something about the views that European merchants and ultimately European societies held on the status of different migrant groups. Few societies in history have enslaved people they consider to be their own. The Salisbury prisoners in Barbados referred to their condition as "a thing not known amongst the cruell Turks," by which they meant "to sell and enslave these of their own Countrey and religion." An almost tangible barrier thus prevented Europeans from becoming

---

[58] Beckles, *White Servitude and Black Slavery*. The thrust of this work is broadly consistent with the positions of Abbott Emerson Smith, *Colonists in Bondage: White Servitude and Convict Labor in America, 1607–1776* (Chapel Hill, N.C., 1947) revised ed., 1966; and Eric Williams, *Capitalism and Slavery* (Chapel Hill, N.C., 1944), pp. 3–29. Interestingly, in a more recent work, Beckles seems to modify his position by arguing that the English elite became sensitive to the poor treatment of whites in Barbados and this influenced their decision to use African slaves ("The 'Hub of Empire': The Caribbean and Britain in the Seventeenth Century," in Nicholas P. Canny (ed.), *The Oxford History of the British Empire* (Oxford, 1998), 4:231–2). This is consistent with Beckles' earlier rejection of Handlin's position that the midseventeenth-century English were not prejudiced against blacks. However, the main concern of the parliamentarians that Beckles cites was the lack of due process accorded to English rebels sent to Barbados, not a humanitarian interest.

chattel slaves unless they were captured by non-Europeans.[59] The relevant issue was who was to be considered "their own." In some African societies shared ethnicity and language might even mean an increased likelihood of enslavement – at least for women and children – given the focus on kin groups and their expansion through absorption of outsiders. In the Americas, slave raids of one Iroquois nation on another were not uncommon. But in western Europe, even the most degraded member of European society was spared enslavement. Only in the rather limited case of Amerindians in the Spanish Americas was such treatment extended to non-Europeans. This barrier was akin to the Muslim bar against the enslavement of non-Muslims, not in the sense that the basis of enslavement was religious, but rather that in both Muslim and Christian societies slavery came to be mainly African despite the fact that in both, slaves often converted to the faith of their owners.[60]

But if all Europeans shared this attitude toward the insider, it is also clear that some societies came closer than others to countenancing slavelike conditions for their own citizens and that Iberians had different views on which non-Europeans could be enslaved. English indentured servants and convicts on average served less than seven years. Effective life sentences, though sometimes providing for exile without labor, were common for Spanish and French convicts, and at least some French engagés were sent to the Americas by the state with a status little different from convict labor. Likewise, slave labor involving non-Europeans was much more common in southern Europe than in the north. The slave markets in Europe from the Middle Ages until the eighteenth century were on the shores of the Mediterranean, not in northwestern Europe. Given the large African slave population in Lisbon, it is hard to visualize a Portuguese counterpart to an incident in Middelburg in 1596 in which 130 African slaves were restored to "their natural liberty" on the grounds that slavery did not exist in Zeeland.[61] Nor is it easy to imagine equivalent action in any part of the non-European world (for example, North Africa) if the slaves had been European. Yet there are abundant instances of ethnocentric attitudes in sixteenth-century Holland, France, and England. In none of these countries were there extensive debates on which non-Europeans could be enslaved such as occurred in mid-sixteenth-century Spain or indeed Islamic societies. France and England in particular provide examples of individual voices opposed to enslavement of others

[59] Foyle and Rivers, *England's Slavery, or Barbados Merchandize*, 7.

[60] Bernard Lewis, *Race and Slavery in the Middle East: An Historical Inquiry* (New York, 1990), pp. 5–15, 54–61; Davis, *Slavery and Human Progress*, 32–51.

[61] A. C. de C. M. Saunders, *A Social History of Black Slaves and Freedmen in Portugal, 1441–1555* (Cambridge, 1982), p. 59; W. S. Unger, "Bijdragen tot de geschiedenis van de Nederlandse slavenhandel," *Economisch-Historisch Jaarboek* 26(1956):136. For this last reference and translation I thank Pieter C. Emmer. For a similar incident in Bordeaux in 1571 parallelling that in Middelburg see Charles de la Ronciere, *Negrés et Négrièrs* (Paris, 1933), pp. 15–16.

but, in general, the English, Dutch, and French saw all non-Europeans as eligible.

Explanations for these attitudes are more difficult to establish than the fact that such attitudes existed. As already noted the difference between Europe and most of the rest of the world on the slavery issue in the early modern period was the conviction that only non-Europeans could be enslaved. Technology gave Europeans the power to sail out and impose this view of the world on others. But in the long run, perhaps the social and economic patterns described in Chapter 2 that were hostile to enslavement of Europeans were eventually hostile to slavery everywhere. In Europe, the system of competitive nation states in an overall balance of power relationship with each other was complemented within each state by an implicit and unusual contract between ruler and ruled that in return for a large share of the peasants' small productive surplus the ruler suppressed random violence and supported a stable legal system. The potential for individual rights was altogether greater in such a system than in a highly centralised empire or in regions where decentralised political power was associated with very low population densities. Conceptions of the individual as owner of himself or herself, owing nothing to society, and of society as a series of "relations of exchange between proprietors," required restraints on political power as well as the encouragement provided by an evolving market society.[62]

A second and perhaps more important implication of comparisons between the early modern European and non-European worlds was the opportunity Europe provided for the pervasive growth of market behaviour. The trading of land, labor, and capital, as well as goods and services was far more extensive in early modern Europe than in any other continent. The ramifications for slavery of an extensive market system are, as noted in Chapter 1, ambivalent. But, in a series of controversial essays on the link between capitalism and abolition, Thomas Haskell has argued that, under certain conditions, markets work against slavery and the infliction of cruelty in general. Haskell has listed preconditions for the historical emergence of humanitarianism as, first, an ethical maxim that makes the alleviation of suffering right, second, a sense of being causally involved in the situation that gives rise to the suffering, and, lastly, possession of a recipe for intervention so easily applied that refusal to employ it might be considered "an intentional act in itself." The market system peculiar to the late-eighteenth-century North Atlantic world "expanded the range of causal perception and inspired people's confidence in their power to intervene." The growth and elaboration of this knowledge incorporates, but is much broader than, technical and scientific learning. For Haskell, it is the link between causal perception and moral responsibility that is important. By the late eighteenth

---

[62] Macpherson, *Political Theory of Possessive Individualism*, especially 46–70. The quote is from p. 3.

century, "recipe knowledge and causal perception," specifically one assumes in long-distance trade, had become so familiar that in the minds of some participants in the North Atlantic economy (noticeably Quakers) action against slavery (and other abuses) had become a moral imperative.[63]

What interests us here, however, are not the implications of this argument for the abolition of slavery but for the origins of the system. Before 1750, these same traits, again as embodied in market behaviour, could have had almost exactly the opposite effect. Until the "recipe knowledge" had become so familiar that not to act became "an intentional act in itself," such knowledge would serve to increase its possessor's power to intervene in the lives of others without generating any feeling of moral responsibility for the suffering that might result. Causal perceptions would lead to moral restrictions on enslaving one's weaker and poorer neighbor (or more broadly, perhaps, one's fellow European) but not to the purchase of a non-European who was already a slave in the Mediterranean, Africa, Asia, and the Americas. The organisational and technical skills of business and the ability to develop long-term projects around scientific knowledge and bring them to fruition could thus disrupt or destroy societies in distant lands without eliciting anything other than indifference on the part of the perpetrators. Dutch slaving activities in the East Indies in the early seventeenth century and English and Dutch use of Africans in the Americas had a larger impact on Asia and Africa than their Iberian counterparts of the previous century but generated no more self-questioning.[64]

Familiarity with "recipe knowledge" would first cross the threshold of action in the domestic rather than the colonial environment and be applied to insiders before outsiders. An increasing regard for the consequences of one's actions at home was thus not inconsistent with continued indifference toward, and indeed encouragement of, slavery overseas.[65] Slave laws were

---

[63] Thomas L. Haskell, "Capitalism and the Origins of the Humanitarian Sensibility, Part 1" and "Capitalism and the Origins of the Humanitarian Sensibility, Part 2," in Thomas Bender (ed.), *The Antislavery Debate: Capitalism and Abolitionism as a Problem in Historical Interpretation* (Berkeley, 1992), 107–60, especially 129–33 and 147–51. These essays were responses to the work of David Brion Davis and first appeared in the *American Historical Review* in the mid-1980s.

[64] J. Fox, "'For Good and Sufficient Reasons': An Examination of Early Dutch East India Company Ordinances on Slaves and Slavery," Anthony Reid (ed.), *Slavery, Bondage and Dependency in South-East Asia* (St. Lucia, Queensland, 1983), 246–62. Fox observes, "The Dutch East India Company embodied new organizational principles whose introduction into Asia had profound effects ... the Company was the first formal slave holding corporation of its kind in Asia" (p. 248). Together with their English counterparts the Dutch West India Companies probably doubled the volume of the transatlantic slave trade in the mid-seventeenth century.

[65] Abolition of colonial slavery may have been the first of the humanitarian reforms of the modern era, but the basic rights of individuals before the law in northwestern Europe were established before the creation of transatlantic European slave colonies.

harsh and barriers to the manumission of slaves particularly strong in the Dutch and English Americas, and it is noteworthy that opposition by slave owners of Dutch descent is credited with delaying the abolition of slavery in New York and New Jersey in the aftermath of the American Revolution.[66] Yet in the European context, countries in which the market was more pervasive, such as the Netherlands and England, might tend to have greater respect for individual rights and more humane treatment of convicts, for instance, than would other countries with a slightly less invasive experience of market institutions. As early as the sixteenth century it was widely believed in England, the Netherlands, and indeed France that no one entering those countries could remain a slave. Curiously, it was thought in England that this had been the case since the advent of Christianity.[67] Again, the line was not absolute. Both the French and the Dutch issued decrees in the 1770s allowing the "warehousing" of slaves for short periods so that those returning from the Caribbean could bring personal slaves with them. While there was no such enabling legislation in England, an English court restored John Hamlet, a St. Kitt's slave temporarily in London, to his master and presumably the West Indies as late as 1799, twenty-seven years after the Mansfield decision.[68] It is ironic and yet not surprising that the English and Dutch not only developed the most absolute form of chattel slavery and the harshest laws against free blacks in the Americas, they also erected the first and most enduring barriers to converting slaves to Christianity. These barriers were logical given that many English and Dutch equated Christian status with freedom. In Catholic and southern European colonial jurisdictions, by contrast, active proselytisation among slaves occurred.

Beyond these common factors, there were important differences. In England the notion that the privileges of the individual are ultimately of

---

[66] Winthrop Jordan, "On the Bracketing of Blacks and Women in the Same Agenda," in Jack P. Greene (ed.), *The American Revolution: Its Character and Limits* (New York, 1987), pp. 277–8.

[67] For a sixteenth-century expression of this view, see William Harrison, *The Description of England* (Ithaca, 1968), p. 118 (I thank David Howard of Houghton College for this reference). In the seventeenth century, a handbook on England partly written for and widely used by foreigners was Chamberlayne, *Angliae Notitia or the Present State of England*. It stated, "Foreign slaves in England are none, since Christianity prevailed. A foreign Slaves brought into England, is upon landing ipso facto free from slavery, but not from ordinary service . . . . " (p. 331). See also Dudley North, *Observations and Advices Oeconomical* (London, 1669), p. 45. For the status of blacks in England prior to the Somerset case see Drescher, *Capitalism and Anti-Slavery*, 25–49.

[68] Sue Peabody, *There are no Slaves in France*, 106–36. For the Dutch case see Seymour Drescher, "The Long Goodbye: Dutch Capitalism and Anti-Slavery in Comparative Perspective," in Gert Oostindie (ed.), *Fifty Years Later: Anti-Slavery, Capitalism and Modernity in the Dutch Orbit* (Pittsburgh, 1996), p. 50. For the Hamlet case see Ruth Paley, "After Somerset: Mansfield, Slavery and the Law of England," in Norma Landau and Donna Andrews (eds.), *Crime, Law and Society* (Cambridge, forthcoming).

greater importance than those of the state or any group was probably more highly developed than anywhere in Europe.[69] Dutch attitudes derived not so much from concern for the individual as from a sense of the fragility of the social compact at a time when the country contained many resident non-Dutch and non-Calvinists. The greater prosperity of the Netherlands attracted large numbers of immigrants but, despite illiberal edicts issued at the behest of the Calvinist church, the Dutch developed a practical tolerance of others unrivalled in seventeenth-century Europe.[70] It would be tempting to see in this a capacity for absorbing outsiders in the sense used earlier, but few of these migrants were in fact non-Europeans. Far more non-Europeans lived in England, where their legal status was clarified only in the late eighteenth century.[71]

The foregoing paragraphs suggest the impossibility of using convicts as a source of permanent colonial labor in England or the Netherlands. Penal transportation did not exist among the Dutch. In the case of England, scholars have until recently disagreed in their interpretations of criminal sanctions. They now seem to accept the view that judges and juries were reluctant to apply the letter of the more ferocious laws, even though scholars are not yet in accord on the reasons. If, for example, judges and juries were slow to enforce branding on the cheek for felons at the outset of the eighteenth century, it is doubtful that they would have sent convicts to chattel slavery in the Americas. If transportation had meant a lifetime of servitude for English people, they might not have convicted anyone.[72]

From one side of the ideological divide such reluctance might appear as a function of shared community values; from the other, it points to the resistance that would have inevitably followed or else manipulation on the part of the elite. The most serious strike in the preindustrial northeastern coal industry occurred in 1765 when mine owners attempted to follow their Scottish counterparts down a road that led to serfdom for workers.[73] But what seems incontestable is that in regard to slavery the sense of the appropriate was shared across social divisions and cannot easily be explained by ideological differences or power relationships among classes. Outrage at the

[69] Macpherson, *Possessive Individualism*, 263–71. See Macfarlane, *The Origins of English Individualism*, 165–88, on the differences between early modern England and continental Europe. Criticisms of the author's attempt to carry the comparison back into medieval times have tended to dominate evaluations of Macfarlane's book.

[70] E. H. Kossmann, "Freedom in Seventeenth-Century Dutch Thought and Practice," Jonathan Israel (ed.), *The Anglo-Dutch Moment: Essays on the Glorious Revolution and its World Impact* (Cambridge, 1991), pp. 281–98.

[71] Drescher, *Capitalism and Anti-Slavery*, 25–49.

[72] Beattie, *Crime and the Courts in England*, 450–519, esp. 490–2; Peter Linebaugh, *The London Hanged: Crime and Civil Society in the Eighteenth Century* (London, 1992).

[73] Michael W. Flinn, *History of the British Coal Industry*, vol. 2, *1700–1830: The Industrial Revolution* (Oxford, 1984), p. 399.

treatment of Africans was rarely expressed at any level of society before the late eighteenth century. The moral economy of the English crowd, like the various Christian churches, was preoccupied with other issues. When the immorality of coerced labor was recognised, the recognition appeared across all social groups at about the same time. Attempts to account for the failure of Europeans to enslave their own in terms of solidarity among the potential slaves do not seem promising. [74] If the elite could kill Irish, Huguenots, Jews, prisoners of war, convicts, and many other marginalised groups, why could they not enslave them? The English considered those from the Celtic fringe different from themselves but, after the eleventh century at least, not different enough to enslave. [75] For elite and non-elite alike enslavement remained a fate for which only non-Europeans were qualified.

[74] "Popular revulsion to bondage and untrammelled private power" that had "long preceded... critiques of colonial slavery" is one of three sources of antislavery sentiment singled out by Robin Blackburn, *Overthrow of Colonial Slavery* (p. 36). He and Seymour Drescher (*Capitalism and Anti-Slavery*) see popular involvement as vital to abolition. Like the churches, intellectuals, and political elite, however, those without property clearly had other priorities before the later eighteenth century. Attempts to enslave Europeans and put them to work on sugar plantations would perhaps have attracted their attention, but were plantation owners, metropolitan merchants, and mercantilist statesmen so apprehensive of popular opinion that not a single one of them dared advocate European slavery in public? A more convincing explanation of the silence, and of course inaction, is simply a shared conception of what was appropriate that easily crossed class lines.

[75] George M. Fredrickson, *White Supremacy: A Comparative Study in American and South African History* (New York, 1981), p. 15.

4

Gender and Slavery in the Early Modern Atlantic World

IF DIFFERENCES BETWEEN European and African concepts of insider made a transatlantic slave trade from Africa possible, then differences in European and African constructions of gender helped determine which Africans entered that trade. As Edmund Morgan argued a quarter-century ago, Europeans put African women to work in whip-driven field gangs in the Americas but were not prepared to see European women work under like conditions, a kind of sexual theory of slavery.[1] As this suggests, Europeans and Africans defined gender as they defined the line dividing insider from outsider – with no apparent reference in either case to maximizing efficiency on plantations in the Americas or, more narrowly, what was in their best pecuniary interest. Once more, the profit-maximizing model of human behavior makes little sense unless it is placed within a cultural framework.

One route into early modern European constructions of gender is provided by the captain of the slave ship *Hannibal*, which sailed from London to the African coast in 1694. "This morning," he wrote,

"we found out that one of the Royal African Company soldiers, for their castles in Guiney, was a woman, who had entered herself into their service under the name of John Brown, without the least suspicion, and had been three months on board without any mistrust, lying always among the other passengers. I believe she had continued undiscovered till our arrival in Africa had not she fallen very sick and needed a glister, surgeon's mate found more sally ports than he expected which occasioned him to made a farther inquiry .... in charity, as well as in respect to her sex, I ordered her a private lodging apart from the men, and gave the taylor some ordinary stuffs to make her women's cloths; in recompense for which she proved very useful in washing my linen and doing what else she could, till we delivered her

---

[1] Edmund S. Morgan, "Slavery and Freedom: The American Paradox," *Journal of American History*, 59(1972):26–7.

85

with the rest at Cape Coast Castle. She was about twenty years old and a likely black girl."[2]

Women passing as men cannot have been common but were probably found most in occupations where individuals were recruited with little reference to their origins and where task performance was more important than social status. The ordinary ranks of the military was perhaps one such occupation. For Captain Phillips, the event was worth a patronising paragraph in a book designed to stave off poverty after a voyage that ended his career, wrecked his health, and shortened his life. But from the late-twentieth-century perspective, the incident highlights larger issues of gender and European views of others. First, that the woman was black but not a slave serves to underline that, as with the black slave-ship captain, the insider-outsider divide explored in the previous chapter was not entirely coterminous with skin colour. However, her presence (and perhaps that of the black captain) undoubtedly reflects the association Europeans made between skin color and resistance to tropical disease, just as her illness illustrates the spurious basis of such a link. The association was nevertheless to survive into the late nineteenth century despite disastrous attempts to use Afro-Americans in the settlement of Sierra Leone in the 1780s and later in Liberia.[3]

More fundamental are the attitudes to gender that Phillips both displayed and assumed existed among his readers. There was nothing that prevented the woman from carrying out the tasks of a soldier to the apparent satisfaction of all. A few years later, a similar case arose when fever in the Bight of Biafra reduced the crew of the *Neptune*, another slave ship, to "three people ... one mate, and one woman, in addition to the captain." The latter had originally dressed as a man and, according to the captain, was not "found out till we were almost on the Coast. (She) has worked as a Sailor, and still does."[4] As in the case of twentieth-century world wars, dire necessity could force a semblance of sexual equality. Nothing, however, could bring Phillips and the society to which he belonged to recognize the inequality. If there was only a social construction keeping women from being soldiers and sailors, then the same could be said for keeping white women from gangs on plantations in the Americas.

---

[2] A. and J. Churchill, *A Collection of Voyages and Travels*, 6 vols. (London, 1744–6)6:195. The voyage id of the Hannibal is 9,714.

[3] Philip D. Curtin, *The Image of Africa: British Ideas and Action, 1780–1850* (Madison, Wis., 1964), pp. 236–7; Antonio McDaniel, *Swing Low Sweet Chariot: The Mortality Cost of Colonizing Liberia in the Nineteenth Century* (Chicago, 1995), pp. 4–6.

[4] *Felix Farley's Bristol Journal*, 28 January 1769. For yet another example of "passing" on a slave ship see Hugh Crow, *Memoirs of the late Captain Hugh Crow of Liverpool* (London, 1830), p. 60. Crow thought it a not uncommon phenomenon. I would like to thank David Richardson and Ugo Nwokeji for bringing these cases to my attention.

A global perspective is useful here. In the late twentieth century, Europe and the Americas are the only continents to sustain the natural sex ratio (i.e., a ratio consistent with both sexes receiving the same care and nourishment) of 105 females for every 100 males (a male ratio of 48.8 percent). Japan also has this rate, the state of Kerala in India has a rate of 103, but the only continental-size area to approach the natural rate is sub-Saharan Africa, with 103. Much of Asia and North Africa have ratios well below 90. Clearly in much of the world mortality rates for females are much higher than for males. Little is known of the gender distribution of the early modern African and American indigenous populations but it is likely that in the African case it was not much different from rural Africa today.[5] Such ratios are usually taken to imply the existence of relatively good economic opportunities for females in both Africa and Europe, at least compared to Asia and North Africa. In the English case there is almost consensus in the literature on women's history that the range of occupations open to women was much greater in the seventeenth century than it was to become. Although hard data on the sexual division of labor before 1700 is scarce, most scholars now argue that first, among the working-class English at least, tasks were assigned on a sexually nonexclusive basis, and second, that during the 150 years after 1700 women came to be excluded from a wide range of occupations.[6]

Yet despite high ratios of females among European and African populations and the relatively abundant opportunities for females, the behavior of Phillips and the young black women points to systemic and overt exclusionary attitudes. Differences between northern and southern Europe in the gender division of labor were probably as marked in 1700 as in 1900, with a greater range of opportunities for women in the north. For England, much of the literature stresses the presence of women before 1700 in occupations often thought of as male, yet the striking feature of the nonanecdotal evidence from the seventeenth century (specifically apprenticeship figures) is how few women were actually to be found in such occupations well *before*

---

[5] Amartya Sen, "More than 100 Million Women are Missing," *New York Review of Books*, 36, no. 20(1991), 61–6; Schofield and Wrigley, *Population History of England*, 224–5, 394. There is no hard evidence for the seventeenth century (Schofield and Wrigley estimate 103 for England and Wales in 1801), but the case for projecting back to the seventeenth century seems strong.

[6] Alice Clark, *Working Life of Women in the Seventeenth Century* (London, 1919) laid out the basic argument. See especially pp. 304–5. More recently see Eric Richards, "Women in the British Economy Since About 1700: An Interpretation," *History*, 59(1974):337–57; B. Ankerloo, "Agriculture and Women's Work: The Direction of Change in the West, 1700–1900," *Journal of Family History*, 4(1979):110–19; K. D. M. Snell, *Annals of the Labouring Poor: Social Change and Agrarian England, 1660–1900* (Cambridge, 1985), pp. 15–66, 270–319. The latest edition of the *Cambridge Economic History of Britain* reflects these views [See Chapter 1 of Roderick Floud and Donald McCloskey (eds.), *An Economic History of Modern Britain* (Cambridge, 1994)].

any hint of the separate spheres associated with industrialization. There may have been more female coopers, weavers, brewers, and wheelwrights before 1700 than after, but there were very few of them in any period. In Tudor and Stuart Salisbury, "[w]omen's work was at the casual, menial end of the market," few widows took over their husband's business, and, in an earlier period, women in guilds were rare.[7] A fascination with industrial capitalism has led historians to see significance in small changes in the sexual division of labor between the eighteenth and nineteenth centuries, when the striking fact is just how small the changes in the range and incidence of skills acquired by women really were. And of course both before and after industrialization, in England and the English Americas, woman lost control of their property upon marriage (though in the Chesapeake they had more rights in widowhood).[8] In the Netherlands, women had a stronger position before the law compared to English women, at least prior to marriage, but a similarly limited range of occupational opportunities.

In short, evidence of a marked pre-1700 sexual division of labor is strong. Distributions of parish apprentices by gender and occupation before 1700 show much smaller numbers of women apprentices than men and a heavy preponderance within the female category of occupations not traditionally associated with males.[9] A great deal of labor in the seventeenth century was organised and carried out in the domestic sphere, and a wide range of income-generating economic activities occurred within the structure, if not the physical limits, of the household. The apprenticeship data may not reflect the full economic importance of women who no doubt labored at a range of heavy tasks. At the extreme, mining – often involving serfdom – and agriculture provided major productive roles for women and children involving severe manual labor. In the century and a half after 1700, the incidence of women and children involved in coal mining, always a regional phenomenon, declined to insignificance.[10]

Nevertheless, the incidence of heavy labor in return for remuneration was much less for women than for men. While prominent in some narrowly

---

7   Sue Wright, "'Churmaids, Huswyfes and Hucksters': The Employment of Women in Tudor and Stuart Salisbury," in Lindsey Charles and Lorna Duffin (eds.), *Women and Work in Pre-Industrial England* (London, 1985), pp. 100–21; quote is from p. 116. Judith M. Bennett, "'History that Stands Still': Women's Work in the European Past," *Feminist Studies*, 14(1988):269–83.

8   Carol Berkin, *First Generations: Women in Colonial America* (New York, 1996), pp. 14–19; Bridget Hill, *Women, Work and Sexual Politics in Eighteenth Century England* (London, 1989), pp. 196–8; de Vries, *The First Modern Economy*, 596–605.

9   Snell, *Annals of the Labouring Poor*, 270–319.

10   Children, however, were unlikely to have ever been of much economic importance. See Hugh Cunningham, "The Employment and Unemployment of Children in England c. 1680–1851," *Past and Present*, 126(1990):115–50.

defined, unskilled tasks such as moss gathering, salt and peat carrying in the Netherlands, women made up a very small share of laborers employed by churches, town councils, and port authorities in the sixteenth and seventeenth century north of England and an even smaller share of building craftspeople. When such female workers appear in the record, their pay was typically three-fifths that of men. Women worked at a wide range of tasks in the countryside including field labor. They produced goods for others within the household, as well as working outside the household for pay. Whether in husbandry, service activities, or manufacturing, however, the heaviest tasks appear to have been dominated by men.[11] The heaviest labor may have been in agriculture, but in the second half of the seventeenth century when the British were establishing their slave system in the Americas, agriculture employed 40 percent or less of either the English or Dutch labor forces.[12] In most other parts of the world, including Europe, agriculture claimed much larger shares of human effort. More important, even where prevalent, heavy labor was never equivalent to working on a sugar plantation in the Americas. Gang labor in the sense of the lockstep organisation of a large group with the pace of work being set by a driver was not widely used in Europe, and where it was, as in the galley ships, for example, women were virtually unknown. Labor in a family unit might be long and heavy but it contained the possibility of some control remaining in the hands of the individual and the unit itself. Overall, heavy tasks claimed the labor of smaller shares of women in England and the Netherlands than in other parts of Europe and, for the purposes of the present argument, West Africa.

Further evidence of strong gender occupational roles in seventeenth-century England comes from migration data – a source not much utilized by those seeking to define the role of women in the preindustrial economy. Table 4-1 shows the occupations of a sample of 4,094 migrants to the Americas given as they left England between 1640 and 1699. It draws on a pool of data that include the pre-1700 Bristol and Middlesex indentured servant sources that David Galenson has already examined but is somewhat larger.[13] Women in the sample are apparently without skills that have much application outside a domestic environment. Female indentured servants

---

[11] Donald Woodward, *Men at Work: Laborers and Building Craftsmen in the Towns of Northern England* (Cambridge, 1995), pp. 23, 53, 108–14; Hill, *Women, Work and Sexual Politics*, 69–84, 148–73.

[12] de Vries, *The First Modern Economy*, 195, 228–9.

[13] Galenson, *White Servitude*, 34–50, 183–6. The Coldham data comprise 32,703 migrants of whom 4,083 have identifiable occupations. Galenson's sample is 13,191 servants, among whom occupation is identified for 3,699. For an earlier discussion of parts of these data see Herbert Moller, "Sex Composition and Correlated Culture Patterns of Colonial America," *William and Mary Quarterly*, 2(1945):113–51.

Table 4-1. *Emigrants from England to the Americas, 1640–1699:*
Occupation by Gender

Occupation	Males	Col. 1/total	Females	Col. 3/total
Farmer	1,011	40.0	3	0.2
Laborer	292	11.5	1	0.1
Food & drink	101	4.0	1	0.1
Metal & construction	308	12.2	1	0.1
Textiles & clothing	544	21.5	0	0
Mining	19	0.8	1	0.1
Services	254	10.0	18	1.2
Spinster	0	0	1,313	83.9
Widow	0	0	113	7.2
Wife	0	0	114	7.3
Total	2,529	100	1,565	100

Source: Eltis and Stott, "Coldham's Emigrants from England, 1640–1699: A Database."

were sought and assigned mainly to household tasks. Once in the Americas, women worked hard, but usually as wives or within a domestic framework. It seems likely that in the early Chesapeake low life expectancy for males meant more economic power for females, at least compared to Jamaica.[14] The migration data, however, suggest nothing remotely approaching equal economic opportunity for females. Indeed, the data reviewed here indicate an economic role for women as severely circumscribed as in any Islamic region long before the later eighteenth and nineteenth centuries.

Opportunity for females in English, Dutch, and eventually in North Atlantic society appears much greater in the reproductive than in the economic zone of gender relations. This is particularly the case if a global comparative perspective is adopted. The exceptional nature of early modern western European marriage patterns is now widely accepted. Compared to women in Asia and Africa, western European women married late, they had considerable choice over whom they would marry, and a large proportion of them never married at all. The space between menarche and the birth of the first child was greater in western Europe than elsewhere, and crude birth rates lower as far back as records reach.[15] Even rough estimates of the

[14]   Lois Green Carr and Lorena S. Walsh, "The Planter's Wife: The Experience of White Women in Seventeenth-Century Maryland," *William and Mary Quarterly*, 34(1977):542–71; Trevor Burnard, "Inheritance and Independence: Women's Status in Early Colonial Jamaica," *ibid.*, 48(1991):93–114; Suzanne Lebsock, *"A Share of Honour" Virginia Women, 1600–1945* (Richmond, 1987). For sexual stereotyping in New England and the limited range of occupations open to women, see Koehler, *A Search for Power*, 28–70, 108–35.

[15]   J. Hajnal, "European Marriage Patterns in Perspective," in D. V. Glass and D. E. C. Eversley (eds.), *Population in History: Essays in Historical Demography*

incidence of mutilation of women do not exist before the twentieth century, but female circumcision and foot binding were unknown in western Europe. Castration, by contrast, was performed routinely in Verdun, France, in the early Middle Ages on North African–bound captives and in modified form (the voice effects may be achieved without the full operation) survived in southern Europe into the nineteenth century, as was the case with the castrati singers in the Vatican. A double standard of sexual morality certainly held in western Europe, but both husband and wife had exclusive rights to the other's sexual activity. In most African societies, the husband was legally injured by his wife's infidelity but the wife had no legal redress for similar behavior by her husband.[16] Within western Europe, the pattern of young adults establishing new households and delaying marriage until this was possible was perhaps – in global comparative terms at least – the key social outcome of the nuclear family.

The nuclear family created some opportunities for decision making by women as well as encouraging companionate marriage. However, this does not mean that the polygyny that held in many African societies necessarily stymied female choice. Polygyny often meant more rather than less economic independence for women, as the husband made fewer demands on each individual wife and wives were able to associate more with their affinal group. Indeed, in some societies, women purchased extra wives for their husband in an effort to bolster their own economic status.[17] Of course, patriarchal power existed in both Africa and in western Europe, but the nuclear family and African polygyny were still preferable to the female seclusion of much of the Islamic world and the extended family structures of, say, India.

Intriguing contrasts and similarities appear in the roles of women in seventeenth-century England and Africa. The nuclear family was much more common in western Europe than anywhere in Africa, and kinship structures were much stronger in Africa than in Europe. Nevertheless the bulk of labor in both continents at this time was performed within the household, however defined. Women in Africa tilled the fields, produced cloth, and had major roles in trade, all of which gave them value as wives. "Polygyny," according to Remi Clignet, "is most tenacious in cultures where economic rights to women can be acquired and have high value."[18] While there are no African occupational breakdowns rivalling those from English apprenticeship data,

---

(Chicago, 1965), pp. 101–35; Ruth B. Dixon, "The Roles of Rural Women, Female Seclusion, Economic Production, and Reproductive Choice," in Ronald Ridker (ed.), *Population and Development: the Search for Selective Intervention* (Baltimore, 1976), pp. 290–305.

[16] Miers and Kopytoff (eds.), *Slavery in Africa*, 7.

[17] See Remi Clignet, *Many Wives, Many Powers: Authority and Power in Polygynous Marriages* (Evanston, Ill., 1970), pp. 46–61 for the theoretical background. I would like to thank Ugo Nwokeji for help on this material.

[18] *Ibid.*, 23.

women were expected to perform a much wider range of occupations than in most other parts of the Old World.[19] Detailed studies of the role of women in seventeenth- and eighteenth-century Africa are rare. For one small community on the western Slave Coast, however, Sandra Greene has shown how the women's economic and reproductive functions varied over time in response to resource availability and an influx of migrants. But even when most restricted by male-dominated patrilineages, the women of Anlo had access to a wider range of skills and a role in economic decision making not to be found in most of early modern western Europe.[20]

Where Europe and Africa came into the most direct contact – the exchange sector on the African coast – the working woman were all African.[21] The wives and daughters of European traders who went to the African coast were considered burdens. Any role that they might have played in the affairs of their husbands and fathers came to an end with the death of the latter.[22] There was no European counterpart to the career of African slave trader Venda Lawrence, who migrated independently to Georgia with her property from the Gambia on the African coast, and probably not in the North Atlantic either.[23] Women were particularly important in African agriculture and textile production, and the former was simply of greater relative importance in Africa than in northwest Europe – no Africanist could argue that agriculture accounted for as little as one-third of economic activity in precolonial times. Given the centrality of the role of women in West African agriculture and textiles, the work of women was closer to the core of the African economy than was its English counterpart. In neither northwest Europe nor Africa was labor performed in a plantation environment. Market relations had a larger role in allocating labor in England than in Africa, but in both areas married women worked for others as part of a relationship that was often defined in non-economic terms and always had a major familial, clan, or, at least, social component. Thus, in eighteenth-century Scotland,

---

[19] Martin A. Klein and Claire C. Robertson, "Women's Importance in African Slave Systems," in Martin A. Klein and Claire C. Robertson (eds.), *Women and Slavery in Africa* (Madison, Wis., 1983), pp. 15–16 and the literature cited there.

[20] Sandra E. Greene, *Gender, Ethnicity and Social Change on the Upper Slave Coast* (Portsmouth, N. H., 1996), pp. 4–6, 20–4, 28–47.

[21] See the essays in Klein and Robertson (eds.), *Women and Slavery in Africa*.

[22] See for example the comment, "By this shipp the St. George ... we send home Letitia Croxton, Daughter to Agent Wm Croxton, Deceased her Diet etc haveing put yr Hons to a Considerable Charge here ...." Greenway, Spurway, Master, Stapleton to the R.A.C., June 3, 1682, T70/16, f. 34. Also "two whitewomen having lost there husbands, he (John Clark, the factor, that is) discharged them," summary of John Clark to RAC, York Fort, Sherbrow, Oct. 24, 1709, T70/5.

[23] Lillian Ashcraft-Eason, "She 'Voluntarily Hath Come to ... [The Georgia] Province': A Gambian-Woman Slave Trader Among the Enslaved" in Paul Lovejoy (ed.), *Constructions of Identity: African Communities in the Shadow of Slavery* (forthcoming).

many of the female colliery employees were bearers drawing coal cut by husbands or fathers.[24] For women of African descent, the familial component reasserted itself when slavery finally ended in the nineteenth century and the former female slaves withdrew not only from gang labor but also from most waged labor of any type.

The direct correlation often made between economic opportunity for women and their standing in society by Amartya Sen and others is thus not evident in early Europe about the time Europeans established the great slave regimes of the Americas. Western women could not, as we have seen, have owed relatively high status to their economic role. European demographic strategies – more specifically, the nuclear family – and a European focus on individualism explored in Chapter 1 are more likely sources of this comparatively elevated status. Economic opportunity seems more influential in explaining female status in the non-European world. If overall sex ratios are any guide, African women have and had more rights and greater status than most of their Asian counterparts. On the other hand most non-European women had much more constrained reproductive options than women in western Europe. In most of sub-Saharan Africa, kinship organizations placed such importance on the acquisition of new members that the reproductive role of women was at least as important as women's central role in production.[25] A simple comparative conclusion would be that in the parts of India and China contacted by early modern Europeans, women had neither the reproductive freedom of western European females nor the central economic role of African women.

We might conclude this brief comparison of intercontinental gender by noting the apparent absence of female resistance to the severely circumscribed roles described here, especially in the case of the women of northwest Europe. Perhaps this is explained by the ambivalent consequences of such circumscription. Put another way, the exclusions were not entirely without benefit for women. Who, as a rule, would not choose to avoid being press-ganged, placed in the front line of an advancing army, or kidnapped into a term of indentured servitude in the colonies? If, as most scholars recognize, the net effect on the position of women of the emergence of separate spheres in the nineteenth century was unclear, then the impact of an earlier value system that severely reduced choices for women but kept them away from forced manual labor was equally ambivalent. Perhaps this is why, before the disappearance of all forced labor for men in the twentieth century, resistance was of the individualised variety of the woman on the *Hannibal*. The liberation of women became an issue only when the ambivalence was

[24] Flinn, *History of the British Coal Industry*, pp. 334–5.
[25] Thornton, *Africa and Africans*, 72–97; Miers and Kopytoff, *Slavery in Africa*, 3–76.

reduced, in other words, when there was something more to which women might escape.

With this as background, we can now turn to a fuller examination of gender in migration before the nineteenth century. If, as argued earlier, one test of a society's commitment to equal care for the sexes is a natural sex ratio in excess of 100, then one test of equal economic opportunity in the early modern Atlantic economy is how closely the sex ratio of migrants approached this natural rate. Simply put, if the capacities of men and women are the same except for a relatively small differential in physical strength (more pertinently, physical endurance), if employers and the state alike wish to maximize profits or output, and if a completely free labor market exists (whether for slaves or non-slaves) with no culturally imposed barriers to participation by any group, then we would expect roughly equal numbers of males and females to be hired (or, in the case of slaves, purchased). The sex differential in muscular endurance might induce some small imbalances, but the extensive use of women of African descent in gang labor on plantations suggests that such differences could not have been too significant.[26] Sex ratios among transatlantic migrants under these conditions would have been close to equality. In the early modern era, we know that the first two of the three conditional statements held. If the relatively equal capacities of women and men and the economic motivations of early modern capitalists can be taken for granted, then the extent to which the sex composition of migrants deviates from equality is a crude indicator of cultural or at least non-economic influences over migration. The fact that one migrant stream, the European, had some choice, and the other, the African, did not, does nothing to invalidate this exercise. *Some* Africans, if not the coerced migrants themselves, had considerable say over who entered the trade, and thus the demographic composition of both coerced and free migrant flows to some extent reflected conceptions of gender in the source societies.

Table 4-2 provides the large overview for the seventeenth and eighteenth centuries. It summarizes the sex structure of European migration, dominated

---

[26]   The differences in muscular strength between men and women are much greater than the differences in endurance. One modern study suggests that women have 58 percent of the strength of their male counterparts but 84 percent of their endurance (Government of Canada, *Fitness and Lifestyle in Canada* [Ottawa, 1983], pp. 24–6), and, presumably, at least 100 percent of male mental capacity. For most physical activity – including most labor down the ages and many modern sports – endurance is much more important than strength. The male world record for the marathon, for example, is just under 0.9 that of its female counterpart. The relatively small endurance differential helps explain the relatively small sex price differential – at least among slaves in the Americas. This argument sets to one side the case where the demand for migrants was for domestic or sexual purposes – as in the trans-Saharan slave trade. Under these circumstances females would predominate. Overall, migration to the Americas was almost entirely shaped by labor, not sexual or even reproductive requirements.

Table 4-2. *Male and Child Ratios of Selected Groups of Migrants Arriving in the Americas, 1638–1860*

	Male ratios	Child ratios (under 15)	No. ('000)[&]
1. Slaves			
To Caribbean, 1663–1700	0.590	0.114	63.4 (60.7)*
To Caribbean, 1701–1800	0.634	0.212	422.3 (367.6)
2. Indentured Servants			
From England, 1640–99	0.753	0.130	16.6 (16.7)
From France, 1638–1715	>0.900	<0.100	6.2
From England, 1700–75	0.902	0.007	7.6**
From Ireland, 1745–73	0.756		1.8
From Germany, 1745–1831	0.671		5.9
From India to B.W.I., 1845–55	0.819	0.123[&]	29.8 (32.4)
From China to Cuba, 1847–60	0.999		49.8
From China to U.S., 1853–60	0.954		42.4

Notes: [&] 10 years old and under. *numbers in parentheses are totals on which child ratios are based where these differ from sample size for male ratios. **1697–1776.
Sources:
Rows 1 and 2, *TSTD*.
Row 3, Calculated from Eltis and Stott, "Coldham's Emigrants from England, 1640–1699: A Database."
Row 4, Debien, "Les engagés pour les Antilles," 5–274.
Row 5, Galenson, *White Servitude*, 24, 26.
Rows 6 and 7, Calculated from Grubb, "Servant Auction Records and Immigration into the Delaware Valley," 164, 167.
Row 8, Calculated from General Reports of Colonial Land and Emigration Commissioners, Great Britain, *Parliamentary Papers*, PP. 1847, XXXIII (809); 1847–8, XXVI (961); 1852–3, XL (1647); XXVIII (1833); 1854–5, XVII (1953).
Row 9, John V. Crawford to Russell, Sept. 30, 1860, British Public Record Office, FO84/1109.
Row 10, U.S. Congress, H. Doc. 57–2, Vol 42, #15, p. 4358.

at this time by indentured servants, and compares seventeenth- with eighteenth-century patterns. A larger proportion of indentured servants were women before 1700 than after. The demand for skilled servants increased after 1700,[27] but as women migrants had few skills before or after 1700, this new twist in the transatlantic markets probably had little effect on the sex ratio of the migrant flow. Exclusion was clearly entrenched *before* 1700. An alternative explanation for the declining ratios (and absolute numbers too) of women servants is that the reproductive and domestic role for women – in the Americas at least – loomed large. In a "new plantation," Virginia planters claimed in 1619, "it is not known whether man or woman be more

[27] Galenson, *White Servitude*, 157–68.

necessary."[28] But for the latter it was positions as wives and family members that the planters and their English sponsors had in mind. The Providence Island Company directed that wives and children work "in the setting of ground, making provision of victuals, washing, and the like for the use of the public servants that the men may wholly employ themselves in the works."[29] By the eighteenth century, high positive rates of natural population growth meant that women of European descent were relatively abundant on the North American mainland. It was no longer necessary to encourage female immigration from Europe for the sole purpose of increasing the supply of housewives. In short, much of the demand for women stemmed from their reproductive role. When such demand declined with the emergence of more balanced sex ratios in white colonial populations, gender roles were such that there was no economic demand to sustain the female component of transatlantic migration.[30]

Indentured servants and convicts, who were heavily male, are probably overrepresented in surviving pre-1800 migration data, and overall, English transatlantic migration may have had a slightly larger female component than Table 4-2 indicates. But the females travelled as family members rather than as unattached individuals, and many were not looking for paid employment outside the domestic sphere. In general, single women formed a significant part of the European migrant flow only when governments intervened; the presence or absence of families largely determined the female component of migration to the Americas.[31]

More important for the present argument, Table 4-2 also suggests that the traditional view of the slave traffic as comprising mainly males and mainly adults needs revision. The table presents male and child ratios for slaves and indentured servants, and it is the latter, rather than the former,

---

[28] John Pory, "A Reporte of the Manner of Proceeding in the General Assembly convened at James City," July 31, 1619, in Kingsbury (ed.), *Virginia Company Records* III, 160, cited in Kupperman, *Providence Island*, 158.

[29] Cited in Kupperman, *Providence Island*, 159.

[30] For eighteenth-century bias against female indentured servants see Sharon Salinger, "'Send No More Women': Female Servants in Eighteenth-Century Philadelphia," *Pennsylvania Magazine of History and Biography*, 107(1983):29–48.

[31] This explains much of the interregional differences in sex ratios (and probably also in child ratios) among European migrants – for example, the differences in eighteenth-century Philadelphia between the German and Scottish in-migrants on the one hand and English on the other. See Farley Grubb, "Servant Auction Records and Immigration into the Delaware Valley, 1745–1831: The Proportion of Females Among Immigrant Servants," *Proceedings of the American Philosophical Society*, 133(1989):154–69. See Bernard Bailyn, *Voyagers to the West: A Passage in the Peopling of America on the Eve of the Revolution* (New York, 1986), pp. 129–203, and the discussions in Galenson, *White Servitude*, 13–14, and Dunn, *Sugar and Slaves*, 55–7, for other regions of the Americas.

that men dominated.[32] For the indentured category, as noted, Table 4-2 shows all streams dominated by adult males. The ratios for slaves on the other hand are much closer to those of family-oriented free migrant streams (for example, to seventeenth-century New England) than to their indentured counterparts. Indeed, the female share of slaves arriving during the seventeenth century probably exceeded the female share of free migrants, and by the nineteenth century the two may well have been similar.[33] Surprisingly, a higher proportion of children left Africa for the Americas than left Europe. In short, compared to the age and sex structure of other migrant flows, slave male ratios appear low rather than high and for child ratios the opposite appears to be the case. The forced migrants from Africa were much more demographically representative of the societies they left behind than were any of the European migrant groupings. Furthermore, because African coerced migrants began to outnumber European migrants a few years after 1650, any attempt to assess the overall role of women in the occupation of the Americas must focus on Africans. Specifically, before 1800 it is likely that at least four-fifths of the females and over 90 percent of the children sailing to the Americas were not European.

When Europeans sought labor from areas other than Africa, the female component of the resulting migrant flow was always much smaller than what was the norm in the transatlantic slave trade. Table 4-2 contains limited data on nineteenth-century Asian migrants. The overwhelming male component is obvious. Indeed, the only reason that nearly one-fifth of Indian migrants comprised females was because the British government required minimum numbers of females in any shipment of contract laborers. The minimum was not always met, but the regulation still resulted in many more Asian women going to Trinidad and British Guiana than went to the United States, Cuba, and probably other American regions that sought Asian labor and were not subject to regulation.[34] Europeans established this pattern of almost

---

[32] The large female component among German indentured servants is explained by the fact that they were really redemptioners and redemption was a device more suited to family migration than the more traditional indentures. See the discussion of this in Galenson, *White Servitude*, 14–15. See also Farley Grubb, "Redemptioner Immigration to Pennsylvania: Evidence on Contract Choice and Profitability," *Journal of Economic History*, 46(1986):407–18.

[33] David Eltis and Stanley L. Engerman, "Was the Slave Trade Dominated by Men?" *Journal of Interdisciplinary History*, 23(1993):237–57.

[34] Dwaka Nath, *A History of Indians in Guyana* (London, 1970), pp. 143–4; Stanley L. Engerman, "Economic Change and Contract Labor in the British Caribbean: The End of Slavery and the Adjustment to Emancipation," *Explorations in Economic History*, 21(1984):146. For sex ratios in the unregulated Cuban traffic see the comments of the U.S. consul in Amoy, China (T. H. Hyatt to Secretary Marcy, May 1, 1855, Sen. Exec. Doc., 99 Sess. 34-1, p. 92). For discussions among British officials on the desirability and difficulty of obtaining female

Table 4-3. *The Sex and Age Structure of Free and Coerced Migration to the English Americas, 1651–99: Major Regions of Disembarkation by Decade (sample size in parentheses)**

A. Male ratio Destination	1651–60		1661–70		1671–80		1681–90		1691–99	
Virginia/Maryland										
Slaves	—	—	—	—	0.543	(541)	0.841	(697)	—	—
Convicts	1.0	(500)	0.837	(43)	0.922	(232)	0.967	(992)	0.930	(299)
Servants	0.718	(1,004)	0.751	(2,498)	0.767	(1,534)	0.708	(1,164)	0.793	(531)
Free migrants	1.0	(1)	—	—	0.885	(26)	—	—	0.667	(6)
Caribbean										
Slaves	—	—	0.536	(7,067)	0.595	(21,188)	0.582	(24,591)	0.611	(10,819)
Convicts	1.0	(82)	0.783	(1,017)	0.705	(837)	0.820	(1,132)	0.700	(789)
Servants	0.709	(5,048)	0.795	(1,639)	0.808	(655)	0.825	(1,345)	1.0	(34)
Free migrants	0.999	(1,511)	—	—	0.750	(4)	1.0	(1)	1.0	(3)
B. Child ratio Destination										
Virginia/Maryland										
Slaves	—	—	—	—	0.044	(541)	0.030	(464)	—	—
Convicts	0.0	(500)	0.0	(43)	0.0	(232)	0.001	(992)	0.0	(299)
Servants	0.0	(1,004)	0.0	(2,504)	0.003	(1,544)	0.049	(1,164)	0.037	(534)
Free migrants	0.0	(1)	—	—	0.041	(122)	—	—	0.0	(6)
Caribbean										
Slaves	—	—	0.121	(7,067)	0.091	(20,763)	0.148	(24,091)	0.106	(10,819)
Convicts	0.0	(82)	0.003	(1,144)	0.0	(841)	0.002	(1,130)	0.0	(789)
Servants			0.001	(1,569)	0.015	(659)	0.030	(1,287)	0.265	(25)
Free migrants	0.0	(1,511)	—	—	0.0	(4)	0.0	(3)	0.0	(6)

*Ratios are for males and children as a proportion of total migrants in the ten-year period. The shares for slaves are thus calculated slightly different from those discussed in Appendix A, where the ratios are means of ship-based data.
Sources: For Europeans, see source for Table 4-1. For slaves, *TSTD*.

exclusively male migration from Asia (in the absence of government intervention, that is) long before the nineteenth century. British, Dutch, and French ships carried slaves from various parts of India to Indonesia and South Africa during the seventeenth and eighteenth centuries. About one-third of the slave arrivals at the Cape of Good Hope between 1680 and 1730 were of Asian origin. These slaves were almost invariably men. Women slaves in Dutch South Africa were almost all African – more precisely in the early days, Madagascan.[35]

A more refined examination of the transatlantic data is possible with Table 4-3, which shows male and child ratios of major categories of migrants into the English Americas broken down by decadal intervals. The sex ratio of arrivals from Africa was close to parity in the 1660s, and while the share

migrants from China, see the letters to Herman Merivale dated May 2, and Sept. 27, 1854 in CO386/91.

[35] Nigel Worden, *Slavery in South Africa* (Cambridge, 1985), pp. 46–8, 52–60; Robert C.-H. Shell, *Children of Bondage: A Social History of the Slave Society at the Cape of Good Hope, 1652–1838* (Hanover, N. H., 1994), pp. 40–8.

of African females declined thereafter, it remained well above that of any category of European arrivals. The sex ratio of servants and convicts arriving in the Chesapeake changed little in this half-century. Among Caribbean arrivals a rising share of female convicts is apparent, but this was offset by a decline in both the absolute numbers and share of female servants so that there was probably little change in the overall sex ratio of European migrants. Table 4-3 lacks much information on free migrants after the 1650s. This omission is less significant for the sugar colonies, where such migrants cannot have been numerous after 1660, than for the Chesapeake. Overall, Caribbean migration became more, rather than less, male oriented in the course of the seventeenth century. On the other hand, children began to show up among servants in the late century (they were mainly boys), and with the child proportion among slaves not changing much, the average age of all migrants probably fell. It is not likely that widespread family migration existed for either free or coerced groups, though for different reasons.

The migration data thus suggest that women of European descent were never a significant part of the labor force of the export sectors of the Atlantic economies. Employers of labor may have accepted women as field workers, especially in the Americas, but not many were forthcoming. Some female migrants specifically excluded working in the fields when signing indentures. Wives of tobacco farmers who employed a small number of servants, and later slaves, might work long hours, many of them spent on manual labor, but the servants themselves, or at least those that worked in the fields, were almost always male.[36] The same was true of employers. Only 6 of the 1,340 persons entering produce in the Barbados custom books of the midseventeenth century were women,[37] and while 100 of the 1,405 pre-1708 Jamaican purchasers of slaves from the Royal African Company were women, almost all were widows who dropped out of the market when an adult male member of the family became available.[38] The high demand for labor in the early modern export-oriented colonies of the Americas provided opportunities for

[36] Lorena S. Walsh, "The Planter's Wife: The Experience of White Women in Seventeenth Century Maryland"; James Horn, "Servant Emigration to the Chesapeake in the Seventeenth Century," in Thad W. Tate and David L. Ammerman (eds.), *The Chesapeake in the Seventeenth Century: Essays on Anglo-American Society* (Chapel Hill, N.C. 1979). pp. 62–5.

[37] "A Coppie Journal of Entries made In the Custome House of Barbados Beginning August the 10th, 1664 and ending August the 10th 1665," Manuscripts English History, b. 122, 205 folios, in the Bodleian Library, Oxford. A second volume, "A Coppie Journal of Entries Made in the Custom House of Barbados, 1665–1667," is located at the Hispanic Society of America, New York (M1480) and covers August 11, 1665 to April 22, 1667. Henceforward referred to as "Custom books." The second book takes up where the first leaves off. For a summary of the first see Puckrein, *Little England*, pp. 57–60.

[38] Trevor Burnard, "Who Bought Slaves in Early America? Purchasers of Slaves from the Royal African Company in Jamaica, 1674–1708," *Slavery and Abolition*, 17(1996):78–9.

females, at least in the English Americas, not available in the Old World. Yet while the separate spheres for the sexes may have been less distinct before 1700 than they were to become in the nineteenth century, it is striking how little impact the strong demand for labor and high wages relative to Europe had on dominant attitudes toward women as either employers or workers in the Americas.[39] Female artisans were no more common in the Chesapeake than in England.[40] Inheritance patterns were more important than employment opportunities in determining the economic status and social position of women of European descent in the seventeenth-century Americas.[41]

African women arriving in the New World had few choices. Europeans carried their conceptions of women's role in society with them when they bought slaves, initially in Africa, and put them to work in the plantations. Slave traders went to Africa looking mainly for men. What they found, in major markets in West Africa at least, was more women offered for sale than they wanted. Europeans wanted males, more males, in fact, than they were able to obtain anywhere in Africa. Indeed, if winds and distance had been slightly different, Chinese and Indians, whose view of the economic importance of women was much closer to Europe's, might have labored on American plantations two centuries before the 1850s. The Royal African Company's standard orders to its captains directed the latter to obtain at least two males for every female.[42] Yet, as Table 4-2 shows, captains and factors managed less than 60 percent male during this period, a ratio that induced the company agents in the West Indies to complain regularly and ineffectually.[43] Planters and slave traders nevertheless made the adjustment. Dealing with African societies where (unlike their own) females had a central productive role and (like their own) were in the majority, Europeans were prepared to bend their attitudes and take on far greater proportions of women from Africa than from Europe. It is striking how quickly the Portuguese in early Brazil, the French and English in the Caribbean, and the Dutch in Surinam all put women to work in the fields. As noted in Chapter 8, the early origins of the gang-labor system are unclear, but by the early eighteenth century the proportion of the female plantation labor force working under the whip in

---

[39]   Salinger, "'Send No More Women': Female Servants in Eighteenth-Century Philadelphia," 29–48; Grubb, "Servant Auction Records and Immigration into the Delaware Valley."

[40]   Jean B. Russo, "Self Sufficiency and Local Exchange: Free Craftsmen in the Rural Chesapeake Economy, " in Carr, Morgan, and Russo, *Colonial Chesapeake Society*, 389–432, especially p. 393, n. 9.

[41]   Walsh, "The Planter's Wife," 555–63.

[42]   See the many letters of instruction from the company to its slave-ship captains in T70/51.

[43]   See, for example, Stede & Gascoigne, Barbados, April 4, 1683, T70/16, f. 50; Stede & Skutt, Barbados, to RAC, August 22, 1688, T70/12, p. 31; RAC to Petley Wyborne and Henry Stronghill, August 8, 1688, T70/50, f. 70; RAC to Browne, Peck, Hicks at Cape Coast Castle, July 23, 1702, T70/51, f. 131.

gangs was very close to that of males.[44] Planters throughout the Americas found that they could make profits with women performing the same labor as men in the fields.

The most plausible indication of this adjustment, apart from the known profitability of the early plantations, comes from an analysis of the sex ratios of African slaves pouring into expanding sugar regions. Planters in these regions – given the particularly hard labor required by the preparation of new sugar estates – might have been expected to put a premium on purchasing young males. In fact, the proportion of women arriving in the newer sugar areas was not significantly different from the proportion arriving on islands with a long history of sugar cultivation. Expanding sugar production was actually associated with fewer men and more children, though perhaps the demand for labor was at root undifferentiated. More formally, the demand for slaves of a particular gender and age was far more elastic than the demand for slaves as a whole. The surprising rise in the proportion of children in the traffic as sugar cultivation increased is probably linked to slave prices and shipping costs rather than crop patterns. The seventeenth century saw the transition of sugar from a medicinal to a consumer product. As the overall market increased, upward pressure on slave prices developed. At the same time, however, transatlantic shipping became more efficient, more than offsetting the pressure on slave prices. It thus became profitable to carry more low-valued slaves such as children across the Atlantic.[45] There is considerable

[44] For Bahia see Schwartz, *Sugar Plantations in the Formation of Brazilian Society*, 151–2; for St. Domingue see David Geggus, "Sex Ratio, Age and Ethnicity in the Atlantic Slave Trade: Data from the French Shipping and Plantation Records," *Journal of African History*, 30(1989):31–3, 42. For Virginia, see Lorena S. Walsh, "Slave Life, Slave Society, and Tobacco Production in the Tidewater Chesapeake, 1620–1820," in Ira Berlin and Philip D. Morgan (eds.), *Cultivation and Culture: Labor and the Shaping of Slave Life in the Americas* (Charlottesville, Va., 1993), p. 177. For a description of women working in the fields in Barbados in the 1650s, see Richard Ligon, *A True and Exact History* (London, 1657), p. 55, and the discussion in Hilary McD. Beckles, *Natural Rebels: A Social History of Enslaved Black Women in Barbados* (New Brunswick, N.J., 1989), pp. 3–11. For Jamaica from the seventeenth to the nineteenth centuries and a striking description of the tension between economic and reproductive roles of slave women (and the predominance of the former) see Richard S. Dunn, "Sugar Production and Slave Women in Jamaica," in Berlin and Morgan, *Cultivation and Culture*, 49–72, especially 55. Bernard Moitt surveys women's work in "Behind the Sugar Fortunes: Women, Labor and the Development of Caribbean Plantations During Slavery," in Simeon Waliaula Chilungu and Sada Niang (eds.), *African Continuities* (Toronto, 1989), pp. 403–26 but assumes that high female ratios on plantations late in the slavery era meant that the slave trade was by then predominantly female.

[45] Galenson, *Traders, Planters and Slaves*, 103–4; Eltis and Engerman, "Fluctuations in Sex and Age Ratios." Analysis of the present data gives partial support for Galenson's assessment of the impact of war on age and sex patterns in the slave trade. See Appendix A.

support in the sources for the connection between the proportion of children carried and shipping costs. Small children, argued the RAC Barbados agents in a typical exchange, are "not worth their freight," to which the captain of the slave ship replied (neatly illustrating the importance of marginal cost in the process), "they cost not much & the shipp had as good bring them as nothing, she (being) paid by the month . . . ."[46] Between 1663 and 1713, the share of children relative to adults in the slave trade increased steadily each year.[47]

Europeans came to accept women workers, but African insistence on offering women as slaves nevertheless created a tension between a chauvinism based on perceived European/non-European differences and a chauvinism based on gender. Only non-Europeans could be slaves, but if many of these slaves were female, could they be put to work in gangs and whipped? Obviously, it was perceptions of gender roles that gave ground. The shift in attitudes remained limited, however. In 1780, Jamaican William Beckford stated that "a negro man is purchased either for a trade, or the cultivation and different processes of the cane," while "the occupations of the women are only two, the house, with its several departments . . . or the field with its exaggerated labors."[48] Non-domestic skilled occupations on the plantations in the Americas continued to be the exclusive domain of males. Europeans were willing to see African, but not European, women working in gangs in the fields but were not prepared to provide opportunities for any women to master skilled tasks outside the domestic environment. Female coopers, carpenters, smiths, and sugar-makers were not just scarce in the plantation Americas, they were unknown.

While Europeans came to accept a wider economic role for women – as long as they were of African extraction – they continued to stress the reproductive aspect of gender relations for their own women. Contact between radically different cultures triggered adjustment but not revolution. If Africans had sailed to Europe and carried off European slaves instead of the reverse, then the slave cargoes would have almost certainly have been mostly females, though unlike the trans-Saharan slave trade, the female migrants would have had a major economic function. Indeed, comparison of the demographic structures of the trans-Saharan and transatlantic slave trades shows how small the reproductive role that plantation owners had in mind for Africans really was. Some historians have interpreted the early prevalence of women from Africa in the British Caribbean as evidence of

---

46   Stede & Gascoigne, Barbados, April 4, 1683, T70/16, f. 50.
47   See Appendix A.
48   Cited in David Barry Gaspar, "Sugar Cultivation and Slave Life in Antigua Before 1800," in Berlin and Morgan, *Cultivation and Culture*, 110–11. See also Gaspar's discussion of this point.

planters wishing to keep the sexes balanced. As shown later, however, there is little evidence in markets on either side of the Atlantic of reproductive functions influencing behavior of European slave owners and traders. Of course, the power of slave owners over slaves was such that widespread sexual abuse of slaves by slave owners may be assumed; the large population of Afro-European descent in the Iberian Americas is testimony to the fact that African women were somewhat more than units of labor to Europeans. But the difference between taking a black mistress or raping a slave on the one hand and establishing the institutions of polygyny, or further, a harem, on the other is of some significance. European settlers in the New World did not reshape European norms in family and sexual conduct whether they were living in predominantly slave or predominantly free societies. Although Elizabeth Fox-Genovese and Eugene Genovese describe the antebellum south as "pre-capitalist," they also recognize that societies north and south of the Mason-Dixon line shared a great deal.[49] The basic European institutions of the nuclear family and serial monogamy were not threatened by African slavery in the Americas, despite the apparently unfettered power of Europeans over Africans in New World.

Much of the recent literature has suggested that African and European demand dovetailed in the sense that Africans wished to retain females (for labor and procreation) and Europeans desired males for plantation work. If this was the case then the fit was not smooth.[50] African traders in some major provenance zones wished to sell far more females than Europeans were prepared to buy, and Europeans wanted more males than Africans were prepared to sell.[51] Clearly, the actual ratio of men, women, and children

---

[49] Elizabeth Fox-Genovese and Eugene D. Genovese, *The Fruits of Merchant Capital: Slavery and Bourgeois Property in the Rise and Expansion of Capitalism* (New York, 1983), pp. 16–17. For a recent careful comparison of colonial and metropolitan societies see James Horn, "Adapting to a New World: A Comparative Study of Local Society in England and Maryland," in Carr, Morgan, and Russo, *Colonial Chesapeake Society*, 133–75.

[50] For evidence of a preponderance of females in the populations of regions supplying transatlantic slave markets, see John Thornton, "The Slave Trade in Eighteenth Century Angola: Effects on Demographic Structures," *Canadian Journal of African Studies*, 14(1980):417–27; and idem, "Sexual Demography: The Impact of the Slave Trade on Family Structure," in Klein and Robertson (eds.), *Women and Slavery in Africa*, 39–48. This evidence is not inconsistent with the findings here. Angola and Senegambia, the regions to which Thornton's evidence pertains, were the regions with the largest male ratios among the sample of deportees analyzed here.

[51] All sides in the debate on the demographic structure of the slave trade seem agreed that Europeans took more females than they would have really preferred. See Joseph Inikori, "Export Versus Domestic Demand: the Determinants of Sex Ratios in the Transatlantic Slave Trade," *Research in Economic History*, 14(1992):155.

traded was a compromise, but one that ensured that far more African than European females crossed the Atlantic before the nineteenth century.

But Europeans and Africans not only differed from each other in their conceptions of gender, they also differed among themselves. Moreover, such differences are just as difficult to explain in economic terms. Women formed a larger share of transatlantic migrants from England than from other European countries. Over 90 percent of French indentured servants were male, and while, in Quebec at least, half or more of the arrivals were not indentured, the female component of this nonindentured group was so low that the French government organised free passages for single women in an attempt to increase the sex ratio of the tiny St. Lawrence settlement.[52] The female component of migration from Spain to the Americas crept from 5 percent to 19 percent in the first post-Columbian century, when Spanish migration was at its height. Indeed, it was only later in the sixteenth century that the Spanish government allowed married men to emigrate, early permits being confined to single men.[53] There are no comparable data for Portugal, but the low incidence of Iberian women in early Brazil has received wide recognition and was for long used to explain a supposedly tolerant Portuguese attitude toward Africans and mulattoes.[54] Women formed a major element of German transatlantic migration when it became significant in the eighteenth century, but the basic unit of such migration was families, not single individuals.[55] The flow from Germany was thus like the Great Migration to New England after 1630. But both the high sex ratios and the religious overtones of these migrations were exceptional in the broad pattern of pre-1800 migration from Europe.[56]

[52] Debien, "Les engagés pour les Antilles," 5–274. The 774 filles du roi had their passage to New France and part of their settlement costs paid by the French government between 1663 and 1673 (Silvio Dumas, *Les filles du roi en Nouvelle France* [Quebec, 1972], pp. 32–3).

[53] Peter Boyd-Bowman, "Patterns of Spanish Emigration to the Indies until 1600," *Hispanic American Historical Review*, 56(1976):584; Ida Altman, *Emigrants & Society: Extremadura and Spanish America in the Sixteenth Century* (Los Angeles, 1989), pp. 176–8, and idem, "Moving Around and Moving on: Spanish Emigration in the Sixteenth Century," in Jan Lucassen and Leo Lucassen (eds.), *Migrations, Migration History: Old Paradigms and New Perspectives* (Bern, 1987), pp. 253–69. See also Magnus Morner, *Adventurers and Proletarians: The Story of Migrants in Latin America* (Pittsburgh, 1985).

[54] See for example the argument and the literature cited in Carl N. Degler, *Neither Black nor White: Slavery and Race Relations in Brazil and the United States* (New York, 1971), 232–9; Galenson, *White Servitude*, 24, 26.

[55] Marianne Wokeck, "The Flow and the Composition of German Immigration to Philadelphia, 1727–1775," *Pennsylvania Magazine of History and Biography*, 105(1981):258–67.

[56] See most recently Virginia DeJohn Anderson, *New England's Generation: The Great Migration and the Formation of Society and Culture in the Seventeenth Century* (Cambridge, 1991), pp. 12–45, especially 21–3.

Table 4-4. *Percentages of African Males, Children, Women, Men, Girls, and Boys Carried to the Americas, 1663–1713, by African Region of Embarkation (sample size in parentheses)*

	Males	Women	Men	Girls	Boys
Upper Guinea	74.3 (7,170)	22.6 (6,937)*	71.6	1.6	4.2
Gold Coast	58.0 (23,026)	39.2 (21,743)	45.8	4.6	10.4
Bight of Benin	62.3 (45,540)	34.6 (40,073)	53.6	3.6	8.1
Bight of Biafra	50.3 (13,024)	46.2 (12,523)	42.2	3.8	7.9
West-Central Africa	64.9 (13,740)	28.5 (13,740)	49.3	6.3	16.0
Africa**	61.5 (111,323)	34.9 (104,151)	51.8	4.0	9.4

*Women, Men, Boys, Girls drawn from same sample. Males includes some individuals identified by sex only. **Includes those from unknown African embarkation zones. African regions are as follows: Upper Guinea is the area north of the Rio Assini and includes the Ivory Coast – though there was very little slave trading between the Rio Assini and Sierra Leone at this time; the Gold Coast comprises the Rio Assini to Cape St. Paul; the Bight of Benin runs from Cape St. Paul up to, but not including, the Rio Nun; the Rio Nun to Cape Lopez, inclusive, makes up the Bight of Biafra; and west-central Africa is the west African coast south of Cape Lopez. *Source: TSTD.*

Government controls help explain the much smaller share of women among Spanish migrants in the first century of the Spanish Americas compared to English departures in the next century. But conventional explanations, whether based on class analysis or neoclassical economics, provide little insight into the reason for those controls. Moreover, the differences between northern and southern Europe in the share of women among transatlantic migrants probably held until the late nineteenth century, despite the fact that migrants from different parts of Europe headed for the same labor markets in the Americas and responded to broadly similar push factors.

At the African end of the slave trade the regional differences are even more striking and even less is known about them. As Table 4-4 indicates, the differences in the age and sex of deportees among African regions were substantial. They were, in fact, much greater than those between regions of arrival in the Americas. The central question is why these differences existed. Were they interactive in the sense that a particular region in the Americas drew on particular regions of Africa? After controlling for region of disembarkation, time, crop type, and war, the distinctiveness of African regions from each other is even more striking. In summary, the proportion of men sailing from Upper Guinea was much larger than elsewhere and the proportion of children smaller. West-central Africa by contrast had much greater ratios of children, especially boys, among their deportees than anywhere else. In the Bight of Biafra the ratio of women leaving was much higher and the proportion of men much lower than elsewhere. The Gold Coast exhibited patterns similar to the Bight of Biafra, though not as extreme. In the Americas, the only regional differences that persist after controlling for region of embarkation, time, crop type, and war are the larger ratios of boys to Barbados and the smaller share of girls absorbed by the Dutch and Spanish Americas.[57]

Most of these regional differences are supported by the contemporary written record. John Tozer wrote from the Gambia that his ship had "never caryed above 60 Men & all ye Rest woomen & children [elsewhere, but] here are all men." Indeed they were male to the point that the latter might even have to prepare their own food: Captain Weaver wrote from Portodally that "he hath not been able to purchase a woman and there must be at least 12 Women to dress the Victuals" on board the slave ship.[58] On the Gold Coast, on the other hand, meal preparation was apparently never a problem as the RAC agents struggled to keep males from minority status. Robert Young's comment from Accra in 1683 that "[w]ee have purchased seaven slaves and Could have had more but wee stand for one man & one woeman, men slaves being verry scarce here" has many echoes from other years and other parts of this coast.[59] "I have now 25 men, 31 women 5 boys 2 girls which is sixty three . . . . I have refused about 30 women, because there is no men, but I shall not let a man pass, if he be anything good. . ." wrote William Piles from Pono in 1697.[60] The RAC had similar problems in the Bight of Biafra. Despite instructions to slave-ship captains and a letter to the largest African slave trader of the region, the king of Bonny, insisting on "three men . . . for two women," Table 4-4 shows that the company barely succeeded in keeping the sexes at parity.[61] On the American side, Jamaica was the chief market after the Dutch islands for purchasers from the Spanish-American mainland;

---

[57] We should note however that a separate equation using male ratios as the dependent variable instead of ratios of men showed no differences between Barbados and other sugar-producing regions. The data thus do not support Beckles' argument that early Barbados planters were unusual in buying more females than planters on other islands in order to sustain a balanced sex ratio (*Natural Rebels*, 7–11).

[58] John Tozer of the *Postillion* at Gambia to the RAC., May 2, 1704, T70/13, f. 71; Thomas Weaver of the *Swan* to the RAC, May 5, 1704, *ibid.*, f. 85. These were characteristics of the slave traffic from Senegambia down to the nineteenth century. Voyage ids and 15,005 and 14,931 respectively.

[59] Robert Young, Accra to Cape Coast Castle, July 22, 1683, Rawlinson manuscript, c. 745, f. 227.

[60] William Piles, Pono, to Cape Coast Castle, June 30, 1697, *ibid.*, c. 746, f. 241. Cf. idem, Tersee to Cape Coast Castle, June 22, 1697, *ibid.*, f. 238; John Groome, Alampo, September 18, 1683 c. 745, f. 290.

[61] RAC to "Great King of Bandie," September 15, 1702, T70/51, f. 150.

the Spanish usually took "choice" slaves on their visits there, which meant more men.[62]

But describing these marked intra-African differences is much easier than explaining them. The dominance of men and the relatively few children in the flow of captives out of Upper Guinea (essentially, Senegambia and Sierra Leone) could well have been influenced by two factors. One was the large distance slave captives travelled in this region before reaching the coast. Longer distances put a premium on the capacity of slaves to carry ivory and other commodities, and children were thus less likely to earn their passage to the coast.

A second possibility is the proximity of the trans-Saharan trade.[63] This traffic absorbed large numbers of females, and African regions of embarkation that fell within its influence may have sent more males across the Atlantic than areas less susceptible to cross-Saharan influences. However, the total number of Atlantic slave departures from West Africa was still only a third or so of what it was to become a century later, and slave prices on the coast were low compared to the eighteenth century. It is not likely at this stage that slave traders were drawing heavily on regions remote from the coast. The traffic to the Arab world would have had a much stronger impact on the mid-Senegal River and the area between the Senegal and Niger Rivers than on the upper Niger and pastoral regions further west. Ocean currents and river systems ensured that the quickest route from the desert fringes to the Americas was via Senegambia. "Bambara" slaves, whether Malinke speakers or the captives of Malinke speakers, appear in transit in the Senegambia in the 1680s but, unlike the nineteenth century, there is no evidence of their departure from Slave Coast and Niger Delta ports at this time.[64] Competition from Arab buyers, or perhaps simply the difficulty in controlling male captives, might have accounted for the fact that in the late 1680s men slaves cost half the price of women or boy slaves at Tarra, 650 kilometres east of the mouth of the Senegal River.[65] Trans-Saharan influence

---

[62] Beckford and Galdy to RAC, January 1, 1708, T70/8. f. 30; Stede and Gascoigne to the RAC, n.d., T70/10, f. 18. Accounts of sales to the Spanish for 1665 indicate male ratios of 62 percent at a time when males comprised just over half of the arrivals in Jamaica as a whole (Entries for May 11, June 5, 1665 in T70/869).

[63] Assuming that data from the late nineteenth century are indicative of earlier trends – and historians have accepted that they are. See Ralph Austen, "The Trans-Saharan Slave Trade: A Tentative Census," in Gemery and Hogendorn, *The Uncommon Market*, 44; Lovejoy, *Transformations in Slavery*, 29–30. The trans-Saharan traffic is cited as the explanation for the high male ratios of transatlantic departures from upper Guinea by Inikori, "Export Versus Domestic Demand," 129, 152–3, 156–7.

[64] Curtin, *Economic Change in Pre-Colonial Africa*, 168–73, 177–9; Eltis, *Economic Growth*, 167–8.

[65] Cornelius Hodge cited in Thora G. Stone, "The Journey of Cornelius Hodges in Senegambia, 1689–90," *English Historical Review*, 39(1924):92.

probably accounts for the large share of males leaving Senegambia for the Americas. But trans-Saharan demand is not likely at this stage to have had much influence on regions farther to the south.

The large proportion of females leaving the Bight of Biafra and the differences between this and the adjacent Bight of Benin are a particular puzzle. Almost half of the slaves from Niger Delta ports were female. Of all the regions in Africa and Europe that were involved in the transatlantic population shift (for which data exist), migrants from this one region come closest to reflecting what must have been the sex ratio of the population of the hinterland that sustained the migration. Joseph Inikori, citing the opinion of a twentieth-century British governor, suggests that European buyers of slaves saw Igbo women (from the Bight of Biafra) as stronger and more resilient than other Africans, and from this single area European traders were prepared to buy women.[66] Yet on board ships leaving the Bight of Biafra there was no sex differential in mortality, and deaths among both sexes were higher than on ships leaving other regions. Further, planters in the early English Caribbean had a poor opinion of slaves from this region, and while later generations of planters apparently had a relatively high opinion of the industry of Igbo females, there is certainly no hint in any of the extensive contemporary comment of a preference for women from there.[67] In the seventeenth century, slaves from the Bight of Biafra frequently sold at a discount in the Caribbean.[68] European traders on occasion saw the Bight of Biafra as a market of last resort and as an appropriate locale for selling off damaged goods.[69]

What alternative explanations are there for the high ratios of women leaving what is now southeast Nigeria? In the nineteenth century the hinterland of the Bight of Biafra, especially the Igbo and Ibibio areas, was (and is) one of the more densely populated parts of West Africa. It is possible that such conditions might support, or be associated with, greater female migration, but population densities in seventeenth-century Africa are necessarily matters of dispute.[70] The most promising approach to the problem is the hypothesis of Ugo Nwokeji that many Igbo societies, particularly the expanding Aro network, placed less value on women's labor than other regions of sub-Saharan

---

[66] Inikori, "Export Versus Domestic Demand," 135–7.

[67] For samples of contemporary comment see "RAC agents at Barbados" to RAC, Nov. 26, 1675, CO 268/1, p. 37; Edwyn Stede, Barbados to RAC, April 20, 1680, T70/10, f. 15; RAC to Charles Chaplin, Jamaica, Feb. 22, 1703, T70/58, f. 28; John Huffam, Nevis, to RAC, May 25, 1710, T70/8, f. 54; idem, December 3, 1711, *ibid.*, f. 60.

[68] Molesworth, Penhallow and Riding, Kingston, Jamaica to the RAC, March 6, 1686, T70/12, p. 71.

[69] Buckeridge, Cooper and Browne, Cape Coast Castle, to the RAC, September 1, 1698, T70/11, p. 126.

[70] David Northrup, *Trade Without Rulers*, pp. 58–65; Inikori, "Export Versus Domestic Demand."

Africa. The reproductive role for females loomed larger here than it did elsewhere, and female slavery was a marginal institution. Much of the internal demand for women that did exist derived from women slave owners who participated in "woman-marriage," thereby obtaining slave "wives."[71] Further, despite the demand for men from across the Atlantic, Cross River Igbo warrior groups accorded high status to the killing of men victims of their raids. For Nwokeji, such factors, together with the already noted remoteness of the region from the trans-Saharan trade resulted in a relative abundance of females leaving Old Calabar, New Calabar, and Bonny.[72]

Other regions have yet to receive the close analysis of indigenous structures that Nwokeji has carried out for the Aro. Differences between patrilineal and matrilineal societies are another promising avenue of investigation. The expectation here is that areas in which matrilineal kinship patterns prevailed were more likely to retain females, and higher male ratios are possible in the transatlantic traffic from such regions.[73] But at first sight this approach also produces inconclusive results.[74] Upper Guinea and west-central Africa, drawing on largely matrilineal hinterlands, fit the expected pattern as far as males are concerned. But once we move the discussion to women, men, girls, and boys, the results are more problematic. The two Bights and the Gold Coast, drawing on heavily patrilineal areas, sent greater shares of females into the trade than the other two major regions of departure. But this is, at best, a broad-brush approach. It cannot explain variations among the three key West African areas of the Gold Coast, the Slave Coast, and the Bight of Biafra. Nor can it explain regional variations in the number of children carried into the trade. In a pattern that was to become even more pronounced in the nineteenth century, between one in four and one in five of those carried from west-central Africa were children, much higher than anywhere else, and most puzzling of all, nearly three-quarters of them were boys.

We should not be surprised that the age and sex of forced migrants varied so much between African regions. Cultural and social diversity within Africa was certainly no less than in Europe. In the African case, migrants did not make the decision to migrate, but the African slave traders that assumed

---

[71] For female husbands see Ifi Amadiume, *Male Daughters, Female Husbands: Gender and Sex in an African Society* (London, 1987) and the convenient survey in Denise O'Brien, "Female Husbands in Southern Bantu Society," in Alice Schlegel (ed.), *Sexual Stratification: A Cross-Cultural View* (New York, 1977), pp. 109–26.

[72] G. Ugo Nwokeji, "Household and Market Persons: Servitude and Banishment in the Making of the Biafran Diasporas, c. 1750–c. 1890" (Paper presented to the Black Atlantic: Race, Nation and Gender Seminar at Rutgers University, October 1997).

[73] Klein, "African Women in the Atlantic Slave Trade"; Geggus, "Sex Ratio, Age and Ethnicity."

[74] For a more formal presentation of these results see Appendix A.

the decision-making role were sellers in a market that allowed full play for African as well as American influences. Yet in one of the great ironies of the slave trade, the gender composition of the plantation work force was shaped in part by the relative economic freedom of women in Africa. It was because African women had a wider range of roles in Africa than Europe that African slave traders – some of whom were women – could envision their sale into the slave trade. The smaller economic role for women in most of the non-African world would have ensured a much larger male presence in the flow of labor to the Americas if Europeans had targeted almost anywhere other than Africa for labor and had organised a non-African slave trade. The African pressure that ensured a large female component in the slave trade also ensured a richer and more enduring African physical and cultural presence in the Americas. Of the thousands of almost exclusively male Chinese who entered Cuba and Peru as contract laborers in the nineteenth century, for example, there is now little trace.

As with the insider/outsider dichotomy taken up in the previous chapter, the major ironies are economic in nature. For Europeans and their descendants in the Americas, an attitude toward women that denied the latter access to full economic opportunities was at least as costly as discrimination built on the European/insider, non-European/outsider dichotomy. First, the cost of labor for export staple producers in the New World (the main employers of indentured servants) would have been lower with no gender occupational barriers in place. Second, prior to the transition to African slaves, plantation produce would have sold for less if Europeans had used female, instead of almost exclusively male, indentured servants in the fields. Third, after the switch to slavery, sugar and tobacco would still have been cheaper if Europeans had put African women to work in skilled occupations. Fourth, as noted previously, the cheapest (and most unthinkable) option of all was the enslavement of other Europeans, men *and* women, instead of Africans, and their distribution across all occupations according to ability.

The foregoing is not an argument against the economic rationality of Europeans and non-Europeans trading for slaves on the African coast or in India (or Arab slave traders operating across the Sahara). Rather it is an attempt to establish the broad cultural parameters within which the market operated and that are sometimes overlooked by economic historians. The composition of the free and coerced migrant flows across the Atlantic does not make sense without taking into account these broader influences, which in a sense help define what was economically rational for particular cultures and epochs. Market analysis nevertheless remains central to any understanding of the slave trade. Labor could simply produce more and was therefore more valuable in the New World than in the Old. Thus, the former was able to attract the most productive part of African labor forces – young women – as well as the most productive part of the English labor force – young men.

In the slave-trade sector the market mediation of cultural preferences is apparent in the long-term steady reduction in transatlantic differentials in the prices of male and female slaves. In the late seventeenth and early eighteenth centuries this differential was much smaller on the American side of the Atlantic than on the African. Young women typically sold for 80 to 85 percent of young men in the late seventeenth and early eighteenth century Caribbean.[75] In Africa, the sex price differential varied considerably, but females sold for just over two-thirds of the male price.[76] The persistence of this cross-Atlantic difference in a competitive market is explained by the large shipping cost wedge. Transport costs accounted for at least half the selling price of a slave newly arrived in the Americas. The cost of selling the slave in the Americas (or distribution costs) and factoring (or bulking) costs on the African coast were also important so that the African cost of the slave formed a relatively small share of the American price. The expense of shipping insulated one price from the other. One hundred years later when transatlantic shipping costs had fallen and African prices of slaves had increased, the male-female price differential on the African coast was similar to the differential in the Americas, which remained at about 80 to 85 percent.[77] The shrinking of shipping costs as technology and organization improved had perhaps allowed the small American differential to exert a stronger influence on its African counterpart.

[75] Galenson, *Traders, Planters and Slaves*, 61–4; Stanely L. Engerman, Manuel Moreno Fraginals, and Herbert S. Klein, "The Level and Structure of Slave Prices on Cuban Plantations in the Mid-Nineteenth Century: Some Comparative Perspectives," *American Historical Review*, 88(1983):1209–13.

[76] The unweighted ratio for the period 1675–1727 calculated from thirty separate market observations and transactions, some involving more than hundred slaves, is 0.688 (sd = 0.11). Fourteen of these observations have been taken from Inikori, "Export Versus Domestic Demand," 137–42. Indrani Sen argues for 0.74 on the Gold Coast for a slightly later period (1712–36) "Trends in Slave Shipments from the Gold Coast: New Evidence on Slave Prices, 1710–1792" (Unpublished paper presented to the Seminar on Atlantic History at Harvard University, September 1996).

[77] Inikori claims that the sex price differential among slaves leaving the Bight of Biafra was very small ("Export Versus Domestic Demand"). The bulk of the data supporting this comment on slave prices in the Bight of Biafra are, however, from the 1790s, whereas data from other regions are from earlier in the century before the rise in African slave prices and fall in shipping costs. In fact, limited data (five observations) from the last quarter of the seventeenth and first quarter of the eighteenth centuries suggest that females sold for 0.76 of males in the Bight of Biafra (see, Elizabeth Donnan, *Documents Illustrative of the Slave Trade to America*, 4 vols. (Washington, 1930–3), 4:69–83; "G. Hingston's Journal," February 11, 1678, T70/1213). Further, the sex price differential appears to have fallen by the nineteenth century (0.93 calculated from David Eltis, "Slave-Price Data Set"), though Indrani Sen notes a widening differential on the Gold Coast in 1768–89 ("Trends in Slave Shipments"), which she attributes to increasing African domestic demand for females.

Any factor that increased shipping costs – effectively the wedge between American and African influences – would have likely reduced the shares of less expensive slaves such as the young and the old. War was the most obvious cost-increasing factor in this period. Increased demand for plantation produce, as described earlier, would tend on the other hand to drive up slave prices and increase the share of less expensive slaves carried across the Atlantic. The current data provide some support for both these arguments, despite the fact that the key variable of slave prices is missing. However, even if it were possible to define exactly the relationship between the demand for, say, sugar and the demand for the labor that produced it, even if we had full details on all the relevant cost functions, even if the competing markets for labor and produce around the Atlantic could be specified with precision, it would still not be possible to address the larger question of why the labor from Africa had a larger female component than that from Europe and Asia without some reference to attitudes to gender.

Nothing here should be construed as supporting a position that Africa determined the demographic structure of the slave trade. Clearly both American and African influences were important in addition, of course, to transportation costs. Sellers as well as buyers of slaves participated in these markets, just as sellers as well as buyers participated in the markets for European labor and to assert the primacy of either is to ignore how markets operate. Because Europeans would have been financially well advised to put women to work in both skilled occupations and the less-skilled field tasks whatever the origins of those women, it is no more possible to explain gender discrimination in terms of the desire of men to improve their economic position than it is to explain the rise and fall of African slavery in the Americas in terms of European merchants rapaciously pursuing profits. The behavior of males in the one case and Europeans in the other was shaped by cultural parameters that are easy to miss if researchers are preoccupied with the profit motive.

In summary, the relative absence of women in transatlantic European migration and their strong presence in the African slave trade provide insight into one of the driving forces behind migration. Ironically, given the enslavement of most African-Americans, women may have had higher status within African-American communities than women of European descent had in their societies. There was no more strictly economic reason for women forming a minor component of European migrant streams than for Europeans not being slaves. The division of labor that kept European women from acquiring skills outside the home and generally kept them from field labor was a purely cultural construct. And like slavery it applied to Europeans but not, in European eyes, to Africans.[78] Europeans were prepared to see African

---

[78] For similar arguments see Morgan, "Slavery and Freedom: The American Paradox," 21; Stanley L. Engerman, "Some Considerations Relating to Property Rights in Man," *Journal of Economic History*, 33(1973):49–51. For the

women work in the plantation fields (though curiously, not to learn skilled tasks on the plantation), but these same Europeans had barriers against using European women for most tasks outside the home. The decisions on both gender and race – in reality more culture-bound assumptions than choices between alternatives – had similar economic implications. They slowed the growth of the plantation Americas, and indeed the whole Atlantic world, by restricting the pool of skilled and unskilled labor. Mercantilist policies adopted by any one European nation designed to extract lifetime streams of plantation labor from European convicts or women would have given that nation an edge in the transatlantic rivalries that dominated the seventeenth and eighteenth centuries. The fact that such issues were not even the subject of serious debate (indeed, could not be so) points to some of the cultural and ideological forces shaping relations between Europe, Africa, and the Americas in the early modern era.

domestic servant orientation of female indentures in a later period at least, see Sharon Salinger, "Send No More Women"; and Grubb, "Servant Auction Records and Immigration."

5

Productivity in the Slave Trade

THE PREVIOUS TWO CHAPTERS have pointed to the shadowy outlines
of cultural norms that neither class nor self-interest can easily explain. Merchants, both European and African, like most others in their community,
spent little time questioning these attitudes. Indeed, we could not describe
attitudes as cultural norms if they had. Rather they got on with the business
of making money, and it is to the relatively precise business of exploring the
consequences of their behaviour that the argument now turns. The European ability to create transoceanic trading networks and establish colonies
of occupation and settlement hinged on first, the rather prosaic issue of shipping technology and second – given the cultural constraints on enslaving
Europeans – the availability of slaves from some non-European source. For
most of the 350-year span of the transatlantic slave trade, increasing demand
for labor from the Americas as the two continents were repeopled and the
increasing value of that labor as technology made people more productive
meant steadily rising prices for slaves. In the 1650–1713 period the explosive
growth of the English plantation system and the discovery of gold in Minas
Gerais in the mid-1690s were specific manifestations of demand pressure.
Any price may be broken down into either demand or supply components,
but the key to understanding the performance of the English, Danish, Dutch,
French, and Portuguese slave traders relative to each other lies largely on the
supply side, and this forms the main concern of the present chapter.

Shipping costs, including labor, provisions, fitting-out costs, insurance,
and port charges, as well as the capital goods involved were of central importance because carrying merchandise to the African coast from Europe
doubled the price of that merchandise and carrying slaves from Africa to the
Americas also doubled the price of slaves. Thus, the transportation component of converting goods in Europe into slaves in the Americas comprised approximately three-quarters of the selling price of an African in the Americas.
Of course, the African cost component was fundamental. If Africans had

sold their slaves on the coast for twice their actual price in the last quarter of the seventeenth century, say, £8 instead of £4, then quite possibly little slave trading would have occurred, given the evidence examined later of a price-sensitive European demand. But the efficiency with which goods were brought to Africa and then slaves to the Americas was nevertheless critical.

This was true for all Atlantic trade. From Columbian contact through to the nineteenth century, shipping costs made up the largest component of the price of all European goods in the Americas, Africa, and Asia and of all American, Asian, and African goods in Europe. Production costs, whether for manufactured or primary products, were always much less important. Four centuries of exchange between European and non-European peoples are in one sense simply the story of falling value-to-weight ratios for merchandise, as transportation costs gradually declined. The piracy that dominated early contact is explained in part by the heavy shipping charges that made the exchange of commodities, as opposed to their theft, almost impossible. This may account in part for the predatory label that many scholars have attached to the activities of the first European overseas merchants. Early trade was confined to high-value merchandise for the same reasons. Gold and silver had the highest value-to-weight ratio and was exceptionally cheap to transport. By the late seventeenth century it could be carried across the Atlantic twice – once from its source in Africa to the Americas and again from the Americas to consumers in Europe – for a shipping charge that amounted to less than one percent of its value in Africa.[1] Plantation produce and manufactured goods by contrast paid freight equal to or greater than the costs of acquiring these goods and putting them on board ship. No other input, including that of labor costs in the production process, was as important as transportation in determining which goods would sell in transoceanic markets, who would do the selling, and what imperial and political structures such activity would support.

The shipping of slaves was a microcosm of the general shipping picture. Shipping productivity shaped the slave empires of the Americas and was, in the early colonial era, the single most important influence over the size and profitability of these empires – and by implication the benefits Europe derived from them. More specifically, as long as transatlantic colonial populations were small and experiencing low or negative rates of natural increase, transoceanic shipping rates comprised the single most important element in the cost of labor in the Americas. The cost of taking a ship from Europe to Africa, loading slaves there, and carrying them to the Americas was critically important to the viability of the plantation complex, especially as European migration fell away in the half-century after 1660.

The importance of shipping costs is demonstrated by patterns in slave prices on both sides of the Atlantic. According to data in Appendix B between

---

[1] Eltis, "The Relative Importance of Slaves in the Atlantic Trade," 240.

1663 and 1698, the average value of goods per person that the Royal African Company exchanged for 77,825 slaves on four major regions of the African Coast was £3.38 in terms of the prime cost of the goods free on board (fob) in Europe (all data in current prices). The company carried the slaves they bought to the English Americas. A weighted price series for Barbados, the major market in the English Americas (as well as the English market closest to Africa), shows average annual prices, 1673–1684 and 1686–1698 to have been £15.22.[2] An inspection of annual average prices over these years shows some large year-to-year changes on both sides of the Atlantic, probably accounted for by sharp changes in the Barbados price, but little or no time trend. Slaves on the African coast thus cost about 22 percent of slaves in the Americas. As noted, the prime cost values would have to be doubled to approximate what the goods were worth off Africa at the point of exchange, which is another way of saying the African price of the slave free on board. By the third quarter of the eighteenth century prime costs had risen to over 40 percent of the American price and increased further to nearly 50 percent on the eve of the abolition of the British slave trade, suggesting the possibility of a long-run trend toward a smaller relative shipping cost. As we shall see, however, this should not be taken as conclusive proof of improving productivity.[3]

The central point is that the merchandise the Europeans supplied and the costs of transporting first the trade goods and then the slaves over the Atlantic shaped the early slave systems of the Americas. Behind the value of the goods exchanged on the African coast lay an African supply network and the ability of the Atlantic economies to produce goods of the type and price that Africans wanted. The more efficient the Europeans and the cheaper the goods, the more African slaves would be delivered to the Americas. Economic progress in Europe thus meant not only more income from which consumers could buy sugar but also cheaper slaves on the African coast. The English in the seventeenth century were among the most productive of Europeans.

As for transportation, European ocean-going sailing ships were by far the most efficient form of long-distance transportation devised before the nineteenth century. Given the outsider and chattel status of the Africans transported, however, efficiency in this context meant ignoring the preferences of the human cargo to a degree not possible in the transoceanic transportation of contract labor and certainly not fare-paying passengers, who had

---

[2] Calculated from Galenson, *Traders, Planters and Slaves*, 65, 67.

[3] Bean, *British Trans-Atlantic Slave Trade*, 158, 210 provides data from secondary sources for 1753–75 suggesting a ratio of 0.401 for Jamaica, equivalent to 0.426 for Barbados. If David Richardson's imputed series of African slave prices is used, the ratio of prime to American cost of the slave (American prices taken from Bean) is slightly lower than Bean's for the years 1753–75 ("Prices of Slaves in West and West-Central Africa: Toward an Annual Series, 1698–1807," *Bulletin of Economic Research*, 43(1991):21–56).

some choice over whether they went on board and thus some control over the likelihood that they were of the same culture or background as those organising the voyage. The degree of crowding on board a slave ship may not explain variations in shipboard mortality but it certainly affected the misery quotient of those on board. European slave traders created shipping conditions, the sheer awfulness of which was unrivalled before, during, and after the era of the transatlantic slave trade. This is not to deny that it was in the interests of the captain, owner, and crew to keep as many slaves alive and in as good health as possible until the ship arrived in the Americas. But the distance between this and having to take some account of the wishes of the people on board allowed ample room for intense suffering. Unlike slave ownership in both Africa and the Americas, slavery in the middle passage provided few opportunities for human contact between master and slave and was probably the purest form of domination in the history of slavery as an institution. It was not just the ability to ignore the preferences of the human cargo that created such conditions. European convicts – also carried across oceans against their will – never had to face slave-ship-like conditions.

The case presented here for the unique severity of conditions in the transatlantic slave trade goes against much of the literature on the shipping of indentured servants and convicts in the seventeenth and eighteenth centuries and the transportation of contract labor from Asia in the nineteenth.[4] The evidence, however, is clear enough at least for the seventeenth century. Between forty and fifty ships a year arrived at Jamaica from England in the 1680s and at least as many again at Barbados and the Leewards. Given the nature of the colonial trade, these one hundred or so ships, aggregating fifteen to twenty thousand tons, always had less merchandise cargo on the westbound journey than when returning. In the same period perhaps two or three thousand migrants per year left England for the Caribbean.[5] More directly, a total of 62 vessels arrived in Barbados and Jamaica between 1683 and 1698 with servants and passengers on board. The density of people on board these vessels averaged less than one sixth the ratio of slaves per ton on

---

[4] Beckles, *White Servitude and Black Slavery in Barbados*, 7–8, 71, although Beckles does note that "traditional ideological restraints within the imported English labor culture kept planters from deriving from servitude the full benefits offered by permanent chattel slavery" (p. 8); Hugh Tinker, *A New System of Slavery: The Export of Indian Labour Overseas, 1830–1920* (London, 1974), pp. 18–19, 177; Coldham, *Emigrants in Chains*, 99–115.

[5] Derived by doubling the net figure of departures estimated at 1,000 to 1,500 in Gemery, "Emigration from the British Isles to the New World," and Galenson, *White Servitude in Colonial America*, pp. 212–18. For the number of ships sailing to Jamaica see Gary M. Walton, "Trade Routes, Ownership Proportions and American Colonial Shipping Characteristcs," in *Las rutas del Atlantico: trabajos del Noveno Coloquio Internacional de História Maritima* (Seville, 1969), pp. 471–502, cited in Walter E. Minchinton, *Naval Office Shipping Lists For Jamaica, 1683–1818* (Wakefield, 1977), p. 9.

slave ships leaving Africa in English ships shown in Table 5-1.[6] Convicts and soldiers might experience on occasion shipboard mortality on the Europe-Americas route as high as slaves going from Africa to the Americas.[7] But English and Irish prisoners alike travelled in convict ships that rarely carried in excess of 150 and on average fewer than 100.

The best documented case of the shipment of prisoners in the seventeenth century arose from Monmouth's rebellion in southwest England. Early in 1686 in the aftermath of the rebellion and at about the time that three hundred of their fellow rebels were executed – many hanged, drawn, and quartered – three ships left Weymouth and one left Bristol carrying 376 rebels to plantations in Barbados and Jamaica. These ships carried from 81 to 103 prisoners each, with a mean of 94. Tonnage averaged 130, so that the prisoner/ton ratio was only 0.72, less than one-third of the 2.3 Africans per ton on 281 English slavers between 1676 and 1700 and far below the ratios for any individual group of slavers shown in Table 5-1. A total of 33 prisoners died on the voyage. Servants and convicts endured experiences they had never before encountered, but transportation history provides no parallel to the transatlantic slave ship.[8]

For a century and a half after 1660 the English dominated all forms of ocean transportation of people. They carried more slaves across the Atlantic than any other nation and shipped more convicts, indentured servants, and probably more fare-paying passengers as well. The nature and extent of the English advantage in the shipping of people may be examined in the slave trade, at least, from the end of the seventeenth century, with newly consolidated data available from the *Trans-Atlantic Slave Trade Database*. It is now possible to compare national groups of European slave traders both with each other and over time. The central indicator of efficiency is what economists call total factor productivity, which computes ratios of physical inputs into a business, such as tonnages and crews of slave ships (adjusted for voyage length) to physical outputs – in this case, number of slaves delivered

---

[6] Thirteen of these vessels reported more than 49 servants each on board. The ratio for this group was 0.86 persons per ton, still less than one-third the mean for slave ships. Calculated from CO 33/13 and CO142/13.

[7] See Raymond L. Cohn, "Maritime Mortality in the Eighteenth and Nine-teenth Centuries: A Survey," *International Journal of Maritime History*, 1 (June 1989):159–91 and the literature cited there.

[8] Calculated from Hotten (ed.), *The Original Lists of Persons*, 317–42, and CO 33/14. The data do not support Beckles' approving quote of a nineteenth-century writer that "one fifth of those who were shipped were flung to the sharks." He is much closer to historic reality when he writes that "[i]n comparison with the slave trade, the numbers were considerably smaller and the conditions less barbaric" in the servant trade (Beckles, *White Servitude and Black Slavery*, 65, 67). For other assessments of mortality on convict ships see Ekirch, *Bound to America*, 98–100; John Mcdonald and Ralph Shlomowitz, "Mortality on Convict Voyages to Australia, 1788–1868," *Social Science History*, 13(1989):285–313.

Table 5-1. *Mean Tonnages, Crew, Slaves per Ton, Tons per Crew Member, and Slaves per Crew Member of Transatlantic Slave Ships by Place of Origin and Quarter Century, 1662–1713*

	Tonnage			Number of crew (at outset)			Slaves/Ton			Tons/Crew			Slaves/Crew		
	mean	S.D.	n	mean	S.D.	n	mean	S.D.	n	mean	S.D.	n	mean	S.D.	n
1662–1688															
London	121.9	71.1	166	31.6	15.9	25	2.3	0.9	149	5.4	2.2	19	8.9	2.8	19
Bristol	51.7	17.6	3												
Brit Amer	60.0	19.3	8				3.2	1.0	8						
1689–1713															
London	142.2	81.3	276	34.7	15.4	144	2.1	1.0	224	4.4	1.6	124	8.5	3.2	115
Bristol	100.3	50.7	68	36.2	6.6	15	2.8	1.1	61	3.8	1.1	15	9.8	2.3	12
Brit Amer	68.3	43.7	129	18.6	10.1	26	2.5	1.0	105	4.2	2.8	24	7.5	2.2	23
France	212.2	87.2	27	82.4	49.0	22	1.3	0.3	21	2.9	1.0	22	3.6	1.3	18

Notes: 1. Tonnage is British registered or official tonnage.
2. Crew is number on board at place of origin.
Source: TSTD.

in the Americas.[9] It is possible to calculate total factor productivity for 1,860 slave voyages after 1676. In addition there are partial data for another 2,000 slaving voyages beginning in 1662, which while not adequate for the calculation of total factor productivity, still provide clues on efficiency trends.

We should begin by noting that English (or indeed Portuguese or Dutch) leadership in efficiency should not have persisted for long in highly competitive market conditions. Innovation in the slave-trading business should have spread quickly, with those failing to adapt choosing to leave – particularly as the cost of the ship was relatively low, and any vessel had so many alternative uses. Likewise, if one African region could provide more slaves faster than another, there should have been movement of traders into the more productive area such as would eliminate differentials in the long run.

International competition for slaves was intense especially among merchants in the same port of departure and on the African coast. As Dalby Thomas succinctly replied from the coast when his London chiefs complained about the low prices he was getting for trade goods, "Unless you sell as other's doe there is no trade."[10] Yet, like most economic activity in the early modern period, the business was subjected to major mercantilist restrictions that fraud and smuggling could never wholly circumvent. Long-term differences in efficiency could survive behind such restrictions. European governments excluded or made it more expensive for the ships of one nation to trade in colonial ports belonging to another. In the French case, transatlantic slave trading became large scale only after the introduction of an elaborate subsidy called the acquits de Guinée based on cargo size before 1784 and tonnage thereafter.[11] Even within the sovereignty limits of individual nations there were market imperfections that produced intramarginal rents for some shipowners. The Royal African Company, which dominated the early London trade, had a monopoly on slave trading from England and the English Americas until 1698 and an effective preference for a further fourteen years thereafter. In France, the internal customs union, the Five Great Farms, inhibited the tendency toward equalisation of costs among French ports prior to the revolution.[12] In both countries, ports located on or east of the English Channel and its prevailing westerlies might be at some competitive disadvantage to those further west.

---

[9] For a fuller description see David Eltis and David Richardson, "Productivity in the Slave Trade," *Explorations in Economic History*, 32(1995):465–84.

[10] Sir Thomas Dalby, Cape Coast Castle to RAC, Sept. 30, 1708, T70/5, f. 36.

[11] Robert Louis Stein, *The French Slave Trade in the Eighteenth Century: An Old Regime Business* (Madison, Wis., 1979), pp. 40–1.

[12] Pierre Boulle, "Marchandises de traite et développement industriel dans la France et L'Angleterre du XVIIIe siècle," *Revue française d'histoire d'outre-mer*, 42 (1975):316.

Even on the African coast, the French reserved Senegambia for the Compagnie du Sénégal during most of the eighteenth century and required other French traders to obtain their slaves south of this region. At the very least we should expect to find more efficiency differences among ports of origin or colonies than among most regions in Africa where ships from all nations tended to mingle. As for changes over time, a prima facie case could be made for secular improvements in the technical efficiency of transoceanic transportation, with setbacks being confined to periods of war. On this latter issue in particular, recent work has suggested a systematic relationship between intra-European hostilities and major cost increases in long-distance transportation.[13]

An initial analysis of the data supports only some of these expectations. English traders, in effect the Royal African Company before 1700, and a mixture of Royal African and Bristol traders thereafter, were nearly one-third more efficient than their counterparts from Nantes, who, in turn, were 15 percent more efficient than traders from other French ports. Differences between African regions were fewer than those among European ports of departure and none were statistically significant. Even more surprising, there is little indication of long-term improvement in productivity: the time-trend coefficient was not significant and its sign was actually negative. For the fifty years from 1676 to 1725, however, efficiency in delivering slaves to the Americas increased about 25 percent.[14]

Data for these individual ports do not overlap as much as we would like. Analysis of a subsample of these data for the period when the overlap between ports was greatest, 1706–29, confirms the earlier findings. The historically maligned Royal African Company, based in London, was between 15 and 20 percent more efficient than the Nantais and between 30 and 40 percent more efficient than all French slave ships combined,[15] while the Bristol group delivered on average 50 percent more slaves with the same quantity of inputs than did the slavers from all other ports in the sample. It might be noted that these were the last years in which the Royal African Company had any presence in the slave traffic. On the English side the comparison here is between a company moving out of the slave business in the face of successful competition from private traders, many of whom were based in Bristol. On the French side, the Nantais at this period were expanding their

---

[13] C. Knick Harley, "Ocean Freight Rates and Productivity, 1740–1913: The Primacy of Mechanical Invention Reaffirmed," *Journal of Economic History*, 48 (1988):851–76; Douglass North, "Sources of Productivity Change in Ocean Shipping, 1600–1850," *Journal of Political Economy*, 76(1968):953–70. On the slave trade in particular see Galenson, *Traders, Planters, and Slaves*, 97–114.

[14] For details see Eltis and Richardson, "Productivity in the Slave Trade."

[15] The breakdown of the sample is Nantes, 160 voyages; other French, 62; RAC, 49; and Bristol, 93 (*TSTD*).

share of the French traffic, but no other port could match the efficiency of the Bristol group.[16]

A further crude comparison of the English slave trade from the late 1680s with that of the French trade from the early eighteenth century suggests that the English, even those trading on behalf of the monopoly Royal African Company, were significantly more efficient than their French counterparts. Moreover the index of English total factor productivity in the slave trade for the 1690s is above that for the French some ten years later, which is when the first French data become available. Data for the Portuguese and Dutch are lacking; not only did the English overtake the Dutch as slave traders no later than shortly after 1660, they also overtook the Portuguese as well. Our main concern here is with productivity rather than with volume. The English slave trade overlapped with the Portuguese less than it did with the Dutch,[17] but one hint of efficiency changes is that prices of African slaves declined or held steady in the Caribbean from the 1650s to the 1680s, while the number of slaves delivered to the Americas increased by at least 50 percent.[18] Part of this may have reflected improving efficiency on the part African suppliers but, as noted earlier, shipping costs formed a much larger share of the final selling price than did African costs. Moreover, slave prices in Africa show no time trend for most of this period. In any event these were the years that the English share of the transatlantic slaving business increased most rapidly. While the overall volume of slaves entering the trade increased by half in the half-century after 1650, the numbers arriving in English slave ships increased between four and five times.[19]

On the African coast business letters written over two centuries give an overwhelming sense of intense price competition among Europeans. There is no significant difference in productivity among regions of African embarkation, a finding that confirms the written evidence from the coast. In the Americas, however, at least before the nineteenth century, each colonial power was able to enforce some mercantilistic restrictions that preserved the

---

[16] Stein, *The French Slave Trade*, 55–8.

[17] Both supplied Spanish America, and there was one unsuccessful effort by the Royal African Company to establish a direct trade with Bahia during the expanding phase of the Brazilian slave trade after 1700 (see the summaries of correspondence for the years 1706 and 1707 in PRO, T70/5 ff. 25–7, 30, 38).

[18] Appendix B suggests little change between 1663–4 and the 1680s in either African or American prices, which, given the large increase in the volume of the trade is enough to suggest improving productivity. Both Manning *(Slavery and African Life*, 178) and Galenson *(Traders, Planters and Slaves*, 67) argue for much higher prices at midcentury. But the evidence for this in both cases appears to be Richard Ligon *(True and Exact History)*. More recent evidence suggesting lower prices is discussed in Chapter 8.

[19] See Eltis, Behrendt, and Richardson, "The Volume of the Transatlantic Slave Trade," for estimates of the size and distribution of the slave trade in the second half of the seventeenth century.

colonial market for its traders. Thus, for example, English ships could not trade freely in the French Americas without first registering as French property – a procedure that was itself hazardous and costly – nor in Brazil and the Spanish Americas. In addition, there was the French subsidy. Such restrictions created barriers around the French and Spanish markets behind which productivity differentials could develop. Consistent with these findings and despite the competitive nature of the transatlantic slaving business in the eighteenth century, slaves were generally cheaper in the British Caribbean than elsewhere. The ability of the French colonial sector to outperform its British counterpart for most of the eighteenth century did not derive from any advantage in labor costs, although a precise evaluation of the impact of the subsidy is not possible at present.[20]

The nature of the English advantage is suggested by disaggregation of the total factor productivity measurement. Breakdowns of slaves per ton, slaves per crew, and voyage time by port of origin are possible for 13,952 voyages drawn from various published and unpublished sources.[21] Because the definition of each of these variables is narrower than for total factor productivity, the data requirements are smaller and the sample sizes are accordingly larger. There are no differences between Bristol and Royal African ships in slaves per ton carried or in slaves per crew member. However, Bristol and RAC ships together carried 50 percent more slaves per ton and twice as many slaves per crew member as did their French counterparts. Yet the English advantage did not carry over into voyage duration. Here, both Bristol and Nantes were faster than their London-based and non-Nantes French counterparts, a result no doubt explained by the location of these ports of origin. Any ship that had to begin its voyage in a port in the English channel with prevailing winds from the west must have expected longer voyages than ships from Nantes and Bristol, and this was undoubtedly a factor in the rise to prominence of both ports in the early eighteenth century.[22]

But for our purposes the key period is before 1710, when the English trade was expanding rapidly, rather than after. Unfortunately only the English records yield sufficient data to permit the calculation of total factor productivity before 1706. Prior to this year, inferences of relative efficiency hinge on trends in the changing shares of the total slave trade carried by each national group, as well as price patterns. However, the data that are available still permit comparisons among English, French, and Dutch traders that are

---

[20] For a review of the literature on this point and a fresh compilation of data see David Eltis, "The Slave Economies of the Caribbean: Structure, Performance, Evolution and Significance," in Franklin W. Knight (ed.), *The UNESCO General History of the Caribbean* 6 vols. (Kingston, 1997–), 3:105–37.

[21] TSTD.

[22] A more refined analysis focussing only on the outbound leg of the voyage is not possible because the Bristol data do not contain the relevant information.

Table 5-2. *Mean Voyage Length in Days of Slave Ships from Port of Origin to the Caribbean via Western Africa, Leg of Voyage by Quarter-Century, 1662–1713*

Leg of Voyage	1662–1688			1689–1713		
	mean	s.d.	number	mean	s.d.	number
1. To Africa:						
London	119	89	24	126	48	91
Brit Amer	60	10	2	92	28	24
France				78	41	22
2. Off Africa:						
London	73	103	23	102	50	36
Brit Amer				95	42	20
France				70	35	22
3. Africa to America:						
London	77	38	89	71	21	107
Brit Amer	54	24	8	65	22	28
The Netherlands	82	22	4	91	35	16
France				66	24	24
4. All voyage legs combined:						
London	309	88	205	297	79	285
Brit Amer	228	141	12	260	110	32
The Netherlands	266	35	4	315	97	23
France				220	58	22

Source: TSTD.

helpful in accounting for the rise to dominance of the English. Tables 5-1 and 5-2 summarize the tonnage, crew size, and voyage length data (and the ratios that these make possible) for the pre-1714 period. The data are broken down into two quarter-century periods roughly coterminous with eras of peace and war, respectively. Within these periods, the data are grouped according to the port or region of origin of the slaving voyage. London slave ships – overwhelmingly those of the Royal African Company in the first of these two quarter-centuries – predominate. But Bristol ships, ships from the British Caribbean, Dutch West India Company ships from the Netherlands and some French voyages, chiefly from Nantes, are also represented.

As in the later period, these data suggest that in the seventeenth century the English had no advantage in speed of voyage. Table 5-2 shows French slave ships reaching the Caribbean over two months (or 25 percent) faster than ships from either London or the Netherlands (differences significant at the 1 percent level). An examination of the breakdown of this voyage into the three stages of port of origin to Africa, time spent off Africa, and the middle passage itself, indicates that most of the faster time was accounted for by the first stage and is explained by the location of Nantes, the port from which most of the French sample sailed, west of the English Channel. Dutch West India ships from Amsterdam and Royal African Company ships from London both had to negotiate prevailing westerlies at the outset of their voyages. In the English case, weeks in the first stage could be spent off the Downs near Deal or in other sheltered anchorages.[23] Nevertheless, French ships also spent less time off Africa in these early days, a pattern determined perhaps by initial French reliance on the high-volume port of Whydah. But if voyage length had been the key determinant of efficiency, most of the European slave trade would have set out from the Americas, specifically the Caribbean, rather than from London.[24]

The major differences in the characteristics of voyages based in different ports, however, were not in voyage length but in size of ship and crew. Before 1714, French ships were three times the size of their counterparts from the English Americas and half as big again as slavers from London. Slave ships were among the smaller of the vessels plying the Atlantic, but English slavers were particularly small by the ocean-going standards of the late seventeenth and early eighteenth centuries.[25] The French ships were not only among the larger slavers in the business, they were crowded even before they took on board slaves, with tons-per-crew ratios one-third smaller than London ships. As a consequence French tons-per-slave and slave-per-crew ratios were only half or less of their English counterparts. Within the English group, Bristol ships were among the smallest of all slavers, and their small crews account for the highest slaves-per-crew ratio of any port in the data set at this time.

Part of the larger French ships and crew may be explained by an early French dependence on piracy. The French created a permanent slave-trading network on the African coast during the mostly war period of 1689 to 1713. This was well after the Dutch and English had established themselves there. But when established on the coast, the French obtained many of their slaves from raids on Dutch and English ships and property. The English factor at Whydah commented that English ships got quicker dispatch than any others from this major port and that the French were only "able to carry on ye [slave] trade to a great degree by their taking so many prizes of other nations

---

[23] See Tattersfield, *Forgotten Trade*, 203–4, for a description of these. Indeed, some of the English outport traffic was in reality London-based ships replenishing supplies and cargo on their way to Africa.

[24] It should be noted, however, that part of the advantage of voyages originating in the Americas is explained by the disproportionate share of Caribbean-based ships that sailed to the Gambia – voyages to which were usually faster than to any other African location.

[25] Davis, *The English Shipping Industry*, 298.

.... The Blacks think ye French are the Masters of ye World by their taking so many prizes."[26] French slavers were probably more heavily armed than their English counterparts, though the evidence on this is impressionistic.[27] It is clear, however, that English slavers carried the same armament during war as in peacetime and perhaps as a consequence lost one out of every eleven slaving voyages to enemy action between 1702 and 1713. Their French rivals, by contrast, lost only one slave ship in fifty over the same period. But if piracy is the explanation for the larger French slave ship and crew, it was not, apparently, the basis of an efficient slave trade. Moreover, it should be noted that the French size differential in both crew and ship persisted for most of the eighteenth century and cannot be tied to the particular circumstances of the French breaking into the trade at the beginning of the eighteenth century.[28]

No tonnage or crew data have survived for the Dutch at this stage, but an outline of a pattern is nevertheless possible. Both the Royal African and Dutch West India Companies used a wide range of ships in the slave trade, most of which were hired rather than owned. Such ships entered the slave trade temporarily before returning to general cargo business.[29] However, there seems little doubt that Dutch company ships were larger than their English counterparts. Johannes Postma's data from the later free-trade era of Dutch slaving indicate a mean displacement of 144 tons for 486 ships sailing between 1731 and 1780 – larger than the pre-1714 London ships shown in Table 5-1. Little data have survived on the displacement of WIC slave vessels, but Royal African Company officials often used the adjective great when describing the arrival and departure of WIC ships.[30]

[26] Richard Willis, to RAC, August 13, 1705, T70/14, f. 110. For similar senti-
      ments from the Dutch side see W. de la Palma, Elmina, to Chamber Amsterdam,
      August 31, 1704; and idem to Assembly of X, March 31, 1705, in Albert Van
      Dantzig (editor and translator), *The Dutch and the Guinea Coast, 1674–1742:
      A Collection of Documents from the General State Archive at the Hague* (Accra,
      1978), pp. 102–3, 110. This was the case despite agreements between French,
      English, Dutch, and the king of Whydah to maintain a ceasefire in Whydah and
      its roadstead.
[27] English slavers averaged one gun for every ten tons before 1714, a ratio that
      was the same in war as in peacetime (n = 268 for the period 1662–1713). French
      ships are nearly always described as heavily armed in this period, though it is
      not possible to calculate a tons-per-gun ratio. The capture ratio was reversed in
      naval conflicts later in the century.
[28] Ratios calculated from *TSTD*.
[29] Postma, *Dutch in the Atlantic Slave Trade*, 142–5; Davies, *Royal African Com-
      pany*, 194–205.
[30] See for example Greenhill, Master, and Stapleton, Cape Coast Castle, to RAC,
      April 19, 1683, T70/16, f. 59; Greenhill, Master, and Adams, Cape Coast Castle,
      to RAC, November 27, 1683, *ibid.*, f. 76. The only tonnage of a Dutch ship I
      have been able to find in the English record at this time is the 250-ton *Maertin
      Van Roffen* (voyage id 21,196) that sold slaves off Jamaica in 1662 (Captain
      Whiting, HMS Diamond, Jamaica, March 10, 1662, CO 1/16, p. 30). Postma,
      Dutch in the Atlantic Slave Trade, 145.

More is known about the number of slaves carried than the tonnage of ships. Before 1714, Royal African Company ships sailing from London carried an average of 330 slaves from Africa. Dutch WIC ships over the same period averaged 488 slaves each.[31] In addition Dutch ships lost a smaller proportion of their slaves during the middle passage than did their RAC counterparts, a pattern determined largely by the fact that Dutch ships almost never sought slaves in the Bight of Biafra – vessels from which usually suffered higher mortality.[32] Taking this together with the information given earlier on size of ship, it is thus probable that, not only were WIC ships larger, their slaves-per-ton ratio was below that of any groupings of the English ships shown in Table 5-1. We have no indication of crew size on Dutch ships, but it is at least clear that English slave ships, even those from the Royal African Company, were on average substantially smaller than those of the French and Dutch and much more lightly manned than French ships.

Finally we should note that these English slave-ship characteristics were particularly pronounced in the substantial branch of the English slave-trade sector based in the Americas. Only the Portuguese and English had an American based branch of the industry, but slavers from the British Americas were particularly small, lightly armed, and dependent on their speed for a successful voyage. The first slaver from the English Americas to enter the record sailed from Boston in 1644, and while there were several others from New England in the next decade and a half, the English American stake in the industry really began to grow after 1680 when a Barbados merchant discovered that Caribbean rum sold much better than English brandy on the African coast.[33] From this point until the Treaty of Utrecht, about one in seven English slave voyages began in the Americas rather than in England

---

[31] RAC ships had a mean of 330.4 and a standard deviation of 164.2 (n = 354). WIC ships averaged 487.6 and a s.d. of 142.7 (n = 212). Differences significant at the 1 percent level (*TSTD*).

[32] Mortality between 1672 and 1688 was 13.6 percent of those embarked on WIC ships (s.d. = 4.7, n = 49), and 23.4 percent on RAC ships (s.d. = 19.7, n = 125). Between 1689 and 1713 the equivalent figures were 14.3 percent for the WIC (s.d. = 7.9, n = 82) and 17.2 percent for the RAC (s.d. = 15.2, n = 104) (*ibid*). In only the first of these periods is the difference statistically significant (at the 5 percent level).

[33] For New England ships in the 1640s and 1650s see James Kendall Hosmer, *Winthrop's Journal 'History of New England, 1630–1649,'* 2 vols. (New York, 1908), 2:227–8; Robert Moody (ed.), *Saltonstall Papers, 1607–1815,* 2 vols. (Boston, 1972–4), 1:138–9; Nathaniell B. Shurtleff (ed.), *Records of the Governor and Company of the Massachusetts Bay in New England,* 5 vols. (Boston, 1853–4) reprinted New York, 1968, 2: 84, 129, 136, 168; John Russell Bartlett (ed.), *Records of the Colony Rhode Island and Providence,* 10 vols. (Newport, 1856–65) 1: 243; 2: 535; 3: 483; 4: 193. For the beginning of the direct trade to Africa from the Caribbean, based on rum see E. Stede and S. Gascoigne to RAC, March 26, 1683, T 70/16, f. 49.

and invariably carried rum rather than the miscellaneous manufactures from England reported on earlier American voyages. Despite the later importance of Rhode Island vessels, English American–based voyages in this period left overwhelmingly from the Caribbean rather than New England. While the data do not allow total factor productivity comparisons, it is worth noting that these ships carried half the crew and armament and were only half the tonnage of the average English slave ship.[34]

It seems unlikely that the smaller English ship was rooted in some English technology unavailable to mainland European competitors. There was no specialised slave ship at this time either in terms of hull or rigging. French and Dutch investors could choose from the same range of ship types as the more successful English competition. A French and Dutch preference for larger ships probably reflected the more specialised nature of their slave trades. Both the Dutch and the French traded between major centers on the Slave Coast, such as Whydah, or Angola and single markets in the Caribbean such as the entrepot of Curaçao in the Dutch case and St. Domingue in the French case (by the end of the first decade of the eighteenth century). These were routes that supported larger ships. The English on the other hand traded on all parts of the African coast that sold slaves and traded all over the Caribbean. Many of these markets on both sides of the Atlantic would not support a large ship trade. Apart from Jamaica, the English markets in the Caribbean and on the mainland were small and dispersed. The English became large-scale slave traders because of their ability to link together large parts of Africa and the Americas.

The English may also have had a larger and more experienced pool of manpower on which to draw for slaver crews and captains. The sheer size of London and the number of voyages it supported ensured economies of scale in the hiring process relative to other ports. Yet the London market for slave-ship crews was integrated with that of Bristol and the Americas. Caribbean slave ships drew on the crews discharged by English-based ships when they had sold their slaves on the islands, and Bristol had strong long-standing trade connections with both Africa and the Caribbean long before its slave trade became significant. Thus the greater English tons per crew and slaves per crew member observed in Table 5-1 were common to all English ports and were not confined to London.

None of these characteristics of English slave trading or indeed the rapid emergence of the industry in the European context seem readily attributable

---

[34] All English ships together averaged 130.7 tons (n = 669); carried 23.4 crew members at the conclusion of the slaving voyage (n = 80) and carried 12.3 guns (n = 449). The equivalent figures for ships from the English Americas were 69.7 tons (n = 138); 12.5 crew (n = 20) and 6.7 guns (n = 114) (*TSTD*). The latter figures have some upward bias imparted by double voyages. In other words the sample contains some ships from England that returned direct to Africa for more slaves after disembarking a first shipment.

to state intervention, but no assessment of the seventeenth-century trade can avoid the issue. An older literature attributed the emergence of the English slave trading sector and indeed the larger English Atlantic system to the Navigation Acts, which for two centuries reserved trade with the English colonies for English ships. Modern discussion has centered on the era immediately preceding the American Revolution, when the burden of the acts is now thought to have been rather small – certainly less than 3 percent of colonial American income.[35] For the years that saw the implementation of the restrictive system, modern scholars have focussed on the motives of the English government rather than its effectiveness. Could the rise of the English shipping industry and English slave traders in particular be explained by the Navigation Acts?

There appears to be a clear chronology, if not a direct cause and effect, in the legislative measures of 1651 and 1660, and the subsequent growth of the English slave trade and Atlantic Empire. Acts of 1650 and 1651 restricted the colonial trade, including the slave trade, unless from the colonies to Spanish America, to English ships. Further measures of 1661 and 1673 elaborated the restrictions and added enforcement provisions. An earlier generation of scholars was in no doubt about the strongly beneficial impact of this legislation for English merchants and shippers.[36] None of this group, however, dwelt on the higher costs for the planters and slower growth of the colonies that must have inevitably resulted if the impact of these acts had been major. The reason for this omission is probably that any deleterious impact on colonial growth was likely to have been minor.[37]

[35] Peter D. McClelland, "The Cost to America of British Imperial Policy," *American Economic Review*, 59(1969):370–81; Gary M. Walton, "The New Economic History and the Burdens of the Navigation Acts," *Economic History Review*, 24(1971):533–42.

[36] Lawrence A. Harper, *The English Navigation Laws: A Seventeenth Century Experiment in Social Engineering* (New York, 1939), pp. 50–62, 231–378, 394–404; George Louis Beer, *The Old Colonial System, 1660–1754*, 2 vols. (New York, 1912), 1:58–85.

[37] Jack M. Sosin, *English America and the Restoration Monarchy of Charles II: Transatlantic Politics, Commerce and Kinship* (Lincoln, Neb., 1980) pp. 68–73. In formal terms the Navigation Acts should have induced restrictions on the supply of slaves, servants, manufactured goods, and imported provisions for the English colonies, as foreign suppliers were excluded (a leftward shift in the supply curve for each of these items). Prices of inputs should have increased; quantity should have fallen. If the Dutch had been supplying, say, one-third of the slaves, servants, and manufactured products before the act, and elasticity of demand and supply was unitary, then prices of slaves should have increased (and quantity decreased) by a like proportion. In fact, prices fell and quantity increased substantially. The historical reality is consistent with a rightward shift in supply (possibly, as argued here, because of increased productivity in the shipping business). Productivity in the slave trade may have improved for both the Dutch and English at the same time and overwhelmed the impact of the acts. But if this did happen, it seems that English productivity went up the faster of the two as

Even though shipping costs formed such a major portion of the prices of slaves, servants, colonial produce in Europe, and European produce in the Americas in the seventeenth century, there are few indications of rising prices for any of these from the mid-century on. Moreover, the years after 1650 saw the rapid expansion of both sugar and tobacco sectors in the English Americas – not something that one would expect if the new Navigation Acts had driven up the price of slaves, servants, and supplies and driven down the net proceeds from colonial produce. Consistent with this, the protests of planters at measures that excluded non-English competitors are muted. English planters pressed for the removal of the RAC monopoly on supplying slaves to the British colonies until that monopoly was finally removed, but there is little sign that what they had in mind was admittance of Dutch traders rather than the legitimisation of English interlopers. The issue of giving the Dutch access to the colonies is rarely mentioned in the numerous position papers on the colonies in the Egerton manuscripts and CO1 series, either favourably or critically.[38]

More direct evidence of the English colonials' relative lack of drive to gain wide-open access to Dutch shipping was the failure of a significant trade in smuggled slaves to develop in the aftermath of the Navigation Acts. A small number of slaves entered the English Leewards from Dutch St. Eustatius, particularly in the later 1680s.[39] Jamaican planters bought direct from a Dutch transatlantic trader in the early 1660s and they also sent to Curaçao for slaves in the early 1690s when wartime severely impeded the transatlantic traffic.[40] But the scale of smuggling was far short of that into the Spanish Americas. Smuggling hinges on the existence of price differentials, and there is little evidence of these between the Dutch and English West

the English gained market share at the expense of the Dutch in markets outside the English colonies. We know that the English slave sector as a whole expanded rapidly when, other things being equal, the Navigation Acts should have caused the shipping sector to expand but the plantation sector to contract as the costs of labor and of delivering the end product increased.

[38] Add ms, 2395, f. 285, "Considerations about the peopling and settling the island of Jamaica," n.d., c. 1660 expresses concern that Jamaica is developing too slowly and is exposed to recapture. One recommended measure is free trade for a limited time so that the Dutch and others can foster trade as in the early days of Barbados and the Leewards. "Whereas no English Merchant yet ever brought to Jamaica eyther slaves, Serv'ts Coppers or such things as tended directly to the settling of the Island, But onely wyne and such things for which they have carried away all the mony that was ever brought to thee Island."

[39] Clement Tudway, Antigua to RAC, January 1, 1687, T70/12, p. 164; Henry Carpenter and Thomas Belchamber, Nevis, to RAC, July 9, 1686 and March 2, 1688, *ibid.*, pp. 128, 131; Thomas Trant to RAC, St. Kitts, March 3, 1714, T70/8, f. 76.

[40] Captain Whiting, *HMS Diamond*, March 10, 1662, CO 1/16 p. 30; *CSPCS*, vol. 5: 36; Charles Penhallow and Walter Ruding to RAC, July 1, 1690, T70/12, p. 84; Walter Ruding to RAC, June 3, 1691, *ibid.*, p. 86. Six hundred were brought from Curaçao in the early 1690s.

Indies. Indeed, contemporary assessments of such differentials indicate that slaves were normally cheaper in Jamaica than in Curaçao.[41] Moreover, the Dutch West Indies remained tiny compared to its English counterpart – an unlikely situation if slaves and transatlantic transportation generally had been so much cheaper there.

Finally, it should be noted that the English were not the only nation to exclude foreigners from their colonial trade at this time. Colbert's *système exclusif*, instituted in 1664, was similarly motivated and structured. The French slave trade is much less well documented than is the English for the period before 1710, but this is partly because there was much less of it to document.[42] While hard data are scarce, it is likely that more slaving expeditions set out from French ports in the two decades after 1664 than in the same period before.[43] But the French slave trade nevertheless lagged far behind that of the English in overall size and rates of growth despite being given similar encouragement. Much of the growth of the French trade that did occur stemmed from expanding demand for plantation produce in Europe and perhaps more generalized improvements in shipping efficiency. All American plantation sectors expanded production in the second half of the seventeenth century, not just those such as England and France that strengthened protective measures for their colonial systems in mid-century. Protective measures would normally cause total production of all the plantation Americas together to decline. If the protective measures were adopted by only one country then there would be a redistribution of output in favor of the protected sector as well as a decline in production of all plantation sectors together. The French, and especially the English, colonies increased their share of the European market at the expense of the Portuguese, despite the fact that France and England instituted restrictions that increased production costs for their respective planters, whereas in Brazil such restrictions were already in place. Higher duties on foreign-produced sugar in France and England certainly discriminated against Brazilian sugar, but the overall European sugar market was increasing strongly in this period. Protection was not as important a factor in the expansion of the English slave trading system as the older literature would have us believe.

If the Navigation Acts and *système exclusif* do not appear to have had major influence over the growth of the English and French slave sectors, African involvement – largely ignored so far – was of obvious significance. European

---

[41] Anon, "Considerations about the Spaniards buying negro's of the English Ro'll Company and receiving 2/3 at Jamaica and 1/3 at Barbados" Jamaica, Feb. 2, 1675, Add ms, 2395, f. 501; Bate and Stewart to RAC, Barbados, July 9, 1709, f. 50. In 1710, the RAC agent in Jamaica reported higher prices but made it clear it was on account of recent severe mortality among the Jamaican slave population (Lewis Galdy, Jan. 14, 1710 T70/8, f. 52).

[42] Eltis, Behrendt, and Richardson, "The Volume of the Transatlantic Slave Trade."

[43] Munford, *The Black Ordeal of Slavery*, 1:155–84.

and African slave traders met as buyers and sellers on the African coast, with, except for temporary circumstances, neither one having much in the way of market power over the other on the coast as a whole. Europeans would build forts only with permission of the African ruler and even then only if they had some assurance of preferential treatment from the African authorities in gaining access to gold or slaves. But promises of such treatment rarely meant much in practice. "Wee take very kindly your Inviting us to send our ships to trade in your Country," the company wrote to the king of Bonny in the Niger Delta,

and the Encouragement you give us to settle with you ... to build a fort, maintain provision grounds and protect our property from robbery, but such a project will be very expensive, and not worth it if you allow other Nations to trade without such an establishment. We need preferential treatment .... no ship that arrives after ours in your river should be allowed to ship a slave while our ship still lacks her complement.[44]

The fort was not built and all African rulers in the Niger Delta states sold to all-comers as long as the trade endured. On the Gold Coast, such forts were established but Europeans were powerless to prevent trade between Africans and other Europeans in the immediate vicinity despite pressure from the Court of Assistants.[45] From much of the African coast – for example, Sherboro, the long littoral between Sierra Leone and Cape Three Points and between Whydah and Calabar – Europeans obtained very few slaves. There were other parts where they could not get the preferred mix of men, women, and children. Even in those areas from which they obtained slaves, the latter were forthcoming only after weeks of negotiation, usually with many different potential suppliers.

The issue of African participation is taken up more fully in Chapters 6, 7, and 9, but we should note here that during the last quarter of the seventeenth century the Slave Coast and the Bight of Biafra had the lowest slave prices on the coast, the northern Angola coast the highest, with the Gold Coast between these extremes. The European demand for slaves was probably fairly elastic. For much of this period the Gold Coast was the preferred region of supply, but if the castles could not accumulate enough slaves – as was usually the case – or if mainly women were offered, Europeans would move on quickly to Offra or Whydah on the Slave Coast for the bulk of their complement.[46] Likewise, the Royal African Company was prepared

44 RAC to "Great King of Bandie," Sept. 15, 1702, T70/51, f. 150.
45 For example, RAC to Joshua Platt, John Gregory, and Willam Ronan, February 14, 1693, T70/50, 142.
46 "If negroes are to be gott upon the Gold Coast on reasonable tearmes. Wee order that you put aboard him ["Sarah Bonadventure"] five hundred and fifty Negroes wch if you doe effect ... take ashore ye Ardra cargoe here shipt. But if Negroes cannot be procured for his supply send away ye Shipp for Ardra with

to pay 25 percent more per slave on the northern Angola Coast but when this differential widened in the 1690s the company stopped trading in the region.[47] Thus while the Slave Coast and the Bight of Biafra supplied slaves steadily down to the last years of the century, the participation of the Gold Coast and to a lesser extent northern Angola was more intermittent. To put this another way, RAC traders in the last quarter of the seventeenth century would have preferred to fill up with slaves from their Gold Coast forts or, alternatively, sail straight to northern Angola and buy slaves for the same price there as on the Slave Coast. Best of all, no doubt, they would have liked to sail to Senegambia – the region closest to Europe and the Americas – and buy all the slaves they needed for say one pound per head prime cost, or better still, for nothing at all. Had they been able to do so, the plantation sector of the Americas, and indeed many nonplantation sectors as well, would have developed much faster than they actually did. African realities, however, did not allow access to any of these options.

Next to the price of the slave, Africa manifested itself in the shipping business chiefly by way of the time taken to obtain a full complement of slaves. Relations among African states through which trade routes passed as well as conditions in the region where enslavement actually occurred exercised major influence over the duration of trade on the coast. Wars among African states were not an unmixed blessing from the European standpoint. Military activity might well increase the flow of slaves but only in the event of a decisive victory. Before this occurred there might be long periods when trade was seriously disrupted, and indeed much European effort on the Gold Coast was devoted to keeping trade routes open. This could involve military action but was more likely to mean prolonged diplomatic efforts to restore peace.[48]

---

ye said Cargoe for ye purchase of ye said number there according to the Charter Party" (RAC to Henry Nurse and Council, Dec. 10, 1685, T70/50, f. 2). The Court of Assistants referred to Whydah as "onely our remedie for want of Gold Coast Negroes," (RAC to Humfries, Wight & Elwes, Sept. 24, 1691, T70/50, 122). Two years later it was asking its agents at Cape Coast Castle (on the Gold Coast) to "send off our Ships directly from the Castle for although quantitys of Blacks are not procurable on the Gold Coast yett there may be care taken to get quantityes from Papa and Arda ...." (RAC to Joshua Platt, John Gregory, and William Ronan, February 14, 1693, T70/50, 142).

[47] See Appendix B. The company wrote the following to the king of Cacongo in 1688: "Some time since we received a letter Signed on your behalfe to acquaint us that you being King of the Cacongo desired us to sende our Shipps into your Countrey where they should receive all sivill usage & Courtisie in their trade & that ye old Customes shall be reduced to what is more reasonable ... the truth is that from all the Govermts on the Coast of Angola we have frequent complaints by every Shipp we send thither that the Slaves cost one third part more there than then at all other places in Guynie ...." February 16, 1688, T70/50, f. 57.

[48] Factors might anticipate military action with some glee.

But the most striking demonstration of the impact of African supply constraints on the slave trade is revealed by changes in productivity over time. Efficiency as measured with a total factor productivity index was subject to major swings between the seventeenth and nineteenth centuries. In the pre-1714 period it declined in the 1670s before recovering at the end of the century. By the 1710s efficiency in the transatlantic shipping of slaves was between one-quarter and one-third greater than in the 1670s. This conclusion holds whether we take into account the English data alone or include the French observations available after 1706. Beyond our period an even greater decline in productivity occurred again on a much larger scale in the middle of the eighteenth century. The intriguing question is how this could happen in an industry where technology and productivity gains appear to have been so closely related over the long term. It is not likely that technical knowledge could have been forgotten.

The answer lies not in the shipping end of the business but rather in the supply of slaves from Africa. The average length of the slave-ship voyage from port of origin (usually Europe) to the Americas via the African coast declined slightly between the seventeenth and nineteenth centuries. But within this long-run trend there were major swings in voyage length largely explained by variations in the time spent on the African coast. Slave-loading time was 50 percent higher in the quarter-century after 1688 than in the same period before. Thereafter it declined, only to increase sharply again, until, by the third quarter of the eighteenth century ships were taking almost twice as long to obtain a complement of slaves than in the first quarter of the century. From 1775, however, despite the volume of the slave trade reaching its all-time peak, time spent on the coast fell back to pre-1750 levels. Moreover, for reasons as yet unclear, these fluctuations occurred at roughly the same time in all African regions and affected all European national groups of slave traders equally.[49] The longer slaving periods do not correlate very well

"Are in Daily expectation of ye Arcanians coming to fight ye Cabesstern people wch if they beat there will be a glorious trade both for Slaves & Gold.... that the trade in slaves increases wonderfully there & that by ye observation has made since there beleives can Ship off 5000 Slaves per ann" (Josiah Pearson, Anamaboo, July 12, 1706, T70/5, f. 18). But there are even more indications of the loss of trade resulting from such activity, for example, "the tedious lying of Ships is occasioned by some disturbances in the Country. But hopes in a little time all things will be setled" (Wyburn, Whydah, Sept. 13, 1688, T70/11, f. 103). Also "... Att present all manner of trade is soe dead yt at all ye forts here has not this two months taken foure ounces: ye reason is Ahensa hath been out against ye Arcanies & akims soe not any Traders from any parts dare adventure to come downe ...." (Ralph Hassell, Jonas Perrin, Richard Griffith, Accra, to Cape Coast Castle, February 1682, Rawlinson manuscript, c. 745, f. 83).

49 A fuller and more technical elaboration of this argument is to be found in Eltis and Richardson, "Productivity in the Slave Trade." For pre-1714 patterns see Table 5–2.

with the peaks in the volume of the traffic. The highest volume decades in the history of the slave trade saw declines in the time spent collecting slaves.

In the second half of the seventeenth century it is likely that the English derived some advantage over other European traders from the range of their operations on the coast. Much later, in the last quarter of the eighteenth century, slave trading had become three or four times more extensive than in the late seventeenth century. As the slave-trading business became much more highly organised and slave supplies in all regions much more dependable, slave-trading firms and captains came to specialize in trading with one or two regions of Africa.[50] In the seventeenth century, however, supplies of slaves from all regions, except perhaps one or two points on the Slave Coast and the eastern section of the Niger Delta, fluctuated considerably from month to month and from year to year. Of all national groups of traders, only the English traded in every part of the African coast that supplied slaves. Of individual European traders, only the Royal African Company routinely visited all slaving regions. When the Court of Assistants met in London, it could review the latest information for the whole of the coast involved in slave trading, as well as call on a pool of men experienced in various regions. Even individual Bristol traders mixed the destinations of their slave ships to a much greater extent than their Dutch counterparts. In the first decade of the eighteenth century the situation changed somewhat as many more French and Portuguese slavers appeared on the coast, but it was always unusual to find French and Dutch, and to a lesser extent, Portuguese ships, in the Bight of Biafra, for example. By contrast, except for a port or two in French Senegambia and Portuguese Angola, at either end of the range of the African coast from which slaves were available, the English were ubiquitous. There were of course many new English slave traders entering the business after 1698 when the trade was thrown open, but the decline of the RAC was probably linked to the ability of major London and Bristol slave traders to match the range of information at the company's disposal – and not just to a legislated reduction of its monopoly power.

Ultimately, the slave trade occurred because African traders could deliver people to the coast at a price that was sufficiently low to allow Europeans to ship those people across the Atlantic. Yet while shipping technology may explain a large part of why it was Europeans rather than Africans and Amerindians who had transoceanic empires, English preeminence among those Europeans probably has other roots. English settlement patterns lay behind the wide range of American slave markets open to the English slave trader. The integrated nature and openness (at least for other English) of the resulting imperial structure encouraged mobility not only of labor but also

[50] Stephen D. Behrendt, "The British Slave Trade, 1785–1807: Volume, Profitability and Mortality" (Unpublished PhD thesis, University of Wisconsin, 1993), pp. 115–24, 315–17.

of capital. The slave trade was anchored in London initially because that city had evolved financial and service structures by the mid and latter half of the seventeenth century that linked the most rapidly growing European settlements in the Americas with the rest of the world. Royal African Company vessels carried back bullion and produce from the Caribbean, but at least as early as the 1670s bills of exchange drawn on London merchants at various terms were common means of payment for slaves carried from Africa.[51] Financial intermediation and the resultant ability to wait for payment developed earlier and further in London than in other centers.

The slave trade was possibly the most international activity of the pre-industrial era. It required the assembling of goods from at least two continents (many different parts of Asia and Europe), the transporting of those goods to a third, and their exchange for forced labor that would be carried to yet another continent. The international contacts, financial services including insurance, and accumulated trading acumen of merchants in London and Amsterdam were clearly of greater importance than a few weeks delay per voyage posed by prevailing westerlies in the English Channel. Ports such as Nantes, Bristol, and Liverpool developed similar structures, but not until the eighteenth century. If London and Amsterdam shared some advantages such as large capital markets, ability to assemble goods, and international service sectors, they did not share them all. The extensive numbers of English overseas relative to the Dutch created a critical mass of a market for slaves with the result that the Dutch, except when they held the *asiento*, always faced the extra cost of selling slaves across international boundaries – an extra cost that pertained whether or not the sale was legal. Once more, at a fundamental level, the roots of free and coerced migration appear the same. The overall pattern and size of transatlantic migration and the resulting societies in the Americas were shaped by profound social forces in western Europe. However, the slave trade was still the result of a partnership between Europeans and elite Africans, and to the African side of this early modern partnership we now turn.

---

[51] See the early folios of T70/15 for several lists of such bills, for example f. 5.

6

Africa and Europe in the Early
Modern Era

I

As Chapter 2 has made clear, after an initial phase in which Europeans first plundered and then traded with the peoples of the overseas world they had contacted, European interest in the Americas and Africa quickly came to center on the production of commodities. From a global perspective this behavior was unusual. It did not characterize the many Chinese expeditions that reached out to East Africa in the early fifteenth century, nor the more enduring trans-Saharan trading diasporas of Islam, nor the Aztec domination of the peoples of what is now northern Mexico. The Inca empire in South America and Arab networks in the Indian Ocean put some stress on production, but the scale of the European commitment remains unmatched. Trade or payment of tribute by the weaker to the stronger power was universal; systematic attempts by the stronger to increase the production of goods in the society of the weaker – with or without the help of the dominated – was not.[1] In the Americas, such a preoccupation was associated with the gradual European conquest of the aboriginal peoples and the establishment of European settlements. With the single exception of the fur trade (always a tiny fraction of total transatlantic trade), trade between American aboriginals and Europeans was never more than trivial. Most transatlantic trade was between communities of Europeans. In Africa, the production of goods (and people) for trade remained in the hands of Africans. The middle ground – that shared cultural space between Europeans and aboriginals – shifted quickly inland in the Americas, as Europeans created their own communities

---

[1] Jones, *European Miracle*, 77–8, 202–6. Other widely read syntheses of European expansion by Wolf, *Europe and the People without History* and Wallerstein, *The Modern World System*, share the conviction that events in Europe are central to explaining the expansion process. They also stress the importance of the European instinct to acquire material goods.

on aboriginal land. In Africa, by contrast, it remained firmly rooted in the littoral – unless we call Portuguese influence in the kingdom of the Kongo a European incursion into the interior.[2]

European and African cultures clashed on almost every level. The differing conceptions of freedom and gender roles explored earlier were symptomatic of what was initially a pervasive and mutual miscomprehension of the other's social structure and value system. This was complicated by differences between propertied and non-propertied Europeans on attitudes toward working for others. The European elite, who dominated initial exchanges with Africans, were as keen to eliminate what they took to be idleness on the part of Africans as they were to banish idleness at home on the part of the European poor. Typical was the report of the 1703 Dutch delegation to the Akwamu Empire, east of the Volta River, which observed much good land but little of it cultivated "because of the laziness of its inhabitants."[3] The RAC's factor in the Gambia wrote that "the Country affords Cotton, Corn & Pepper etc., but natives are slothful ...."[4] First contact between peoples has always tended to generate mutual feelings of superiority. But in this case, until late in the nineteenth century, neither side had the ability to dominate the other in any sense.

Given the mutual interest of each in the commodities the other had to offer, such a balance ensured that pre-colonial relations between elite Africans and elite Europeans were characterized by compromise and accommodation. In some regions, mediation in the process of developing that accommodation came in the seventeenth century from the community of Afro-Portuguese – the product of marriages going back for generations before the English arrived, though on the Gold Coast there was a class of Dutch- and English-speaking mulattoes by the end of the seventeenth century on whom both Africans and Europeans relied.[5] These communities played a role similar to the métis in the fur-bearing regions of North America, especially in Senegambia and Angola. They would act as translators, advisers, and traders in their own right, penetrating regions too remote for the agents of the chartered companies.[6] In the 1660s and 1670s, the

---

[2] For the application of this concept to the region south of the North American Great Lakes, see Richard White, *The Middle Ground: Indians, Empires and Republics in the Great Lakes Region, 1651–1815* (Cambridge, 1991), pp. 50–93.

[3] Van Dantzig, *The Dutch and the Guinea Coast*, 94.

[4] Quoted in RAC to Bradshaw, Rayne and Oakly, Gambia, February 24, 1702, T70/51, f. 119.

[5] Kwame Yeboa Daaku, *Trade and Politics on the Gold Coast, 1600–1720* (Oxford, 1970), pp. 96–114.

[6] Portuguese and some French carried on trade with "ye remotest part of ye river, where Teeth & Slaves are b[u]t cheap" (John Snow, Gambia, to RAC, December 29, 1707, T70/5, f. 44). See also Thomas Chidley, Gambia to RAC, April 26,

RAC did more business in the Gambia with this community than with Africans.[7]

From a transatlantic and European perspective, what happened in the Americas was what Europeans wanted to happen in Africa but could not bring about.[8] European expansion began with the offshore Atlantic islands. Northern Italians and Portuguese created an almost complete plantation complex, including massive exports of sugar and a partly slave labor force that could not reproduce itself, well prior to the first New World manifestation of this phenomenon in Brazil.[9] The geographic movement of the plantation complex in the fifteenth and sixteenth centuries was toward Africa rather than the Americas (see Map 1 in the map section following appendices). The "African wing" of the European sweep into the western ocean was far more important than its Atlantic (or American) counterpart until the second half of the sixteenth century.[10] Sugar production in the Atlantic shifted first to Madeira and then to São Tomé in the Gulf of Guinea in the course of a century or so. In effect, the plantation complex had circumvented the arid zone of the African continent by the first quarter of the sixteenth century and was poised to make the small step on to the African mainland where land, labor, and rain were even more abundant than on São Tomé. At this point, however, the movement of the complex toward Africa abruptly halted, and plantations appeared next, not on the African mainland, but on the part of the Americas closest to Africa – still four thousand miles distant from supplies of dependable slave labor. In fact, the plantation complex died out in São Tomé for an extended period and did not appear on the African mainland for a further three centuries – by which time it had changed character and embodied neither sugar nor slaves.[11]

What can explain the transatlantic lurch of the plantation complex? It was certainly not a lack of will on the part of Europeans. Given a backdrop of bankruptcies in European financial centers and mortality rates in

1704, T70/13, and John Booker, James Island to RAC, June 17, 1691, T70/17, f. 26 on the key position of the Portuguese community.

7 Thomas Thurloes, Gambia to RAC, March 15, 1678, T70/10, f. 1. For the 1660s see the many Afro-Portuguese names in the account book, T70/544.

8 Henry A. Gemery and Jan S. Hogendorn, "Comparative Disadvantage: The Case of Sugar Cultivation in West Africa," *Journal of Interdisciplinary History*, 9 (1979):429–49.

9 Philip D. Curtin, *The Rise and Fall of the Plantation Complex: Essays in Atlantic History* (Cambridge, 1990). For the genesis of some of these ideas see Verlinden, *The Beginnings of Modern Colonization*, and for the best current survey of the literature see Blackburn, *The Making of New World Slavery*.

10 Thornton, *Africa and Africans*, 29–36.

11 The Dutch were still shipping sugar from São Tomé to Europe in the late seventeenth century.

West Africa, which was the more astonishing – European willingness to risk savings or lives? There was rarely a shortage of capital or labor in Lisbon, London, Amsterdam, – or indeed in Berlin, Paris, and Copenhagen - for speculative ventures in the tropical and subtropical areas of the world. The only successful voyage of an English company formed in 1630 returned £30,000 in 1636 – enough to give the company a surplus overall in seven years of operation.[12] Returns for the few who succeeded were thus commensurate with the risks for the many who did not, and seventeenth-century New England and Quebec suggested that one could not expect great wealth without venturing into tropics. In the very early days, at least, the risks in Africa to life and financial well-being must have seemed little different from those, say, in Virginia, Surinam, Batavia, or the Amazon. The Portuguese and Spanish, who ejected the northern Europeans from the Amazon, played a role similar to Africans in Africa.[13]

A fresh perspective is possible if the focus is switched from the activities of the Europeans when they crossed the oceans – particularly when the slave systems of the Americas were fully operational – to their early intentions. Europeans had an obsessive concern with settlement and increasing production wherever they went. This was true not only for the Atlantic offshore islands where only one of the three island groups – the Canaries – was inhabited at contact and where Portuguese interest in growing grain and sugar was clearly evidenced,[14] but also for the African mainland. The sixteenth century Portuguese saw Angola as an alternative to Brazil for settlement and obsessively pursued silver mines up the Kwanza River. In the English case, Hawkins aside, the English Elizabethan ventures brought back pepper, palm oil, and ivory but no slaves or even gold at first. In 1597, the Queen was being urged to settle Guinea rather than Guiana. Africa, it was argued, may "turn it to her best profit and commodity, as to plant such things as the earth will bear." As for the inhabitants of Guinea, any problems were rooted "in the neglect of [English] people in not labouring to bring the blacks to civility by courteous conduct."[15] Of slaves there was scarcely a mention. By 1618 a London African merchant was claiming to have had "people in that country" (probably the Gambia) who were bent

---

[12] Scott, *Joint-Stock Companies*, 2:15.

[13] For early Dutch efforts see Van Cleaf Bachman, *Peltries or Plantations: The Economic Policies of the Dutch West India Company in New Netherland, 1623–1639* (Baltimore, Md., 1969), pp. 47–9. For Dutch, Irish, and English efforts on the Amazon, see Joyce Lorimer, *English and Irish Settlement on the River Amazon, 1550–1646* (London, 1989), pp. 35–125.

[14] Pierre Chaunu, *European Expansion in the Later Middle Ages* (Amsterdam, 1979), pp. 104, 150.

[15] "A project in the Days of Queen Elizabeth for the Settling her Subjects in Guinea; shewing of what conveniency it would be, Writ in the year 1597" in Churchill, *Collection of Voyages*, 5:428–30. For Portuguese priorities see David Birmingham, *The Portuguese Conquest of Angola* (London, 1965), pp. 1–23.

"upon the discovery of the gold mines," and the 1630 charter specified gold and provided for the holding of African territory. Thirty years later the territorial claim was much wider as the crown granted a new Company of Royal Adventurers title to the whole of the west coast of Africa.[16] However absurd, the intention was "the encouragement of ... undertakers in discovering the golden mines and the setting of plantations there." The private instructions of Robert Holmes, the commander of the 1660 expedition that established the English fort at James Island in the Gambia, focussed on bringing back casks of sand for analysis. Holmes was to "trade with all in your gooing & returne, provided yt it hinder not ... or retard the discovery (of gold)."[17] Trade in redwood, hides, and ivory was seen as a by-product of gold production. Slaves were not written into the charter until the 1662 reorganization.[18]

The distinction drawn between "companies formed for foreign trade" and "companies for planting or colonization" by earlier historians is misleading. Even the expedition initiating the permanent settlement of Virginia occurred only after several successful transatlantic trading voyages. In conception, the charter that established the English colony of Virginia in 1606 and, say, its 1660 African counterpart differed little. The very different outcomes on opposite sides of the Atlantic were due to the political, geographic, and epidemiological realities that faced the English, not the intentions of their governments and investors.

The intention of the French, too, was to assume control of gold production. While French efforts to establish even a trading presence on the Gold Coast failed in the seventeenth century, the first permanent French presence in West Africa, embodied in the Compagnie du Sénégal, spent heavily on expeditions up the Senegal River in pursuit of gold and had elaborate plans to develop agriculture.[19] There seems little doubt that these companies would have been more viable if they had concentrated on trade alone. The evidence of an initial focus on production – of gold, at least – is weaker in the Dutch case, but in 1673 the West Indian Company contracted to "extract with little cost gold from earth and sand which may be invisibly contained in it," a commitment that continued after the company reorganized. The RAC

---

[16] Scott, *Joint-Stock Companies*, 1:xlviv, 10–17; Hilary Jenkinson, "The Records of the English African Companies," *Transactions of the Royal Historical Society*, 6 (1912):194; George F. Zook, *The Company of Royal Adventurers Trading into Africa* (New York, 1919), pp. 9–10.

[17] "Private Instructions for them that goe up to the Myne" in "Capt. Robert Holms his Journalls of Two Voyages into Guynea ... in the Years 1660/61 and 1663/64," Magdalene College Library, Cambridge.

[18] Cecil T. Carr, *Select Charters of the Trading Companies, 1530–1707* (London, 1913), 174, 180.

[19] Abdoulaye Ly, *La Compagnie du Sénégal* (Paris, 1993), pp. 267–73. For English counterparts in the Gambia, see Stone, "The Journey of Cornelius Hodges," 89–95, and the correspondence in T70/11, pp. 65, 69.

instructed its factors to assess cultivation possibilities for a variety of crops from at least the mid-1680s.[20]

Even as the chartered companies participated fully in the expansion of the slave trade, they continued to probe the productive potential of sub-Saharan Africa. Efforts to find precious metals predominated, notwithstanding earlier failures. "Men skill'd in digging in mines" were sent to the coast, samples of gold, silver, and copper ore were shipped to Europe frequently, and silver works were undertaken, the biggest being at the so-called Mony Hill at Commenda, where both Dutch and English were active.[21] The "Company of Adventurers to the Gold Mines of Africa" was formed in 1714, and batches of Cornish miners (with some wives) went to the Gambia and the Gold Coast in 1715, 1721, 1722, and 1723.[22] But, like later colonial officials, the Royal African Company also attempted to co-opt the African population. In a letter that could have emerged from any later Colonial Office, the Royal African Company's Committee of Assistants told its chief factor, "[w]e are of the opinion that as you have Negroe towns adjoyning to our castles, so there may be some Method taken to make ye Natives Under our protection Useful and profittable, and that by Degrees they may be brought to contribute a small matter for benefitts they enjoy and wee apprehend it may but be effected by agreeing first wth yr Capasheers [African officials] that are over them." To make Africans "usefull," the company urged a small annual tax on each canoe or inhabitant, payment of which would entitle an individual to "a freedom and our allyance" – in other words full citizenship – with the proceeds to be shared with the Cabasheers. The proposal embodies all the elements of the head taxes levied by colonial governments from the late nineteenth centuries as a means of forcing people into the labor market.[23]

The Royal African Company saw indigo and cotton as commercial crops. The RAC factor in the Gambia sent to Barbados for a "Cotton Gynn" as early as 1680 for use on cotton grown by the local population.[24] "Wee . . . . designe of making Indico in your parts" the Committee of Assistants wrote to the factor in the Sherboro River area in 1692. "Wee fixed our thoughts on York Island as a place . . . that we might the better traine up some people in that art & secure our Materials from violence . . . ." The company sent

---

[20]   Van Dantzig, *Dutch and the Guinea Coast*, 20, 25, 95.

[21]   RAC to Factors Buckeridge, Freeman and Willis, Cape Coast Castle, January 1, 1699, T70/51, f. 14; idem, November 7, 1699, *ibid.*, f. 30; idem. December 12, 1699, *ibid.*, f. 35; RAC to Factors Lewis, Crossley and Scott, Sierra Leone, January 2 1700, *ibid.*, f. 40; RAC to Joseph Baggs, Cape Coast Castle, October 3, 1700, *ibid.*, f. 70.

[22]   Tattersfield, *The Forgotten Trade*, 295, 320–1.

[23]   RAC to Spencer Boughton, Cape Coast Castle, February 23, 1703, T70/51, f. 167. Daaku in *Trade and Politics on the Gold Coast*, pp. 48–50 draws interesting parallels between the seventeenth-century company and nineteenth-century colonial officials but without noting their common desire to extract labor.

[24]   Edmond Pierce, Gambia, to the RAC, January 5, 1681, T70/10, f. 56.

skilled dye extractors at great wages who promptly died.[25] Yet promising reports resulted in further seeds and personnel arriving from Montserrat and Antigua (and no doubt further deaths), and in 1698 a mill was dispatched from England.[26] In 1706, the RAC ordered its agents in the Caribbean to supply Cape Coast Castle with "all sorts of seed of their best kind, fruit etc & of things that won't increase by seed, to send Roots in boxes & Tubbs which should be growing in them two or three months before they are shipt."[27]

More striking yet, the chief factors at Cape Coast were told to focus their efforts on Whydah, from which more slaves and perhaps less produce left than from any other port on the west coast. The Whydah factor was to "purchase all the Cotton Yarn he can, & encourage the Natives to spinn it, and that he buy it of them white, That he get also the wild Indico he can & pepper & send them to you by Canoes, ... or otherwise to us by the way of barbados ... Let them prepare ... to receive Indico and Cotton and give the natives an encouraging price to gather it & the like for yarn."[28] The instructions were repeated a few months later with phrases that could have been taken from the many late-seventeenth-century pamphlets urging spinning as an appropriate activity for the idle poor in England. "[E]ncourage the natives to as much as you can spinn Cotton & improve that Comodity to the utmost."[29]

Surprisingly, the factors themselves waxed only slightly less enthusiastic. The "land about Sera leon (as also elsewhere)," wrote one, "is very good & seemingly will bear anything especially ye sugars or Rice plantations."[30] The influential Dalby Thomas, one of the longest-lived of all the RAC's chief factors at Cape Coast Castle, was particularly supportive. "Everything that thrives in ye West Indias will thrive here," he wrote.[31] If high prices, good examples, and encouragement were not enough, then coercion was required. Thomas cleared ground around Cape Coast Castle and used "castle" slaves from the Gambia to cultivate a variety of crops. He asked for increased supplies to extend his plantations for sugar, indigo, cotton, and ginger, as well as provisions.[32] "Sir Dalby," wrote a slave-ship captain to the Committee

---

[25] RAC to Henry Gibbs, York Island, February 9, 1692, T70/50, f. 133. There are similar letters to other parts of the coast in this volume.
[26] RAC to Thomas Corker, Sherboro, October 16, 1694, T70/50, f. 158; "Directions how to fix the Indico Mill," n.d. but November, 1698, T70/51, ff. 11–12. This was probably sent to the Sherboro with the letter dated November 24, 1698. Cf. RAC to William Fry, Montserrat, January 25, 1705, T70/58, p. 82.
[27] RAC to Bullard, Bate and Stewart, September 9, 1706, T70/58, f. 126.
[28] RAC to Buckeridge, Freeman and Willis, November 7, 1699, T70/51, f. 30.
[29] RAC to Scott and Greenway, July 1, 1701, T70/51, f. 98. Cf. RAC to Loadman, Coats and Wilcocks, January 2, 1700, T70/50, f. 44.
[30] John Fletcher, Scarcies, to RAC, April 11, 1706, T70/5, p. 26.
[31] Dalby Thomas to RAC, May 10, 1706, T70/5, p. 26.
[32] Dalby Thomas to RAC, September 24, 1708, T70/5, f. 49; idem, July 28, 1708, *ibid.*, 47–8; idem, May 21, 1709, *ibid.*, f. 58.

of Assistants, "imploys your slaves in Planting when they might be better imployed (in) the repair of your forts wch are in ruinous condition."[33] The English slave traders who pressed for an end to the privileges of the Royal African Company in the early eighteenth century lobbied for a ban on the growing of sugar in Africa.[34]

Dutch efforts were similar in conception and endured longer. The Dutch began planting cotton at Butri and Axim (the fort) in the 1650s.[35] Renewed efforts in the late 1690s centered on Shama, and in 1701 they began planting sugar cane at Butteroe. By 1705 a full-time commies, or underfactor, was responsible for cotton on the coast. Like the English, the Dutch sent for slaves to work on these crops, mainly from Whydah, but included a dozen from Surinam sugar plantations to act as instructors – possibly the only time that slaves were carried from the Americas to be put to work in Africa. A cotton mill arrived from the Americas in 1703, a sugar mill after 1705, and indigo equipment and personnel from Curaçao no later than 1712. Optimistic assessments abound in Dutch and English correspondence; Gold Coast cotton "had a ready market in Amsterdam" in 1714.[36] Efforts to establish plantations in Africa, usually with slave labor, continued through the eighteenth and early nineteenth centuries, though, as the history of the Americas suggests, with little success.[37] Nineteenth-century efforts might be explained in part as attempts to develop alternatives to the transatlantic slave trade, but the vision of African plantations had never dimmed. In 1768, as the Liverpool slave trade approached its acme, *The Liverpool General Advertiser* ran a long article entitled "Remarks relative to the Extension and Improvement of the African Trade." The trade at issue was not the slave trade but the potential trade in coffee, sugar, and tea from African plantations.

The shortness of the distance, and the safe passage between England and the African coast, compared to the whole voyage, which is at present made from hence to the coast, and from thence to the West Indies is such as would give the African sugar a great advantage at our market over our rivals the French, in which case there

---

[33] Charles Hayes to RAC, January 13, 1708, T70/5, f. 42.
[34] Dalby Thomas to RAC, October 22, 1709, T70/5, f. 63. In fact, the legislation was not passed. Instead the RAC's right to a levy of 10 percent of the value of all cargoes bound for the west coast of Africa was not renewed in 1711.
[35] Daaku, *Trade and Politics on the Gold Coast*, 44–5.
[36] *Ibid.*, 45; Dalby Thomas to RAC, October 22, 1709, T70/5, f. 63–4; Van Dantzig, *Dutch and the Guinea Coast*, 84, 92, 113, 130. For Dalby Thomas' opinion on Dutch efforts see his letter to the RAC, July 28, 1708, T70/5, ff. 47–8.
[37] R. Baesjou and P. C. Emmer, "The Dutch in West Africa: Shipping, Factories and Colonisation, 1800–1870," in J. Everaert and J. Parmentier (eds.), *Shipping, Factories and Colonization* (Brussels, 1996), 199–200. For the better-known later Danish efforts see Edward Reynolds, *Trade and Economic Change on the Gold Coast, 1807–1874* (London, 1974).

would be no difficulty in finding a vent for three times the quantity of sugar we import.[38]

In the 1790s the Danes renewed efforts to establish plantations in Africa.

Overall, the explanations that scholars have provided for the failure of the plantation complex to take root on the African mainland have tended to stress European rather than African factors. Serious texts no longer give Europeans center stage in the enslavement or capture of Africans prior to their embarkation on slave ships. The Africans-as-victims paradigm is now less pervasive than it once was. Nevertheless, Europeans are still assigned a more active role in the creation of post-Columbian societies than the peoples with whom they came into contact. At one level this is appropriate. It was the Europeans who visited Africa and the Americas, not Amerindians and Africans who established bridgeheads in Europe. But while the expansionary impulse was clearly European in origin, the direction it took – geographically, materially, and ideologically – was heavily shaped by non-European influences. The recent literature acknowledges this to some extent. While echoes may be found in an earlier historiography, environmental factors have come to the fore since the 1960s. The epidemiological hypothesis, whereby Europeans could survive better in the Caribbean than in West Africa, and Africans did better than either Amerindians or Europeans in the Caribbean, took on its modern form in Curtin's seminal 1967 article.[39] A different environmental approach stresses soil acidity, poor drainage, and the monthly distribution of rain in West Africa, which, taken together, meant that sugar would be grown elsewhere.[40] Arguments that focus on the higher labor productivity possible in the Americas relative to Africa also have a strong ecological component even when the stress is on technological differentials.[41] Implicit in this third approach is the reasoning that African slaves could produce sufficiently more in the Americas than in Africa, to more than cover the cost of an expensive transatlantic crossing. When political factors are brought into the discussion it is usually in terms of disagreements among Europeans. Thus, Daaku argued that

[38] *Liverpool General Advertiser*, April 8, 1768, p. 2. I would like to thank Stephen D. Behrendt for drawing my attention to this reference.
[39] Philip D. Curtin, "Epidemiology and the Slave Trade," *Political Science Quarterly*, 83 (1967):190–216, summarized in *Plantation Complex*, 38–40.
[40] Gemery and Hogendorn, "Comparative Disadvantage," 429–49, especially 439–47.
[41] Manning, *Slavery and African Life*, 33–4; Jack Goody, *Technology, Tradition and the State in Africa* (Cambridge, 1971), pp. 24–6; Stefano Fenoaltea, "Europe in the African Mirror: The Slave Trade and the Rise of Feudalism" (Unpublished paper, 1991). Henry A. Gemery and Jan S. Hogendorn argue for relatively low productivity in West Africa in "Assessing Productivity in Precolonial African Agriculture and Industry, 1500–1800," *African Economic History* 19(1990–1):31–5, as well as making the more narrowly ecological argument already noted.

West Indian planter opposition inhibited the growth of plantations in West Africa.[42]

It is not that these arguments are wrong, although aspects of them are certainly questioned here. In Angola in particular the required combination of reliable rainfall and suitable soil was not to be found anywhere. When the Portuguese replicated their early efforts to generate plantation-based exports in the mid-nineteenth century, they again failed. In West Africa, however, ecology and epidemiology need to be supplemented with recognition of African agency in the shaping of the larger Atlantic World.[43] In short, Europeans did not have the power to move into West Africa. This is not to maintain that sugar plantations would have thrived in West Africa, though on strictly ecological as opposed to social grounds this was not impossible. Only a small part of the land area of the Caribbean was devoted to sugar, and suitable tropical microclimates existed in West Africa as well as in the Caribbean. Rather, the argument is that after due allowance for epidemiology and the ecology of sugar production, the absence of any plantation-grown commercial crop in any part of West Africa in the seventeenth and eighteenth centuries reflects the inability of Europeans to penetrate beyond the littoral.[44] As with the total absence of Europeans in the ranks of slaves in the Americas, the lack of any significant attempt to establish export sugar production on the African mainland provides a key insight into the forces that shaped the early modern Atlantic world. Twelve million people were forced on to ships bound for the Americas. African influence over this movement began with the enslavement process, as is now well known, but African agency extended far beyond the activities of African slave traders. Resistance on the part of many Africans and cooperation by some meant that European traders and ultimately consumers had to bear the costs of African agency. Africans, as much as Europeans, shaped who entered the trade, the geographic patterns

---

[42] *Trade and Politics on the Gold Coast*, 44–7. Daaku also notes the difficulty of keeping slaves in West Africa when slave prices were so high in the Americas.

[43] This critique is consistent with Thornton, *Africa and Africans*, especially pp. 13–71, 152–82.

[44] On epidemiology, it should be noted that the five hundred to one thousand Europeans living on the Gold Coast in the early seventeenth century could have just as easily supervised plantations as trading posts. Soil and climate were of course critical, but if the experience of the Americas from Louisiana to Campos in Brazil is a guide, sugar culture simply required a few microenclaves of favourable conditions. Thus while most of mainland Africa does not have the combination of soil, rainfall, and temperature for cane-sugar agriculture, the same may be said of, say, northeastern Brazil or even Jamaica. There was certainly no doubt in the minds of pre-nineteenth-century Europeans that these microclimates existed on the Gold Coast. On the drainage issue, the extensive capital investment in, say, fifteenth-century Madeira or eighteenth-century Demerara suggests that secure European political structures might have created an environment in which these problems would have been solved.

of the traffic, the conditions under which slaves travelled to the New World, and, indeed, what slaves did when they arrived in the New World.

All European activity on any part of the West African littoral was a result of negotiation with local African authorities. Forts were built after payment of what Europeans took to be rent or purchase money, and the close proximity of several forts belonging to different European nations indicates that the African interpretation of these contracts was the one that prevailed.[45] Theft by the local population meant either that Europeans had to rely on Cabasheers for the punishment of perpetrators or had to pay strict attention to "this country's customs" in the limited areas under direct control.[46]

Despite a fortified presence on the coast stretching back sixty-five years, a Dutch factor stated in 1702 that "no European nation can feel safe on this Coast unless the surrounding Natives are on its side."[47] Almost every European settlement in Africa north of the Gold Coast (and in the early days in Angola too) was located on an island, and personnel could be at risk when they left these havens. The director of the Compagnie des Indes and his staff were arrested at the mainland port of Rufisque in 1701 by Latsukaabe Faal, the founder of the dual Wolof monarchy of Kajoor-Bawol, because the French company was trying to monopolize Atlantic trade with the area.[48] On the Gold Coast, islands were scarce, so the Europeans fortified their settlements heavily or ensured they could leave quickly. Even small polities such as Fetue (where Cape Coast Castle was located) could lay siege to the largest forts, and "at any time a concerted effort on their (African peoples') part could have driven the Europeans into the sea."[49] West and south of the Gold Coast, except for Angola and the tiny trading posts at Whydah, European establishments did not exist.[50] At Whydah, a free trader explained that the "King ... of the Country with great justice protects the traders and prevents any unfair Practices and maintains an exact Neutrality both at sea

---

[45] Daaku, *Trade and Politics on the Gold Coast*, 51–60. For a contemporary discussion of the rent issue see W. Cooper, Winnebah, May 3, 1695, Rawlinson manuscript, c. 746, f. 94. For a recent assessment of European power consistent with that offered here see Robin Law, "'Here is No Resisting the Country': The Realities of Power in Afro-European Relations on the West African 'Slave Coast'", *Itinerario: European Journal of Overseas History*, 18(1994):50–64.

[46] Van Dantzig, *Dutch and the Guinea Coast*, 130. John Browne, Agga, January 1, 1696, Rawlinson manuscript, c. 746, f. 139.

[47] Van Dantzig, *Dutch and the Guinea Coast*, 81.

[48] James F. Searing, *West African Slavery and Atlantic Commerce: The Senegal River Valley, 1700–1860* (Cambridge, 1993), pp. 23–4. The eventual French enforcement of exclusive trade hinged on European naval power, not territorial holdings, but even then the French had to increase their payments to the African monarch.

[49] Davies, *Royal African Company*, 263.

[50] Goree, St. Louis, James Fort (Gambia), Bance Island (Sierra Leone), York Island (Sherboro) are the major examples.

and ashore . . . ."[51] A summary of the RAC establishments on the coast shows one carriage gun for every two Europeans in residence.[52] It was not disease and not just other Europeans that dictated this pattern.

Plantations, when they were attempted, were plagued by problems unknown in the Americas. The labor problem was solved with castle slaves or gromettoes.[53] These were invariably people from other regions of Africa whom, as Chapter 3 suggests, the local population would find almost as alien as Europeans. The English put slaves from the Gambia on the Gold Coast and, less frequently, vice versa. The Dutch supplied their Gold Coast forts from the Slave Coast and points east. But theft by the local population was beyond the power of Europeans to control. According to minutes of the council at Elmina, "the difficulty in the cultivation of sugar is that much of it is stolen by the Negroes themselves, as they have a very great liking for it."[54] Despite bringing in labor from many hundreds of miles away, in 1712, the local population "harbouring all ours and the Dutch Comp's Rebellious Black Servts," attacked Dixcove fort and blew up the powder turret, killing the factor, Timothy Fish.[55]

As the earlier discussion suggests, trading relations were those of equal partners. When the RAC complained in 1682 that slaves and hides in the Gambia were so expensive that they "turned to no acct," their factor at James Island responded "[t]hese things I cannot help, it is the traffique of the country & such Goods must be bought if you will Trade at all . . . . [W]ith teeth & Wax (which was what the Company really wanted) some hides must be bought . . . slaves likewise."[56] Two key factors weakened the European hand in their relations with Africans. Paradoxically, one of these was what helped make European expansion possible and what separated it from its fifteenth-century Chinese counterpart. The fractured political structure in Europe provided an opportunity for a multitude of relatively small-scale European business and military initiatives and maximum dissemination of feedback of the results of these. It also ensured that when Europeans arrived off the African coast, Africans would be able to play off one group

---

[51] "Answers of Mr. May to Queries," December 15, 1707, Doc. 112, CO388/11.

[52] "Reasons Humbly offered by ye Royal African Company of England for their Ships to Proceed on their Voyages" petition to the Queen, March 13, 1703, T70/170, f. 36.

[53] *Grometto* is an anglicized form of *grumete*, a Portuguese fifteenth-century term for a sailor's slave. For the origin and functions of castle slaves see Walter Rodney, "African Slavery and Other Forms of Social Oppression on the Upper Guinea Coast in the Context of the Atlantic Slave Trade," *Journal of African History*, 7 (1966):437–9.

[54] Van Dantzig, *Dutch and the Guinea Coast*, 130.

[55] Seth Grosvenour and James Phipps to RAC, March 15, 1712, T70/5, f. 81. For similar links between slaves and the local population in the Gambia see John Snow to RAC, Fort James, June 8, 1708, T70/5, f. 52.

[56] John Kastell to RAC, October 14, 1682, T70/16, f. 44.

of Europeans against another. Of course, African political structures were also fractured and Europeans took similar advantage of this. Much of the English and Dutch factors' correspondence home was preoccupied with the shifting political alignments among Africans and Europeans. But this was a symptom of weakness, not a means of building overwhelming strength. The second and related factor was the impossibility of Europeans imposing their military power beyond a cannon shot from the coast. Africans and European elites wished to dominate each other, but Europeans no more had the military power to occupy the major gold-producing regions of Axim and Denkyra (just a few days journey from the coast) than Africans could contemplate laying siege to London or Amsterdam.[57] Even as late as 1852 the commodore of a British naval squadron, amounting to one-tenth of British ships on active service, found it impossible to bring Whydah – located five miles from the ocean lagoon – under his control.[58] And only a few years before, a Dutch observer reported Africans in the vicinity of Elmina stating "the forts don't protect us – we protect the forts."[59]

Convinced of the potential of Africa, Europeans wanted mines and plantations. Africans did not want to give up the sovereignty that this would have entailed, and they certainly had no interest in working voluntarily on such operations. Europeans failed completely to gain control or even access to the production of African gold. Possibly the only gold to leave Africa, produced under European direction, came from Brazil, beginning at the end of seventeenth century, and was carried to Africa to pay for slaves. Aided by the epidemiological factor (though there was certainly no shortage of Englishmen prepared to go to the coast), West Africans were able to resist European incursions. African resistance resulted in Europeans taking slaves away in ships as a second-best alternative to working slaves on African plantations or mines. From this perspective the slave trade was a symptom of African strength, not weakness.

II

But was the price of this independence necessarily the *African* slave trade? Put differently, why was it African labor that Europeans carried to the

---

57 Van Dantzig, *Dutch and the Guinea Coast*, 105; idem, "The Ankobra Gold Interest," *Transactions of the Historical Society of Ghana*, 14(1973):169–70.

58 Eltis, *Economic Growth*, 92, 162.

59 J. A. de Marée, *Reizen op en Beschrijving van den Goudkust van Guinea*, 2 vols. (Amsterdam, 1817–18), 1:72, 183 cited in Douglas Coombs, *The Gold Coast, Britain and the Netherlands, 1850–1874* (London, 1963), p. 6. These arguments have some implications for the debate over reparation payments that might be made to descendants of victims of the slave trade. Both European consumers and African elites benefited from slave trade. For a recent discussion of the reparations issue see Clarence J. Munford, *Race and Reparations: a Black Perspective for the Twenty-First Century* (Trenton, N.J., 1996).

Caribbean? European captains were part of a culture that had learned how to navigate the world's oceans. They could have taken their ships to almost any part of the globe to get labor for their plantations. Indeed, as argued in Chapter 3, they might have ignored the non-European world altogether and made slaves of members of their own societies convicted of serious crimes or forced European instead of African prisoners of war to work on their sugar estates. The second of these options clearly required a shift in cultural parameters that Europeans were never prepared to make. But the first – drawing on, say, the peoples of China or India, who formed the bulk of the immigrant labor to the Caribbean in the mid-nineteenth century instead of Africans – would surely have been more likely in the absence of the initial African decision to enslave.

Thus, the decision to enslave and ship was taken and executed jointly by Africans and Europeans, albeit with some specialization of function. But what is most striking is the shared assumption that underlay the decision. Initial African enslavers and European slave traders had identical attitudes toward the people they enslaved and shipped. Despite the use of the terms Africa and Africans here, modern conceptions of Africa and Africans did not exist in the seventeenth and eighteenth centuries. The vast majority of African slaves were originally members of a society almost as alien to the individual who carried out the act of enslavement as Africans as a whole were to Europeans. The only difference between African and European lay in the relative size and definition of the group that was defined as outsider and was thus eligible for slave status. Nor was it just African and European elites that thought in these terms. The idea that it was inappropriate or immoral to enslave anyone did not exist anywhere in the world during the expansionary phase of the transatlantic slave trade.

Slaves emerged as the dominant element in the middle ground of African and European interaction on the West African littoral at the end of the seventeenth century. Despite European failure to tap gold supplies, the volume of West African gold exports to Europe continued to increase until late in the century, reaching perhaps a value of £250,000 per annum. Overall, commodity exports were much more valuable than their slave counterparts in the last third of the seventeenth century.[60] The precise point at which the value of slaves leaving Africa surpassed the value of gold and produce exports was probably in the interlude of European peace between the Treaty of Ryswick in 1697 and the outbreak of the War of the Spanish Succession

---

[60] Eltis, "The Relative Importance of Slaves," 337–49; Ernst van den Boogart, "The Trade Between Western Africa and the Atlantic World, 1600–90," *Journal of African History*, 33(1992):369–85; Richard Bean, "A Note on the Relative Importance of Slaves and Gold in West African Exports," *ibid.*, 15(1974):351–6; Walter Rodney, "Gold and Slaves on the Gold Coast," *Transactions of the Historical Society of Ghana*, 10(1969):17.

in 1702 when slaving activity increased dramatically. Thereafter the value of slaves leaving Africa remained far higher than that of commodities until the mid-nineteenth century.[61]

It was the English who led the way in replacing gold with slaves. They were the first European power to move voluntarily from produce trading to slave trading. The Portuguese had probably already attained this position earlier in the seventeenth century but had done so as a result of being driven out of the gold trade by the Dutch. The Portuguese switch to an African trade dominated by slaves was accompanied by a large decline in the combined value of their slave and produce trades. In the British case the switch from gold to slaves occurred with a much smaller and more temporary dip in combined values. Slave prices and volumes in the English slave trade had risen sufficiently by the end of the first quarter of the eighteenth century to push the combined value of slaves and gold to new heights – a situation that it took the Dutch some time to emulate.

How and why the switch occurred seems fairly clear. Table 6-1 provides estimates of slave prices and the numbers of slaves carried from Africa between 1681 and 1710. Between 1681 and 1697, 13.6 thousand slaves a year left for the Americas. Between 1698 and 1703, the annual average almost doubled to 25.4 thousand, and in the 1698–1710 period (in effect, five years of peace and seven of war) annual mean departures were only slightly lower at 23.3 thousand. This major increase was clearly in response to a large increase in slave prices. Prices in the Americas (taking Barbados as a proxy), after remaining stable in the 1680s (£13.2), increased strongly in the 1690s (£17.6) as war increased shipping costs such as insurance and labor. But the trend continued during the subsequent interlude of peace. In the six years from 1698 to 1703, slaves cost 10 to 15 percent more than they had in the earlier 1690s (£19.8) and were higher again (£20.6) in the seven years from 1704 to 1710 when war returned once more. Such a pattern is consistent with a major increase in demand over the whole period, reflecting the discovery of gold in Brazil, with attendant increases in the Portuguese slave trade, as well as the beginning of rapid expansion of the St. Domingue plantation sector and a newly systematic French slave trade.

African prices tracked those in the Americas in the 1680s and 1690s, and, while the series ends in 1698, there is some evidence that they increased strongly after 1697, more strongly, in fact, than did their American counterparts. African prices – more accurately, the price in London of a bundle of goods exchanged for a slave on the African coast – averaged 25 percent of slave prices in the Americas between 1681 and 1697 but 35 percent of

[61] David Eltis, "Trade Between Western Africa and the Atlantic World before 1870: Estimates of Trends in Value, Composition and Direction," *Research in Economic History*, 12(1989):197–239.

Table 6-1. *Slave Prices on the African Coast and Barbados, Selected Years, 1663–1697 (Current Pounds Sterling) and the Volume of Slaves Leaving Africa* *

	Prices in Africa	Prices in Barbados	Col. 1/Col. 2	Slaves leaving Africa (thousands)
1681	2.96	13.21	0.224	17.3
1682	3.27	14.08	0.232	13.6
1683	3.78	12.41	0.305	18.5
1684		12.78		12.4
1685	3.41			17.0
1686	3.21	13.28	0.242	13.9
1687	3.10	12.42	0.250	17.0
1688	3.10	13.15	0.236	14.7
1689	3.49	14.17	0.246	11.0
1690		16.27		5.0
1691	4.15	14.29	0.290	11.2
1693	4.22	16.22	0.260	13.7
1694	4.16	16.94	0.246	12.2
1695		20.44		13.2
1696	4.90	23.16	0.212	13.8
1697	4.62	17.48	0.264	14.8
1698	5.45	15.80	0.345	13.8
1699		15.19		18.5
1700		24.71		21.9
1701		20.21		26.3
1702		21.77		33.7
1703		20.87		26.6
1704		26.28		17.1
1705		26.22		20.9
1706		17.90		23.6
1707		13.65		19.7
1708		19.17		20.6
1709		19.88		27.4
1710		20.97		21.5

*Africa defined as a weighted average of the Slave Coast, Bight of Biafra, and west-central Africa.
Source: For African prices, see Appendix B; for Barbados prices see Galenson, *Traders, Planters and Slaves*, 65. Total slaves leaving Africa (col. 4) are calculated as follows:
For British ships, estimates of slaves leaving Africa are calculated from slaves arriving in the Americas taken from Eltis, "The British Transatlantic Slave Trade Before 1714," divided by 1 minus the mean shipboard mortality loss ratio (or 0.793). (See Eltis, "Volume and African Origins of the Seventeenth Century English Trans-Atlantic Slave Trade," 620, for the voyage mortality rate of 0.207.) For non-British ships, the estimate is based on a count of imputed slave departures made from the *TSTD*, with the addition of Postma's estimates of Dutch interloper activity in *Dutch in the Atlantic Slave*, 110. This series is not a complete record of slaves leaving Africa. Departures on Dutch ships are fairly complete, but departures on French, Portuguese, Danish, and Brandenburg ships are less so. However, the sample is large enough to be of use in reflecting the true trend.

American prices in the 1698 to 1710 period.[62] The chartered companies found themselves squeezed as hundreds of separate traders from England and the Netherlands – the former encouraged by the effective ending of the RAC monopoly – joined first-time French and Portuguese slave traders on the West African littoral.[63] Slave prices in the coastal markets increased, regions that had not supplied many slaves, such as the Gold Coast, now became significant provenance areas, and African commodity traders now turned to the slave trade. The additional slaves were not sufficient to keep the African-American price ratio constant. The transatlantic cost wedge (the difference between the African and American price) came under pressure. "The low-price Slaves sell for at Barbadoes will never answer the high price Given on the Coast," wrote the RAC's chief factor.[64] The RAC instructed its chief factors that "Since the procuring of Negroes is so difficult And the prizes so high Wee shall not so much covet them but rather advise you to use yr utmost dilligence to Improve our Trade in all other Commodities and Employ all our Vessels in Search thereof."[65]

III

Trade among equals in this context meant the most extreme commodification of labor possible and put millions of Africans into the New World, but the relative strength of Africans had effects beyond the exclusion of the

---

[62] There is no consensus in the literature on the cause and magnitude of the rise of slave prices at this time. Using British customs records David Richardson has estimated a series that yields prices for 1701–10 not much different from the 1690s estimates presented here ("Prices of Slaves in West and West-Central Africa," 52). Marion Johnson has much higher estimates for five of these years for the Gold Coast ("The Ounce in Eighteenth Century West African Trade," *Journal of African History*, 7(1966):197–217). Robin Law concludes a discussion of the evidence from the Slave Coast with an agnostic position *(The Slave Coast of West Africa, 1550–1750* (Oxford, 1991), pp. 173–4). The most systematic set of actual price data for this period begins in 1712 – again for the Gold Coast. These data are consistent with the position taken here that prices increased sharply at the beginning of the eighteenth century. See Sen, "Trends in Slave Shipments from the Gold Coast," Appendix II.

[63] The Royal African Company's monopoly was curtailed by withdrawal of royal support following the Glorious Revolution – the monopoly had never had parliamentary sanction. In 1698 the trade was officially thrown open to any slave trader who would pay a levy of 10 percent of the value of the outbound cargo to the company to be used for the support of their forts on the coast. The RAC accounted for just over 17 percent of British slaving voyages between 1699 and 1703 (54 in a sample of 344). In the 1680s it had accounted for close to three-quarters. See the *TSTD* and Eltis, "The British Transatlantic Slave Trade Before 1714."

[64] Dalby Thomas to RAC, February 6, 1710, T70/5, p. 66.

[65] RAC to Gresham, Pile, and Rayner, October 3, 1700, T70/51, f. 75.

plantation complex from Africa itself. African influence over the transatlantic flow of coerced labor began with the enslavement process, but, as already hinted, African agency extended far beyond this. Resistance on the part of many Africans and cooperation by others meant higher costs for European traders and ultimately consumers.[66] Thus, Africans, as much as Europeans, shaped who entered the trade, the geographic patterns of the traffic, the conditions under which slaves travelled to the New World, and, indeed, what slaves did when they arrived there. Both sides had to take into account the wishes of the other, but there were substantial cultural misapprehensions between Africans and Europeans based in part on the fact that the African coast represented an absolute barrier rarely crossed by either side except, of course, by the human commodities themselves. African merchants living in European countries were as rare as Europeans dwelling in Asante or Dahomey, neither of which was very far from the coast. Trade had to get by without the cross-cultural diasporic merchant communities that Curtin describes for other parts of the globe. Trading diasporas in Africa were peopled by other Africans, not Europeans, and an analogous situation existed in Europe.[67] The basic structure of European travellers' books on Africa remained unchanged from the seventeenth to the nineteenth centuries, suggesting that neither side learned much about the other in this time. The potential for conflict in this market relationship was accordingly great and unlike anywhere else in the Atlantic system the main cargo traded was human, which increased the potential for misunderstanding even further.

While the two peoples developed systems of credit and other market institutions, these arrangements could founder as one side or the other got into financial difficulties. Such situations were normal *within* the separate cultures – say, between Europeans or between Africans. Contact across the cultural divide, however, augmented the normal stresses of a business relationship, so that there was a greater incidence of such breakdowns than in transactions where only Africans or only Europeans were involved.

The chartered companies cultivated African leaders and sent captains back to the parts of the coast and dealers they already knew. Later, with the demise of the companies, strong links developed between particular ports in Europe and particular coastal regions in Africa as personal contacts maintained over the years came to form the basis of the Afro-European business relationship.

---

[66] The literature on resistance before Africans reached the Americas is not extensive. Until recently, contributions tended to catalogue instances of resistance and rebellion and remind readers that Africans did not go gently into the night. Modern and more sophisticated assessments are Richard Rathbone, "Some Thoughts on Resistance to Enslavement in West Africa," *Slavery & Abolition: A Journal of Comparative Studies*, 6(1986):11–22 and Winston McGowan, "African Resistance to the Atlantic Slave Trade in West Africa," *ibid.*, 11(1990):5–29, though neither of these essays attempts a formal restatement of African agency.

[67] Philip D. Curtin, *Cross-Cultural Trade in World History* (Cambridge, 1984), pp. 38–59.

Yet personal ties were not entirely adequate. In the absence of formal courts, financial intermediaries, and credit markets, disagreements led to the pan-yarring or kidnapping of principals. On some parts of the coast such acts became formalised into pawning practices in the eighteenth century. Credit relationships would take on real physical and personal forms as family members became temporary hostages. As this suggests, physical violence was never distant. At such times each side often ceased to see the other as individuals and would launch retaliatory actions against all Africans, in the European case, and all Europeans, in the African. Panyarred Africans might spend the rest of their lives on plantations in the Americas, Europeans could be captured, held and perhaps put to the death; goods and ships would be confiscated, and trade might be halted for extended periods.

From the European perspective a more insidious ploy was the attempts by African authorities to foment mutiny among the African employees in European establishments, as in the Gambia and Gold Coast forts or, at Bonny, rebellion among the slaves already in European hands.[68] In addition, if a ship ran aground, or became disabled because of storm damage or the effect of African fevers on the crew, then Africans simply took possession of ship and cargo. This was not different in principle from the situation in European waters (or, indeed, anywhere else in the world) where some shore-based communities drew steady income from shipwrecks. In the maritime world, stranded or wrecked ships were routinely plundered. There were simply a larger proportion of such incidents on the less familiar African coast, and in Europe, at least, disablement short of shipwreck did not always mean the total loss of the venture or the death of the crew at the hands of the local inhabitants.[69]

A second form of African resistance – really an extension of the previously described African ability to resist European territorial encroachment – was thus a capacity to resort to non-market means when market negotiations broke down or when market outcomes were deemed unacceptable. If Europeans carried away African pawns or otherwise treated free Africans badly, the African response was swift and effective. Respect for African

[68]   John Snow to RAC, June 8 and June 14, 1708, T70/5, f. 52 recounts a mutiny at Fort James in the Gambia provoked by the king of Barra from which the latter gained directly. For the Bonny incident see Starke to Westover, October 22,1700, in Donnan, *Documents*, 2:80. For mutineers at the Brandenburgh fort on the Gold Coast supplying ammunition to the African authorities see Seth Grosvenour and James Phipps to RAC, March 15, 1712, T70/5, f. 81.

[69]   For the African coast, many of these incidents are catalogued in Joseph Inikori, "The Unmeasured Hazards of the Atlantic Slave Trade: Sources, Causes and Historiographical Implications," *Revue Française d'Histoire d'Outre Mer*, 83(1996):64–74. For a fuller example see Suzanne Schwarz, *Slave Captain: The Career of James Irvine in the Liverpool Slave Trade* (Wrexham, 1995): pp. 33–60. For parallel incidents on the British coast involving regular merchant ships see *Lloyd's List*, Nov. 17, 1749, and Oct. 11, 1763.

For
Rev
or
Sion

power was such that in 1747 the British government prohibited British ship captains from unjustly seizing African peoples.[70]

Put baldly, the costs to Europeans of doing business were higher in Africa than in Europe itself where market participants shared cultural values, and could call on risk-reducing financial intermediaries. Using people as security for credit was always likely to be more troublesome than using property, and, like all credit systems that do not call on third (or risk-spreading intermediate) parties, it was expensive. Costs to Europeans must have been higher here than in the aboriginal Americas where European conquest meant the steady expansion of European influence and the imposition of forms of the credit markets and legal recourses that already existed in Europe. As a consequence, wages paid to European personnel would have to be higher to offset personal risk, losses of merchandise and ships would have to be discounted, ultimately through higher insurance premiums, and direct costs of armaments for ships and personnel would be higher than for equivalent trade in Europe or the Americas. As explained later, any increase in costs would mean higher prices for slaves on both the African coast and the Americas. Given a downward sloping demand curve for slaves in the Americas this meant fewer slaves carried across the Atlantic.

If the need to guard against market breakdown had cost-increasing effects, the need to control the slaves was even more expensive. "The Negroes rising, and other disappointments, in the late [slave] voyages ... have occasioned a great reducement in our Merchant's gains," reported a New England newspaper in 1731.[71] Slaves may have had fewer choices than migrants from Europe, but their wishes nevertheless shaped the volume and direction of the slave trade. The nature of the interaction among slave traders/crews and the Africans that comprised the transatlantic cargo was unique in the early modern Atlantic world. These were cargoes with wills of their own.

The relationship between those charged with carrying the slaves to the Americas and the African slaves themselves was among the most uncomplicated of all forms of human interaction. Unlike the slaves and masters in the Americas (or in Africa) or master and servant in the rest of the early modern Atlantic world, the two groups had little opportunity to get to know each other.[72] The average middle-passage voyage lasted two to three months in

---

[70]   The law reads "no Commander or Master of any Ship trading to Africa, shall by fraud, or Violence, or by any other indirect Practice whatsoever, take on Board, or carry away from the Coast of Africa, any negroe or Native of the said Country, or commit, or suffer to be committed, any Violence on the Natives, to the Prejudice of the said Trade; and every Person so offending shall, for every such Offence, forfeit the Sum of One hundred pounds of lawful Money of Great Britain." T70/1585, *Act for extending and improving the trade of Africa*. Parliament modified this act in 1749 and 1761 (5 Geo III c. 44).

[71]   Reported in Donnan, *Documents*, 2:431, n.

[72]   Sexual abuse of the slaves by the crew adds another dimension to the relationship, equally elemental perhaps. Slaves were valuable and sexual interference with them

the early sixteenth century, and by the midnineteenth century slavers were routinely crossing to Bahia in less than three weeks and to Cuba in five. Behavioural motives on both sides remained straightforward and sharply confrontational. Slaves hated their captors, and their wish to escape was uncluttered by slave family ties or, indeed, affective associations of any kind. Resignation, despair, and suicidal tendencies were constant but not usually dominant.[73] The crew faced economic necessity – they could hardly expect to be paid in the event of a successful slave revolt – reinforced by terror. The vast majority of rebellions resulted in inordinate bloodletting, whatever the outcome. If the slaves got the upper hand, even temporarily, most of the crew could expect to be killed. If the crew retained control, the death of the rebel leaders was almost inevitable, and the actual numbers of slaves put to death would be limited only by the need to get enough slaves to the Americas to ensure a profit in what was a highly competitive business. Naked physical force determined who would be in control of a slave ship; any relaxation of vigilance or reduction in the amount of force available would mean rebellion.[74]

This unrelenting application of force separates the slave ship from the plantation in the Americas, where force defined the system but might be supplemented by incentives in day-to-day operations. It also makes the slave trade different from the transatlantic traffic in indentured servants or free migrants – where the vast majority of travelers had chosen to be on board – as well as the nineteenth-century traffic in contract labor from Asia to the Americas. There were revolts on ships carrying indentured servants and convicts and more again on vessels bringing Asian contract workers to the Americas in the nineteenth century, but these were not as frequent. Slave

was analogous to damage of a non-human cargo, yet there are many incidents on record. It is noteworthy that the women were held separately from the men, adjacent to the officer's quarters.

73 W. W. Piersen, "White Cannibals, Black Martyrs: Fear, Depression and Religious Faith as Causes of Suicide Among Slaves," *Journal of Negro History*, 62(1977):147–59 and much of the popular literature argue for widespread suicide on the part of Africans. An analysis of ninety-two surgeons' logs from 1792 to 1796 that recorded the causes of slave deaths indicates that 5.7 percent of slave deaths during loading and 2 percent of those on the middle passage were suicides. As less than 5 percent of all slaves taken on board ship in these years died, these figures suggest that for every one thousand slaves taken on board ship between one and two committed suicide in these years. Calculations made from Steckel and Jensen, "New Evidence on the Causes of Slave and Crew Mortality," Tables 1 and 3. For a late-seventeenth-century discussion of suicide among slaves on a slave ship see "Journal of Captain Phillips," in Churchill, *Collection of Voyages* 6:235.

74 There is no indication in the records of cooperation between ordinary seamen and slaves against authority (slave-ship officers in this case) of the kind posited in port cities by Peter Linebaugh and Marcus Rediker ("The Many-Headed Hydra: Sailors, Slaves and the Atlantic Working Class in the Eighteenth Century," *Journal of Historical Sociology*, 3(1990):225–51).

ships were more heavily armed than vessels carrying indentured, contract, or free labor, and also had a higher crew-per-tons ratio. But perhaps the best comparison is between slave ships and non-slave ships sailing to Africa from Europe – the latter trading for ivory, hides, and other produce. Both types of ships had to cope with the cross-cultural difficulties of trade that might degenerate into violence. Produce ships were just as likely as slave ships to be cut off when this happened. It is hardly surprising to find that there is no statistically significant difference between the tons-per-gun ratio of a produce ship going to Africa and a slave ship in the eighteenth century, whereas both types of ships were more heavily armed than ships sailing to other parts of Europe or the Americas at this time. The major difference between a produce ship and a slave ship was in manning, a clear reflection of the human nature of the latter's cargo. The crew-per-tons ratio on a slave ship was only 75 to 80 percent of that on ships purchasing only African produce. The armament differential between African- and European-bound ships reflects in part the cross-cultural trade problem. The tons-per-crew differential is indicative of the human versus non-human element in what these ships carried.[75]

The significance of these patterns for costs is readily apparent. The costs of going to Africa to trade, as well as the costs of going to Africa to trade for people, were higher than elsewhere. A rough assessment of how much higher is not only possible but these higher costs may also be attributed to the ability of Africans, slave and non-slave, to resist European encroachment. If cut-offs forced Europeans to recognize the equal status of Africans in a trading relationship, revolts reflected the cost of forcing Africans to do something they manifestly did not want to do. Shipping costs made up about half the price of an African slave newly arrived in the Americas. During the eighteenth century – when 95 percent of the slave revolts discussed here occurred – labor costs made up about half of this shipping cost.[76] Slave ships were larger and carried 60 percent more crew than non-slavers. Owners also paid higher wages to that crew and allowed the captain to take 5 percent of the slaves arriving in the Americas for himself – a practice for which there is no parallel in the African produce trade.[77] Good quantitative evidence on wage differentials is unavailable, and such differentials are not taken into account in the

---

[75] David Eltis, Stephen D. Behrendt, and David Richardson, "The Impact of Slaves on African Atlantic Trade" (Unpublished, 1998).

[76] Eltis and Richardson, "Productivity in the Transatlantic Slave Trade," 469.

[77] For wage differentials see Shiela Lambert (ed.), *House of Commons Sessional Papers*, 145 vols. (Wilmington, De, 1975), 68:173, 177, 178. These may have just offset the fact that part of the wages were paid in devalued colonial currency when surplus crew were paid off in the West Indies at the end of the middle passage. The 5 percent allowance for captains is one of the constants in the transatlantic slave trade. See Davies, *Royal African Company* for the seventeenth century; Behrendt, "The British Slave Trade, 1785–1807: Volume Profitability and Mortality" for the eighteenth; and Eltis, *Economic Growth* for the nineteenth.

formal analysis that follows. In addition, a major part of the captain's allowance, comprising 10 percent of labor costs (captain's allowance as share of total costs/labor as share of total costs) was an incentive to the captain to care for the health of the slaves and not just to keep control of them. Arbitrarily assigning half the allowance to resistance (5 percent) and combining this with the 60 percent extra crew for a slave compared to a non-slave ship gives additional labor costs attributable to resistance of about two-thirds.

The remaining expense of mounting a slave voyage, after deducting labor, was the cost of the ship itself, or more precisely, the rental price of capital per voyage. How would this be affected by resistance? The two major elements to consider here are armaments and insurance. Ships arriving in the English Caribbean from Africa carried 20 percent more guns per ton than those coming direct from Europe and guns comprised about 10 percent of the costs of the ship. This estimate excludes small arms, which would have been particularly important for close-quarter control of the slaves. Insurance contracts either excluded losses that resulted from slave revolts or provided only partial coverage, a strong indication in itself of the high probability of such events. Insurance against the normal hazards of a voyage to Africa was typically 5 percent in peacetime and considerably higher during periods of European war. A direct estimate of the costs of slave losses from resistance is thus not possible, and the best proxy is an estimate of the number of slave deaths that were due to acts of resistance. If shipboard mortality among slaves in the nineteenth century averaged 14 percent of those taken on board, a sampling of ships' logs suggests that only 1 percentage point of this may be attributed directly to acts of violence, including suicide. The capital costs of the slave ship were thus not heavily affected by the human nature of the contents of the cargo hold and cannot have been increased by more than 4 percent.[78]

If labor costs were two-thirds higher and capital costs were 4 percent higher because of resistance, an average of the two (labor and capital each comprising 50 percent of transportation costs) yields an additional total shipping cost of 35 percent. As shipping costs made up in turn half the total costs of the slaving voyage (the trading cargo accounting for the rest), then we might estimate crudely that the cost of taking unwilling people to the New World was almost one-fifth higher than the cost of transporting indentured servants or free laborers. Is this significant? Elementary economics suggests that for Africans entering the trade it was of the greatest possible

---

[78] Additional armaments would have increased capital costs by 2 percent (20 percent additional guns multiplied by the 10 percent share of total costs that armaments comprised). To this should be added the 1 percent of the slaving cargo taken on board that was lost as a result of slave deaths attributable to acts of violence, adjusted for the 50 percent of total costs that was absorbed by the trading cargo (share of violent deaths/trading cargo's share of total costs).

importance. As noted earlier, anything that increased costs and thus prices of slaves reduced the numbers of Africans entering the trade. An estimate of how many hinges on the elasticity of the demand for and supply of slaves and an estimate of the numbers of slaves carried to the Americas during the eighteenth century. Between 1700 and 1800, 5.5 million Africans were carried off from Africa. In the absence of resistance this figure would have been 9 percent greater.[79] Thus, in the eighteenth century alone, resistance ensured that half a million Africans avoided the plantations of the Americas (and European consumers were forced to pay higher prices for plantation produce). In effect, Africans who died resisting the slave traders, as well as those who resisted unsuccessfully but survived to work on the plantations of the Americas, saved others from the middle passage.

IV

In summary, European-African relations in the seventeenth century may be grouped according to whether or not Europeans occupied territory. In three regions, Senegambia, the Gold Coast, and particularly in Portuguese Angola, Europeans had some territorial presence. In three other regions, the Slave Coast, the Bight of Biafra, and west-central Africa north of Portuguese Angola, commerce between the two peoples was largely ship-based or was only temporarily based on land. Except in Angola, however, Europeans were unable to take over much resembling sovereignty on the African mainland. Even the smallest West African polities were capable of holding Europeans at arm's length and in the seventeenth century Europeans did not come into much contact with any large African states. Even where a European presence existed, as in Senegambia and the Gold Coast, Africans limited the relationship to trade, and a fairly small trade at that. African ability to resist European encroachment and the availability of slaves on the African littoral,

---

[79] The relevant formula is

$$Q^* = \frac{e}{e + y} S^*,$$

where Q^* = percentage change in quantity of slaves entering the slave trade
 e = elasticity of demand
 y = elasticity of supply
 S^* = percentage increase in costs as a result of resistance.

e is estimated at -1.95; y is 2.0. For a discussion of elasticity see David Eltis, "The British Contribution to the Transatlantic Slave Trade," *Economic History Review*, 32(1979):225–6, which is based in part on E. Phillip LeVeen, *British Slave Trade Suppression Policies* (New York, 1977). For the model and general approach see S. L. Engerman and R. W. Fogel, "A Model for the Explanation of Industrial Expansion during the Nineteenth Century," in idem (eds.), *The Reinterpretation of American Economic History* (New York, 1971), pp. 150–1; and Eltis, *Economic Growth*, 343–4.

combined with European demand for slave labor (ultimately for plantation produce) and the inability of Europeans to extend to Africans domestic conceptions of freedom, created a transatlantic slave trade. How many slaves would be carried and at what prices, the regions from which they would be removed, and the timing and demographic composition of the transatlantic flow were the result of interaction between Africans and Europeans.

The plantation complex thus made the large leap from São Tomé to the Americas instead of the small one to Africa in part because of relative European weakness. The intriguing question is why the outcome of European expansion was so different in the Americas compared to Africa. European mortality rates were higher in Africa than in the Americas. Yet the relevant comparison is not between West Africa and, say, the mid-Atlantic colonies of North America but between West Africa and the early Chesapeake or the Caribbean, where transatlantic mortality differentials for Europeans were much narrower. European settlement of Africa is not the issue here; a plantation economy needs relatively few managers, and the Europeans who staffed the castles, or later, the mixed commission courts and colonies, could just as easily have run plantations. The impact of epidemiology on Europeans seems less critical than most scholars assume, but it takes on greater importance when attention swings to the indigenous inhabitants. The mortality differential between Africans and aboriginal Americans faced with European contact was far larger than that between Europeans in the tropical Americas and Europeans in tropical Africa. Population initially declined drastically in the Americas after transatlantic contact. The European epidemiological impact on Africa by contrast was negligible.

But geosecurity concerns must also form a critical element of the explanation for the diversion of plantations to the Americas. A larger part of the tropical and sub-tropical Americas than of sub-Saharan Africa comprised islands more easily policed by European naval powers.[80] Indeed, perhaps all slave plantations of the type developed by Europeans needed to be either on geographic islands or islands in a sea of insiders, as on the North and South American mainlands.[81] Yet this latter option was not entirely impossible in

---

[80]   The best discussion of the role of islands in the plantation complex is in Arthur L. Stinchcombe, *Sugar Island Slavery in the Age of Emancipation: The Political Economy of the Caribbean World* (Princeton, N.J., 1995), pp. 29–56.

[81]   Soil and climate were of course critical, but given these, as long as slave labor was possible, sugar was usually a crop grown on islands – in the Mediterranean, Atlantic, Caribbean, and Indian Ocean. It was also the crop associated with the worst working conditions. Rice, tobacco, coffee, cotton, and cacao, also employing slave labor, were much more frequently grown on continental land masses. Is there a point to be made here linking working conditions with security considerations? The major exceptions were Brazil and nineteenth-century Louisiana. In both cases, however, the sugar sectors were, in effect, islands, at least in the

Africa: none of the slaves that Europeans held along the western African coast were from the local population. There may be room, accordingly, for a cultural argument. Would the plantation sector have made the step from São Tomé to the African mainland if Africa had been populated by people like aboriginal Americans, a good part of whom had not completely emerged from this side of the agricultural revolution? There were probably as many Europeans in the haute pays south of the North American great lakes as on the western African littoral through most of the seventeenth and eighteenth century. Europeans did not establish plantations in what became the American Midwest either, but their economic and cultural influence in the pre-settlement era seems of a greater order of magnitude there than it was in pre-colonial West Africa. More specifically, environmental conditions in say Guiana and Guinea were similar and cannot explain why European plantation activity should have been so much greater in the former than in the latter. The swing of the plantation complex across the Atlantic makes full sense only when we take into account the greater capacity of the African population to resist European encroachment prior to the nineteenth century.

In the short run, those Africans who did not enter the Atlantic slave trade clearly gained from European failure to move beyond the western African littoral. However severe the impact of the slave trade, slave plantations on that littoral (or in the interior) would have been worse. Compared to the indigenous Americans, Africans gained three centuries of further independence. Moreover, during both the gold and slave phases of European-African Atlantic trade, Africa participated in the rapid expansion of world trade that was associated with European expansion. For Africans who did not enter the trade, the increase in the flow of imports into Africa from the Atlantic exceeded population growth and probably income growth too.[82] The relevant question, of course, is how these long-run trends – the social costs of slave trading, in particular – would have differed if European and African elites had cooperated to bring the plantation complex to the African mainland or, second, if there had been no European contact at all.

On the first of these it is worth noting that while African trade volumes increased during the slavery era, trade with the plantation Americas increased much more rapidly yet. In 1700, trade between Europe and the Caribbean was thirty times greater than that between Europe and Africa. This ratio was not much different one century later when both the volume of the transatlantic slave trade and the prices of slaves on the African coast were at the highest levels they were ever to attain. The African ability to deflect the

sense that the people who comprised the labor force were marked off from the dominant population by skin colour.

[82] David Eltis and Lawrence C. Jennings, "Trade Between Western Africa and the Atlantic World in the Pre-Colonial Era," *American Historical Review*, 93(1988):957–9.

plantation system to the Americas thus meant smaller trade flows and wealth than would have occurred if the complex had forced its way into West Africa. It was the Caribbean rather than West Africa that provided the jewels in European crowns before 1800, and in the very long run per capita incomes have correlated strongly with the value and volume of external trade – unprecedented levels of exploitation notwithstanding.

On the second of these issues, what would have happened without any European contact? Some scholars have argued that West Africa would have experienced strong economic development, indeed industrialisation, in the absence of the slave trade or any European contact.[83] Any judgment on these large issues is beyond range of the present work. At the very least, however, the moral issues involved in these alternatives to the historical reality are clearer than the economic. It is easier to condemn the way some Europeans and Africans created and sustained the Atlantic slave system than to spell out the economic consequences of the alternatives.

[83] Joseph E. Inikori, "Slavery and the Development of Industrial Capitalism in England," in Barbara L. Solow and Stanley L. Engerman (eds.), *British Capitalism and Caribbean Slavery: The Legacy of Eric Williams* (New York, 1987), pp. 79–101; James M. Blaut, *The Colonizer's Model of the World: Geographic Diffusionism and Eurocentric History* (New York, 1993), pp. 152–213.

7

The African Impact on the Transatlantic
Slave Trade

THE AFRICAN CAPACITY TO influence the early modern Atlantic world
is nowhere clearer than in the highly individualised regional diversity that
developed in Afro-European relations. As long as Europeans wanted plantations in the seventeenth-century sense then, as in the Americas, the natural
resource base of the continent would have a major influence over the geography of trade. But once Africans made it clear that Europeans could
have no significant settlements and little political power, and once slaves
became the dominant commodity, as in Africa by 1700, then trade should
have followed the distribution of the population in Africa or perhaps wind
and ocean currents in the Atlantic. In fact, European-African trade patterns
were not consistent with these expectations. To explain the historical reality
of trade, scholars must look beyond geophysical and narrowly economic
factors. Physical and cultural anthropologists recognise that greater human
diversity exists in Africa than in any other continent. Such diversity meant
a wide variation in the human needs and preferences that provide the foundations of all trade and also, perhaps, helps explain the narrower concepts
of insider that held in Africa compared to Europe.

Each segment of sub-Saharan Africa developed its modus vivendi with
early modern Europeans. While all regions saw slaves emerge as the dominant export, each reached that point via a different route. Senegambia
demonstrates this point best (see Map 2 in the map section following appendices).[1] This region was the part of sub-Saharan Africa closest to both Europe
and the Americas. Ships sailing from Europe and North America (including
the Caribbean) had to sail past the region in order to reach other parts of

---

[1] See Curtin's discussion of the atypicality of the Senegambian-European trading
patterns in "The Abolition of the Slave Trade from Senegambia," in David Eltis
and James Walvin (eds.), *The Abolition of the Atlantic Slave Trade: Origins and
Effects in Europe, Africa and the Americas* (Madison, Wis., 1981), p. 83.

tropical Africa. On average, slave ships leaving Senegambia took only 48.3 days to reach their destinations in the Americas, compared to 74.4 days for all African provenance zones combined.[2] Trips from slaving ports in the North Atlantic to Africa and then to the Americas took eight months on average when the ship went to Senegambia, ten months if the vessel obtained its slaves at Sierra Leone, and twelve months if at any port to the south. The navigable range for ocean-going vessels of the Gambia river was greater than that of any other internal waterway in the sub-Saharan region.

Yet the most striking advantages for the European slave trader lay not in geography but in what was seen as the human product. The coastal areas of Senegambia were linked with a wide range of ecological zones and peoples. By far the greater part of the major groups of Fuulbe, Malinke, Sereer, Wolof, and Soninke nations, amounting in all probably to between 1.5 and 3 million persons, lived within easy reach of these rivers.[3] This region yielded the mix of gender, age, and size that planters in the Americas – if the instructions given to slave-ship captains are reliable evidence – wanted most. An analysis of over one hundred thousand slaves taken from five major regions of Africa between 1662 and 1713 indicates that men made up over three-quarters of those leaving Upper Guinea (and children less than 6 percent), while no other area in Africa had much more than half of its deportees comprising men or less than 10 percent comprising children.[4] These were large men, perhaps reflecting the relatively high animal protein in the diet of much of this region. "[T]he Slaves in this country," wrote a slave-ship captain from the Gambia as he complained about the space available on his ship, are "as large as one & a half in any [other] part of Guinea."[5]

If the foregoing suggests that Senegambia should have been a major provenance zone for people travelling to the Americas, Table 7-1 shows that the reality was the opposite.[6] Upper Guinea was, in fact, the least important of all major African slave provenance zones. Records survive of only one thousand slaves per year leaving for the Americas and, even after allowing for missing data, the total is not likely to have approached two thousand per

---

[2] Calculated from a sample of 2,706 voyages in the *TSTD* covering the period 1662 to 1864. For Senegambia, n = 299, sd = 32.5. For all African regions n = 2706, sd = 42.0.

[3] Curtin, *Economic Change*, 333–4 for a discussion of population estimates.

[4] See Appendix A.

[5] John Tozer, "Postillion," to R.A.C., May 2, 1704, T70/13, f. 71. Voyage id, 15005.

[6] Table 7-1 is not a complete record of departures. If it were, the French and Portuguese components would be much larger, but the missing data would not be enough to double the totals presented here. The major omissions from the table are national carriers trading more heavily to areas south of Senegambia – Portuguese Angola was particularly important. If this trade were included, Upper Guinea – effectively Senegambia – would be even less important in relative terms.

Table 7-1. *Estimated Slave Departures from Africa to the Americas by African Region of Departure and Nationality of Carrier, 1662–1713*

	Upper* Guinea	Gold Coast	Bight of Benin	Bight of Biafra	West-Central Africa	South-East Africa	Total
1662–70							
English	1,496	7,997	13,727	32,497	4,083	91	59,891
Dutch**	1,736	4,170	9,294	1,974	5,612		22,786
Total	3,232	12,167	23,021	34,471	9,695	91	82,677
1671–80							
English	5,072	17,518	17,174	22,944	8,315	309	71,332
Dutch	770	2,976	5,579	1,077	7,479		17,881
Other		103					103
Total	5,842	20,597	22,753	24,021	15,794	309	89,316
1681–90							
English	10,599	12,676	40,089	18,219	19,826	5,392	106,801
Dutch	235	1,807	22,102	470	12,934		37,548
Portuguese			9,542		2,936		12,478
Other		850					850
Total	10,834	15,333	71,733	18,689	35,696	5,392	157,677
1691–1700							
English	13,141	17,097	33,434	10,544	17,153	190	91,559
Dutch	235	310	15,665	470	9,616		26,296
Portuguese			49,412	1,101	3,303		53,816
Other			4,802				4,802
Total	13,376	17,407	103,313	12,115	30,072	190	176,473
1700–7							
English	8,366	38,016	35,041	12,481	7,476	3	101,383
Dutch		2,928	11,895		10,835		25,658
Portuguese			54,316	367	367		55,050
Other			2,565				2,565
Total	8,366	40,944	103,817	12,848	18,678	3	184,656
1708–13							
English	3,681	40,441	20,529	4,214	3,677	5	72,547
Dutch		949	9,671		2,874		13,494
Portuguese			52,481	2,202		4,037	58,720
French	3,078	591	4,559	266			8,494
Other			2,112	426	1,329		3,867
Total	6,759	41,981	89,352	7,108	7,880	4,042	157,122
1662–1713							
English	42,355	133,745	159,994	100,899	60,530	5,990	503,513
Dutch	2,976	13,140	74,206	3,991	49,350		143,663
Portuguese			165,751	3,670	6,606	4,037	180,064
French	3,078	591	4,559	266			8,494
Other		953	9,479	426	1,329		12,187
Total	48,409	148,429	413,989	109,252	117,815	10,027	847,921

Notes: *For slave departures, Upper Guinea at this period means effectively Senegambia. Very few slaves left from the long coastline between the southern rivers of Senegambia and the western limits of the Gold Coast prior to the eighteenth century. **The Dutch data are for the years 1658 to 1670.

Source: Computed from *TSTD*.

annum. Probably fewer than 5 percent of total departures from Africa left Senegambia at this time. Those leaving the Slave Coast were eight or ten times more numerous, despite the much longer ocean voyages that participation in such a market dictated. The number of slaves leaving the region did increase over time, and Senegambia was one of the first areas in which the value of slaves entering the Atlantic trade exceeded that of produce, probably in the 1680s.[7] Moreover, after 1713, warlord operations turned producers of commodities into human commodities.[8] But the scale of departures and a regional population of 1.5 to 3 million suggest that this was not the situation in the seventeenth century. The basic point is that despite favorable geography, European forts, and the attention it has received from historians, the region did not have strong trade connections with the Atlantic before 1700. Atlantic trade on both the Gold and Slave Coasts was several times more valuable.[9]

What accounts for the paradox? Seventeenth-century European merchants had the same problem in Senegambia that they had in the Far East. Whereas many Amerindians were understandably keen to acquire textiles and cooking containers in place of animal skins, people of Senegambia found that many European products offered little advantage over what they already had. Table 7-2 provides a breakdown of merchandise that the Royal African Company shipped to West Africa in the second half of the seventeenth century.[10] The Senegambian column in Table 7-2 suggests that Europeans could supply only two broad product categories that were of interest to the people of Senegambia – personal decorator items such as beads and coral, and metals, or in this case iron bars. Even the demand for the latter was highly localised and, between 1662 and 1697, Senegambians imported no more than a few

[7] Curtin has argued for slaves making up 55 percent of the value of total exports from Senegambia in the 1680s (*Economic Change*, 327).

[8] Boubacar Barry, *Senegambia and the Atlantic Slave Trade* (Cambridge, 1997), translated from the French by Ayi Kwei Armah, pp. 42–5.

[9] Table 6-1 suggests that slave prices averaged £4 in the 1680s. Slave departures in Table 7-1 suggest the total value of the slave trade in the 1680s was thus £43,550 in Senegambia, £61,600 in the Gold Coast, and £288,300 on the Slave Coast. To this must be added produce, the most valuable being gold. Slaves were more valuable than produce in Senegambia at this time, but the reverse was true on the Gold Coast, which shipped at least 80 percent of African gold entering the Atlantic (Philip Curtin, "Africa and the Wider Monetary World, 1250–1850," J. F. Richards (ed.), *Precious Metals in the Later Medieval and Early Modern Worlds* (Durham, N.C., 1983), pp. 247–8). It seems likely that the value of Atlantic trade to Senegambia was only one-third that of either the Slave Coast or the Gold Coast.

[10] The quantity of English cloth shown here is probably understated. This was a period when cloths of English manufacture were replacing those of continental European origin. Unfortunately the name of the cloth, for example, annabasses, remained the same during this process so that the name of the cloth does not necessarily reflect its provenance (Davies, *Royal African Company*, 166–79).

Table 7-2. *Relative Shares of Types of Merchandise Shipped to West Africa by the Royal African Company, 1662–1703, by African Region of Import (columns sum to 100)*

	Upper Guinea	Gold Coast	Slave Coast	Bight of Biafra	West-Central Africa	Total
Textiles	12	77	27	1	54	56
Metals	27	6	8	80	12	17
Cowries	1	1	44	1	0	6
Personal Decorator Items	27	1	8	14	1	5
Containers*	5	2	4	1	17	4
Guns & gunpowder	3	5	1	1	6	4
Spirits	8	2	1	0	1	2
Misc	17	5	8	1	9	6
Total	100	100	100	100	100	100

Notes: *Basins, pans, kettles, mainly brass and pewter.
Source: Computed from Appendix C.

hundred tons in total from the Atlantic.[11] These products formed over half by value of total imports into the region. Textiles accounted for just 12 percent of all imported goods, and among these the cheaper East Indian cloths outsold all the European varieties. For the region as a whole such items must have had curiosity status only; most inhabitants would never see imported cloth. Indifference to what the other had to offer may also be seen on the European side, as planters in Barbados and Jamaica were reluctant to buy slaves from the region.[12] Indeed in the seventeenth century the major market for slaves from the Gambia was Virginia.[13] One reason given for such reluctance was the meat-eating predilections of Senegambian people (in contrast to those from the tsetse fly regions to the south), which increased maintenance costs for owners of slaves.[14]

[11]   Curtin, *Economic Change*, 314. For a discussion of beads and coral see *ibid.*, 315–19.
[12]   A view widely held across the English Caribbean. See RAC to John Case, August 24, 1686, T70/50, f. 25; Philip Brome, Nevis, to RAC, May 17, 1697, T70/12, f. 141; Molesworth, Penhallow, and Riding, Jamaica, to RAC, April 7, 1684, T70/16, f. 80; Edward Parsons, Montserrat, to RAC, December 24, 1686, T70/12, p. 100; Thomas Mackley, Jamaica, to RAC, December 5, 1707, T70/8, f. 28; Bullard, Bate, and Stewart, Barbados, to RAC, December 7, 1707, T70/8, f. 29.
[13]   RAC to Alex Cleeve, Gambia, December 23, 1686, T70/50, f. 29, and idem, January 6, 1687, *ibid.*, f. 30.
[14]   Jamaican planters had "noe esteeme for those sorts of negroes [Gambia] who are used to eat soo much flesh in theire own country that they seldom proove

If the price had been right, European merchants would no doubt have purchased in Senegambia rather than, say, the Slave Coast. Slave prices, however, were never below those of other regions despite the relatively small number of slaves carried across the Atlantic.[15] Such a combination of high prices and small numbers of slaves traded (relative to other regions) suggests strongly that the reason for the small market lay on the African rather than on the European side of the transaction. More specifically, a large proportion of slaves leaving the region appear to have journeyed from Segu and Kaarta far inland (or rather upstream). The ratio of slaves originating within 100 kilometers of the coast to those travelling from farther afield was lower here than from any other region, except perhaps for west-central Africa.[16] Universalist religions such as Islam tended to widen the conception of who could not be enslaved in lower Senegal without diminishing demand for the unfree.[17] High slave prices thus reflected the combined pressures of local, transatlantic, and trans-Saharan demand for a relatively small number of high-cost slaves from the interior. High transport costs associated with long-distance travel from the upper regions of the major rivers helps explain the large proportion of more valuable men leaving Senegambia for the Americas.

Once away from the river estuaries where naval technology gave some advantage, European initiatives were strictly circumscribed. "[A] factor once settled ashoare is absolutely under the command of the King of the Country," wrote the RAC chief at James Island, "in the case of mortality it is very

well under a dyet except it be for house negroes" (Molesworth, Penhallow, and Riding to RAC, April 7, 1684, T70/16, f. 80). The early Virginia connection is interesting in the light of the taller stature of slaves in the United States compared to their Caribbean counterparts (Fogel, *Without Consent or Contract*, 138–42).

[15] Price data for the Gambia are easy to obtain but usually are quoted in terms of bars of varying values, which makes a sterling equivalent difficult to derive. The one cargo labelled specifically for slaves that the RAC sent to the Gambia at this time suggests slave values 20 percent higher than for other regions (T70/1222). The Senegambian slave prices that Curtin quotes are 36 percent higher than those for the rest of Africa shown in Table 6-1 for the 1680s and 39 percent higher for the 1690s (*Economic Change: Supplementary Evidence*, 51).

[16] Slaves were available for the Atlantic trade mainly when African merchants arrived from the interior (March-April in the Gambia) or when Europeans returned from their seasonal voyage to the upper reaches of the rivers (August-September in the Gambia): "Your Ships being ordered here in March may Prove well if the Merchants bring downe a store of slaves. Butt... a Ship in May for goods nor Slaves I desire you will not send. For our Vessell goes up to trade in the River this month and they come downe in August soe that if you order me two Ships in September one for slaves and another for goods I shall be able to comply with them. Butt I begg that you will order it soe that noe ship shall come for more than two hundred negroes and the ship for goods one hundred tuns" (John Kastell, James Fort to RAC, March 2, 1681, T70/1, 83; see also John Chidley, Joar to RAC, June, 1704, T70/14, f. 68). This was a different pattern from the rest of west Africa.

[17] Searing, *West African Slavery*, 28–31.

difficult to recover of the Negroes any thing that was in the hands of ye deceased."[18] Given the scarcity of local slaves, the lack of enthusiasm for European and East India merchandise that sold well in other parts of West Africa, and the resistance of Senegambians, Europeans could get neither settlements and plantations nor large numbers of slaves in this region.

Between the southern rivers of Senegambia and the western limit of the Gold Coast, there was little slave trading before the eighteenth century – this despite the large numbers the British carried away from the Sierra Leone region later in the 1700s. Apart from the Portuguese post at Cacheo, which seems to have had little regular contact with Lisbon, the RAC had forts at Bance Island in Sierra Leone and York Island at Sherboro. While the latter was home port for twenty-six vessels carrying on an extensive coasting trade, the commodity basis of this trade is obvious from the fact that we have records of only nineteen slave ships leaving these two trading centres between 1663 and 1713 – each ship carrying only 124 slaves on average.[19] A Gambia-type pattern of trade apparently held here into the eighteenth century.

The ability of Africans to resist was a key factor in the distinctive pattern of Afro-European relations in both Senegambia and the Windward Coast. The previous chapter examined the overall effect of African resistance, but no one has assessed the regional imbalances in the nature and instances of that resistance. Market breakdowns, with its risks of costly violence, as well as slave rebellions were considerably more frequent in some regions than in others. Such imbalance led in turn to regional cost differentials and variations in the number of slaves carried into the Atlantic trade. Trading rules had to be learned, which put a premium on the factor. "[T]o send him (an inexperienced man) abroad is the same thing as to kill him," wrote the RAC factor at James Fort, "for the natives will soone do it for the Goods he carryes with him as soon as they find he doth not understand them nor the Custom of the countryes."[20] Tied selling was as likely to be an African as a European practice. At one stage the company told its agent not to buy slaves, to which the factor responded, "although yor Slaves as you write me yields you but little after Freight and Charges paid & that Hides turn to no acct .... [t]hese things I cannot help, it is the traffique of the country & such Goods must be bought if you will Trade at all ...."[21] Fever-afflicted ships were at continual risk. In 1715, a nonslave ship with its crew disabled was

[18]   Thomas Thurloes, Gambia, to RAC, May 28, 1678, T70/10, ff. 2–3.
[19]   *TSTD*. Mean = 123.7, sd = 30.4, n = 16. The nineteen voyages is not a complete record, but the slave trade from Sierra Leone and Sherboro is unlikely to have attained an average of as much as one small ship a year in the half-century before 1714.
[20]   John Kastell, James Fort to RAC, October 14, 1682, T70/16, f. 44.
[21]   *Ibid.*, See also RAC to Gresham, Pile, and Rayner, James Fort, October 3, 1700, T70/51, f. 75.

taken over by the king of Barra, when "his people going on board with teeth to trade .... seeing (the) condition (of the crew) seized on them without doing any hurt to any of them and run her ashore." The following year the fort was in danger. "I have but four men in all," the factor wrote, "the negroes Dayly threaten us with cutting off ...."[22] Francis Moore's proposal a few years later to reduce such risks by having all slaves acquired upstream shipped directly to James Fort was thus not a complete answer.[23] During the seventeenth and eighteenth centuries sixty-one instances of slave ships being cut off by shore-based Africans exist. Senegambia and the Windward Coast are hugely overrepresented in this admittedly small sample. In the *Trans-Atlantic Slave Trade Database* these two northern trading regions account for less than 10 percent of departures from Africa but nearly 60 percent of all attacks by shore-based Africans.

As with the incidence of violent disputes between African and European market participants, ships that experienced slave revolts were also distributed unequally across regions. Resistance per se was, of course, universal. Forcing people against their will to board cramped ships required unrelenting vigilance on the part of those in control. The shackles and elaborate baricados erected while slaving was in progress, designed to prevent slaves from even seeing the land and people they were about to leave, are testimony to this. Captains in all regions had to cope with slaves refusing to eat, attempting to escape, and assaulting crew members. The incidence of rebellion was not, however, the same everywhere. Records of 382 slave-ship revolts exist and, given the fact that two-thirds of revolts occurred at the port of lading or within a week of setting sail, it is possible to identify the African region of departure for 342.

Table 7-4 (p. 181) compares the distribution of regional origins of all slave ships leaving Africa with the distribution of those experiencing slave revolts. Column 3 in this table provides a crude index of representativeness of the data on revolts. A figure of one here indicates that the proportion of voyages experiencing slave revolts was the same as the proportion of all slave voyages leaving the region. Less than one indicates fewer revolts than the number of voyages known to have left the region would lead us to expect, and greater than one indicates a greater probability of revolt. Only three regions have values in column 3 in excess of one, the same three in fact that are prominent in the small sample of ships that were cut off as discussed earlier – though the Windward Coast is the least prominent of the three in this instance and the Senegambia and Gabon regions by far the most overrepresented.[24] Moreover,

---

[22] David Francis, Gambia, January 28, 1715, CO388/18 pt. 1, Document O27; idem, December 21, 1716, T70/26, p. 55.

[23] Francis Moore, *Travels into the Inland Parts of Africa* (London, 1738), p. 57.

[24] Lambert, 73:376.

it is likely that when rebellions did occur, they were more severe on ships leaving at least one of the higher risk areas than those leaving elsewhere. An average of fifty-seven slaves per incident died in eighteen revolts on ships in Senegambia region compared to twenty-four per incident in forty-nine revolts elsewhere on the coast. The only records of the manacling of female slaves – women and children were normally unshackled – are in the Gambia region.[25]

Nor was the resistance limited to slave ships. Some of the bloodiest incidents occurred before the slaves embarked. The ferocity of the resistance – in effect, the determination of the slaves not to give up whatever the odds – appears large even against the broader backdrop of the annals of slave resistance in the Americas. It is worth quoting one early incident that took place at James Fort in the Gambia in 1681.

On the 24 November I had 105 Male slaves on the Island. They all tooke an Oath to rebell & Drink the blood of the White men [T]hey begun their Rebellion at 3 o'clock in the Afternoone. I had yn 19 whitemen on the Island & they continued the fight till 7 a Clock then I held a Parly with them. [T]heir answer was that they rebelled wth a designe to dye & dye they would. In the Morning I had severall of the Natives came to assist me then I drew up my men & winged them the length of the Houses were ye Slaves were and told them they were all to dye in a moment [if] they did not yield. [T]hey still continued their resolution then I entered Their Houses & seized them, at the same time they begged all to dye per my hands for they had Deferred it. But in entring ye Houses I did not kill or wound one of them by reason they were soe few in Number .... in the first 4 howers [hours we had] Killed 34 & wounded 40.[26]

The account points to the exceptional number of male slaves in captivity, but what is most striking compared with later accounts of rebellions in the Americas is the tone of the report. The account is written without any of the moral outrage that colours its New World counterparts put together by planters and colonial officials. The latter often communicated a sense of betrayal. The RAC factor in the Gambia by contrast wrote matter of factly with the implication that such incidents were to be expected.

While historians have made little of the regional differentials discussed here, contemporaries were not unaware of them. Any ship in the Gambia with more than thirty slaves on board should expect a rebellion according to the RAC factor at James Fort.[27] Moore's injunction to move purchased slaves quickly downstream came from the rebelliousness of the slaves as well as what he perceived as the latent hostility of their sellers. In 1717 the South Sea Company hired the *Clapham* to carry slaves to the Spanish Caribbean, but when the owner discovered that the company wished to send the ship to

---

[25]   Calculated from David Eltis, Stephen D. Behrendt and David Richardson, "Revolts on Board Slave Ships; A Database," (unpublished, 1998).

[26]   John Kastell, James Is, to RAC, January 24, 1682, T70/16, f. 21.

[27]   David Francis, December 21, 1716, T70/26, p. 55.

the Gambia he threatened to withdraw his vessel and the company sent it to the Gold Coast instead.[28]

The Gold Coast proper (see Map 3 in the map section following appendices) contrasted sharply with Upper Guinea but from a European viewpoint nevertheless contains elements of paradox. Here a different Euro-African compromise occurred. The two peoples had an interest in what the other had to offer to a much greater extent than in Senegambia. Table C-1 (see Appendix C) contains English data only and, given non-RAC trading on this coast, not a complete picture of that. Nevertheless, the preeminence of the Gold Coast in European-African relations suggested by the table is no doubt accurate. Dutch trade conducted by the West Indian Company and others rivalled the English in scale and was even more focussed on the Gold Coast than its English counterpart. Thus while Table C-1 shows that 60 percent of the RAC's African trade was with the Gold Coast, a rough allowance for other European nations suggests that at least two-thirds of all merchandise arriving and leaving sub-Saharan Africa in the second half of the seventeenth century passed through the Gold Coast. Put another way, before the great surge in the Atlantic slave trade in the eighteenth century, the rest of Africa, including Senegambia, generated far less Atlantic trade than did the Gold Coast alone. The sustained European efforts to establish a permanent presence on the Gold Coast reflect this reality.

On the import side, the earliest European contacts on the Gold Coast had involved Portuguese and later Dutch ships carrying textiles and slaves into the region from other parts of Africa, a continuation of even earlier precontact coastal patterns.[29] Benin cloths continued to be in demand in the late seventeenth century despite the availability of European and East Indian cloth, and estimates of imports based on European exports alone will understate the true import level. The distribution of merchandise categories in Table C-1 thus shows a continuation of a well-established pattern. No less than 85 percent of all textiles that the Royal African Company shipped to West Africa were absorbed by a mere 300 kilometers of coastline that constituted the Gold Coast. Put another way, as Table 7-2 shows, over three-quarters by value of all the RAC's merchandise imports into the Gold Coast were textiles, and the company went to great lengths to ensure that they kept abreast of shifting African tastes.[30] However, Atlantic trade did bring something new that is not shown in either Table 7-2 or C-1. Two products of the

---

[28] Add ms, 25,497, pp. 145, 178, 188, 198. The riverine environment may have been a key factor here. The company minutes make clear the profound unhappiness of the owner but not its cause.

[29] Daaku, *Trade and Politics on the Gold Coast*, 24.

[30] Davies, *Royal African Company*, 177. Davies' discussion of European textiles, indeed merchandise, intended for Africa in the early modern period (pp. 165–79) can hardly be bettered.

Americas, rum from the British Caribbean and Brazil and rolls of tobacco from Brazil, though far behind textiles in value, were probably the second and third most important commodity imported along the Gold Coast. More than 60,000 gallons of rum a year arrived after 1698.[31] Prior to 1700, the Portuguese sold their tobacco on the Gold Coast (mostly to the Dutch) and then bought their slaves on the Slave Coast. If the Portuguese accounted for as much as half the slaves taken from the Slave Coast (as Table 7-1 suggests for the years after 1680) and brought cargoes in exchange comprising 80 percent tobacco, then produce from the Americas may be estimated at between 5 and 10 percent of Gold Coast imports at the end of the seventeenth century.[32]

Africans initially obtained these goods with gold carried down to the coast by the Arcany and Denkyra merchants in whose territory most of the deposits were to be found. It was this commodity that led to the second largest European presence in numbers and largest in fortifications anywhere in sub-Saharan Africa. At the beginning of the eighteenth century there were twenty-three occupied European forts and factories from Dutch Axim, a few kilometres east of Cape Three Points, to Christiansborg or Danish Accra, less than 300 kilometers to the west. Twelve were English and nine were Dutch, with the two largest, Dutch Elmina and the English Cape Coast Castle, each holding up to five hundred so-called castle slaves (none of them local to the area) as skilled craftsmen, laborers, and soldiers.[33] The number of European permanent residents is unlikely to have exceeded five hundred on the whole of the Gold Coast at this time so that the ratio of Europeans to African slaves (within the European settlements) was not unlike that in the

---

[31] For the calculations supporting this statement see Appendix C.

[32] For tobacco on the Gold Coast see Thomas Bucknell, Succondee, to CCC, April 22, 1686, Rawlinson manuscript, c. 745, f. 343; idem, February 20, 1687, *ibid.*, c. 745, f. 437, "here hath lately passed by three Pourtugues one from Lisbon haveing only a slave cargo aboard, ye other two had tobacco . . . ." When an RAC captain took a Bahian ship in 1690 it contained "gold, rum and tobacco" (RAC to Humfries, Wight, and Whiting, CCC, March 19, 1691, T70/50, ff. 117; RAC to Platt, Ronan and Melross, CCC, March 19, 1695, T70/50, ff. 162). Bosman wrote "For the Portuguese come on this coast . . . selling their American Commodities viz Brazil Tobacco, Brandy and Rum," *A New and Accurate Description of the Coast of Guinea* (London, 1705, reprinted 1967), p. 89; see also Paul Hair (ed.), *Barbot on Guinea: The Writings of Jean Barbot on Africa* (London, 1992), p. 419, though, as the editors note, this passage may have been cribbed from Bosman. See also John Brown, CCC, to RAC, December 16, 1703, T70/28, ff. 14; Dalby Thomas, CCC, to RAC, February 12, 1704, T70/14, f. 23.

[33] Davies, *Royal African Company*, 240–64 describes these establishments. For additional detail see the various petitions in T70/170, ff. 6, 36, and T70/175, ff. 65–88, which Davies appears not to have used. For maps see Van Dantzig, *The Dutch and the Guinea Coast*, facing p. 1; and Davies, *Royal African Company*, 246.

Caribbean islands.[34] While the larger establishments had extensive cultivated areas around them, no fort commanded much more than a few square miles of territory and, as noted earlier, despite the best efforts of the Europeans, the latter were centers of trade, not production. The initial reason for constructing such large establishments was to secure the gold from pirates, other European merchants, and Africans until it could be shipped to Europe. Despite the forts, however, a much larger share of the gold than the slaves of the region was bought by interlopers – non-company vessels operating chiefly out of England and the Netherlands.[35]

By the second half of the seventeenth century, slaves were of growing significance with perhaps an average of one thousand five hundred people a year entering the traffic from this stretch of coast. Both the Dutch and English used their major forts as collecting points for slaves; the smaller forts send their slaves to headquarters rather than loading them directly on to the company ships.[36] The forts thus came to assume a secondary and slave-trading role. Prior to the great increase in the non-company trade after 1698, probably over half of all Gold Coast slaves bound for the Americas passed through Elmina or Cape Coast Castle. Only after 1709 did other embarkation points, especially Anomabu, emerge. But this did not entail any shift in the finely balanced trading relationship between Europeans and Africans. In contrast to Senegambia, Africans on the Gold Coast offered more women than men for sale, about whom Chapter 4 indicates that Europeans were not enthused. If Europeans had accepted more women, then the numbers entering the Atlantic trade would have grown faster than they did on this part of the coast. In the seventeenth century, Gold Coast slaves were highly prized in the British Caribbean, but so also were men slaves. Nevertheless, Europeans did, perhaps, adjust their preferences gradually. The proportion of men slaves leaving the Gold Coast fell from 52 percent of all slaves between 1662–97 to 47 percent in the 1698–1713 period, and the proportion of children doubled from less than 6 percent to 12 percent.[37]

---

[34] For its Gold Coast forts the RAC listed 226 European personnel in 1698 and 218 in 1703 (see T70/170, ff. 6 and 36). The 1703 figure is nearly 50 percent greater than the one Davies cites for that year (*Royal African Company*, 248).

[35] The English factors in the smaller Gold Coast forts almost always complained about the lack of gold, not slaves, when an interloper ship appeared on the coast. For a similar assessment for Dutch interlopers see Postma, *The Dutch in the Atlantic Slave Trade*, 80–1.

[36] The Rawlinson manuscripts, which contain the letters written by the factors at the smaller forts to the chief factors at Cape Coast Castle, provide a detailed micro-level view of this process. Some transatlantic vessels received a few of their slaves at these places, but most slaves were sent to the castle on coasting sloops.

[37] Based on a *t*-test of mean men and child ratios of twenty-eight shipments before 1698 (8,807 slaves) and fifty shipments, in the years 1698–1713 (15,210 slaves). Differences statistically significant at the 5 percent level. All data are from the *TSTD*.

Table 7-3. *Relative Shares of Types of Merchandise Traded for Gold and
Slaves on the Gold Coast, 1662–1703*

	Slaves	Gold
English textile @ £2 per piece or more (wool)	41.2	28.7
East Indian cloth @ less than £1 a piece	19.4	22.5
Iron	7.5	3.0
English textile @ less than £2 a piece (sheets)	7.3	15.8
Cowries	5.9	0.3
Gunpowder	5.7	1.9
European cloth	5.6	17.0
Guns	3.8	2.9
Brandy	1.3	2.6
Pewter containers	0.7	1.0
Manilos	0.5	0.6
Knives	0.5	1.9
Beads	0.3	0.2
Brass basins	0.1	1.0
Other	0.2	0.6
Total	100.0	100.0
Number of cargoes in sample	23	30
Total value of cargoes (in current £s)	11,676	78,345

Source: T70/1222 and 1223.

This happened despite war at sea, which increased transportation costs and
put a premium on carrying higher-value slaves. In fact, everywhere else on
the coast the ratio of men rose temporarily and that of children fell between
these periods.[38] As Europeans sought more slaves from what had been an
underutilized provenance zone, they accommodated themselves to African
preferences for selling women slaves.

Table 7-3 provides a summary of the types of goods making up a total
of fifty-three cargoes that the RAC carried to the Gold Coast in the late
seventeenth century. Thirty of these were for gold and 23 for slaves. The
overwhelming preponderance of textiles to be exchanged for both slaves and
gold is striking, as is the fact that textiles formed a larger share of the typical
slave cargo (84 percent) than of the cargo intended for gold (74 percent).
Clearly, there were differences between goods intended for slaves and goods
intended for gold, otherwise the RAC would not have gone to the trouble
of separating out the cargoes. But the differences do not seem related to the
nature of the African commodity offered in exchange, at least in this period.
Guns and gunpowder were twice as important in the slave than in the gold
cargoes but together they comprised less than 10 percent of the total traded
for either gold or slaves and, if we allow for rum imports (not shown here),

[38]   See Galenson, *Traders, Planters and Slaves*, 93–114 for a discussion of this issue.

they would be even smaller. In fact differences are more likely related to the region of origin of the slaves and gold than to the fact that it was slaves rather than gold that was being traded. Most of the gold came from the eastern part of the Gold Coast, "windward" of Cape Coast Castle in the English parlance, whereas before the 1690s most of the slaves came from the central or western region.[39] The relative importance of cowries in the cargoes exchanged for slaves may be accounted for by the proximity of this region to the cowrie-consuming Slave Coast. Overall, the distribution of major product types shown in Table 7-3 is not much different from that for exports from England as a whole. The share of English and European cloth and metals among all RAC exports was similar to the share of textiles and metals among all English exports at the end of the seventeenth century. On the Gold Coast, 47 percent of total exports were categories of English woollen cloth (including the Castle cargoes not shown in Table 7-3), with perpetuanas (a durable English woollen cloth, usually dyed blue) accounting for just under one-fifth of all merchandise. Woollen cloth comprised 46 percent of all English exports and reexports combined in 1697–9.[40]

As already noted, the slave-gold mix shifted sharply at the end of the century in response to a change in the relative price of gold to slaves. From the Gold Coast, the Dutch director-general commented that "the natives no longer occupy themselves with the search for gold, but rather make war on each other to furnish slaves."[41] Slave departures between 1700 and 1713 were quadruple those of the previous four decades, with Table 7-1 showing nearly six thousand a year entering the Atlantic trade in these years.[42] Less is known of the types of goods shipped in this period than in the previous decades, but sample cargoes and trade statistics later in the century show guns and gunpowder rising to nearly 10 percent of the total,[43] though textiles continued to be by far the largest import category on the Gold Coast. The

---

[39] The term "windward cargo" in the RAC records invariably means a cargo intended for gold. Occasionally, part of such cargoes were used to buy slaves. The largest example of this I have found was for *Princess Ann* (voyage id 9,821) in 1689, which bought fifty-eight slaves with about one-fifth of the cargo. See August 19, 1689, T70/968.

[40] For British exports, 1697–9 see Brian R. Mitchell, *British Historical Statistics*, second ed. (Cambridge, 1988), pp. 448, 468. RAC exports calculated from T70/1222 and 1223.

[41] Van Dantzig, *The Dutch and the Guinea Coast*, 112. See also Davies, *Royal African Company*, 360.

[42] As there are more likely to be gaps in the estimates in Table 7-1 in the later period than in the earlier, the slave trade probably more than quadrupled in the early eighteenth century.

[43] Ray A. Kea, "Firearms and Warfare on the Gold and Slave Coasts from the Sixteenth to the Nineteenth Centuries," *Journal of African History*, 12(1971): pp. 185–213. Eltis, "Trade Between Western Africa and the Atlantic World Before 1870," 218, estimates between 8 and 9 percent by value of all imports for the 1780s.

rise in both the price and the quantity of slaves shipped was probably not enough to sustain trade at the value Atlantic trade had attained in the 1680s. Total gold exports are more difficult to track than slave departures, but in the first decade of the eighteenth century the Dutch West India Company carried only half the volume of gold from the coast that it had in the 1680s.[44] If this mirrored the overall trend – and Curtin estimated that the Dutch Company accounted for more than half the gold leaving the coast – then the rise in the value of slaves leaving the Gold Coast after 1700 could not at first have been nearly sufficient to offset this decline.[45] Thus, unlike other parts of sub-Saharan Africa, the Gold Coast experienced a declining rather than an increasing capacity to pay for imported goods after the 1680s. From this perspective, then, the rising volume of slave departures from the Gold Coast may be seen as an ultimately unsuccessful attempt to maintain the flow of Atlantic imports threatened by diminishing gold production. The increased warfare that the Dutch and English factors observed in the early 1700s could have been struggles over a smaller and shrinking export pie as much as an attempt to capture more slaves in response to higher slave prices. From the African standpoint, slaves were an alternative way of obtaining the same broad type of goods that were traded for gold.

The accommodation between Africans and Europeans on the Gold Coast was thus more complex than just an African response to rising prices for slaves in the Americas. The extent of the interchange between the two peoples was greater here than in any other region, and in scale was a polar opposite to the position in Senegambia. In contrast to Senegambia, Europeans had a much clearer idea of the source of the gold, they had a wider military presence on the coast, and they had a product that at least some part of the population apparently desired. Yet two points stand out. First, Europeans came no closer to gaining control of production – of gold or anything else of commercial value – than they did in Senegambia. The slave trade here emerged as a second-best alternative for both sides. For Europeans it was a recognition that they could not establish viable productive enterprises on the African mainland. They could control African labour for such activities only by removing it from Africa. For Africans, selling slaves was a way of offsetting the effects of declining gold output. Africa's share of world gold output was too small for fluctuations in African output to have any impact on

---

44 Johannes Postma, "West African Exports and the Dutch West India Company, 1675–1731," *Economisch en Sociaal-Historisch Jaarboek*, 36(1973):71. As some of this gold may have originated in Brazil, the decline in African exports may have been even greater than these figures suggest.

45 Even if slave exports had been running at ten thousand a year instead of the six thousand suggested in Table 7-1, and, in addition, slave prices had doubled in 1700–13 period compared to the 1680s, the additional value of the slave trade to the Gold Coast would still have amounted to less than half of the drop in gold exports.

the world price of gold. By contrast, Africans comprised at least 95 percent of the slaves in the Americas. When demand for slaves from the Americas increased, the impact on prices was immediate and facilitated the switch from gold to slaves. But Europeans also adjusted to African preferences on the age and sex of slaves in this region, and this also facilitated the increased flow of people into slavery in the Americas.

The second key point is that, even on the Gold Coast, Africans were not dependent on Europeans. Curtin has estimated total African gold exports in the 1680s at 1,700 kilograms a year, 95 percent of this from the Gold Coast. The price of gold on the Coast through the 1680s was £3.75 an ounce or £30 per mark. Total annual gold exports were thus approximately £215,000. Total slave departures are not known, but Table 7-1 estimates 1,500 a year with the real total not likely to have been in excess of 2,500. Table 6-1 suggests slave prices in the 1680s averaged £3.29 prime cost or £6.6 on the coast. Taking 2,500 as the upper limit, then the value of slaves leaving the coast was £16,500 – less than one-tenth the value of gold exports. Capital inflows in the form of fort construction as well as servicing those forts would have been significant at this time, but the value of goods carried to the Gold Coast in the 1680s by Europeans could well have approached £400,000 per year.[46] The seventeenth-century population of what is today an area somewhat larger than Ghana must have numbered in the millions.[47] Per capita exports into the Atlantic area would thus have been less than £0.4 and probably in the range of £0.1 to £0.3. This compares with per capita exports from England and Wales of about £1 in 1700, from the Chesapeake of about £2.25, and from Barbados of about £7.3.[48] Given the two-thirds share of European–sub-Saharan African trade going to the Gold Coast and the absence of any indication that other parts of the West African littoral were populated more lightly than the Gold Coast, per capita exports from the rest of sub-Saharan Africa at this time were much smaller. No other region could have shipped as much as £0.1 on a per capita basis, and the Bight of Biafra and west-central Africa would have been exporting far below this level.

It is thus hard to imagine that, overall, imports from the Atlantic world made much of an impact on the lives of African residents of the Gold Coast

[46] For explanations of the valuations used here as well as some indication of the value of RAC castle cargoes – the merchandise intended for the maintenance of forts as opposed to purchasing gold or slaves – see Eltis, "The Relative Importance of Slaves and Commodities." For gold exports see Curtin, "Africa and the Wider Monetary World," p. 247.

[47] Patrick Manning estimates between 2.5 and 3 million (*Slavery and African Life*, 65–6).

[48] See David Eltis, "New Estimates of Exports from Barbados and Jamaica, 1665–1701," *William and Mary Quarterly*, 53(1995):646–8, for a discussion of per capita exports.

in the late seventeenth century. Those living in the vicinity of the forts (for example, the king of Fetue and his immediate entourage) would have had daily experience of European goods, as would the gold producers and merchants of Arcanie. Given the quantities discussed here, as well as the relatively high quality of the imported textiles discussed later, the non-elite could have had direct experience of the Atlantic trade only if they entered that trade as a slave. At this time, with departures in the 1,500 to 2,000 a year range and a population greater than one million, the risks of this were not as high as they were later to become.

It is hardly surprising to find that violent confrontation during trade and transportation from the Gold Coast was well below the levels experienced in (for Europeans) the high-risk regions. A much greater proportion of disputes were settled by negotiation. The practice of pawning, with its potential for disputes, had a long African lineage in this region but does not appear to have had as wide a usage in commercial relations between Africans and Europeans.[49] Europeans advanced credit from their shore-based establishments, and the permanence and relative extensiveness of these perhaps removed the need for pawning. English, Dutch, Danes, Brandenburgers, and Africans frequently accused each other of bad faith, but Afro-European incidents of the kind that plagued Upper Guinea were neither common nor enduring in their effect. In 1702, inexperienced tenpercenters (non-RAC traders allowed on the coast from 1698 in return for payment to the chartered company of 10 percent of the outbound cargo) carried people to Barbados that Africans deemed not to be slaves nor even in this case had been held as pawns. The company had to expend considerable effort and resources to return seventeen individuals to their homeland. Newcomers eventually learned the rules.[50] Gold Coast Coromantines had a reputation for resisting, especially among Jamaicans, but Table 7-4 shows that not only were cutoffs from the shore less frequent here than in Upper Guinea, but also the ratio of ships experiencing revolt was about average for West Africa as a whole. It is hard to believe that the Gold Coast would have claimed such an exceptionally large proportion of all Euro-African trade in 1700 if violence had been as common as in Upper Guinea.

---

[49] For examples of pawning on the Gold Coast see Ray A. Kea *Settlements, Trade, and Polities in the Seventeenth Century Gold Coast* (Baltimore, 1982), pp. 235, 237. However, the total amount of debt outstanding (pawns were security for debt) does not appear large relative to total trade (*ibid.*, 240 for estimates of amounts owed to the Dutch and English companies on the Gold Coast). Moreover, pawns do not figure prominently in either the Rawlinson or T70 correspondence at this time.

[50] For one of several instances see RAC to Browne, Major, and Willis, May 29, 1703, T70/51, 187; Charles Thomas, Barbados, to RAC, May 3, 1703, T70/13, f. 18.

Table 7-4. *Regional Origins of All Slave Voyages Leaving Africa Compared to Regional Origins of Slave Voyages Experiencing Slave Revolts, 1595–1867*

	All Slave Ships (%)	Slave Vessels with Revolts (%)	Col.2/Col.1
Senegambia	3.3	21.7	6.6
Sierra Leone-Windward Coast	6.0	19.1	3.2
Gold Coast	11.5	15.5	1.3
Bight of Benin	22.7	18.4	0.8
Bight of Biafra*	13.2	7.3	0.6
Gabon-Cape Lopez	0.5	4.7	9.4
West-Central Africa	37.6	10.8	0.3
Southeast Africa	5.1	2.6	0.5
Totals	100.0	100.0	1.0
Sample Size	14,491	342	

Note: *Bight of Biafra except for Gabon and Cape Lopez.
Sources: TSTD; "Revolts on Board Slave Ships: A Database" (unpublished, 1998).

To the west and south of the Gold Coast lay the Slave Coast (see Map 4), the Bight of Biafra (see Map 5), and west-central Africa (see Map 6), three regions that according to Table 7-1 supplied 80 percent of the slaves going into the Atlantic trade. Yet commodity exports from all these regions were so small and gold exports from the Gold Coast so large that even including slaves, these regions accounted for less than one-third of total trade between the Atlantic world and sub-Saharan Africa.[51] Of the three regions, Table 7-1 shows that despite its total lack of harbours, the Slave Coast earned its name. About half of all slaves leaving Africa by sea between 1662 and 1713 left from the Bight of Benin. West-central Africa is clearly underrepresented in Table 7-1 because data on the Portuguese are not as abundant as that for the Dutch and English, but correcting this bias would in no way threaten the Slave Coast's position as the major source of slaves in western African.

More striking even than the predominance of the Slave Coast at this time is the extraordinary geographic concentration of slave departures within the region. Before 1681, thirty-three out of thirty-five English vessels identified

[51] See Eltis, "The Relative Importance of Slaves and Commodities," 245, for RAC exports of merchandise broken down by region. If we accept the RAC aggregates as a proxy for English exports to Africa and take into account that non-English trade at this time (especially the Dutch and French) focussed on the Gold Coast and Senegambia, then the Slave Coast, the Bight of Biafra, and west-central Africa may well have absorbed far less than a quarter of all sub-Saharan Africa's Atlantic imports.

as embarking or intending to embark slaves on the Slave Coast went to Offra in Ardra, on the eastern Slave Coast. In the 1680s, equal numbers of English ships went to Offra and Whydah (thirty-five each) with only two Slave Coast vessels *not* going to these ports. Thereafter, Whydah accounted for all but four English ships going to the Slave Coast. Grand and Little Popo and Jakin appear only occasionally as embarkation points. A similar breakdown for other nationalities is not possible, but the Dutch began drawing on Whydah shortly after the English (trading little at Offrah after 1692), the French had only an intermittent presence anywhere before 1700, and the Dutch restricted Portuguese access to only four ports, one of which was Whydah.[52] In other words, the English pattern is broadly representative of the overall trend. By the end of the first decade of the eighteenth century it was not unusual to have over a dozen slave ships at one time waiting for dispatch at Whydah. The Dutch, French, and especially the Portuguese had joined the English at Whydah by 1710 with, of course, the active encouragement of the king, who sent a Whydah delegation to the French court. For Europeans, Whydah promised a large volume of slaves and a delivery time that compared well with the Gold Coast, as well as slave prices that were below those of any other region except the Bight of Biafra.[53] Preconquest Whydah dominated not just the Slave Coast but the coast as a whole. It is possible that in most years between 1690 and 1713 the port accounted for half of all Africans entering the Atlantic slave trade.

Whydah was not a major African power in its own right. It was loosely subject to the kingdom of Allada, the latter perhaps twice its size; Allada and Whydah together were smaller than the Dahomey state that absorbed them in the eighteenth century. Whydah's subjection to Allada became weaker in the late seventeenth and early eighteenth centuries, a process that might be connected with the increasing volume of Whydah's Atlantic trade but at 25 miles across and a population not likely to have exceeded two hundred thousand, it had as much in common with the trading states of the Niger Delta or even the Fetue kingdom on the Gold Coast than with the major empires of West Africa. It was often at war in this period as a consequence of Akwamu conquests on the Gold Coast and was frequently under threat.[54] Yet it was never at risk from Europeans. Despite the latter's increasing interest

---

[52]   *TSTD*. Unfortunately, a similar breakdown for Dutch and Portuguese ships is not possible because the data provide only the broad designation of Slave Coast or Elmina for these ships.

[53]   For slave prices, see Appendix B. For loading times, a small sample of ships with data on days spent on the coast between first slave purchase and departure to the Americas yields the following means (in days):
The Gambia 73.6 (sd 21.4, n = 17)
Gold Coast 93.9 (sd 44.2, n = 23)
Slave Coast 85.1 (sd 70.1, n = 18)

[54]   See Law, *Slave Coast of West Africa*, 225–60.

in Whydah as the slave trade expanded in the seventeenth and eighteenth centuries, Whydah eventually lost its independence to Dahomey, not to some transoceanic power.

Europeans, either individually or collectively, had no significant land-based power on the Slave Coast. Each of the major companies had establishments at Whydah after 1700 but these amounted to mere trading posts and were not comparable to the forts of the Gold Coast. They had few resident personnel and little fortification. Ships might be assigned temporary warehouses and lodgings but nothing more.[55] For protection, the Europeans were dependent on the king of Whydah, with the only European sanction being to quit the location and seek trade elsewhere. Such action was conceivable; as noted, between 1671 and 1692 the French, English, and eventually the Dutch switched from Offra to Whydah, but by the early 1700s the dominance of Whydah was such that real alternative markets appeared to lie outside the Bight of Benin altogether.[56] There was thus never any possibility of any European group excluding others from trade here or gaining privileges not available to all, though all Europeans tried "to ingross the trade."[57] In contrast to the Gold Coast and Angola, Europeans were sideline observers of relations among African polities in this region, not participants. Europeans could never contemplate breaches of African sovereignty of the kind that occurred before partition in the late nineteenth century. Whydah was thus a port in the European sense in that it was open to the ships of all nations but on terms laid down by the country in which the port was located. The duties and customs were set by the king of Whydah, and when European nations captured each other's ships during the War of the Spanish Succession, the king successfully imposed a moratorium on such activities in his waters that was respected throughout the hostilities.

If the king could impose such conditions on warring Europeans then he could enforce rules on Afro-European commerce, even though this commerce was in unwilling people. When John Wortley, the Royal African Company's factor, attempted to circumvent these rules in 1682, he was first imprisoned and then expelled. The king's subjects could expect equivalent treatment for similar transgressions. Table 7-4 also shows Europeans could expect a lower proportion of slave rebellions here than elsewhere on the coast.

Neither here nor in the Bight of Biafra was there a middle ground of any significance, either in the cultural or economic sense. Europeans simply did not have a large enough presence for one to develop. Plantation activities were never an option. Dalby Thomas, the chief factor at Cape Coast Castle, sent indigo plants to Whydah shortly after his arrival from England

---

[55] See Phillips' description of this process described in Churchill, *Collection of Voyages*, 6:233–4.
[56] Law, *Slave Coast of West Africa*, 127–33.
[57] William Hickes, Whydah to RAC, March 15, 1711, T70/5, f. 78.

and urged the RAC factor there, Capt. Willis, to explore the prospects of a commercial crop. The latter's restrained response was that "he fear[ed an] Indicao Plantation will not turn to acct" – an understatement given what the English controlled – and there is no evidence that the plants were ever put into the ground,[58] just as there is no indication that his more enthusiastic predecessor organized the locals to collect cotton in response to an earlier request. Europeans, indeed, could not even manage provision grounds, and all provisions, including those for slaves dispatched to the Americas, were sent to Whydah from the Gold Coast or Europe. The issue here was security rather than soil or climate. This was a trading relationship only; capital inflows were either very limited or nonexistent.

On the African side there was the familiar, strongly marked, differentiated, regional demand. Again, one or two product categories predominated. Table 7-2 suggests that cowries (virtually unknown anywhere else on the coast) and textiles made up between two-thirds and three-quarters of all goods imported by value.[59] A third product, rolls of tobacco from Bahia (not shown in the table), became important at the end of the period. Even then, however, it is not likely to have approached the second-ranked textile category.[60] Among textiles, East Indian products were most in demand. Comprising less than a quarter of the textiles traded on the Gold Coast, Asian textiles here claimed two-thirds of the import market (by value). With cloth from continental Europe accounting for most of the remainder there was little demand here for the English woollens so common on the Gold Coast.

Seventeenth- and eighteenth-century memoirists, nineteenth-century abolitionists, and twentieth-century scholars have written at length on Whydah and the Slave Coast in general. The question of why this small African state was so dominant in the slave trade still has no answer. The question of why, with all the income from its Atlantic trade and a significant military capability, Whydah was unable to retain its independence or, indeed, become a major power has yet to be addressed. Could it be that even on the Slave Coast the transatlantic slave trade was not the central event shaping African economic and political developments?

In the adjacent Bight of Biafra, the patterns of European-African relations were once more different from elsewhere. The European land-based presence was weakest of all here. There does not appear to have a been permanent European post in any Delta state at any point before the mid-nineteenth

---

[58]   Dalby Thomas, Cape Coast Castle, to Capt. Willis, Whydah, September 5, 1705, T70/5, p. 5.

[59]   For cowries see Jan S. Hogendorn and Marion Johnson, *The Shell Money of the Slave Trade* (Cambridge, 1986), though this work and, indeed, most discussions of cowries exaggerate their significance. In the late seventeenth century, cowries could not have comprised as much as 10 percent of total imports into sub-Saharan Africa as a whole.

[60]   Law, *Slave Coast of West Africa*, 203–4.

century, and crews spent little time ashore.[61] In short, there was no one here to whom the RAC could send its boxes of experimental plants. The king of Bonny invited the English to establish a fort and provision grounds here in 1701 and sent members of his family to London and Paris on separate occasions to encourage trade, but while relations among governing elites were cordial, the trade remained a modified *troque sous voile*.[62] The English dominated here more than in other regions, despite the fact that the Dutch had been the most important traders at New Calabar in mid-century and the Portuguese, probably from São Tomé rather than Brazil, were frequent visitors. Ivory made up 5 percent of the seventeenth-century English Chartered Company cargoes from the region, with slaves accounting for the remainder.[63]

But what really separates the region is the pattern of slave departures. Table 7-1 shows that while almost every other coastal region saw rising numbers of slaves entering the Atlantic slave trade between 1662 and 1713, the trend line for Bight of Biafra ports is in the opposite direction. Departures in the last decade of this period, 1704–13, while somewhat higher than the total for the 1690s, were still well below those of the 1660s and 1670s. From the long perspective, even the level of slave departures of the 1660s was only one-sixth what it was to become 120 years later, and for most of the 1660–1720 era was only one-tenth of later levels.[64] As noted earlier, the data are incomplete, but there is little mention anywhere of French- and Brazilian-bound Portuguese trade here. More complete data would not likely change the trends described earlier.

European slave traders found many aspects of the Bight of Biafra slave-trading environment relatively uncongenial. Among slaves, shipboard mortality was the highest of all the major regions. Almost one-third of the slaves leaving Bight of Biafra ports between 1663 and 1713 never made it to the Americas, whereas in no other region was the ratio higher than one-fifth.[65]

---

[61] For one of the few seventeenth-century descriptions of the Delta ports, mostly drawn from a voyage made in 1699, see Hair, *Barbot on Guinea*, 670–713.

[62] RAC to the "Great King of Bandie," September 15, 1702, T70/51, f. 150.

[63] The first recorded ivory cargo (that is merchandise to be exchanged for ivory) from England was 1663, and T70/1222 contains 38 ivory cargoes compared to 113 dispatched for slaves, but in constant pounds the former amount to only 5.4 percent of all RAC and Company of Royal African Adventurer trade goods sent into the Bight of Biafra before 1700.

[64] Richardson, "Slave Exports from West and West-Central Africa."

[65] TSTD. For the Bight of Biafra there are records of thirty-one voyages, mean 0.313, sd 0.191. The overall mean for 517 voyages sailing from all regions was 0.1836, sd 0.166. The Bight of Biafra sample is small but the differences are statistically significant at the 5 percent level, and the pattern is well established for other periods as well. See Stanley L. Engerman and Herbert S. Klein, "Long-Term Trends in African Mortality in the Transatlantic Slave Trade," *Slavery and Abolition*, 18(1997):44.

As most slaves died from dehydration arising from gastrointestinal disease, more Bight of Biafra survivors arrived in the Americas in a highly emaciated condition than those from elsewhere. Further, almost half the slaves supplied in this region were females, with the prevalence of the Bight of Biafra being largely responsible for the nearly balanced sex ratio of the early slave trade to Barbados. While the male ratio rose slightly over time, the planter ideal of obtaining mainly men slaves looked particularly unrealisable in this region. Between 1662 and 1713, this was the only region on the African coast where more women than men left for the Americas, and the male ratio reached 50 percent only because of the boys in the trade. Indeed, throughout the slave-trade era, the forced migrant stream from the Bight of Biafra always contained fewer men (and males) than elsewhere on the African coast.[66] And when men were available in sufficient numbers, they tended to be of shorter stature than in other regions, reflecting in part, perhaps, the yam-based diet of the Igbo lands closest to the embarkation points as opposed, say, to the higher protein diets in the Gambia.[67] These characteristics helped contribute to planter aversion for people from "the Bite" as the region was known in the Caribbean. "Wee shall find miserable sales for those that come from Callabare, unless they bee of better stature and in better condition than they have yett come thence," wrote the Barbados agents of the RAC in 1675.[68] As we might expect, prices in the Americas were somewhat lower for slaves from this region.[69]

Within the Bight of Biafra slaves left from only three embarkation points: Old Calabar, New Calabar, and Bonny.[70] Few ships took on slaves at Bonny,

---

[66] Appendix A; Eltis and Engerman, "Was the Slave Trade Dominated by Men?"

[67] David Eltis, "Nutritional Trends in Africa and the Americas, 1819–1839," *Journal of Interdisciplinary History*, 12(1982):453–75.

[68] Letter dated November, 26, 1675, CO268/1, p. 37. For similar comments from other parts of the Caribbean see John Huffam, Nevis, to RAC, May 25, 1710, T70/8, f. 54; idem, December 3, 1711, *ibid.*, 60; RAC to Charles Chaplin, Jamaica, February 23, 1703, T70/58, f. 28.

[69] Why did the English take so many slaves from this region, both in 1660s and 1670s as well as in the eighteenth century? In the mid-1660s, a report on the activities of the Company of Royal Adventurers referred to "the Byte, from whence so many more Sarvants may easily be procured" (CO1/19, f. 7v). Estimates from a later period suggest larger ships as well as faster loading rates coupled with the manning and efficiency advantages of the English as slave traders that perhaps counted for more here than elsewhere on the coast.

[70] The coast toward Cape Lopez, including the Gabon estuary, an important source of slaves later in the eighteenth and nineteenth centuries, was at this point used for wood, water, and provisions though it supplied some slaves to the offshore islands of Principe and São Tomé. See Michel François and Nathalie Picard-Tortorici, *La Traite des Esclaves au Gabon du XVIIe au XIXe Siècle: Essai de Quantification pour le XVIIIe siècle* (Paris, 1993), p. 37; and Henry Bucher, "The Atlantic Slave Trade and the Gabon Estuary: The Mpongwe to 1860," in Paul E. Lovejoy (ed.), *Africans in Bondage: Studies in Slavery and the Slave Trade* (Madison, Wis., 1986): pp. 137–8.

and none at all before 1699, according to the RAC records at least. Thus New Calabar dominated the 1660s and Old Calabar the rest of the period.[71] Indeed, about one-third of the decline in Bight of Biafra departures may be attributed to the demise of New Calabar as a major embarkation centre and the apparent failure at this time of the adjacent port of Bonny to compensate. Changes in demand cannot explain this unusual phenomenon. As already noted, English planters preferred slaves from the Gold Coast and the Bight of Benin, but this was true as long as the slave trade endured. Slave prices in Biafran ports held up fairly well after 1690 despite declines in numbers of departures.[72] The major reason for the pattern thus appears to lie on the supply rather than the demand side. The small polities that dealt with the Europeans obtained most slaves by canoe from the Igbo areas upstream. They were quintessentially trading communities, buying most of the slaves they sold rather than carrying out the enslavement themselves. African authorities at all three embarkation points oversaw relatively orderly trading. Despite the fact that Europeans did not establish a land-based presence here, there is little evidence of pawning in the seventeenth century and, when these practices developed later, they were largely confined to Old Calabar. The area was not without disputes, but the best-known incidents, involving both slave traders and slaves, occurred later in the eighteenth century.[73] Europeans and Africans arranged credit, the order in which ships were slaved, and customs levies without recourse to frequent violence, and as Table 7-4 shows, the proportion of ships experiencing slave revolts here was among the lowest on the coast.

As elsewhere, Biafran slave traders required particular trade goods in payment for slaves. As Table 7-2 indicates, in sharp contrast to other parts of West Africa, they did not want textiles. Eighty percent of the merchandise that the English chartered companies carried into the three Bight of Biafra ports comprised metals, with, by value, twice as much copper as iron arriving at this period. A further 14 percent comprised manillas (decorator armlets and anklets) and rangoes. While the region accounted for less than

---

[71]   A detailed survey of the coast, c. 1665, suggests the Company of Royal Adventurers did not trade at Bonny ("A Brief Narrative of the Trade and Present Condition of the Company . . . ," CO1/19, ff. 7–8). On the other hand, one of chief men at Bonny was known to Europeans by a name derived from an English slave captain who traded at Bonny in the 1660s (Hair, *Barbot on Guinea*, 708). This trade does not, however, show up in the slave-ship data set. Only about one-quarter of the English records for this region give the specific point of embarkation. The generic "Bite" is the usual designation for vessels from the Bight of Biafra. The term "Old Calabar" may have included Bonny at this time. See infra, p. 249.

[72]   Hair, *Barbot on Guinea*, 698–700 cites prices in bars for 1700–4 suggesting prices had not declined, although, as is often the case, the composition of the bar in these transactions is not specified.

[73]   See Eltis, Behrendt, and Richardson, "Africa in the Atlantic World: Slave Ship Revolts and African Agency in the Early Modern Era" (forthcoming).

15 percent of all goods carried to sub-Saharan Africa from London before
1700, it absorbed two-thirds of the copper and iron bars. A rough calculation using the prices, quantities, and values of metals shown in Tables 6-1,
7-1, and 7-2 suggests that Old and New Calabar and Bonny imported on
average about 60 tons of iron and 42 tons of copper per year between 1662
and 1713.[74] If this metal was made up into tools, implements, and weapons
it would have provided the materials for perhaps eighty thousand iron and
copper items per year, which, depending on one's estimate of the population,
appears large enough to have had some impact on life in the area over the
course of several years.[75] At the very least, it would seem that the supply
of these semi-processed materials was a central part of the accommodation
between Africans and Europeans and that failure to supply them would have
meant far fewer slaves for the English. Textiles, pans and kettles, cowries,
miscellaneous manufactured goods, tobacco, and alcohol (locally produced
palm wine remained the preferred stimulant) would not sell here. If for any
reason a ship headed for the region was forced to unload its goods at Cape
Coast Castle, the factors there would immediately ask for a replacement ship
to complete the journey, for "wee shall never sell them (the goods) here."[76]

Gabon, at the southern limits of the Bight of Biafra, was different from
the rest of the region. The volume of trade here in both commodities and
slaves was low in this period, a pattern that was no doubt connected with
the high incidence of violence in the region. Problems in the Gabon River
began early and persisted throughout the slave-trading era. African authorities "panyarred" not just individual Europeans but five complete vessels
and their crews in 1683, with no apparent distinction as to nationality –
Portuguese, English, and Dutch were among the five.[77] For reasons that had
more to do with European power relations, the Portuguese government tried
without success to channel the slave trade to Bahia into routes leaving the
Senegambian (actually Cape Verde) and Cape Lopez regions. They created
a Corisco Company in 1723 (Corisco Island is a few miles from the Gabon
estuary) and planned a fort in the region. Not surprisingly, planters and
shipowners ignored the initiative and continued to draw overwhelmingly on
the Mina Coast and Angola.[78]

---

[74] This estimate assumes an average price for slaves of £4 and that the English
Chartered Companies accounted for one-sixth of the merchandise carried into
the Bight of Biafra.

[75] These estimates assume implements each taking up three to four pounds of iron
and two to three pounds of copper.

[76] Bradley, Hollis, Harbin, and Spurway, CCC, to RAC, October, 20, 1679, T70/20,
f. 38.

[77] Thomas Woolman, São Tomé, August 25, 1683, Rawlinson manuscript, c. 745,
f. 283.

[78] Verger, *Trade Relations Between the Bight of Benin and Bahia* 42–65, but especially p. 55.

Finally, in Angola, a term broadly applied to the region south of Cape Lopez but fronting the largest slave provenance zone in sub-Saharan Africa, European-African relations were a curious amalgam of the patterns on the Gold Coast on the one hand and in the Bight of Biafra on the other. The Luanda enclave was more akin to the former. Luanda town was described, perhaps optimistically, in the mid-1660s as having three thousand whites and a prodigious multitude of blacks; most of the latter were slaves of the former.[79] This was the largest concentration of both Europeans and European-owned slaves in Africa at this time. As a result of their conquest of the kingdom of the Ndongo and their weakening of the Kongo state, the Portuguese had consolidated their hold on Angola by 1683. Atlantic trade was confined entirely to slaves who, except during the wars of conquest, originated beyond the frontiers of Portuguese influence. Portuguese Angola became a conduit for trade and in itself yielded nothing that the Atlantic economy valued.[80] Only the Portuguese carried slaves from Luanda, most of them to Brazil, mainly Bahia. Table 7-2 does not take into account any of this trade but, given the depressed state of the Brazilian economy before the Minas Gerais gold boom, the numbers cannot have matched those carried by the Dutch and English to the Caribbean. Nevertheless, this was the one area in western Africa where the European-African frontier moved a couple of hundred kilometres inland and where traders on the African coast sent their own shipments of slaves to the Americas.[81]

North of the Congo River, at Cabinda and Malimbo chiefly, the Dutch, English, and eventually the French bought slaves and small quantities of ivory. In this period, European-African relations mirrored those in the Bight

[79] Michael Angels of Gatlina and Denis de Carli of Piacenza, "A Curious and Exact Account of a Voyage to Congo In the Years 1666 and 1667," in Churchill, *A Collection of Voyages*, 1:491; Charles R. Boxer, *Portuguese Society in the Tropics* (Madison, Wis., 1965), pp. 120–34, though Boxer reflects older interpretations of the effects of the slave trade on white society.

[80] Birmingham, *The Portuguese Conquest*, 31–41. Records of actual slave voyages, as opposed to annual summaries of slave departures or impressionistic estimates, scarcely exist before the 1720s. Thereafter, Herbert S. Klein presents data for 1723–71 in *The Middle Passage: Comparative Studies in the Atlantic Slave Trade* (Princeton, N.J., 1978), p. 28. For a review of estimates derived in part from summaries, often taken from customs records, see most recently Jose Curto, "A Quantitative Reassessment of the Legal Portuguese Slave Trade from Luanda, Angola, 1710–1830," *African Economic History*, 20(1992):1–25.

[81] Joseph C. Miller, "Capitalism and Slaving: The Financial and Commercial Organization of the Angolan Slave Trade, According to the Accounts of Antonio Coelho Guerreiro (1684–1692)," *International Journal of African Historical Studies*, 17(1984):1–52. For early African-European relations here see John Thornton, *The Kingdom of the Kongo: Civil War and Transition* (Madison, Wis., 1983), pp. 69–83. For the slaving frontier at this period, see Joseph C. Miller, *Way of Death: Merchant Capitalism and the Angolan Slave Trade* (Madison Wisconsin, 1988), pp. 140–53.

of Biafra to the north but without much of the cordiality between European and African slave traders. In 1708 the Lords Commissioners of Trade and Plantations criticized the RAC's failure to establish a fort in the region.[82] The king of Kongo had invited the company to erect such a structure as early as the mid-1680s, and the Dutch actually did have a trading post at Loango in the 1670s. The English company, however, declined the invitation, citing the high prices of slaves, the preferential treatment that the king's representatives expected, and the lack of "Security and Faithfulness (such) as we find in other places."[83] The company could have added that Angolan slaves ranked only slightly higher than Gambian and "Bite's" slaves in the main markets of the Caribbean, though a settled trading relationship and planter acceptance of slaves from the region developed quickly after 1700.[84] In the seventeenth century, however, ships from private traders preferred the better-known Slave and Gold Coasts, leaving this region to the chartered companies.[85] This decision had little to do with slave resistance. Unlike other parts of the Atlantic coast there is no correlation here between violence arising from trade and the incidence of slave rebellions. The ratio of ships experiencing rebellion was the lowest of any region, a pattern that was not lost on purchasers in the Americas.[86]

Complaints of high prices for Angolan slaves were common at this time and, taken together with the modest volume of the trade, point to two tentative conclusions. First, slaves travelled long distances in the Zaire basin and beyond (and thus incurred high transportation costs) before reaching the coast. Such an assessment is supported by the fact that the Angolan hinterland likely had the lowest population densities of any sub-Saharan provenance zone. Second, Europeans could not afford to obtain slaves in this region until slave prices in the Caribbean (and behind these, consumer demand for plantation produce in Europe) had increased. In broad terms this is what happened in the eighteenth century; west-central Africa became

---

[82] "Copy of ye Report from ye Lords Commissioners of Trade and Plantations," February 3, 1708, T70/175, f. 11.

[83] The company's response is in RAC to King of Cacongo, February 16, 1688, T70/50, f. 57. Note also the comments of the captain of the *Providence* (voyage id. 9,951) in 1679, in David Bodkin to the RAC, July 23, 1679, T70/1, p. 27, and the logbook of the *Carlisle* (voyage id. 9,897) in T70/1216 on the lack of security at Malimbo.

[84] "[W]ee spent much time to sell them (newly arrived slaves from Angola), being a sort of negroes utterly disliked in this countrey" (Stede and Gascoigne, Barbados, to RAC, March 15, 1684, T70/16, f. 78).

[85] "A State of the Trade to Africa presented to the House of Commons by the Council of Trade," Jan. 27, 1709, CO 390/12, p. 192.

[86] The Portuguese government instructed the Viceroy of Bahia in 1725 "to send Angola Negroes into the mines for they go there with more confidence and are more obedient than the Minas." Cited in Verger, *Trade Relations Between the Bight of Benin and Bahia*, 56.

the leading regional supplier of slaves to the Americas. Although estimates of slave departures in Table 7-1 are incomplete, it is probable that the number of people leaving west-central Africa for the Americas at this time was only one-eighth what it was to become in the 1780s, 1790s, and 1820s.[87] Despite the presence of early Portuguese missions on the coast and in the Kongo Kingdom, Atlantic trade cannot have provided much of a base for a major European economic influence.

From the African perspective, the merchandise Europeans supplied in the seventeenth century appears of less importance than elsewhere. Unless the trade was much larger than suggested here, the size of the provenance zone was such that the quantity of Atlantic goods flowing into the area must have had little overall impact. It would have been easy to live in the vast hinterland without seeing any non-African merchandise at this time. Further, the composition of these goods was not as specialized as in other regions in sub-Saharan Africa, suggesting nothing approaching the metals shortages of the Bight of Biafra or the currency requirements (cowries) of the Slave Coast. Table 7-2 shows textiles accounting for over half by value of all RAC merchandise, with metals (chiefly iron bars) and brass and pewter containers comprising most of the remainder.[88] Once more, American produce – this time in the form of cachaça, the Brazilian counterpart of West Indian rum, going into Luanda from Brazil – is missing from the table, but estimated breakdowns for the later eighteenth century suggest that this would not have approached textiles in importance.[89] As on the Slave Coast, the textiles were mainly of East Indian origin. European woollens were no more popular here than on the Slave Coast and in the Bight of Biafra. But the range of goods imported here, especially if the cachaça is taken into account, is wider than in other regions. The value and composition of imports into Angola, especially the region north of the Zaire River, is such that had there been no trading contact between Europeans and Africans of any kind in the late seventeenth century, the implications for either side would not have been great. Those who found themselves forced into the transatlantic slave trade would no doubt have disagreed with this assessment.

The regional differences in trading patterns, resistance, and demographic characteristics of deportees discussed previously are so pronounced that it makes far more sense to talk of Europeans as a group than it does Africans in the early modern period. Overall, what emerges here is a larger role for

---

[87] If the estimates in Table 7-1 are only half the true figure, departures in 1790s would have been six times larger than those of the 1680s (Richardson, "Slave Exports from West Africa," for the 1790s). If Table 7-1 captures two-thirds the true figure then departures in the 1790s would have been eight times the true figures.

[88] The breakdowns here are similar to the fragmentary accounts of one Luanda trader in the 1680s and 1690s. See Miller, "Capitalism and Slaving," 33–7.

[89] Eltis, "Trade Between Western Africa and the Atlantic World," 218.

Africans in shaping the slave trade and, beyond this, the Atlantic world, than even the more recent literature concedes. On the resistance issue, Africans were depicted in the previous chapter as holding Europeans at bay as far as the mainland of Africa was concerned and, in one of the larger ironies in the history of African-European relations, thereby helping ensure that a slave trade would occur. Thereafter, resistance held down the numbers entering the trade by raising the costs of carrying on the business. In the present chapter, the regional imbalances in the ability of Africans to resist are shown to have determined the direction and composition of the transatlantic slave trade. Many factors influenced how many Africans were forced into the slave trade. It is nevertheless striking that the regions with the strongest records of resistance were also the regions with smallest number of slave departures. Of the six regions in western Africa that featured prominently as provenance zones for the Americas, Senegambia, Sierra Leone–Windward Coast, Gold Coast, Bight of Benin, Bight of Biafra, and west-central Africa, the first two are estimated to have supplied only 10 percent of the slaves. Moreover, one of these regions, Senegambia, was the area in which the slave trade ended first, and the second, the Windward Coast, was the one in which the traffic grew to significance last. In other words, the two had the shortest acquaintanceship with the traffic of the six. Yet it should be noted that while cost-enhancing acts of resistance reduced the total volume of the trade, the regional bias in this resistance also meant that the slave trade was redirected. Angola, the Bight of Biafra, the Slave Coast, and the Gold Coast probably sold more slaves into the trade than they would have done if this regional imbalance in resistance had not existed. In the larger picture, these findings should force us to see the slave trade as a product of bargaining between equals as far as African and European elites are concerned, but as the evidence of shipboard resistance suggests, and ignoring for the moment the activities of European consumers of plantation produce, there was far more shaping the transatlantic slave trade than just negotiation between elites.

8

The English Plantation Americas in Comparative Perspective

INITIALLY, THE ENGLISH FACED the same dilemma as other Europeans in seeking to create transoceanic empires. For those with little property, lightly populated territories represented an opportunity to acquire land and independence from others – a chance to avoid wage slavery in Christopher Hill's characterization. The high cost of transatlantic travel, however, prevented the mass migration of individuals free of obligations to others before the nineteenth century. For the propertied classes (in other words, from an imperial perspective) transatlantic land was useful only if trade and labor supplies were possible. As noted in Chapter 5, shipping costs before 1650 were such that only the highest-value produce could be traded. Even if commodities were stolen or pirated, they still had to be carried to a market; if that market was across the Atlantic then their value would have to exceed at minimum the cost of transportation. Atlantic trade and empires could be based on plunder, exchange with indigenous populations (for example, gold from West Africa), or production within a new colony, but in each case the product had to warrant shipping. Individuals working by themselves or with family members on their own plot of land did not normally produce high-value products. Given the failure of Europeans to establish plantations in Africa described in Chapter 6, the third of these options, production for export, thus meant one group working for another – initially Europeans working for Europeans, at least outside Iberian America.

The plunder option was used first and, as one might expect of first-comers when there was still something to plunder, to greatest effect by the Spanish. From the second half of the sixteenth century to the 1640s and stimulated by their war of independence against the Spanish and the union of the Portuguese and Spanish crowns, the Dutch were the quintessential plunderers of at least the sea lanes to the Americas. Trade was not the primary goal of the Dutch West Indies Company for the first quarter-century of its existence. In the third quarter of the seventeenth century, however, the English spearheaded piracy beyond the line, especially in the western Caribbean. For the first decade of British rule in Jamaica and probably through to Henry Morgan's last attack on Panama after the 1672 peace treaty, commodities stolen from the Spanish and sold or deposited in Jamaica exceeded in value exports of the produce of that island. In 1669 the Jamaican governor wrote, "Most of our privateers are turned merchant."[1] But as late as 1676, his Barbados counterpart could write that Jamaica's "chiefest dependence (was) upon a difference with Spain that they may make up with rapine what they cannot obtain by industry."[2] Nevertheless, it is highly unlikely that the value of pirated commodities ever approached the level of legitimate trade in the English Caribbean as a whole.[3] Buccaneering by this time was a predominantly French activity or at least based on the part of Hispaniola that became French (St. Domingue) at the end of the seventeenth century.

The second option of exchange or trade with indigenes was least significant to Europeans. Indeed if it meant respecting the territorial integrity of indigenous communities, such activity could be antithetical to strong transatlantic ties. Only in the case of the Canadian Shield did this option have more than temporary significance. Yet even here, despite its crucial importance to the Huron and Iroquois, and to a lesser degree the European polities that eventually formed part of the United States and Canada, the trade in beaver skins, even at its peak, was always a trivial component of overall transatlantic commerce and an even more trivial contributor to European welfare. In one respect, to anticipate a later argument, the importance of the Caribbean to Europe may be reduced to what it provided in the way of sweetening for food and drink, sugar products habitually accounting for over 90 percent of exports from the region after 1660. From the broad perspective of what Europeans consumed in the process of feeding, sheltering, clothing, and providing whatever other amenities for themselves that they could afford, such an addition to European welfare does not loom large.[4]

---

[1] Thomas Modyford, Nov. 30, 1669, CO1/24, f. 166.

[2] Sir John Atkins, CSPCS, 9:368.

[3] Estimates of produce exports from Jamaica begin in 1671–5 (see Table 8-1). Certainly in various surveys of the worth of the Caribbean to the English made until 1672, Jamaica is scarcely mentioned. Nevertheless without any chance of evaluating total proceeds from piracy, this assessment must remain impressionistic. See A. P. Thornton, *West India Policy Under the Restoration* (Oxford, 1956), pp. 67–123 for a good discussion of the private and public dependence of the colony on freebooting.

[4] The counterfactual here is not European consumers doing without sweeteners but rather putting up with less sugar or less convenient alternatives to sugar, such as honey, until the explosion of sugar beet production in the nineteenth century. The relatively trivial addition to European welfare that slavery in the Americas brought about is staggering when it is compared to the non-pecuniary costs of enslavement in Africa, the middle passage, and plantations in the Americas. Such

By the late seventeenth century sugar was at least a common grocery item. It is harder to envisage a smaller increment to European welfare than that represented by the slightly smoother texture (compared to alternative pelts from northern Europe) of a few thousand expensive hats.

In the long run, as both the Dutch and Spanish discovered in different ways, the sustenance and strengthening of links across the Atlantic and the empires these made possible hinged not only on European settlement but also on production for export within those settlements. The question was who would provide the labor? As earlier chapters suggest, it was the size of its labor pool that distinguished the English system from the others, as well as the weakness of traditional ties between the propertied and the non-propertied classes. Spanish transatlantic migrants commonly moved as social dependents of others, whereas the English were more likely to have associations forged in the marketplace. Free European migrants everywhere supplied much less labor than merchants and landowners wanted, and ultimately – in a pattern repeated as long as a temperate frontier remained open to European migrants – they farmed for themselves. The Caribbean provided a market for North American foodstuffs grown on small farms, but before the nineteenth-century wheat booms family farms were not likely to contribute much to the transatlantic export sector.

As discussed in Chapter 2, white indentured servitude provided the labor that guaranteed first the survival and then the success of the early English colonies. In the absence, initially, of Indian and African labor, the viability of English settlements in the Atlantic world hinged on the indenture contract. The English appear to have been the first Europeans to have used it widely, though the French also relied on it heavily. Indentured servants provided the basis for the establishment of tobacco production in both the Caribbean and mainland North America and constituted an expanding source of new labor in Barbados for a decade or perhaps two after the beginning of the switch from tobacco to sugar in this first English sugar colony. At some point in the 1660s, however, the annual number of Africans arriving in the English Americas began to exceed the number of Europeans, a pattern that quickly came to hold for the Americas as a whole until the slave trade was suppressed in the decades after 1807.

The conversion from tobacco to sugar in Barbados has been tracked with deed records. Land consolidation (to provide the basis for economies of scale possible in the production of sugar), rising land values, and the use of sugar

a comparison yields a sharp insight into the widespread acceptance of slavery and the failure of seventeenth-century Europe to perceive the evil of slavery – slavery at least for non-Europeans. A similar argument may be made for the impact of the fur trade on Huron and Iroquois societies. The devastation of the latter is outlined in Richard White, *Middle Ground*, 1–49.

as unit of account and medium of payment began about 1645.[5] The switch to slaves began in the early 1640s, before the switch to sugar; as noted in Chapter 2, increasing numbers of slaves and servants arrived on the island in the 1640s and 1650s, the former expanding the faster of the two groups. However, while the arrival of sugar in the English Caribbean between 1643 and 1660 was dramatic, sugar output in the mid-1660s was still small compared to what it was to become. London imports of sugar from the English West Indies tripled between 1665 and 1700. Even in the most developed colony, Barbados, both the value of plantation output and the size of the slave labor force more than doubled in the half-century after 1660 and doubled again by the end of the eighteenth century. In the Leewards, except for Nevis and, of course, Jamaica, sugar production was still insignificant in 1660. As late as 1700, the value of all Jamaican plantation produce was only one-ninth what it would become just seventy years later.[6] In short, in 1660 the development of the English sugar complex had scarcely begun.

The English Americas in the second half of the seventeenth century comprised four relatively distinct trading zones: Barbados, Jamaica, the Leewards, and the Chesapeake colonies (see Maps 1 and 7 in the maps section following appendices). Table 8-1 shows estimates of the value of trade from these colonies in the second half of the seventeenth century. By 1700, Virginia was exporting more than Jamaica but less than the Leeward Islands as a group, and far less than Barbados. More interestingly, the development of each one of the four zones displayed patterns not apparent in any of the others, despite the fact that all regions came to specialize in one of two crops, tobacco and sugar. All the Caribbean islands included in Table 8-1, for example, came to concentrate on sugar products in this period, but they reached that point by different routes. Specifically, they exported different combinations of sugar products, and this in turn hints at social differences among the islands.

Barbados was clearly the regional and perhaps, in terms of productivity, the global economic giant in the second half of the seventeenth century. By the 1660s, Barbados land was already fully claimed, though not yet fully cleared. The wooded areas were actually worth twice as much per acre as cleared land, which suggests that the cost of clearing the land was less than the initial premium available for growing sugar cane on virgin soil.[7]

---

[5] Emily Mechner, "Paupers and Planters: The Transition to Sugar in Barbados, 1638–1674" (Paper presented to the Cliometric Conference, Toronto, May 1997); Menard, "Sweet Negotiation of Sugar."

[6] For 1770 values see Eltis, "The Slave Economies of the Caribbean."

[7] "Standing wood here [Barbados] is now worth £20 sterling per acre and other land £10 per acre . . . ." Thomas Modyford to Sir Henry Bennett, May 10, 1664, CO1/18, ff. 135–6.

Table 8-1. *Average Annual Values of Exports from the Major Colonies of the English Americas for Selected Years in the Second Half of the Seventeenth Century (values fob Caribbean in thousands of current pounds sterling)*

	1665–66	1671–75	1675–78	1678–79	1682–83	1689–91	1698–1700
Barbados							
Sugar products	259.6					163.0*	423.5
Nonsugar	24.9					15.0*	19.5
Total	284.4					178.0*	443.0
Sugar as % of total	91.2					91.6	95.6
Jamaica							
Sugar products		10.8	23.7	50.4	53.2	105.5	110.0
Nonsugar		60.6	60.7	74.7	44.0	30.8	45.4
Total**		72.1	85.2	126.3	98.2	137.7	155.4
Sugar as % of total		15.0	27.8	39.9	54.2	76.6	70.7
Leewards							
Sugar products							235.1
Nonsugar							6.7
Total							241.8
Sugar as % of total							97.2
Chesapeake							
Tobacco		108.8***					218.3****

Notes: *for 1688, 1690, 1691   **Total includes an allowance of one percent to allow for missing minor products   ***for 1669 and 1672   ****for 1699–1700 only.

Sources: Panels 1 and 2, David Eltis, "New Estimates of Exports from Barbados and Jamaica, 1665–1701," *William and Mary Quarterly*, 52(1995):631–48.

Panel 3, Appendix D.

Panel 4, Calculated from Russell R. Menard, "The Tobacco Industry in the Chesapeake Colonies, 1617–1730," *Research in Economic History*, 5(1980):159, 160 with an allowance of 50 percent to convert farm gate prices to free on board (fob) values.

Table 8-1 shows that annual total exports from Barbados in 1665–6 averaged £284.4 thousand sterling, over 90 percent of which stemmed from the sugar crop.[8] The equivalent value of total exports in 1688, 1690–91 was £178 thousand, and in 1699–1701, £443 thousand. The exports of no other

---

[8] Converting this into London prices of £1.5 per cwt. yields a total value £427 thousand for Barbados and (allowing a further 15 percent for the other sugar colonies) £491 thousand for all English sugar. This might be compared with an estimate in a broadsheet in the Rawlinson papers, "The State of the Case of the Sugar Plantations in the Americas," c. 1670, Rawlinson, A 478, p. 63, which states, "In the year 1666 the English were possest of Barbados, the better half of St Christopher's, Nevis, Mountserrat, Antigua and Surinam. These plantations

European colony approached the value of that of Barbados in this era.[9] Table 8-1 shows that in 1700 the island was exporting more than the rest of the English Caribbean, including Jamaica. Barbados was probably exporting more relative to its size and population than any other polity of its time or indeed any other time up to that point – the Hong Kong of the preindustrial era in a sense. In 1699 and 1700, Chesapeake tobacco exports brought in £145.5 thousand sterling per year and an increase in the order of 50 percent to convert to free on board values (fob) would still leave Chesapeake exports at about half those of Barbados.[10] The Recònçavo of Bahia, the major sugar-growing region of Brazil, exported sugar and tobacco worth £227.4 thousand in 1700 from an area far larger than Barbados.[11] Contemporaries made

did then employ above 400 sayl of English ships annually, and in them above Ten thousand English seamen and did also furnish a Native Commodity of above 800,000 Pounds value per annum to this nation besides a considerable revenue to the crown [in the margin here a handwritten note adds "of wch 400,000 was transported to forraigne markets"]. Of which 800,000 pounds there was not above Forty thousand . . . clear gain to the planter . . . ." The writer was obviously using London rather than Barbados prices in the estimate and throughout the sheet appears concerned to maximise the importance of the Caribbean to the English and likely ignored the leakage-in-transit problem. The sheet's estimate of £800,000 (or £720,000 arriving in London after leakage) might be compared to exports of just under £500,000 (London prices) estimated from the customs books.

9 It is probable that Table 8-1 understates the value of sugar exports from Barbados. The sugar prices used to calculate these values (adjusted for freight, etc., from the Caribbean) are taken from McCusker's compilation of Davies' prices paid at the Royal African Company's auction sales (McCusker, *Rum Trade*, 1140–3). These prices mixed together muscovado and clayed sugar, whereas a much larger share (perhaps one-third in 1700) of Barbados than Jamaican sugar was of the more highly valued clayed variety. It might also be noted that the charts in Frank Wesley Pitman, *The Development of the British West Indies, 1700–1763* (New Haven, 1917), facing pp. 99 and 108, which provide annual values of imports into England from Barbados and Jamaica respectively, indicate much lower values than the estimates presented here. However, the valuation procedures used by Pitman are unclear, nor does he appear to make allowance for losses in transit or exports from the Caribbean to the rest of the Americas – a major omission for Barbados at least.

10 Calculated from Russell R. Menard, "The Tobacco Industry in the Chesapeake Colonies, 1617–1730: An Interpretation," *Research in Economic History*, 5 (1980):160. Menard uses farm gate prices to compute export values. Transportation and shipping would probably have added less than 50 percent.

11 Schwartz, *Sugar Plantations*, 186, 502. Conversions to sterling using the average exchange rate, sterling to milreis, from John J. McCusker, *Money and Exchange Rates in Europe and America, 1600–1775: A Handbook* (Chapel Hill, N.C., 1978), p. 111. Schwartz gives only quantities of tobacco, and these have been converted directly to sterling using Menard's price series (Menard, "The Tobacco Industry in the Chesapeake Colonies," 160). It is likely that the Barbados advantage was even greater than the data in this paragraph suggest. As already noted, Barbados exported increasing quantities of clayed, or semiprocessed, sugar, more valuable than muscovado, which does not appear as a separate product category

similar comparisons. Barbados planters claimed in 1655 that "they ship out yearly as many Tunns of goods as ye King of Spain doth out of all his Indian Empires."[12]

In per capita terms Barbados was even more exceptional. The population of Barbados in the mid-1660s is taken here to have been forty-six thousand, of whom approximately twenty-five thousand were slaves.[13] The island exported £6.2 per person in 1665–6 and £7.3 in 1699–1700. Indeed, by the 1660s, Barbados had already matched or exceeded average exports per person attained in the eighteenth- and nineteenth-century Caribbean.[14] These values per person were also far in excess of what was to be found in any European country. In the Americas, the Chesapeake was exporting only £1.55 of tobacco per person in 1699–1700 or perhaps £2 to £2.25, fob – probably more than any mainland colony except for South Carolina before or indeed after the Revolution.[15] Per capita values for the Chesapeake did not

in the naval office shipping list (the source of the estimates for 1699–1701). There is no way of knowing the proportion of exported sugar that was, in fact, clayed, and the value of Barbados exports for these years in Table 8-1 should be regarded as a lower-bound figure. On the other hand, little is known of the sugar output of Pernambuco and Rio de Janeiro at this time, except that they were below that of Bahia. In 1710 Bahia was estimated to have produced almost 40 percent of Brazilian sugar (calculated from Schwartz, "Colonial Brazil, c.1580–c.1750: Plantations and Peripheries," 430–1). If this ratio held in 1700 for all plantation produce, then the value of Brazilian exports would have exceeded that of Barbados (£568,000 v. £443,000), but Brazilian exports as a whole would have been below those of the British Caribbean as a whole.

[12] Thomas Povey, "Book of Entrie of Forreigne Letters," Add. mss., 11,411, f. 9.

[13] Dunn, *Sugar and Slaves*, 87, 312. Dunn's acceptance of the general validity of the 1673 census of Barbados is persuasive. This gives 33,184 slaves. Slave arrivals from Africa between 1666 and 1672 were about two thousand a year on a net basis. A population of twenty-five thousand in 1665–6 is thus consistent with a natural rate of decrease for the slave population of c. 4.0 percent a year, working back from the 1673 figure. See Curtin's discussion of rates of population change in the early slave colonies in *Atlantic Slave Trade*, 58–64. Such a figure also interpolates well between the 1673 estimate of 21,309 whites, 33,184 blacks, and that for 1655 of 23,000 whites and 20,000 blacks (Dunn, *Sugar and Slaves*, 87).

[14] Stanley L. Engerman, "Notes on the Pattern of Economic Growth in the British North American Colonies in the Seventeenth, Eighteenth and Nineteenth Centuries," in Paul Bairoch and Maurice Levy-Leboyer (eds.), *Disparities in Economic Development since the Industrial Revolution* (New York, 1981), pp. 46–57. Engerman's series are for sugar only, but total values are computed using a London price series. The discussion in the present text attempts to take into account all produce and uses local prices to compute total values.

[15] Calculated from Menard, "The Tobacco Industry in the Chesapeake Colonies, 1617–1730," 160. For per capita exports in the United States before and after independence, see James F. Shepherd and Gary M. Walton, "Economic Change after the American Revolution: Pre- and Post-War Comparisons of Maritime Shipping and Trade," *Explorations in Economic History*, 13(1976):413. Cf. McCusker and Menard, *The Economy of British America*, 85.

change much in the next century, and no other part of the British Americas approached this level of involvement in Atlantic trade before 1700.[16] In Bahia, per capita produce exports cannot have been more than £4.[17]

Yet there was much more going on in Barbados in these years than just a simple expansion of semi-processed or muscovado sugar. As noted earlier, Barbados was the first of three sugar frontiers in the early English Caribbean. The Barbados sugar complex began by producing muscovado sugar and initially much of the molasses generated by the production of sugar must have been consumed locally or wasted. Despite this, Barbados sugar came to dominate the market. "Scarce any island in the world," claimed Barbados sugar producers in 1661, "yields so great a revenue or employs so much shipping and stock (capital); that the price of sugar has thereby been reduced from three pounds, ten shillings to per hundred to less than half ...."[18] The Commissioners of the Customs agreed. They reported that in the same year sugar "pays more custom to His Maj than the East Indies four times over." The price decline continued for another two decades and, by the late 1660s, prospects were less bright. In 1668, the governor of Barbados noted that the island "declines from its Ancient fertility not rendring ... by two-thirds its former production by the acre."[19] Thus, in the thirty-five years after 1665 – indeed for much of the balance of the period of slavery – the first West Indian sugar island had to cope with three major pressures. The first was increasing competition from the Leeward Islands, Jamaica, and eventually the non-English Caribbean, second, diminishing soil fertility, and third, declining sugar prices.

In response to these pressures, Barbadian planters demonstrated striking flexibility. Their basic strategy was to diversify the product they exported. This meant first switching to more refined sugars – if not white sugar, then at least clayed. They invested more capital and produced a higher-valued product that was cheaper to transport, in the process overcoming an imperial duty in favor of muscovado sugar that had been in place since 1649. In the mid-1660s neither refined nor clayed sugars were of major importance. Unlike Brazil, its main rival in European sugar markets at this time, Barbados shipped little of these sugars. But between the mid-1660s and

16 Engerman, "Notes on the Pattern of Economic Growth in the British North American Colonies," 48.

17 There are no population data for Bahia in 1700. A reliable census taken about 1724 indicates a total population of 79,864. Slave arrivals at Bahia from Africa in the first quarter of the eighteenth century were at least 180,000, and free migration from Portugal was also strong, though perhaps most migrants, both slave and free, passed through Bahia to other regions of Brazil, especially the gold-producing areas (Schwartz, *Sugar Plantations*, 88, 343). If we assume a population of sixty thousand in 1700, per capita exports are £3.79.

18 "Petition of the Planters of Barbados," July 12, 1661, CSPCS, 5:46–7.

19 "Report by the Commissioners of Customs," Nov. 6, 1661, *ibid.*, 58; CO29/1, f. 59.

1700 the exports of Barbados sugar increased by 40 percent and the quality of that sugar appears to have improved. While the naval officers' data on exports from the island do not reflect this change (the returns seem to include clayed sugar in the muscovado category), the evidence is fairly strong.[20] By 1691, despite the preferential duty, the island was exporting so much clayed, or partly refined, sugar that English sugar refiners pressured the English government for relief from the competition. In a classic mercantilist statement they singled out the clayed sugars of Barbados as particular offenders, pointing out that "one ship of white (sugar) brings the lading of three of brown" and asked "[i]s this the way to maintain Nurseries for our Seamen?" More important, "[s]ince refining in England hath been a trade before ever we had plantations," it was absurd that "it should be lost by the having them."[21]

The second major Barbadian innovation, connected to the first, was the marketing of sugar by-products. In 1665–6, exports of molasses and rum accounted for less than 7 percent of total exports by value. By the end of the century, these two products accounted for nearly 28 percent of total exports. By 1770, molasses exports had disappeared altogether, but the more highly processed product of rum took up 47 percent of total exports from Barbados. Put another way, sugar exports may have increased by 40 percent in volume between 1665 and 1700 (though somewhat more than this if we allow for its higher clayed content), but exports of molasses increased tenfold and exports of rum by between five and six times. In the Leewards in 1700, these products accounted for just over 5 percent of exports, and in Jamaica, about 1 percent.[22] Although Barbados had no rival in total product, it is remarkable that if we look at sugar alone (and ignore the clayed nature of some of the Barbados product), the island had actually been overtaken by Jamaica and the Leewards together. Barbados was still the dominant plantation colony in the Americas as late as the beginning of the eighteenth century, but this dominance no longer rested upon muscovado sugar. On the soil fertility issue, Barbadian planters did what the rest of the Caribbean came to do eventually

[20] John Oldmixon, *The British Empire in America*, 2 vols. (London, 1741), 2: pp. 154–7; McCusker, *Rum Trade*, 201–4. The impression was also shared by some contemporaries: "Two thirds of the Planters of the Sugar colonies do turn into whites or Sun dry'ds all their sugars they send to England," Broadsheet. "The State of the Case of the Sugar Plantations in the Americas," c. 1670, Rawlinson manuscript, A478, p. 63; and Edward Lyttleton, *The Groans of the Plantations* (London, 1689), pp. 11–12.

[21] Anon, *The Interest of the Nation as it Respects all the Sugar-Plantations Abroad and Refining of Sugars at Home* (London, 1691). The only copy I have found of this is in CO5/1. McCusker's careful review of this problem suggests that one-quarter of Barbados sugar exported in 1690 was clayed (*Rum Trade*, 201–4).

[22] All ratios calculated from Table 8-1 and Eltis, "New Estimates of Exports from Barbados and Jamaica," and idem, "The Slave Economies of the Caribbean," Table 1.

in the wake of the sugar juggernaut. They practised "a strict husbandry" at the heart of which was careful manuring.[23] Thus, Barbados maintained its exports and high income level during the slave regime with a measure of innovation and diversification that gets lost when observers see no further than the labels monoculture and sugar. Looking only at trends in the production of muscovado sugar is almost bound to yield an interpretation of Barbadian decline based on the presence of inefficient production techniques and an entrepreneurial inability to adjust, when the reality was quite the opposite.

Thus, Barbados had no rival as the richest English colony well into the eighteenth century. The great wealth of the island was generated by relatively few large planters, but it is also clear, first, that the export sector was broadly based and second, that poverty in the old-world sense of the term scarcely existed.[24] On the first point, 1,353 people, almost all adult males, entered produce in the Barbados custom house between 1664 and 1667. These comprised about one in four of all men on the island. While the top fifth of those entering produce supplied 87 percent of all produce handled by the customhouse, even the poorest of the remaining four-fifths managed to supply some rum and in some cases even sugar. For this, they required a primitive grinder and still, but if they wanted to make sugar, they would use the equipment of others. In contrast to the claims of the Bridenbaughs and others, the Barbados smallholders produced cane and rum, not just minor staples such as cotton and tobacco.[25] In 1714, a visitor to Antigua, which by that time approximated the stage of development reached by Barbados fifty years before, commented,

[t]he richest planters have large sugarworks, which require a great many slaves to manage ye business, the poorest sort content themselves with one or two horses & requires but little attendance; if ye man has no slaves, Himself with his wife & children manage it. These seldom make anything but rum, & ye trash and ye Cane after grinding serves for fewel under ye still.[26]

Clearly, the economies of scale possible in sugar production that ensured the emergence of the planter class were not as marked in the production of rum.

Barbados was a nursery for the rest of the English Caribbean after 1660[27]

---

[23] Lord Willoughby, July 9, 1668, CO29/1, f. 59. For detailed instructions on making and using manure see the instructions of Col. Henry Drax to an overseer during the 1670s (Rawlinson manuscript, A348, pp. 8–10). For soil exhaustion in this period and its control, see Bridenbaugh, *No Peace Beyond the Line*, 289–90.

[24] This paragraph is based on David Eltis, "The Total Product of Barbados, 1664–1701," *Journal of Economic History*, 55(1995):321–36.

[25] Bridenbaugh, *No Peace Beyond the Line*, 403–4.

[26] Add ms, 39,946, "Narrative of Voyages to the Guinea Coast and the West Indies, 1714–1716," p. 14.

[27] "Petition of the planters ... of Barbados," July 12, 1661, CSPCS, 5:46–7.

in terms of supplies as well as migrants. Not all small proprietors were excluded, as Pitman implied.[28] As late as 1679 there were still 1,041 planters holding less than 20 acres of land each, and this does not include rental property.[29] The initial expansion of rum exports from Barbados and later Antigua must have come from smallholdings as well as large estates, and the former switched into rum from tobacco and cotton rather than hanging on to the latter crops or resorting to a subsistence existence. Time-expired indentured servants left Barbados in the second half of the seventeenth century in search of land, yet the white population changed little in the last third of the century. As in Virginia and Maryland at this time, there was still room in the export sector for the small producer.

For the bottom fifth of those entering produce into the custom house of the mid-1660s, rum generated a per capita income below what the vestry of St. Michael's allowed the indigent of Bridgetown as relief payments. Such revenue is unlikely, however, to have been the only income of the smallest of the smallholders. The booming Barbados economy generated employment for free labor as well as for slaves, and smallholdings that grew cane also grew subsistence food crops. Jerome Handler's comment on midtwentieth-century Barbados, that whereas "small-scale cane farming can rarely suffice as a ... livelihood, a farmer can expect some cash from his cane-producing activities" is applicable to the 1660s.[30] A study of the occupational class of buyers and sellers of land during the sugar revolution concludes that the rise of a plantocracy did not necessarily mean the impoverishment of smallholders.[31] In any event, the numbers receiving poor relief in the mid-1660s were small.[32] Indeed, seventeenth-century Barbados contained features that we associate with the nineteenth-century antebellum society of the South in the United States in that there was a large number of free whites with some access to land who did not own slaves but who could not conceive of a society without slaves. Unlike the later South, however, these whites participated directly in the export economy. Only large planters clayed and refined sugar but even in export terms there was more to

---

[28] Pitman, *Development of the British West Indies*, 91–2.
[29] Dunn, *Sugar and Slaves*, 91. Cf. Puckrein, *Little England*, 148. For new information on small tenants see Menard, "Sweet Negotiation of Sugar," pp. 31–2.
[30] Jerome S. Handler, "Small-Scale Sugar Cane Farming in Barbados," *Ethnology*, 5(1966):264–83. Ninety percent of Barbados farmers grew cane in the early 1960s.
[31] Mechner, "Paupers and Planters."
[32] Only thirty-three adults received outrelief in St. Michael's in 1665 and 1666, computed from "Records of the Vestry of St. Michael," *Journal of the Barbados Museum and Historical Society*, 15(1948):98–104, 119–27. Governors in 1672 and 1677 claimed that no one was to be seen begging. See Vincent T. Harlow, *History of Barbados, 1625–1685* (Oxford, 1926), p. 331; Bridenbaugh, *No Peace Beyond the Line*, 279.

Table 8-2. *Estimates of Exports from the Antigua, Montserrat, Nevis, and St. Kitts, 1700 in thousands of pounds sterling (current values)*

	Sugar	Molasses	Rum	All other	Total
Antigua	88.0	8.1	4.8	5.9	106.8
Montserrat	31.6	0	0	0.1	31.7
Nevis	85.4	0.3	0	0.3	86
St. Kitts*	15.9	0.6	0.3	0.5	17.3
Leeward Is	220.8	9.1	5.2	6.7	241.8

Sources: Appendix D.

Barbados than sugar and slaves. There were some parallels in the Leeward Islands and early Jamaica. "What makes ... New England, Jamaica and the Plantations abroad, increase so fast but that they have employment and estates for all people, and no poor among them," noted an English observer in 1674.[33] Extensive poverty among whites was perhaps a later development both in Barbados and Kingston, Jamaica.[34]

The Leeward Islands as a group were second in importance in the English Americas, producing exports worth 241.8 thousand pounds sterling by 1700.[35] Table 8-2 shows that collectively the Leewards were far more important than Jamaica at this time, exported more than the Chesapeake, and shipped produce worth over half that of Barbados exports. Indeed, by themselves, Antigua and Nevis each exported almost as much sugar as did Jamaica, and it was only Jamaica's nonsugar exports that put the larger island's export values ahead of its much smaller Leeward counterparts. Like Barbados, these islands began with tobacco, though Antigua also specialized in cattle, which were sold in Barbados.[36] As this suggests, in the last thirty years of the seventeenth century, produce exports from the Leewards grew

[33] Carew Reynell in J. P. Cooper and Joan Thirsk (eds.), *Seventeenth Century Economic Documents* (Oxford, 1972), p. 760.

[34] For Jamaica see Trevor Burnard, "'The Grand Mart of the Island': Kingston, Jamaica in the mid-Eighteenth Century and the Question of Urbanisation in Plantation Societies," in Kathleen Monteith and Glenn Richards (eds.), *Aspects of Jamaican History* (forthcoming, UWI Press). For Barbados see Jill Shepherd, *The "Redlegs" of Barbados. Their Origins and History* (Millwood, 1981). For a corrective of the "redlegs" image see Donald Harman Akenson, *If the Irish Ran the World: Montserrat, 1630–1730* (Montreal, 1997), pp. 48–51.

[35] See Appendix D for the derivation of this estimate. The importance of the Leeward Islands as a sugar frontier between the development of Barbados then Jamaica was pointed out in Stanley L. Engerman, "Europe, the Lesser Antilles, and Economic Expansion, 1600–1800," in Paquette and Engerman, *Lesser Antilles*, 147–64.

[36] "Most humble Proposals of merchant planters and traders of the island of Antigua," n.d., but c. 1660, Add ms, 2395, f. 288.

much more rapidly than those from Jamaica or Barbados. Some idea of the relative position of the Leeward Islands in the late 1660s is provided by the returns of the Crown's 4.5 percent duty on exported produce that all the islands except Jamaica were required to pay. For 1668–9, Barbados paid almost ten times as much as Antigua, Montserrat, and Nevis together, while St. Kitts, because of the devastating French attack in 1668, paid nothing at all. Nevis was by far the most important of the Leewards at this stage and, after Barbados, had been the first English colony in the Americas to receive slaves direct from Africa (the first recorded being 1662). Nevertheless, Nevis still generated only 8 percent of the revenues of Barbados at the end of the 1660s.[37] Thirty years later, revenues of all the Leewards together had grown to equal 55 percent those of Barbados. Yet despite this growth, the Leewards remained a frontier region – indeed, *the* frontier region of the English Caribbean. Tobacco was still a major crop in Antigua in the late 1680s.[38] A decade later it had sunk to insignificance, but the sugar that had replaced it was entirely muscovado; rum and molasses accounted for the same tiny proportion of total exports as they had in Barbados in the mid-1660s. Moreover, as in Barbados thirty-five years earlier, most of the expansion of the Leewards still lay ahead.

But to treat the Leewards as a unit means missing key details. As Table 8-2 suggests, major differences existed within the group. While sugar appeared in significant quantities on Nevis first, expansion was slower there than on either Antigua or Montserrat when it eventually reached those islands. Antigua was the leader in terms of export growth and overtook Nevis before 1700, a position it maintained throughout the slave era. In addition, the diversification apparent when the island first turned to sugar never completely disappeared in this period. Rum, molasses, and lignum vitae had replaced tobacco, cotton, and cattle by 1700, but non-muscovado items remained important. Where 99 percent of the exports of Montserrat and Nevis were muscovado sugar in 1700, sugar accounted for just 82 percent of Antigua exports. As noted earlier, Antigua had a broader-based economy than the rest of the Leewards in the sense that small producers sold into the export market, though this process had not proceeded as far as in Barbados. Unlike Barbados, sugar production in these islands was entirely muscovado at the end of the seventeenth century.[39]

Jamaica was relatively slow to develop in plantation terms and obviously did not, as is sometimes assumed, begin to take over the role of Barbados in

---

[37] Unsigned accounts for 1668–9, dated Oct. 6, 1669, CO1/24, f. 160.

[38] Quantitative assessments are not possible but see the numerous references to tobacco in the correspondence of the Antigua factor in T70/12, especially pp. 150–70.

[39] Anon, *The Interest of the Nation*. For more precise estimates based on the fragmentary naval officer returns in CO157/1, see Appendix D.

the last quarter of the seventeenth century.[40] At the end of the seventeenth century, nearly a half-century after the English acquired the colony, Barbados produce exports were nearly three times and sugar products were nearly four times as valuable as their Jamaica counterparts. Jamaican exports were markedly below those of the Leeward Islands as well. Jaundiced assessments of the island's agricultural potential are not hard to find in the late 1660s and 1670s.[41] The basic problem was location, as a careful assessment of the island's prospects made clear in the late 1660s. "[S]ervants (and especially negro servants) are most considerable in the making all plantations and Colonies florish," but the island was "too far to the leeward" to tap into cheap supplies of either. Returning ships could not make the Windward Passage (between Cuba and Hispaniola) and Jamaica, in any event, was far from being the only source of pirates in the western Caribbean at this time. Shipping costs, whether for inputs or outputs of the plantation sector, were thus too high, and sugar prices in the late seventeenth century would not easily cover these costs.[42] In short, in the third quarter of the seventeenth century Jamaica (like the future St. Domingue) lay beyond the western limits of large-scale sugar production for export.

As noted in Chapter 5, English slave traders were very efficient at getting slaves into the western Caribbean at prices that sugar planters could afford, and Jamaican produce exports grew strongly in the later 1670s and 1680s. Yet, as Table 8-1 suggests, the sugar sector in particular appeared to have stalled in the 1690s, probably in response to the higher shipping costs associated with war. After discussing the activities of privateers, Thomas Modyford wrote from the island in 1669 that "[s]ome of the best monyed are turned planters here."[43] If pirates' loot did jump-start Jamaica's sugar sector, then the jump was extremely modest in comparison to Barbados and the Leeward Islands. The major generation of capital and inflows of labor that were to turn the island into a major sugar producer came after 1700, when the returns from piracy were negligible, not before.[44] Almost

[40] Or even earlier. Jack P. Greene has written recently that "[b]y 1670 ... Barbados was already losing its position as England's leading sugar-producing colony to Jamaica." [Changing Identity in the British Caribbean: Barbados as a Case Study," in Nicholas Canny and Anthony Pagden (eds.), *Colonial Identity in the Atlantic World, 1500–1800* (Princeton, N.J., 1992), p. 216.]

[41] For example, Sir John Atkins wrote in 1676 "the expectation which was great fades, the land proving very sterile ... for canes ...." (CSPCS, 9:368).

[42] The quotes and the arguments are taken from "Proposalls and Reasons for the encouragement of the trade of Jamaica, the peopling and improvement thereof," Rawlinson manuscript, A478, f. 85. N.d., but context suggests 1669.

[43] Thomas Modyford, Nov. 30, 1669, CO1/24, f. 166.

[44] The argument that piracy established the plantation system in Jamaica is in Nuala Zahedieh, "Trade, Plunder, and Economic Development in Early English Jamaica," *Economic History Review*, 39(1986):205–22. Allan D. Meyers, accepts this argument in "Ethnic Distinctions and Wealth among Colonial Jamaican

one-third of Jamaica's exports in 1700 still had nothing to do with the sugar sector.

Jamaica, moreover, was actually quite isolated from the rest of the English Americas in this early period. One indication comes from naval office shipping list data on intra-American trade. The figures for 1688–91 are distorted by the impact of war in Europe on shipping lanes to England. Setting those years aside, New England received less than 5 percent of the exports of Barbados and Jamaica, and Virginia and Maryland received less again. The North American mainland took mostly rum and molasses, with most of the former going to Virginia and most of the latter to New England.[45] But the location that delayed the development of plantation agriculture and restricted trade with the rest of the English Americas also meant the island was an ideal entrepot for the Spanish Americas.

This last assessment points to a second key function of the English Caribbean in the early modern Americas. Not only did the English establish the leading plantation colonies at this time, the productivity advantage in slave trading examined in Chapter 5 also allowed them to assume a major role supplying slaves to other parts of the Americas. Between 1662 and 1713 the English carried about four hundred thousand Africans to the Americas. Table 8-3 shows the primary destinations of these slaves but not the fact that many of these were taken to other parts of the Americas within a few weeks of their arrival.[46] One indication of entrepot trade is that a comparison of Table 8-1 with Table 8-3 suggests that slave arrivals at the various colonies do not jibe well with estimates of produce exports. By 1700, Jamaica had received three times as many slaves as the Leeward Islands, yet was exporting less than two-thirds of the produce of these islands. It had also received almost three-quarters of the numbers entering Barbados but was exporting, as we have seen, only one-third as much produce as that island, although the discrepancy was much reduced between 1700 and 1714. Clearly, the Leeward Islands ultimately received more slaves and Jamaica, and possibly Barbados, received fewer than Table 8-3 indicates. The question is how many Africans were resold and where did they go?

The major resale market for the English, as for the Dutch at this time, was Spanish America. Spanish purchases were frequently disrupted by mistrust

---

Merchants, 1685–1716," *Social Science History* 22(1998):47–81, while putting a little more stress on the entrepot trade with Spanish America. But even apart from the issue of timing, neither author evaluates the possible magnitudes of such activity compared to the plantation economy.

[45] "An Accompt of Goods entered in His Maj Custom Houses in the American Plantacons as exported from one plantacon to another ..." (1677–8), CO1/43, f. 356.

[46] For comparisons of the estimates in Table 8-1 with other estimates of the English slave trade at this period see Eltis, "Volume and African Origins," 620–5.

Table 8-3. *Estimated Slave Arrivals in the Americas on English Ships,*
1662–1713

	Barbados	Jamaica	Leewards	Virginia Maryland	Other Regions	Total Arrived
1662–70	30,318	11,031	2,801	0	412	44,562
1671–80	21,400	20,323	9,566	3,082	318	54,689
1681–90	39,101	27,730	14,146	3,450	288	84,715
1691–00	29,394	35,945	5,304	3,391	2,104	76,138
1701–07	25,629	30,808	10,414	8,515	1,423	76,789
1708–13	10,167	34,711	7,048	5,273	2,110	59,309
1662–1713	156,009	160,548	49,279	23,711	6,655	396,202

Source: Calculated from Eltis, "The British Transatlantic Slave Trade Before 1714," 196–200.

and political intervention but a tendency to pay cash ensured quick
attention when the Spanish did enter the market. Records of the Company
of Royal Adventurers and Royal African Company sales to Cartagena, Portobello, and Vera Cruz exist for about seven thousand Africans carried into
Jamaica and about two thousand who arrived at Barbados. These transactions are almost all before 1700 in the Jamaican case and before 1682
in Barbados.[47] This is not, however, the sum total of company sales to the
Spanish and the company was far from the only English source of Spanish
slaves. Most RAC slaves arrived from Africa on "hired" ships the payment
for which was made direct to the captain in the form of "freight negroes,"
usually one-fifth of all slaves delivered. Captains sold these slaves separately
from the company, some of them to Spanish agents or representatives of the

[47] For the earliest sales see Zook, *Company of Royal Adventurers*, pp. 79–80, 87–
96. Zook stresses sales from Barbados, but an entry in the Jamaican ledger shows
£75 for provisions for "negroes sent to Cartagena," T 70/869, f. 14 (June, 1665),
which must have been for several hundred people. After the 1660s see "Considerations about the Spaniards buying negro's of the English Ro'll Company
and receiving 2/3 at Jamaica and 1/3 at Barbados," Jamaica, Feb. 2, 1675. Add
ms, 2395, f. 501. Also in CO1/31, ff. 6–7, though after the 1660s the ratio of
Jamaica to Barbados sales to the Spanish must have been far greater than two
to one. Also Stede and Gascoigne to RAC, March 17, 1681, T 70/15, p. 51, and
the correspondence summarised in T 70/10, pp. 17–20, and CO268/1, pp. 73–5.
For Jamaica see H. Molesworth and Chas Penhallow to RAC, Oct. 20, 1683,
T 70/16, f. 69 and the correspondence summarised in T 70/12, ff. 61–73. For
the 1690s see *ibid.*, ff. 94–96 and Walter Ruding to RAC, July 27, 1691 and
Jan. 7, 1692, T 70/17, ff. 26, 40. Also Chas Whittall to RAC, Aug. 8, 1695,
T 70/12, p. 151. For background to this trade and a low assessment of its extent
(the author does not appear to have consulted the T70 records) see A. P. Thornton,
"Spanish Slave Ships in the West Indies, 1660–1685," *Hispanic American His-*
torical Review, 25(1955):374–85.

Asiento holder (the licensed supplier of slaves to the Spanish Americas).[48] Non-RAC ships were another major source. In the 1700–14 period, before the South Sea Company established its operations, these became the major suppliers to the Spanish in Jamaica.[49] Finally, there were Jamaican planters, many of them investors in interloping voyages, who in 1681 when slave prices were high supported the assembly's imposition of a £5 duty on all slaves sold off the island but who two years later, when prices had moderated, repealed this act.[50] By 1686, they were petitioning London to stop the governor of Jamaica from interfering with "the spaniards who come to purchase negroe slaves & that noe seizure may be made of their shipps."[51]

None of the foregoing permits a precise estimate of the size of the trade, but it does suggest that the total leaving for the Spanish Americas must have been several times the seven thousand that appear in the RAC's records. Perhaps thirty thousand left before 1700 and twenty thousand between 1701 and 1714.[52] In Barbados, a much smaller market for the Spanish, the latter bought perhaps five thousand slaves, most before 1686. If these figures approximate reality then, as well as meeting all the needs of their colonies, the English may well have supplied fifty-five thousand overseas slaves to the Spanish American, sharing that market with the Dutch before virtually taking it over after 1714. Between 1662 and 1714, ninety thousand slaves arrived in Dutch ships at Curaçao or directly at the Spanish Main, but many of these would have gone to the French and a few to the English Leeward Islands.[53]

The English Leewards got most of their slaves direct from Africa. Nevis received the first direct shipments in the 1660s and, by 1672, had three times as many slaves as any of the other Leewards.[54] As sugar became established in the rest of the islands the market for direct shipments expanded. In 1675 the Royal African Company decided to order a ship direct to Antigua and instructed its Nevis factor to supply "Antigoa, St. Kitts & Montserrat with such quantities of good negroes as they can find payment for."[55] Some

[48]   Molesworth and Penhallow, Oct. 20, 1683, T70/16, f. 69.
[49]   Molesworth and Penhallow to RAC, Feb. 20, 1683, T70/10, f. 30; Samuel Bernard to RAC, August 20, 1692 and Sept. 16, 1692, T70/11, p. 92.
[50]   Molesworth and Penhallow to RAC, Sept. 26, 1682, T70/10, 29; idem, June 4, 1683, T70/10, f. 30.
[51]   T70/169, ff. 54–55. The petition was actually from the RAC but they appended a certificate "signed by the principall men of Estates . . . In Jamaica." The governor had seized two Spanish sloops that had arrived for slaves.
[52]   Stephen Fuller's widely cited annual series of the Jamaican slave trade shows 18,090 reexported from Jamaica, 1702–14. See Pitman, *Development of the British West Indies*, 391.
[53]   Calculated from Postma, *Dutch in the Atlantic Trade*, 45, 48, 54.
[54]   "A Particular of the Leeward Islands," July 17, 1672, Add ms, 2395, f. 530.
[55]   Minutes of Court of Assistants, T70/76, ff. 55, 58.

company ships from Africa divided their slaves among Barbados and one or more of the Leewards, and these are included in the appropriate columns of Table 8-3. Before 1700 none of the Leewards was as capable of handling complete transatlantic shipments of slaves as they were to become later, and the islands drew on Barbados[56] and, to a much lesser extent, the Dutch island of St. Eustatius.[57] Slaves from these areas arrived in small batches and on inter-island sloops that have left behind little record of their activities. Precise estimates are thus even more difficult to make for this traffic than for the Spanish trade, but the fact that sugar exports were twice those of Jamaica in 1700 suggests that slave arrivals between 1662 and 1700 must have been at least double the thirty-two thousand indicated as arriving by 1700 direct from Africa in Table 8-3. Moreover, a much larger share of both Leeward Island and Barbados slaves worked in the sugar sector than did their Jamaican counterparts.[58]

All but a few thousand of the inter-island arrivals would have come from Barbados, with the remainder from St. Eustatius. There were also a few hundred slaves carried from Barbados to the Chesapeake, probably less than five hundred in the 1698–1714 period and even fewer before 1698.[59] Some speculative adjustments for these intra-Caribbean movements of slaves leave

---

[56] For Barbados as an entrepot for the Leewards see Clement Tudway, Antigua, to RAC, Jan. 1, 1687, T70/12, p. 164; Bullard, Bate, & Stewart, Barbados, to RAC, Dec. 12, 1707, T70/8, f. 29; Bate & Stewart, Barbados, Oct. 12, 1708, *ibid.*, f. 41; idem, May 9, 1709, *ibid.*, f. 41; John Huffam, Antigua, to RAC, Aug. 8, 1708, Dec. 3, 1711, *ibid.*, ff. 40, 60.

[57] Thomas Trant to RAC, March 3, 1714, T70/8, f. 76; Clement Tudway to RAC, Jan. 7, 1687, T70/12, p. 164; Carpenter and Belchamber, Jul. 7, 1686, T70/12, p. 128; Philip Brome to RAC, May 17, 1697, *ibid.*, p. 141; Bate and Stewart to RAC, Oct. 12, 1708, T70/8, f. 41.

[58] Direct comparisons between Jamaica and the Leewards at this time are hard to make. Slave populations were likely not much different in the early 1660s but thereafter Nevis, the major sugar producer among the Leewards before 1690, became for twenty years the major Caribbean destination for indentured servants (Dunn, *Sugar and Slaves*, 123). Antigua, which took over Nevis' leading role and, like Jamaica, relied heavily on slave labor, developed only from the 1680s. By 1700, the slave population of the Leewards was somewhat below that of Jamaica (42,000 compared to 50,000), but, unlike Jamaica, almost all the islands' exports comprised sugar, implying that all Leewards slaves and perhaps servants were on sugar plantations. Moreover, Jamaican planters used slaves to grow provisions, whereas Leeward Island planters, and especially their Barbadian counterparts, relied more on imported foodstuffs.

[59] A count from Walter Minchinton, Celia King, and Peter Waite (eds.), *Virginia Slave Trade Statistics, 1698–1775* (Richmond, 1984), pp. 2–23, indicates seventy-nine slaves on ten vessels arriving from Barbados for Virginia alone. In addition, another eighteen vessels arrived with unspecified numbers of "negroes" from Barbados. Imputing an average of slaves on board for these eighteen from the ten with known quantities suggests 250 slaves to Virginia alone. Maryland is not likely to have taken in more than this. Fewer than thirty slaves arrived from Jamaica and the Leeward Islands.

us with Barbados retaining about ninety thousand slaves between 1662 and 1700, and Jamaica and the Leewards absorbing perhaps sixty thousand each in the same period. Between 1700 and 1713, however, even after adjusting for Spanish America, Jamaica absorbed more slaves than either Barbados or the Leewards, but the latter areas combined remained ahead of Jamaica. Thus, for the complete half-century, 1662–1713, 156,000 are estimated as arriving in Jamaica, with the island's slaveowners actually retaining closer to 100,000. Barbados was the single most important market on a net basis, absorbing perhaps 120,000 new arrivals from Africa over the same period. This made the English Caribbean and certainly the English Americas the major transatlantic market for slaves at this time and very nearly the major entrepot as well. No one could have imagined this happening a few decades earlier, in Richard Ligon's day.

This activity generated a per capita income in Barbados estimated at £16.0 in 1665–6, which increased by about one-third over the next thirty-five years, or just under 1 percent per annum.[60] As with any export economy producing a commodity the price of which was set on world markets, there were severe fluctuations. The onset of war induced a major decline in exports in 1688–9 to 60 percent of values in 1665–6, or less than half what they were to become in 1699–1701. While no income estimates are available for any war years, it is safe to assume that incomes, too, must have been severely affected by hostilities. Comparisons with other late-seventeenth-century groups are not easy. The Chesapeake colonies had three-fourths of the Barbados population in the mid-1660s but exported about half Barbados' total export values. By 1700, Virginia and Maryland had 80 percent more people than Barbados, yet exported nearly 40 percent less by value. It is likely that in both per capita and aggregate terms the tobacco colonies lagged behind Barbados. Turning to England, a recent revamping of Gregory King's social tables for England and Wales yields a real per capita income in 1688 of £11.7 (1700 − 02 = 100).[61] Barbados was thus one- to two-thirds better off than the society that spawned it even when slaves and servants are

---

[60] This paragraph, including all estimates, is based on Eltis, "Total Product of Barbados."

[61] Peter H. Lindert and Jeffrey G. Williamson, "Revising England's Social Tables, 1688–1812," *Explorations in Economic History* 19(1982):387, 393; for per capita estimates of GNP in the thirteen continental colonies expressed in 1980 dollars, see John J. McCusker and Russell R. Menard, *The Economy of British North America, 1607–1789* (Chapel Hill, N.C., 1985), p. 57. A conversion of these to prices in 1699–1700 yields a range for per capita GNP in 1700 of $51.4, assuming a 0.6 percent per annum growth rate from 1700 to 1774, to $64.1, assuming a growth rate of 0.3 percent per year – all estimates of income and wealth in thirteen colonies hinge on Alice Hanson Jones' estimates for 1774 (*Wealth of a Nation to Be: The American Colonies on the Eve of the Revolution*, New York, 1980). Converting dollars to pounds at 4.5 produces a highly speculative per capita range of £11.4 to £14.2, which places the continental colonies closer to England than to the sugar colonies.

included in the per capita count. If slaves and servants are excluded from the computation, then per capita income becomes £55 in 1665–6 and £82 in 1699–1700. Although the number of servants declined and the slave population increased strongly, the free population actually changed little after the 1660s. The small share of the Barbadian population that held the large estates obviously had extraordinarily high incomes. Late seventeenth- and eighteenth-century observers tended to look only at this group when contemplating West Indian society, and their concept of West Indian well-being was probably consistent with the per capita income measurement that excluded slaves. If per capita exports are any indication, whether with or without slaves, Barbados incomes were substantially higher than those in Bahia.[62]

What was behind the spectacular yet, from a modern perspective, obscene explosion of English economic power in the post-1650 Americas? As already noted, the ability of English slave traders, including the supposedly inefficient Royal African Company, to bring slaves cheaply from Africa was a vital part of English success in the great increases in their plantation production while at the same time sharing the Spanish-American slave market with the Dutch. It is striking that English domination of plantation production in the Americas – a domination not to be seen again until the collapse of St. Domingue in the 1790s – was built on the back of one of the great chartered companies of the mercantilist era. But if cheap slaves had been the only issue presumably the Spanish Americas and Bahia would have experienced comparable growth. In fact the English Americas received twice as many slaves from Africa as the Spanish Americas between 1660 and 1700 and quite possibly close to what the rest of the Americas received altogether. As Table 1-1 shows, a parallel situation existed for white transatlantic migration between 1640 and 1700. An efficient slave trade does not by itself account for the growth of the English plantation Americas. At least some of the key developments must have taken place on the plantations rather than on board slave ships.

The emergence of Barbados as the dominant plantation colony and rising imports of sugar into England came about in an era of declining sugar prices. Reliable annual series on sugar prices begin in 1673 and 1674, respectively, but scattered evidence from earlier years suggests an intermittent decline from midcentury, when Barbados sugar began to reach London in larger quantities.[63] There was a substantial decline during the third quarter of the seventeenth century (perhaps 50 percent), much of it in the 1650s,

[62] Eltis, "New Estimates of Exports from Barbados and Jamaica," 646–7.

[63] McCusker, *Rum Trade*, 1143; Galenson, *Traders, Planters and Slaves*, 65, 67. There has been little progress on finding earlier data since Pares commented, "Something very serious must have happened to the prices in the ... generation" of 1640s to 1670s, but "the course of sugar markets is very hard to trace" ("Merchants and Planters," *Economic History Review, Supplement,* 4(1960):70.

which was the subject of contemporary comment and shows up in London, Amsterdam, Lisbon, and, after a lag, in Bahia.[64] When usable annual data appear they show a 14 percent fall from 1674–8 to 1683–7. For slave prices a decline of perhaps one-third after midcentury ended by 1663–4. When annual data began in 1673 the downward trend had flattened, and there may even have been an increase from these years to the late 1680s.[65]

What is the significance of these trends? Taken together with the rapid expansion of exports of plantation produce from the English colonies, the faster decline in the prices of the planter's major output (sugar) than that of the major input (slaves) for thirty to forty years from midcentury is strongly suggestive of productivity improvements on the plantation. Moreover, this a different pattern from that faced by the Brazilian producer. In Brazil, prices of slaves and sugar remained in step until the Minas Gerais gold boom sent slave prices soaring late in the century.[66] Those supplying slaves and receiving payment in sugar in the English Caribbean felt intense pressure. The Royal African Company complained in a petition that they were "Great losers" because the sale of negroes in the Leewards "hath alwayes been for pounds of sugar (the accompts in those islands being kept in suger onely, & not in mony..)... yett the Prices of Negroes are but as formerly ...."[67] The company nevertheless supplied more slaves than any other business in the history of the Atlantic world and managed an average return on paid-up

---

[64] Falling sugar prices form one of the main themes of Lyttleton, *Groans of the Plantations* and Dalby Thomas, *An Historical Account of the Rise and Growth of the West India Colonies* (London, 1690). In the mid-1660s an English writer argued for a two-thirds price decline from midcentury ("True state of the manufacture of sugar in our plantations," n.d., c. 1667, Add ms, 2395, f. 636). As early as 1661, Barbados planters pointed to a 50 percent fall (CSPCS, 5:46–7). For a long-run Brazil and Mexico price series, see Ward J. Barrett and Stuart B. Schwartz, "Comparación entre dos Economías Azucareras Coloniales: Morelos, México y Bahía, Brasil," in Enrico Florescano (ed.), *Haciendas, Latifundios y Plantaciones en América Latina* (Mexico, 1975), p. 565.

[65] David Galenson relied mainly on Richard Ligon's estimate of what slaves cost in mid-century Barbados (*Traders, Planters and Slaves*, 64–5). New evidence from Larry Gragg ("'To Procure Negroes': The English Slave Trade to Barbados, 1627–60," *Slavery & Abolition*, 16(1995), 74–5) and Russell Menard ("Sweet Negotiation of Sugar," 46) based on actual transactions in Barbados in 1644, 1645, 1654, and 1658) indicate somewhat lower prices than Ligon's observation for 1647. The "Mary Bonadventure" (voyage id = 21,581) sold 244 slaves for £22 each in 1645. Ligon suggested £27 pounds for a prime male and £27 for a female equivalent in 1647 or perhaps £25 for a more typical adult. Bridenbaugh (*No Peace Beyond the Line*, p. 78) notes two transactions in 1644, one of thirty slaves sold for £660 and one of thirty-four slaves for £726. For the late 1650s, Gragg estimates a price of £17.

[66] Stuart B. Schwartz, "Free Labor in a Slave Economy: The Lavradores de Cana of Colonial Brazil," in Dauril Alden (ed.), *Colonial Roots of Modern Brazil* (Berkeley, 1973), p. 194.

[67] "Terms on which the Compa desire to furnish the Leeward Islands," April 19, 1687, T70/169, f. 47.

capital of 7 percent in the 1672–91 period.[68] Moreover, in the words of a 1670 broadsheet, the English had become "the best planters in the world" having reduced Portuguese imports from seventy thousand to twenty thousand chests a year, "and have caused the French and Dutch not to make new sugar plantations in the West Indies."[69] This was an overstatement. The French and Dutch expanded more slowly than the English. Brazilian sugar output did not decline, though it did, as we have seen, stagnate while Barbados and eventually other English sugar islands greatly increased their market share. Price declines or not, both slave trader and slave user did well.

After 1688 war increased freight prices and distorted the price trends for both sugar and slaves. When peace returned in 1697, sugar prices were double what they had been in the 1684–8 period in both Barbados and London while slave prices had increased by only 50 percent.[70] Given the much larger quantities of sugar shipped in 1698–1702, this suggests a surge in demand for the product or at least rebuilding of inventories. But Barbados prices declined again with the renewal of war and did not rise above 1680s levels permanently until after 1713. One interpretation of this pattern is that the dominance of Barbados was built on an efficiency or productivity advantage. Jamaica participated in this advantage, of course, but the emergence of the larger island (and of course, St. Domingue) after 1713 hinged in addition on a price rise for sugar sufficient to offset the extra expense of setting up a plantation complex in the western Caribbean. Productivity improvements in the delivery and use of slaves may well have continued after 1713 but the dominant long-run factor in European sugar markets had become rising demand by European consumers, no doubt linked to higher incomes in Europe. From a broader perspective, Barbados sugar prices were, by the early 1730s, almost back to where they had been in the mid-1680s. The English, and by this time the French, had come to dominate world sugar production without any permanent upward movement in the price of sugar occurring – indeed in the face of a price decline if we go back to the mid-seventeenth century.

There are no plantation records for this early period that would allow us to even verify the existence of productivity improvements, much less pinpoint their source. Detailed comparative work on early sugar operations in the Americas has generated output per slave and output per acre ratios, but these do not allow us to construct a total factor productivity index similar to

---

[68] Davies, *Royal African Company*, 72–4, 79; idem, "Joint-Stock Investment in the late Seventeenth Century," *Economic History Review*, 4(1952):291.

[69] "The sugar trade and the influence of the last Act of Navigation upon it especially in confining the growth of plantations in England" Rawlinson manuscript, A 478, n.d., but c. 1670, f. 88.

[70] For a price series for sugar in Barbados dating from 1678, see Robert Nash, "English Transatlantic Commerce, 1680–1750: A Quantitative Study," (Unpublished DPhil thesis, Cambridge University, 1982), pp. 65, 151.

what is possible for the slave trade.[71] Thus while the English contribution to the decline in the price of slaves is assessed in Chapter 5, there is no matching calculation possible for the even greater and more enduring concurrent decline in the price of sugar. Neither the quality of the soil nor the technology of sugar preparation are likely to have been major factors in the emergence of the English plantation colony. Virgin soils anywhere gave higher initial yields, but the advantage of Barbados over the Bahian Recònçavo is not obvious. The Barbadian ascent continued long after yields per acre had begun to decline, and both regions maintained profitable sugar sectors for centuries, not just decades. Sugar-making technology spread rapidly, even in the seventeenth century, and in this instance it spread from the region that lost market share to the region that gained it.

Adam Smith observed that "the prosperity of the English sugar colonies has been in great measure owing to the great riches of England, of which a part has overflowed upon those colonies."[72] What Smith meant here was that English consumers could afford to buy sugar but, to put a different sense on his words, could the close connections between London merchants and Barbados have provided planters with streamlined access to what was emerging as the world's major capital market, and could this have been the critical advantage? Cheaper capital would, of course, have meant no more than a substitution of capital for labor but, given the novelty of sugar in Barbados, this process could have been associated with innovation and improved technical efficiency. Cheap capital and new technology are common themes in the older literature on the emergence of the Barbados sugar sector, but the older literature stressed the Netherlands and Dutch merchants from Brazil as the source, rather than London.

New information has recently come to light on the early English sugar sector. An earlier generation of historians may have exaggerated the Dutch role in supplying both slaves and credit to the early sugar planters. From the Genoese in fifteenth-century Madeira, outside capital was important in the establishment of sugar cultivation, but, as with slaves, London was more important than Amsterdam.[73] After examining land transactions on Barbados during the period of the sugar revolution Russell Menard has concluded that

[71] J. Ward Barrett, "Caribbean Sugar-Production in the Seventeenth and Eighteenth Centuries," in John Parker (ed.), *Merchants and Scholars: Essays in the History of Exploration and Trade* (Minneapolis, Minn., 1965), pp. 147–89; J. R. Ward, "The Profitability of Sugar Planting in the British West Indies, 1650–1834," *Economic History Review*, 31(1978):203, 206.

[72] Smith, *Wealth of Nations*, (New York, 1937), pp. 625–6.

[73] The strongest recent statements on the influence of the Dutch in Barbados are J. H. Galloway, *The Sugar Cane Industry: An Historical Geography from its Origins to 1914* (Cambridge, 1989), pp. 77–83; and Matthew Edel, "The Brazilian Sugar Cycle of the Seventeenth Century and the Rise of West Indian Competition," *Caribbean Studies*, 9(1969):24–44.

if "the Dutch ... did play such a role, (they) have left few tracks in the surviving records in England or at the island."[74] This assessment is confirmed
by the Barbados customs books, which contain barely half a dozen names
that have any possibility of being Dutch in origin. On the Dutch side, there
is much more evidence of French planter indebtedness to Dutch merchants
than there is of English indebtedness. Guadeloupe and Martinique emerge as
far more important to Dutch merchants than the English islands, and even
in the French islands it is ordinary trade goods, not capital equipment for
making sugar, that appear in accounts of sales from the Netherlands to the
mid-seventeenth-century Caribbean.[75]

How important was direct investment from England? Menard has traced
twenty London merchants and a further two from outside London purchasing 1,800 acres of prime Barbados land in 1647. Total investment was
£25,000 sterling, and this was just the culmination of earlier activity. Four
brothers of the London-based Noell family alone invested nearly £10,000
in the island in 1646 and 1647.[76] Direct investment from London had a
major role in the process of buying equipment and consolidating land into
units capable of supporting sugar cultivation. But how many were still operating on the island in the mid-1660s? Of thirty-two London merchants
mentioned in Barbados deeds in the 1640s, only fourteen individuals with
the same family names may be identified in the Barbados customs books of
the mid-1660s, and the elimination of common family names such as Black,
Cooke, Andrew, and Ellis reduces the number to ten. Moreover only one of
these ten was in the top hundred entering produce into the Barbados custom
house. A further test of the London connection is possible with the aid of
the London port books. A comparison of the customs books with a list of
all 408 merchants importing sugar into the port of London in 1672 reveals
only 23 names common to both sources.[77] Ten of these names have broad
currency, and all 23 account for less than 23 percent of all sugar entered
for export. The largest Barbados planters may have been well connected in
England but by the mid-1660s they were not as a rule London merchants or
members of London merchant families.

---

74 Menard, "Sweet Negotiation of Sugar," pp. 30–6. On the unlikelihood of large
   Dutch slave sales in Barbados, see Gragg ("To Procure Negroes," 68–9).
75 Wim Klooster, "Dutch Trade, Capital and Technology in the Atlantic World,
   1595–1667" (Paper presented to the American Historical Association Annual
   Meeting, 1998), p. 7. It is also significant that among the English it was the
   Leeward Islanders, adjacent to St. Eustatius, rather than Barbadians who are
   mentioned as debtors. For the general background to illegal Dutch trading activity
   in the seventeenth-century Caribbean see idem, *Illicit Riches: Dutch Trade in the
   Caribbean, 1648–1795* (Leiden, 1998), pp. 18–71.
76 Menard, "Sweet Negotiation of Sugar," pp. 30–6, Table 7.
77 Jacob Price and Paul Clemens, "A Revolution of Scale in Overseas Trade: British
   Firms in the Chesapeake Trade, 1675–1775," *Journal of Economic History*,
   47(1987):36. I wish to thank the authors of this study for making the list of
   sugar merchants available to me.

Metropolitan capital was important in other ways. London capital markets formed the ultimate source of the credit critical to the functioning of long-distance trade upon which the planters depended. English shipping carried almost all merchandise, slaves, and plantation produce across the Atlantic; English insurance underwrote most ventures; brokerage activities, mail, and a host of other services were likewise supplied from the metropolitan centre of the empire to a much greater extent than was the case in any other European slave system, with the possible exception of the Dutch. These items are all current account entries on the balance of payments but clearly depend on the existence of the saving and investment of capital in a domestic environment.

Capital inflows continued after the initial switch to sugar. Governor William Willoughby raised £50,000 sterling by mortgaging and selling his English estates and spent the whole amount in Barbados on his plantations and on expeditions to other parts of the Caribbean, the ultimate aim of which was to add to his estates.[78] Among merchants, slaves were sold on credit, supposedly short, but in reality, long term. By 1680, with the RAC charter just eight years old, the company was owed £66,000 in Jamaica, almost £50,000 in Barbados, and over £56,000 in the Leeward Islands.[79] The terms under which the debt was contracted would suggest commercial credit, but planters had incurred more than two-thirds of this debt in the period 1673 to 1679, not the selling season of 1679–80. Given the fact that the company was prepared and able to carry the debt over a period of years, these funds should perhaps be reclassed as long-term capital inflows into the English Caribbean. Indeed, planters may have complained of the company monopoly, but it is hard to imagine a large number of small private companies carrying this long-term debt. In fact the company did in the end take possession of estates on the basis of non-payment.[80] As early as 1680, then, credit on slaves was comparable in amount to what London merchants put into Barbados estates three decades earlier. It is difficult to believe that slave traders supplying the Bahia market had anything like this ability to underwrite Brazilian sugar planters.

Despite this evidence, however, it is probable that the rapid expansion of English plantation output after 1660 in Barbados and a little later elsewhere was financed mainly by the planters. New reconstructions of balance of payments suggest that, overall, capital flows to the Caribbean from England in the later seventeenth century were not large.[81] Moreover, many of the larger

---

[78] Pares, "Merchants and Planters," 58.
[79] About one-third of these amounts were for slaves that the company knew to have arrived in the course of 1680 but whose accounts had not yet come in. Some of these slaves would have been sold for cash or produce. ("Debts," Nov. 4, 1680, CO268/1, pp. 69–70.)
[80] For an example of the RAC taking possession of an estate see Lewis Galdy, Kingston, Oct. 3, 1710, T70/8, f. 55.
[81] Nash, "English Transatlantic Commerce," 1–40 reconstructs the late seventeenth-

planters of the pre-sugar era in Barbados became major sugar producers. Between one-third and one-half of the big planters of the 1660s belonged to this category, which, allowing for normal attrition over two decades, suggests that the sugar revolution occurred without large-scale ownership change and that any debt was retired, or at least carried, with some ease.[82] There are strong parallels here with the Bahian sugar complex where, if the senors of the *engenhos* (sugar mills) did not always finance themselves in the late seventeenth and early eighteenth century, overseas capital was of trivial significance compared to local sources of credit.[83]

More generally, both Barbados and Jamaica had significant commercial sectors with a range of potential lenders separate from the planter class. If per capita income in Barbados was one- to two-thirds higher than in England, surplus spenders would not have been in short supply.[84] There are no Caribbean counterparts to the work of Bernard Bailyn on early New England merchants and Jacob Price on the tobacco merchants to the south.[85] It is perhaps for this reason, as well as the modern wealth of mainland North America compared to the Caribbean, that the West Indian commercial sector is viewed as having been behind that of its mainland counterpart. In fact, the commercial nexus in the English Caribbean was much bigger and more complex than its east coast mainland counterpart until at least the mid-eighteenth century.

Examples of the size and sophistication of the Caribbean commercial sector abound. The first bank in the English Americas, more properly a device to cope with a wartime induced shortage of hard currency, opened in Barbados, not the mainland; while it survived for only a few months in 1706, it had been

century balance of payments between England and the plantation Americas and argues partly on the basis of these estimates and partly on qualitative evidence that capital inflows from Britain into the Caribbean were non-existent after 1680. Apart from ignoring the role of the RAC in advancing credit, he also overvalues the slave trade. He does this by taking fob values of English exports to Africa as a proxy for the slave trade when at the beginning of the period more than half of these exports were exchanged for African gold. His broad conclusions are nevertheless accepted here.

[82] Dunn, *Sugar and Slaves*, 57–8.

[83] Schwartz, *Sugar Plantations*, 204–12.

[84] Eltis, "Total Product of Barbados." It is striking that the high per capita income of Barbados throughout the later seventeenth century did nothing to counter the decline in immigration from Europe. As noted in Chapters 1 and 2, what migrants wanted was land and, by the last quarter of the century, Barbados had none that was freely available.

[85] Bernard Bailyn, *New England Merchants in the Seventeenth Century* (Cambridge, Mass., 1955), especially, pp. 16–44. For a slightly later period in the Chesapeake see Price, *Capital and Credit in British Overseas Trade: The View from the Chesapeake, 1700–1716* (Cambridge, Ma., 1980), pp. 124–41, 156–7; idem (ed.), *Joshua Johnson's Letterbook, 1771–1774: Letters from a Merchant in London to his Partners in Maryland* (London, 1979), pp. vii–xxviii.

first proposed in 1661.[86] About ten times more transatlantic slave ventures left the Caribbean (mainly Barbados, Jamaica, and Antigua) than left the North American mainland prior to 1725.[87] In the third quarter of the seventeenth century, Bridgetown was the largest English town in the Americas and was overtaken by Port Royal in Jamaica thereafter. Both were principal port towns in the fullest sense before Boston and Philadelphia attained such status.[88] Bridgetown was the major distribution center for merchandise and slaves destined for the English Leeward Islands. Port Royal had a similar role for the Spanish Americas. Barbados was the base for most of the large number of English military and colonising ventures to the rest of the Caribbean and to the southern mainland until 1700. After 1700, Kingston became the third most populous city in the Anglophone Americas, its merchants even wealthier than those in Charleston, and the range of services the city provided comparable to those of Philadelphia.[89] As noted earlier, however, establishing the source of the capital does not show whether there were improvements in technical efficiency, much less the source of such improvements.

What this last comment implies is that comparing the sources, cost, and quantities of the three factor inputs in Brazil and the English Caribbean is not going to answer the question of why the English plantation sector grew explosively in the second half of the seventeenth century. Capital from outside sources was likely cheaper and more abundant in the English Caribbean than in Bahia at this time, but this by itself would lead only to a substitution of capital for labor and land, not necessarily technological advance. Put another way, at a time of expanding demand for sugar and mercantilist inhibitions of capital movements, cheap capital (and slaves) might have ensured an English presence among sugar plantations in the Americas but not the partial displacement of Brazilian producers. If English slave traders could deliver slaves to the New World more cheaply than could their Brazilian counterparts and were kept out of Brazilian ports by imperial regulations, such an advantage might only have served to counteract the fact that Bahia

---

[86] Pitman, *Development of the British West Indies*, 140–4.

[87] Between 1701 and 1725, 19 voyages left the North American mainland for slaves from Africa, compared to 208 from Caribbean ports. About 10 percent of the latter were by ships that had originally left Europe and were making a second voyage to Africa without returning to Europe. Between 1726 and 1750 these numbers were reversed. Only 21 left from Caribbean ports compared to 174 from the North American mainland (*TSTD*). The collapse of the Caribbean-based slave trade, indeed also its growth, requires further study.

[88] Bridgetown functioned much as did Philadelphia and Boston in the second quarter of the eighteenth century. See Jacob Price, "Economic Function and Growth of American Port Towns in the Eighteenth Century," *Perspectives in American History*, 8(1974):138–42.

[89] See the recent work of Trevor Burnard, especially, "The Grand Mart of the Island," and "Prodigious Mine: The Wealth of Jamaica Once Again" (Unpublished paper, 1998).

and Pernambuco were substantially closer to Africa than was the English Caribbean.

It would seem therefore that there is a strong presumption of productivity gains on the part of English planters from the mid-seventeenth century but, unlike the European-based slave trading industry, no clear idea of its source. We need data from, or at least more descriptions of what went on in the early sugar plantation. More specifically, as Stuart Schwartz has noted, there is much more information available on what happened in the sugar mill than there is of activities in the cane fields of early plantations.[90] From these we know that at a given point there were no great differences in roller technologies or in sugar-making equipment across the Americas. Almost all the descriptions of slaves at work in the fields come from late in the slave era, and these establish the existence of a whip-driven lockstep gang labor regime on most plantations, whatever the product and wherever the location. But for the period under consideration here, there is nothing except indications that slave drivers were key personnel, the labor they extracted was forced, and the punishments well in excess of what were the norm for whites.[91] The central question is the extent to which slavery and sugar production in the European-dominated Americas was coterminous with gang labor as described by later observers or did the latter evolve over time. At the moment, the answer is not known.

On the basis of earlier chapters, it appears that the high productivity of the Barbadian system was not possible in either England or Africa. No economic activity in the Old World could match the productivity possible on New World plantations. It is even possible to note real differences between Portuguese and English attitudes to non-Europeans that would have had some implications for the cost of operating a sugar plantation. As discussed in Chapter 3, the English regarded African slaves as quintessential outsiders or people without rights and values worthy of recognition. Lorena Walsh has argued for increased labor productivity in the Chesapeake as a result of switching to slaves, partly because English masters could ignore labor practices and rhythms that English indentured servants brought with them from the Old World.[92] Put another way, working with slaves provided masters with an opportunity to ignore cultural norms established in an environment where everyone was an insider. One of these cultural norms was the seventeenth-century notion of the freeborn English. In the Caribbean too, Africans, as a matter of course, could be made to function outside the conventions, especially those of gender, that the English had constructed for

---

[90] Schwartz, *Sugar Plantation*, 106.
[91] The most detailed description of plantation tasks and the earliest reference to a black slave driver in the English Caribbean appears to be in "Instructions which I would have observed...," n.d., but context suggests early 1690s, Rawlinson manuscript, A348, pp. 8–11, 14.
[92] Walsh, "Slave Life, Slave Society, and Tobacco Production."

themselves in the centuries before reaching overseas. Chapter 3 has shown that the English excluded non-Europeans more rigorously from membership in their social system than did other Europeans. They intermarried with non-Europeans less than did, say, the Portuguese. When progeny of mixed relationships appeared on the scene anyway (though always in fewer numbers than in the colonies of the Iberians), they were less likely to give such progeny full rights of citizenship. They were less likely also to give freedom to slaves to whom they were not related, whether through wills or through the self-purchase schemes that persisted in Iberian Americas through to the end of the slave era. It is entirely plausible that the English were less constrained than the Portuguese in their attitude toward Africans working in the field under their control.

But did the English introduce gang labor into the Americas, for this was the major source of high productivity on plantations? If they did not introduce it, did they at least systematize it so that slaves worked in rigidly controlled teams?[93] English attitudes suggest that the English Americas was the most likely point of evolution for such labor practices, a payoff for racism. While the awful conditions associated with sugar cultivation ensured the early disappearance of voluntary labor, in the absence of evidence either way it is more plausible that factory-like conditions in the plantation fields evolved over time, rather than were imported full-fledged into Brazil from São Tomé. There is no firm evidence of gang labor being used in the earlier Mediterranean sugar complexes.

Apart from the question of how work was organized in the early cane fields of the larger plantation, there is the related issue of the Brazilian *lavradores de cana*. These were small farmers without mills who would grow cane and give up a substantial share of what they grew in return for access to the sugar-making capabilities of an *engenho*. Some *lavradores de cana* owned slaves, in Bahia averaging, in fact, four slaves per cane farmer, but with highly unequal distribution. In the later period at least, the average number of slaves per owner was 7.2 in Bahia (1816–17), similar to the South in the United States in 1830 at 8.7, but whereas U.S. slave owners grew mainly tobacco and then cotton, for both of which potential economies of scale were less than for sugar, Bahian owners grew sugar. Compared to Barbados in 1679–80 where owners held 19.9 slaves per owner and Jamaica, at 25.0 slaves in 1832, average slave holdings in Bahia may not have been optimal for sugar production, though the larger plantations certainly had sufficient slaves to realize efficiency gains.[94] The one *engenho* that yields ratios of

---

[93] And if they did, to repeat a question asked earlier, can there be any doubt that the productivity gains would have been even larger and European expansion more rapid if they had used white slaves in this fashion, the Irish in particular?

[94] For comparative slave holdings in the Americas, see Stuart B. Schwartz, "Patterns of Slaveholding in the Americas: New Evidence from Brazil," *American Historical Review*, 87(1982):82. For *lavradores de cana* see idem, *Sugar Plantations*,

lavradora-produced sugar to total sugar produced shows that cane farmers grew all sugar produced in 1655–6 but only 22 percent in the years 1704–12. However, as there is abundant evidence that cane farmers were supplementary to the main cultivation activities on most *engenhos* before 1650, these ratios are likely not typical.[95] Thus while we do not know what was happening in seventeenth-century cane fields, circumstantial evidence suggests that a different and lower-cost system emerged in Barbados. The number of Barbados smallholders notwithstanding (making rum, it should be noted, rather than sugar), Brazil had both smaller average slave-holdings and more small sugar producers than Barbados, with the implication that full economies of scale were less likely to be realized in the Portuguese Americas.

The English Atlantic system had several novel features that separated it from the others. All European powers strived for the ideal most fully articulated by Colbert of a colonial system complementary to, and wholly dependent on, the European homeland. It is ironic that the two countries that came closest to achieving it in the seventeenth century – the English and Dutch – did so with fewer of the subsidies and direct restrictions that others, such as the French and Spanish, employed. It might be argued in fact that the English did not take over leadership of European slave systems from the Portuguese and Dutch; rather they created something new. Significant sugar production in the Dutch Americas (Dutch Brazil apart) did not get underway until the eighteenth century, and even then was always less, usually much less, than a fifth of the output of the British system.[96] Moreover despite the Dutch role in selling slaves to all-comers in the Caribbean, the focus of Dutch trade with Africa (defined by value) remained commodities, particularly gold, rather than slaves until as late as 1720. The English by contrast had switched to predominantly slave trading by the 1680s and perhaps the 1670s. Further, in the seventeenth century no part of the Dutch Atlantic (indeed the Dutch overseas empire as a whole) was seriously involved in production for export as opposed to trading with aboriginals or non-Dutch Europeans and, like the French, few Dutch migrated to the New World. The Dutch are usually put ahead of or bracketed with the English as leaders of seventeenth-century European capitalism, but the importance of gold and the relatively small share of nonspecie items in Dutch imports from the Atlantic evokes the pre- rather than post-seventeenth-century Atlantic world, a Spanish past rather than an English future.[97] There was nothing inevitable about this. Indeed,

295–312, and idem, "Free Labor in a Slave Economy," pp. 147–97. Barbados ratios calculated from Puckrein's summary of the 1680 census in *Little England*, 148. These sources unfortunately do not provide any indication of dispersion around the mean, a critical omission in the context of the present argument.

95 Schwartz, "Free Labor in a Slave Economy," 194–5.

96 Postma, *The Dutch in the Atlantic Slave Trade*, 174–200, 411; McCusker, "The Rum Trade and the Balance of Payments," 891–3.

97 Of course if the Dutch had managed to hold on to Brazil it might have been a different story.

without the efficiency advantage at shipping slaves, and given the massive decrease in English migration after 1660, it is possible that the English might have started down the Dutch road of global trading rather than global settlement and agricultural production after 1660, at least until migration began to recover in the second quarter of the eighteenth century. In comparison to the Portuguese, the English Caribbean plantation complex was not only part of a self-sufficient system it was also an extension of a financial, manufacturing, and transportation European hub.

But the most important innovations of the English system stemmed from the links explored in Chapter 1 between the evolution of free labor in the metropolitan economies and the tight control of slaves in the Caribbean colonies, as well as the cultural attitudes that ensured Africans would be slaves in the Americas. Both English and Portuguese operated in the Americas relatively free from government supervision, certainly imperial government supervision. What separated the English from the Portuguese was the fact that the former had less familiarity with people different from themselves or, alternatively, a more highly developed sense of separateness from non-Europeans. The oppressive conditions of gang work, which few peoples in history have voluntarily accepted, were more likely to evolve first in territories under English control. More and cheaper sugar was a tangible economic consequence of a more exclusive and tightly defined sense of insidership, especially when this was allied to local political autonomy, meaning the untrammelled freedom to exploit people different from oneself. Thus, the crucial contribution from Europe was not capital, nor even in the end plantation innovations, but the value system that made exploitation on this scale possible. The same system that countenanced more rights for workers in Europe (and we might add rising living standards in the long run) also ensured slavery in the Americas. The central practical distinction between the freedom to exploit others and the freedom from exploitation by others is how society defines others. As noted earlier, the story of the rise and fall of European slavery in the Americas is the story of how people defined themselves and identified with others in the Atlantic world, and this issue is the subject of Chapter 9.

9

Ethnicity in the Early Modern Atlantic World

EUROPEAN OVERSEAS EXPANSION and the slave systems in particular triggered an unprecedented intermixing of peoples in the Atlantic world. Social identity (more broadly, ethnicity), nationhood, or the way peoples group themselves beyond the confines of their extended family or kin, was probably more important than the profit motive in reshaping that early modern world.[1] Chapter 3 has argued that European-controlled slavery in the Americas cannot be understood without recognizing the differences between the nature of European and African self-identification. Europeans defined as insider anyone brought up as European. Africans drew the insider line around an area somewhat less than subcontinental in scope. Without such marked differences between these two self-concepts, slavery would not have been confined exclusively to Africans. Europeans thus entered the era with a conception of self that included some recognition of the subcontinent in which they lived as a defining entity. For Africans, no comparable perception existed and, initially, the terms Africa and Africans had meaning only to Europeans. Conceptions of separate group identities were no less pronounced in Africa than in Europe, but in Africa functioned without any overarching sense of the African continent as a whole. Elizabeth Isichei has convincingly argued

[1] Until recently much of the work on identities in the early modern period has focussed on how outside observers constructed the identity of others rather than on how individuals saw themselves (or self-identity). See for example Nicholas Canny and Anthony Pagden (eds.), *Colonial Identity in the Atlantic World, 1500–1800* (Princeton, N.J., 1987), especially Jack P. Greene, "Changing Identity in the British Caribbean: Barbados as a Case Study," pp. 213–66. In Africa the issue is often debated in terms of how colonial agents and elites shaped the identities of indigenous peoples, particularly in later southern Africa. See, for example, Leroy Vail (ed.), *The Creation of Tribalism in Southern Africa* (London, 1989). Here the question is rather how Europeans and Africans defined themselves and is consistent with the approach of Greene, *Gender, Ethnicity and Social Change*.

that the Igbo came to see themselves as a people or nation only in the aftermath of European contact.[2] Obversely, loyalties to kinship and, secondly, more distant associated lineages that were so important in Africa, had only weak echoes in Europe. Three centuries of contact, exchange, and violence among the indigenous inhabitants of Europe, Africa, and the Americas is at root the story of the impact of these competing conceptions on each other. Except for the Boers and Quebecois, the long-run outcome was that people widened the identities they created for themselves; nevertheless the more interesting impacts were short term and run counter to the direction modern observers might expect.

When Europeans dealt with other Europeans, and Africans with other Africans in the early modern era, national identity was usually paramount. In 1683, a pirate ship crewed by 150 men described as being "of all nations" captured the *Merchant Bonadventure,* a Royal African Company vessel carrying gold from Cape Coast Castle crewed entirely by Englishmen and waiting for its slaves off Whydah. Eager to find the gold on the ship – presumably a preliminary to sharing it equally among themselves – the pirates "seized all (the) officers to ye Gunnell to shoote (them) to Death to confess (its whereabouts)." In fact, "they only shott (the) Gunners mate to Death .... ye others (being) prevented by ye English Pyrates that was aboard, otherwise all ye Rest had dyed."[3] The incident encapsulated the tensions between class and a sense of nationality, with, in this instance, the latter emerging as dominant. African national identities were just as strong. Shortly afterwards, as the local population besieged the English fort of Commenda on the Gold Coast the factor complained of his servants, drawn from that population, "standing trembling and ... not fir[ing] a Gun at yr [their] countrymen, if you would hang them"[4] – circumstances that explain the European use of grometto, or castle slaves, discussed later.

It was only when Europeans and Africans dealt with each other that they tended to emphasize characteristics that they shared with other Europeans and other Africans, respectively. The resultant behavior often qualified as ethnocentric. Ethnocentrism among Europeans evolved most fully in the plantation Americas, though it might be argued that even here it was more severe after the end of slavery than before. Outside the plantation Americas (and perhaps the small African enclaves in which Europeans supervised African slaves), it became less pronounced as European conceptions of insider slowly broadened after 1600. In Africa, some Africans dealt with Europeans on equal terms. Without such relations, no trade with Africa would have been possible. The impact of this trading as well as some cohabitation

---

[2] Isichei, *A History of the Igbo People* (London, 1976), p. 20.
[3] John Lowe, Whydah, to the RAC, June 10, 1683, Rawlinson manuscripts, c. 745, ff. 209–11.
[4] Thomas Willson, Commenda, Feb. 19, 1696, *ibid.,* c. 746, f. 51.

was to break down the European sense of separateness despite the fact that the major items of trade were human beings from sub-Saharan Africa.

On the African side, the major effect of the African-European exchange that developed out of European contact from the Atlantic was dramatically different. If Europeans had an effect on how Africans defined themselves, it was to encourage an elementary pan-Africanism rather than to foster tribalism and attach inaccurate ethnic nomenclatures to African groups. The initial and unintentional impact of European sea-borne contact was to force non-elite Africans to think of themselves as part of a wider African group. Initially, this group might be, say, Igbo or Yoruba and, soon, in addition, blacks as opposed to whites. At the most elemental level the slaves at James Island, as we have seen, vowed to drink "the blood of the whitemen." In Gorée, a little later, one-third of the slaves in a carefully planned conspiracy "would go in the village and be dispersed to massacre the whites." When asked, albeit by the Europeans who had been at risk, "[w]hether it were true that they had planned to massacre all the whites of the island .... [t]he two leaders, far from denying the fact or looking for prevarication, answered with boldness and courage: that nothing was truer."[5] On board a slave ship with the slaves always black and the crew largely white, skin colour tended to define ethnicity. "[Y]e Chaldron Sloope, Capt. Latton, Commander," wrote the factor at Accra, in a typical report, "[Y]e slaves ryse on board her and killed all the white men."[6]

But through most of the early modern period there were limits to such inclusive identities among Africans that not even the traumatic experience of confinement on a slave ship could breach. Europeans were well aware of this and benefited from the relatively slow development of a broader sense of Africanness or even blackness. Throughout the period covered here all Europeans used grommettos, or castle slaves. Even before Europeans had established their bases on the Gold Coast, they had carried on a successful trade with slaves brought from other parts of Africa for sale on the Gold Coast. Carrying castle slaves into the area was simply a continuation of this pattern, except that the slaves were now put to work for the small European contingents who took up residence on the coast. The principle was the same, however. Slaves were carried far enough away from home to be sold into a strange environment and to people, white or black, whom they could only see as foreigners. Given that all non-slave inhabitants in the new environment were also foreigners, this increased the dependence of the slave on the owner and reduced the possibilities of escape. [7]

[5] For the full account see Pruneau de Pommegorge, *Description de la 'Nigritie'* (Paris, 1789), pp. 104–18.

[6] Marke Bedford Whiteing, Jan. 24, 1686, Rawlinson manuscripts, c. 745, f. 321.

[7] Ivana Elbl, "The Volume of the Early Atlantic Slave Trade, 1450–1521," *Journal of African History*, 38(1997):44–6 for the early trade, and Robin Law, *The Kingdom of Allada* (Leiden, 1997), pp. 90–2, for the later use of Allada slaves by all Europeans on the Gold Coast.

The initial victims of this trade came from São Tomé, but by the second half of the seventeenth century most gromettoes employed in the European Gold Coast forts were collected from Gambia and Windward Coasts by ships on their way to the Gold Coast from Europe or, alternatively, were brought from the Slave Coast. Cape Coast Castle had several hundred in residence, far outnumbering those slaves normally being held for the slave ships at this period. The castle served as a distribution point for the smaller forts along the Gold Coast.[8] The Dutch held 348 trainslaven or company slaves on the coast in 1703, most of them from points east.[9] The English establishments at Whydah and James Fort in the Gambia River in turn received their castle slaves from the Gold Coast.[10] Gambia slaves were used in the canoes, but the range of duties was wide and included the supervision of slaves being held in the forts prior to their embarkation for the Americas as well as defence against outside attack. The Royal African Company told its agents to obtain the "most fitt persons you can, such as understand armes if to be gott."[11] The strategy was effective, at least some of the time. From the Gambia, factor David Francis wrote:

I must needs Confess I have always had ye good fortune to prevent their [the slaves' rebellious] designs, the Slaves informing the Inhabitant Gromiettoes of their Designs, who have So much Affection for your Hon's Interest, that they always discover that their Designs to me, Whether out of fear, Love or Interest I cannot say.[12]

"Fear" or imagined "Interest" seem more likely than "Love" here, but in either case the motivation would seem to have more to do with the African perceptions of themselves and other Africans than to have been inspired by the Royal African Company. Dalby Thomas, the chief English factor on the Gold Coast, actually used castle slaves as unsupervised agents to trade gold and slaves with merchants in the interior.[13] There is no record, in this period at least, of castle slaves being dispatched to the Americas.[14] If they did

---

[8] Hayes, Chaigneau, and Hickes to R.A.C., March 7, 1708, T70/26, f. 22; Howsley Freeman, Commenda, May 1695, Rawlinson manuscripts, c. 746, f. 93; William Cross, Commenda, Oct. 27, 1686, *ibid.*, c. 745, f. 383; Ralph Hasell, Feb. 13, 1681, *ibid.*, c. 745, f. 94.

[9] Postma, *Dutch in the Atlantic*, 72.

[10] Edward Jacklin (Whydah, Oct. 13, 1692, Rawlinson manuscripts, c. 747) wrote that he needed all fifty of his castle slaves to repair the fort. For Gold Coast slaves at Gambia see John Booker, Gambia, Feb. 12, 1689, T70/11, p. 66 and R.A.C. to Humfries, Wight, and Boylston, June 11, 1689, T70/50, f. 93.

[11] R.A.C. to Humfries, Wight, and Boylston, June 11, 1689, T70/50, f. 93.

[12] David Francis, James Fort, to R.A.C., Dec. 21, 1716, T70/26, p. 54. It is not absolutely clear whether these gromettoes sailed with the ship as in the previous example or remained behind. For similar incidents at Whydah see Phillips' comments in Churchill, *Collection of Voyages*, 6:245.

[13] Dalby Thomas, Cape Coast Castle, Feb. 22, 1709, T70/5, f. 54.

[14] When they were too old for fort work, they were too old for the Americas. "Would have a new supply of Gambia slaves for ye use of ye forts, those they

join forces with their Americas-bound charges in acts of resistance against
Europeans, instances have not survived in the historical record. Indeed, as the
above suggests, quite the contrary; gromettoes, far from home and usually
preserved from the transatlantic market, were more likely to betray than
foment rebellion.

Guardians, or slaves taken on board slave ships for the explicit purpose of
controlling other slaves, had much in common with gromettoes. However,
they are even more useful to the historian in the effort to plot the evolution
of how slaves viewed themselves. Many of the slaves obtained on the Gold
Coast in the seventeenth century were in fact purchased to keep the larger
numbers obtained on the Slave Coast under control. Royal African Company
ships destined for the Windward and Gold or Slave Coasts were ordered to
use part of their Windward cargoes to buy such slaves. "If you meate with
Stout Negroes," the company wrote to Captain Ingle of the *Princess Anne*,
"you may buy to ye number of 40 for your Guardians out of said (Windward)
Cargoe .... [I]f you have not purchased ye full number of 40 negroes for
Guardians we order them (the Cape Coast Castle factors) to make up that
number."[15] The ship was then to go to the Slave Coast to buy 360 slaves for
Nevis. The practice was standard in the late seventeenth and early eighteenth
centuries, and before 1700 it is likely that nearly all male slaves that Slave
Coast–bound ships obtained from the Ivory and Gold Coasts west of Cape
Coast Castle, as well as many of those from the vicinity of the Castle itself,
were given roles supervising other slaves.[16] Different configurations held
elsewhere on the coast. Slaves from Sherbro, just south of Sierra Leone,
were used as guardians for slaves from the Bight of Biafra. Gold Coast
slaves were similarly employed in the Gambia. Indeed, the company used the
terms *guardians* and *gromettoes* interchangeably in a 1689 letter ordering
an exchange of slaves between the widely separated Gambia and Gold Coast
regions.[17] The distances involved were so great and the cultures involved so
diverse that guardians had diets quite separate from the main body of slaves.
Along with the guardians, the captains were invariably ordered to obtain
the appropriate provisions as well. People from the rice-growing regions of
upper Guinea, for example, could not be expected to live on yams.

have being superannuated." Dalby Thomas, March 6, 1707, T70/5, f. 40. For
parallels in the Dutch case, see Postma, *Dutch in the Atlantic*, 72.

[15] R.A.C. to Captain Joshua Ingle, May 22, 1688, T70/61, ff. 63–4. Voyage id is
9,821.

[16] In 1687 the company complained that "you (the factor at Cape Coast Castle) take
noe bills of Lading for Corne & a few Negroes for Guardians wch you deliver to
almost all ships that goe to Arda & by wch wee are uncertaine of our businies,
wch you ought to remedy ..." (R.A.C. to Humfries, Wight, and Boylston, May 3,
1687, T70/50, f. 38).

[17] R.A.C. to Humfries, Wight, and Boylston, June 11, 1689, T70/50, f. 93. For
Sherbro slaves see R.A.C. to Thomas Corker, Sherboro, Oct. 16, 1694, T70/50,
f. 157.

The duties and fate of these slaves may appear astonishing to the late-twentieth-century observers. Captain Phillips of the *Hannibal* wrote of the

30 or 40 Gold Coast negroes which we buy, and are procur'd us there by our factors, to make guardians and overseers of the Whidaw [Or Slave Coast] negroes ... [They] sleep among them to keep them from quarrelling and in order as well to give us notice, if they can discover any caballing or plotting among them ... when we constitute a guardian, we give him a cat or nine tails as a badge of his office ...."[18]

No instance has surfaced of guardians being given firearms, yet it is surprising that none of the 383 slave-ship revolts in a slave-ship-revolt data set appears to have originated among the guardians.[19] It is even more surprising when we take into account what happened to the guardians when they reached the Americas. Without exception they were sold into the same slavery that awaited the slaves that were put under their control. The guardians may have received better treatment on board ship but they could expect no benefits thereafter. They were bought with the same cargoes of trade goods as other slaves, consigned to the same factors in the West Indies, and sold into the same slavery as their charges.[20] In principle, there is not much difference between the functions of these guardians and the "slaves in redcoats" that the British used later or the Janissaries in Islamic armies.[21] All, in effect, sustained a slave system, and often helped acquire new slaves for that system. Yet in this case the poor future prospects of the guardians, no different to the slaves they were expected to guard, are rather striking. Slavery in the early English Caribbean was as closed (i.e., provided poorest prospect for a slave changing status) as in any society in human history.

As already noted, slave-ship revolts occurred regularly despite the precautions. Yet this did not guarantee unanimity among the slaves, much less between slaves and indigenous populations when the resistance occurred on shore. The captain of the *Brome* survived a revolt in the Gambia in 1693 largely because of differences among his slaves. When "the Jollofes rose," stated the cryptic report, "the Bambaras sided with the Master,"[22] thus

---

[18] Churchill, *Collection of Voyages*, 6:245–6.
[19] Eltis, Behrendt, and Richardson, "Revolts on Board Slave Ships: A Database."
[20] Though often purchased on the Windward Coast – the chief source of gold at this time – guardians were usually obtained with the goods set aside for slaves (see R.A.C. to Platt, Ronan, and Melross, October 16, 1694, T70/50, f. 155). For their consignment and sale in the Caribbean see R.A.C. to Thomas Corker, October 16, 1694, T70/50, f. 157. See also the letters to Francis Battram, Oct. 25, 1687 and to Nathaniel Bradley, May 24, 1687, both in T70/61.
[21] For later parallels see Roger Norman Buckley, *Slaves in Red Coats: The British West India Regiments, 1795–1815* (New Haven, 1979), especially pp. 1–19, 130–44.
[22] John Booker, April 25, 1693, T70/11, p. 76. This incident occurred on voyage number 9,706. There may or may not have been confusion as to the definition of the ethnic label Bambara in the Americas, but resident factors and some captains

saving not only the master's life but ensuring the successful (from the owner's standpoint) completion of the slave voyage. The Jolloffes were known for holding themselves separate from others, and in this instance, it perhaps cost them dearly. When the *Lady Mary* arrived in Montserrat in December 1686, 53 of the original 150 taken on board had died and "severall" of these deaths had resulted from fighting among the slaves.[23] The slave revolt at James Fort in 1681 was put down with the help of the local population. This brings to mind Cornelius Hodges' comments on the distance Gambia captives travelled, as well as John Thornton's assessment that upper Guinea was the most culturally and linguistically diverse part of sub-Saharan Africa. Such slaves were as foreign to the local population, and perhaps to other slaves, as were the Europeans.[24] Even when there are no references to dissension among slaves, the sources for the earlier period often indicate that slaves from a particular region had combined to start rebellions.[25]

These cases become intelligible only if we recognize that African identities did not assume a subcontinental scope until the twentieth century. We do not know how Africans at the time thought about themselves, but their actions suggest that over time Africans from different backgrounds gradually assumed elements of identity encumbering wider geographic and cultural boundaries. There is some parallel here with the process noted by the governor of Barbados at the end of the first generation of the expansion of slavery in the island and seven years before the first major slave conspiracy. "[T]he Blacks' ... different tongues and animosities in their own Country have hitherto kept them from insurrection, But I fear the Creolian generation now growing up ..."[26] On the African side of the Atlantic it was not

in the Gambia, unlike today's scholars, apparently had very clear conceptions of differences among peoples of the Senegambia region. For different interpretations of the meaning of Bambara see Gwendolyn Midlo Hall, *Africans in Colonial Louisiana: The Development of Afro-Creole Culture in the Eighteenth Century* (Baton Rouge, La., 1992), pp. 97–118 and Peter Caron, " 'Of a nation which others do not understand': Bambara Slaves and African Ethnicity in Colonial Louisiana, 1718–60," *Slavery & Abolition*, 18(1997):98–121.

[23] Edward Parsons, Montserrat, to R.A.C., Dec. 24, 1686, T70/12, p. 100. The voyage id is 21,026.

[24] Stone, "The Journey of Cornelius Hodges," 92–3. Referring to slave traders coming down from Jarra, 650 kilometers from the coast, Hodges wrote, "we never find yt in a Thousand they [bring] either woman boy or girle but in generall men slaves Such as they Know not what to doe with all, either through stubborness or feare of theire Runi'g, otherwise [than] to bring them to us to sell." For the assistance of the local population in suppressing the rebellion see Kastell to R.A.C., January 24, 1682, T70/10, f. 58.

[25] For example in 1701, after a revolt on board the *Don Carlos* (voyage id, 20,207) as it left Cabinda, the captives "unanimously, declar'd, the Menbombe slaves had been the contrivers of the mutiny," Churchill, *Collection of Voyages*, 5:512.

[26] Ld. Willoughby to Lords of HM Councill, July 9, 1668, CO29/1, f. 59. Shortly after the 1675 conspiracy, a subsequent governor, Sir John Atkins, could still write

creolisation so much as greater awareness of European activities and attitudes that increased the possibility of a successful slave-ship revolt. While the slave trade was already two centuries old in the late seventeenth century, for most of this period there were very few ports where departures exceeded a few hundred slaves a year. Fewer than half a dozen relatively small slave ships a year on average left all the rivers of Senegambia together – the locations of a disproportionate share of the evidence presented earlier – before the last quarter of the seventeenth century. As we have seen, the Gold Coast, the major source of guardians, was not a major provenance zone for slaves prior to the last quarter of the seventeenth century.

The point at which African levels of awareness of European activities began to affect behavior cannot be pinned down easily. We do know that during the first three-quarters of the eighteenth century decadal volumes of departures from Africa quadrupled. Although the Atlantic slave trade lasted four centuries, nearly two-thirds of it occurred between the years 1698 and 1807. By the end of the second decade of the eighteenth century, the English, at least, were no longer using guardians, and the practice slips from the historical record without any discussion. The slave trade of the Royal African Company declined precipitously after 1711 – it had already been dwarfed by the traffic of the independent traders – before reviving strongly in the 1720s. When it revived, however, guardians were no longer mentioned. In many respects the 1720s and 1730s are the most poorly documented decades of the transatlantic slave trade after, say, 1670, but what documents survive, noticeably the Nantes records and the South Sea and Royal African companies' material, contain little hint of shipboard use of one group of slaves being used to guard another.[27] Slaves were taken on as sailors on occasion, and fort slaves continued in use until the nineteenth century and beyond. Yet given the rapid expansion of the trade outside those areas in which forts were located, the fort-based gromettoes became much less important in the overall picture.[28] In all other African provenance zones, the Slave Coast, the Bight of Biafra, and the Angola region either side of the Congo River, slaves remained under the control of local slave merchants until just prior to embarkation. The latter were, presumably, better able to control the slaves than their European counterparts.

"They sleep not so unquietly as the rest of their neighbours in the Americas, from whence they receive nothing but il news of daily devastations by the Indians ..." (CSPCS, 9:368 letter dated April 3, 1676). An analogous process of black cultural integration in Virginia is one of the themes in Gerald W. Mullin, *Flight and Rebellion: Slave Resistance in Eighteenth Century Virgina* (New York, 1972).

[27] One exception to this assessment was the *L'Amitié*, (voyage id, 32,398) which had on board "les nègres quartiers maîtres" in 1787, the functions of which are not specified.

[28] Postma, *Dutch in the Atlantic*, 72.

Patterns of resistance on board slave ships after 1700 fit well with the disappearance of the office of guardian on board slave ships. There were few successful slave revolts in the sense of Africans returning to the African coast free of their European jailers, and even fewer where those who returned spent the rest of their lives free of reenslavement, but there were none in the early modern period, that is, before 1716. Of 383 slave revolts recorded in the slave-ship revolt database, only 23 are known to have resulted in some of the slaves on board returning to Africa or disembarking in Europe or the Americas free of slave status. One dates from 1820; almost all the others fall into the last three-quarters of the eighteenth century.[29] The key period, in fact, appears to have been 1750–94. Thirty-six percent of all vessels that actually took slaves on board (and were therefore at risk of rebellion) appear to have sailed in this period, according to the *Trans-Atlantic Slave Trade Database*. Yet no less than 54 percent of all recorded slave-ship revolts occurred in this period and a staggering 75 percent of all successful rebellions. Indeed, the twelve years from 1766 to 1777 account for 43 percent of cases of successful resistance. While fewer revolts occurred in the nineteenth century than the eighteenth, the most successful revolt currently known was in 1858, when 270 engagés (actually slaves) killed all but two of the French crew of the *Regina Coeli* and ran off in the environs of Monrovia when a British packet boat brought the ship to shore. [30]

Despite this last spectacular case, why did this trend to rebellion not continue into the nineteenth century? There are several plausible hypotheses, though no firm answers. We know that slave ships, for reasons not yet absolutely clear, began to carry far more children after 1800 than before.[31] Between 1810 and 1867, nearly half of those on board were children and only one-third were adult males. Second, from the early 1790s until 1807, the data on the slave trade have a heavy British bias. The British were subject to legislative restrictions after 1788, the effect of which was to reduce the number of slaves carried per ton of shipping and arguably made revolts less likely. Third, after 1775, the slave trade shifted away from the Upper Guinea region, ships from which were most prone to revolts and from where nearly half of all ships experiencing successful revolts originated. Fourth, and perhaps not entirely independent of the first three points, there would certainly

[29]   One of the more successful was on the London ship *Industry* (voyage id, 24,700 in *TSTD*) in 1772 where "the slaves killed all the white people except two, and carried the ship into Sierra Leone, where they ran her ashore and made their escape. A few of them were taken ..." (*Gentleman's Magazine*, 43 (1773):469). Data on revolts are in Eltis, Behrendt and Richardson, "Revolts on Board Slave Ships."

[30]   *The Times*, June 18, 1858; François Renault, *Liberation d'Esclaves et Nouvelles Servitude* (Abidjan, 1976), pp. 66–7.

[31]   David Eltis and Stanley L. Engerman, "Fluctuations in Sex and Age Ratios in the Transatlantic Slave Trade, 1663–1864," *Economic History Review*, 46(1993):310.

have been a learning curve for slave-ship owners and captains in dealing with revolts such that their incidence would decline. Owners and captains had more power and resources at their disposal than the slaves they moved. Fifth, and perhaps most important, a vessel took less time to obtain slaves after 1807, partly because of the attempts of slave captains to avoid capture when the traffic became illegal. The length of time a ship had slaves on board thus fell substantially in the nineteenth century.

Dissension among slaves did not disappear, but the last case of shipboard tensions resulting in the failure of a rebellion was on the Nantes ship *Levrette*, carrying slaves from various parts of the Windward and Gold Coasts. Incredibly, after five days in control of the ship and a violent fight among themselves, a group of slaves surrendered the vessel to the nine surviving crew members.[32] Nor are there cases of slaves dying as a result of internecine on-board strife after 1750 even though the historical record gets stronger over time. On the other hand, there is some evidence of improved cooperation in the later period. Not only do guardians disappear but when officers attempt to co-opt slaves to play the role of crew, usually because of sickness, instances of revolt appear that never occurred under the old guardian system.[33] In a related case in 1773, Captain Stephen Deane, who had already made seven voyages to the Gambia for slaves, found himself short of crew and took on board free blacks as replacements to help get his cargo of 230 slaves to South Carolina. This was a captain with a track record of dealing with free Africans (at least free African merchants) as equals.[34] As the ship began its voyage from Africa

some of his black boys belonging to the ship (free Africans) found means to furnish (the slaves) with carpenters tools, with which they ripped up the lower decks, and got at the guns and gunpowder; being overpowered, however, by the crew, they then set fire to the magazine, and blew up the vessel, by which not less than 300 souls perished.[35]

Slaves who escaped from slave ships to the African shore continued to be liable to reenslavement.[36] On board ship, however, slaves came to recognize a common white enemy and in the process modified their identities.

The same outward movement of barriers dividing insider from outsider may be seen within European communities in the Americas. Identifying

---

[32] And were taken back to Ile Principe and sent to the Americas on other vessels (Mettas, *Répertoire des Expéditions Négrières Françaises* 1:382). Voyage id is 30,658.
[33] Eltis et al., "Revolts on Board Slave Ships," voyage ids are 17,243 and 36,299.
[34] Ashcraft-Eason, "She 'Voluntarily Hath Come . . .'" Voyage id is 78,101.
[35] *Gentleman's Magazine*, 43(1773):523.
[36] Joseph Inikori speculates that some rebelling slaves received assistance from the local inhabitants ("Measuring the Unmeasured Hazards of the Atlantic Slave Trade: Documents Relating to the British Trade," *Revue Française d'Histoire d'Outre Mer*, 83(1996):63, 75). However, none of the 23 cases of successful resistance involved the assistance of local inhabitants, as far as we know.

oneself in relation to the peoples among whom one lived or, alternatively, did not live, was a universal phenomenon. The plantation Americas, however, especially the Caribbean, quickly came to contain an ethnic mix beyond parallel in the early modern world. As the story of the *Merchant Bonadventure* and the recent debates on European migration imply, ethnicity, or nationhood, was a powerful force in the Atlantic even before the arrival of large numbers of Africans in the Americas.[37] Scholars have naturally focussed on European-African relations in the Caribbean or more recently on similarities and differences between African groups. As already suggested, however, some reexamination of how Europeans saw themselves is relevant to a fresh assessment of African identity.

Whites in the early modern Americas had what Philip Curtin has called the "peculiar European sense of ethnic solidarity."[38] Yet a sense of nation was already highly developed, especially in England with its common language, centralized administration, and single large city. The colonies that Europeans established in the Americas could never have been European as opposed to French, Dutch, English, or Spanish, Except perhaps in the Spanish case (and even then only if we discount the Indian component), overseas settlements were generally more ethnically diverse than were the respective countries that had established them. The seventeenth-century English mainland colonies – which have the best evidence on the origins of whites – came closest to mirroring their Old World antecedents.[39] But even here, at least in the areas that became slave societies, people came together from dispersed English locations, though mostly passing through London and Bristol, to form communities. Free migrants to the Chesapeake tended to use family connections but, overall, a migration flow dominated by indentured servants did not lend itself to chain migration.[40]

Moreover, in sixteen cases where slaves reached the shore (nine of them after 1750), the local inhabitants reenslaved some of slaves. The voyage ids for these cases are 7,551, 11,178, 16,838, 16,873, 24,700, 25,310, 25,340, 30,445, 33,119, 33,131, 77,218, 87,001, 91,098, 91,415, 91,480, 91,564.

[37] Ethnicity or nationhood may today be used almost interchangeably in that, as social constructions, they have no genetic or even physical reality. As noted earlier, however, the bulk of the construction was carried out by the groups themselves whether they lived in Europe or Africa. Thus the composition of people living on either side of the English and the St. George's Channels was physically identical, but this did not prevent them from seeing each other as being very different.

[38] Curtin, *Pre-Colonial Africa*, 93.

[39] T. H. Breen, *Puritans and Adventurers: Change and Persistence in Early America* (New York, 1980), pp. 107–8. Carole Shammas, "English-Born and Creole Elites in Turn of the Century Virginia," in Tate and Ammerman, *Chesapeake in the Seventeenth Century*, 274–96.

[40] James Horn, *Adapting to a New World: English Society in the Seventeenth Century Chesapeake* (Chapel Hill, N.C., 1994), pp. 39–48, 109–11. Russell R. Menard, "British Migration to the Chesapeake Colonies in the Seventeenth

There was greater diversity in the English West Indies than in the Chesapeake. In one of the most widely cited comments on early Barbados, Henry Whistler, who visited the island in 1655, wrote, "This Island is inhabited with all sortes: with English, french, duch, Scotes, Irish, Spaniards thay being Jues ...."[41] The bulk of white migration to Barbados occurred before the more restrictive Navigation Acts of the early 1660s cut off the influx of Scottish indentured servants and after the flow of prisoners from Scotland and Ireland had ended. Yet most of the 903 names in the customs house entries for 1664–6, almost all those on Ford's map of 1672, and the property-owners listed in the 1680 census appear to be English.[42] Barbados deeds from the 1640s show strong connections with London merchants; before 1650, 80 percent of the servants originated in London. Despite the overall diversity, the core English migration to Barbados likely drew on a more limited catchment area than did its Chesapeake counterpart.

Jamaica was similar but became so via a different route. The island began to draw migrants after English migration had peaked and after Bristol and Liverpool began to reduce London's preponderance in the West Indian trade. Nevertheless, most of the Bristol and Liverpool connection with Jamaica developed after 1700 rather than before,[43] and the island had strong early links with London and the Home Counties. More than two-thirds of a sample of 2,077 European immigrants to Jamaica before 1720 came from London and its immediate environment. If David Hackett Fischer had included Jamaica in his studies, he would have found a fifth folk byway to the Americas connecting London and surrounds with that island.[44] A similar pattern is to be found in the French islands. The great majority of seventeenth-century French transatlantic migrants left from La Rochelle – most of them going to St. Domingue, St. Kitts, and Guadeloupe. Almost half of the engagés portion of the emigrants came from provinces in the immediate hinterland of La Rochelle.[45]

Between the mid-seventeenth and late eighteenth centuries, European Caribbean populations became more diverse (although in early St. Domingue the

---

Century," in Carr, Morgan, and Russo, *Colonial Chesapeake Society*, N.C., 122–6.

[41] "Extracts from Henry Whistler's Journal of the West India Expendition," in Charles H. Firth (ed.), *The narrative of general Venables, with an Appendix of Papers Relating to the Expedition to the West Indies and the Conquest of Jamaica, 1654–1655* (London, 1900), p. 146.

[42] Customs books. For Ford's map see Dunn, *Sugar and Slaves*.

[43] Kenneth Morgan, *Bristol and the Atlantic Trade in the Eighteenth Century* (Cambridge, 1993), p. 14 shows the growth of the Jamaica connection.

[44] Trevor Burnard, "European Migration to Jamaica," *William and Mary Quarterly*, 53(1996):769–96; David Hackett Fischer, *Albion's Seed: Four British Folkways in America* (New York, 1989).

[45] Debien, "Les engagés pour les Antilles (1634–1715)," 98–112.

opposite occurred as French migrants replaced freebooters). In the Dutch case, given that few citizens of the Netherlands could be persuaded to migrate, the mixture of peoples from around the Atlantic basins that lived in the Dutch Antilles and Surinam was always greater than elsewhere.[46] Deported Scots and Irish prisoners to Barbados in the 1650s were followed by subsidized Huguenot migrants to the British Americas in 1670s.[47] Colonial property-owners came from an increasingly wide range of geographic origins. British immigration policies and British military success in acquiring French and Spanish territories after 1756 reinforced this tendency. Part of the increasing diversity came from the slaveholding classes' capacity to absorb into their ranks people who were different from themselves. The most extreme example was in St. Domingue where, according to a free-colored deputy to the National Assembly, free coloreds owned one-third of all slaves in the colony. Faced with a tension between slave owner solidarity and white solidarity, the leading white planters plumped for skin color, and helped precipitate the sudden demise of the plantation regime.[48]

Like all Europeans, the English imposed restrictions on foreigners in their colonies. Paradoxically, Africans were not affected by this process, so that the tendency to base legislation on whom a person was, rather than on what that person did, had its largest impact on the Irish rather than on Africans. Because Europeans assumed that only Africans could be slaves, there was no need for legislation that singled them out (as African, as opposed to slaves) for particular treatment. For Africans, the English used a slave code to convert an insider/outsider divide into an apartheid-type legal environment.

For non-English Europeans, restrictions tended to be severe when the slave trade was beginning to change the ethnic composition of the new colonies, then weakened later, both in terms of formal legislation and the application of that legislation, as the influx of Africans reached its peak. In the early 1650s, English planters may not have been able to conceive of the Irish as slaves, but initially they found it almost equally as difficult to think of them as anything other than bound servants. An Irishman who arrived in the English West Indies without a contract was likely to be forced into one. Thus, in the aftermath of the Cromwellian deportations the Barbados Council

Ordered, that the three Irishmen, by name, Garrett Plumbett, Freman, Marsh Owen Carthy, Devenish Oye O'mehegan, which came over free (that is without indentures)

---

[46] Cornelis Ch. Goslinga, *The Dutch in the Caribbean and the Guianas, 1680–1791* (Assan, 1985), pp. 231–66.

[47] See for example "The humble Peticon of Rene Petit yo maj agent at Rouen ...," 1679 (arranging the settlement of several hundred Huguenots in South Carolina), CO1/43, ff. 246–51. In direct contravention of the Navigation Acts, a French citizen was registered as a ship owner in Barbados in the 1690s (Pitman, *British West Indies*, 221).

[48] Robert Stein, "The Free Men of Color and the Revolution in Saint Domingue, 1789–1792," *Histoire Sociale*, 14(1981):14.

do put themselves into some employment with some Freeholder of ye English nation, and that they do bring with them before ye Governor on Monday next their Masters, with whome they do agree to put in security for their good demeanour for the time they stay on the land.[49]

Despite these restrictions and the general hunger for labor in the plantation colonies, if Barbados is representative, English colonists despised the Irish as servants.[50] Moreover, they were not allowed to command seagoing vessels of any kind nor to bear arms unless enlisted. If enlisted, then, "Field officers of Every Regiment (were to) take an Exact list of what Irish ... are in their particular ... and to give an account of the Number of them .... as also their place of abode ...."[51] Infractions of a Barbados Statute of 1652 "impowering the Governor and Councell to inflict corporal punishment on such persons that give out mutinous language ..." involved far more Irish than other groups, including African.[52] Whether cause or effect of this policy, the Barbados Council noted in 1655 various reports of "severall Irish Servants and negroes out in rebellion in ye Thickets and thereabouts."[53] In this pre-1688 era, the Barbados authorities made no distinction between Catholic and Protestant Irish.

In the Leeward Islands, a large and divided Irish population earned a reputation for supporting whoever would serve their interests. Some sided with French invaders, others the English colonial administration, and in Montserrat, some conducted guerrilla campaigns against plantation owners. But Irish, both Catholic and Protestant, were to be found on each side of these divides.[54] As late as 1689 some Irish Catholics on St. Kitts rebelled

[49]   P.R.O., "Minutes of the Council of Barbados, 1654–58 From the Original in Barbados, 1654–1658" (henceforth "Barbados Minutes") Vol. 1, p. 53, December 6, 1854.

[50]   "(As) for Irish servants wee find them of small value, our whole dependence is therefore upon negroes." "Grievances of Barbados about negroes," April 6, 1676, CO 268/1, p. 43. See Burnard, "European Migration to Jamaica," 780 for comparisons between Jamaica and Barbados on this.

[51]   "At a meeting of Rt Hon Daniell Searle, Esq, Governor ... and ... his Counsell," June 11, 1660, P.R.O. CO31/1, p. 10. The occupational restriction reads "It is orderd that noo Irish bee comander ... of any Shallopp or boate belonging to or in this Island." For restrictions on arms see CSPCS, 1:487, June 11, 1660.

[52]   "Barbados Minutes, 1654–58," 1:121, Jan. 15, 1656.

[53]   "Barbados Minutes, 1654–58," 1:108, November 6, 1655. For other evidence of the position of the Irish see Hilary McD. Beckles, "A 'riotous and unruly lot': Irish Indentured Servants and Freemen in the English West Indies, 1644–1713," *William and Mary Quarterly*, 47(1990):503–22; and idem, *White Servitude and Black Slavery*, pp. 102–4.

[54]   C. S. S. Higham, *Development of the Leeward Islands under the Restoration* (Cambridge, 1921), pp. 40–60; Akenson, *If the Irish Ran the World*, 85–7. See also Aubrey Gwyn, "Documents Relating to the Irish in the West Indies," *Analecta Hibernica*, no. 4 (1932):243–9. Beckles writes of "Irish rebellions under Searle's administration in the 1650s" in Barbados (*White Servitude and Black*

in response to the accession of William of Orange. While the Royal African Company was hired to carry some of the rebels to Jamaica, we may be certain that they were not sold as slaves there. Further afield, in Maryland, any ship's master bringing in Irish servants had to pay 20 shillings per servant to the Naval office.[55]

Despite this seventeenth-century background and the increasing formal barriers against Roman Catholic land and officeholders thereafter, the Irish nevertheless quickly became almost fully integrated into white Caribbean society. The Irish have usually been depicted as remaining at the lowest levels of West Indian society, eventually migrating out of the Caribbean, or at least Barbados and the Leewards.[56] But large numbers remained. Beginning with the restoration of the right to bear arms in Barbados as early as 1660, the integration process moved farthest in Montserrat. The formal barriers against Roman Catholic officeholding emanated from London and were laxly enforced or overlooked in the Caribbean. Richard Dunn described the Montserrat Irish, comprising over two-thirds of the white population in 1678, as second-class citizens. Yet by the time the detailed 1729 census was taken on Montserrat, where they accounted for the largest share of the population of any Caribbean island, the Irish had become the island's major slaveholders and sugar producers. More specifically, they were "on average, bigger planters, and owned more slaves, than did their English counterparts."[57] Further, the Irish were disproportionately represented among eighteenth-century Jamaican officeholders.[58] It might be argued that the first great transatlantic Irish diaspora (that of 1650s) integrated more quickly than some later migrations from Ireland. Integration, indeed, was probably easier in a predominantly slave society (like the Caribbean) than a predominantly free society (like the northern United States), though that did not make slave societies any more attractive to immigrants.[59] As in Jamaica, descendants of the forty thousand Irish that moved to the Spanish Americas with Spanish government support in the 1650s filled many official positions in the colonies in the eighteenth and nineteenth centuries, especially in Cuba.[60]

Slavery, 122). This assessment seems to be based on a free interpretation of the use of the term rebellion in the Barbados Council Minutes. The context suggests the council meant runaways, rather than active resistance.

55 Dunn, *Sugar and Slaves*, 133–4. Henry Carpenter and Thomas Belchamber to RAC, Aug. 19, 1689, T70/12, p. 134. Anno 11, WIII, 1699, in *An Abridgement of the Laws in force in Maryland* (London, 1704), p. 77.
56 See most recently Beckles, "A 'riotous and unruly lot'," 508–9.
57 Akenson, *If the Irish Ran the World*, 117–53; quote is from p. 149; Dunn, *Sugar and Slaves*, 130.
58 Burnard, "European Migration to Jamaica," 780.
59 Thomas Sowell, *Ethnic America: A History* (New York, 1981), pp. 35–41.
60 See the Irish names in Allen J. Kuethe, "Los Llorones Cubanos: The Socio-Military Basis of Commerical Privilege in the American Trade Under Charles IV," in Jacques A. Barbier and Allan J. Kuethe (eds.), *The North American Role*

Discrimination against Jews, whatever their country of origin, was even more overt. Dutch and English conceptions of citizenship meant that the potential for full civil rights was greater in northwest Europe than in, say, the Iberian peninsula. In 1650 the Barbados Assembly passed legislation permitting the immigration of Jews and other religious minorities. Five years later the Barbados Council, in response to a petition, ostensibly put Jews on the same footing as foreigners in England, by resolving that "ye (Jewish) Petitioners behaving themselves civilly, and compartable to ye Government of this Island, and doing nothing tending to ye disturbance of the peace and quiet thereof during their stay, shall enjoy ye privileges of laws and statutes of ye Commonwealth of England & of this Island, relating to foreigners and strangers."[61] Surinam, in British hands between 1650 and 1666, followed suit and went even further in offering incentives to Jewish migrants. The contrast with the Portuguese and Spanish colonies is stark. An Italian capuchin wrote of the extensive forced labor in Portuguese Luanda at this time – he was observing deported Jewish degredados, not African slaves.[62] The striking point here is not the contrast between Luanda and Barbados but rather that when the Barbados resolution passed it was still illegal for Jews even to reside in England. Not until 1656, six years *after* the council decision, were Jews given the right to take up residence in that country for the first time since their expulsion in 1290. This suggests that the Jews sought out, and often found, a measure of civil liberties in the English Americas that was not possible in England itself.[63] They sought the same in the smaller Dutch colonies and received rather more initially; in the Netherlands there had never been any counterpart to the English expulsion.

Barbados and Surinam were ahead of their respective mother countries in offering some security for Jews, yet reference to the cited legislative decrees alone gives a misleading impression. Throughout the English Caribbean what was offered fell well short of equality. In Barbados, Jews were not allowed to hold more than one slave and could not own any Christian servants.[64] As he prepared to leave Barbados to take up the governorship of Jamaica

---

in the Spanish Imperial Economy, 1760–1819 (Manchester, 1984), pp. 142–57. For the 1650s migration see Abbot Smith, *Colonists in Bondage*, 162–74.

[61] Sheldon J. Godfrey and Judith C. Godfrey, *Search Out the Land: The Jews and the Growth of Equality in British Colonial America, 1740–1867* (Montreal, 1995), p. 38; "Barbados Minutes, 1654–58" 1:60, Jan. 9, 1655.

[62] Michael Angels and Denis de Carli, "A Curious and Exact Account of a Voyage to Congo In the Years 1666 and 1667," in Churchill, *A Collection of Voyages*, 1:491–2.

[63] Godfrey and Godfrey, *Search Out the Land*, 38; Stephen A. Fortune, *Merchants and Jews: The Struggle for British West Indian Commerce, 1650–1750* (Gainesville, Fla., 1984).

[64] P. A. Farrar, "The Jews in Barbados," *Journal of Barbados Museum and Historical Society*, 9(1942):130–4; Jerome S. Handler and Frederick W. Lange, *Plantation Slavery in Barbados: An Archaeological and Historical Investigation* (Cambridge, Mass., 1978), pp. 180–1.

in 1664, Sir Thomas Modyford noted that "Strangers (including Jews) are allowed to Live and Plant amongst us, but not in Separated Plantations."[65] In effect, the rights extended to Jews were that of residence and denization only, but even the Jews who were born in England received rights only on application. Nor were Jews secure in the economic enclave into which they were forced. In the late 1680s the Jews of Jamaica had to petition the crown against

english marchants and others who ... desirous to have the Jews deprived from their priviledges they enjoy ... did to that purpose petition that counsell, wherein the petition was at their request so earnestly admited that many members of the counsell did signe to it ....

The petitioners pointed out "they are allowed ... to be shopkeepers and to sell by the Retayle, a great many poore people of them having that onley way of living to maintaine their familyes ...."[66] The petition was successful, yet the Jamaican government was still able to levy a tax on Jews. Clearly, the Jewish presence was a privilege advanced rather than a right recognized.

Jews remained a small minority but were not at the bottom of the socioeconomic scale. In Jamaica, the small and urban-based community of Jewish merchants accounted for 6.5 percent of all slaves sold by the Royal African Company between 1674 and 1708.[67] It was wealthier, on average, than the English merchant community on the island.[68] The Barbados community was about three hundred strong or about 2 percent of the white population in 1679. It already had a representative among the ten largest Barbados sugar exporters between 1664 and 1666, and the forty Jewish family names in a list of exporters at that time (903 individuals listed) accounted for 3.3 percent of all exports.[69] At the end of the detailed 1679 census manuscript, a breakdown of a sugar levy (in effect a summary return of tax revenues) on the island lists Jews separately and shows them holding about one-fifth of the urban wealth of the island. There is only a single documented case of a Jewish owner of a slave ship but, given the restrictions discussed earlier, no Jewish planters.[70] Under the circumstances, Jews did well. Three of the four

---

[65] Thomas Modyford to Sir Henry Bennett, May 10, 1664, CO1/18, ff. 135–6.

[66] "Copy of petition to the Crown on behalf of the Jews in Jamaica against a proposal to withdraw letters of denization and other privileges granted to them" (n.d., but about 1688–90), Rawlinson manuscripts, D.924, p. 431.

[67] Trevor Burnard, "Who Bought Slaves in Early America? Purchasers of Slaves from the Royal African Company in Jamaica, 1674–1708," *Slavery and Abolition*, 17 (1996):74, 79–80.

[68] Meyers, "Ethnic Distinctions and Wealth," 54–75. Meyers stresses the disabilities of Jews in Jamaica, but the broader imperial perspective suggests an opposite conclusion at least in relative terms.

[69] Calculated from Customs books.

[70] For the tax summary and census see CO1/44, ff. 242–4. For the Jewish slave trader, see Stede and Gascoigne to R.A.C., March 31, 1685, T70/12, p. 10. For a

communities located on English territory that were large enough to support a synagogue before 1689 were in the Caribbean.

In no English possession in the Americas was there complete equality for Jews such as existed in the Dutch Caribbean by 1730, but over the course of the slavery era disabilities became fewer.[71] More important, the movement toward equality was strongest in the slaveholding colonies. South Carolina had a general naturalization law as early as 1697. Maryland had de facto, if not de jure, religious toleration. Barbados finally moved to treating Jewish and non-Jewish traders equal before the courts in terms of oaths in 1786. Pennsylvania, with few slaves but many Quakers, was the exception to this pattern in that it offered the most complete resolution to the thorny issue of oath-taking. The piecemeal approach to removing disabilities in the colonies was overtaken in part in 1740 by imperial legislation that extended naturalization to any Jew or foreign Protestant who had resided in the British possessions for seven years. The oath of abjuration, necessary for naturalization, was amended, though the wording was ambiguous with respect to the oaths required to exercise other rights of citizenship. In effect, the act encouraged a Jewish presence without guaranteeing equality, but while less equality was offered than to Jews in the Dutch Americas, it was more than was available in Britain before the nineteenth century.

The main motive behind the Plantation Act, as the new legislation on "foreign Protestants" and Jews became known, was to attract merchants to British possessions. For the British Isles, similar legislation was repealed almost immediately after it became law in response to popular protest. Indeed, for Roman Catholics generally and the Irish in particular the eighteenth century was an era of growing rather than diminishing disabilities.[72] For the English, at least, the Irish and Jews were the hardest to absorb. Outside these groups, naturalization in the English Americas quickly became a formality available to other Europeans in the plantation colonies upon payment of a smallish fee and an oath of loyalty.[73] Indeed the Jamaican government in the 1690s launched what was possibly the first broad-based assisted immigration scheme complete with dedicated revenue and named agents in Europe. The scheme reimbursed masters of ships for the cost of the passages of immigrants

useful summary of disabilities on religious minorities see Godfrey and Godfrey, *Search Out the Land*, 42.

[71] This paragraph is based on Godfrey and Godfrey, *Search Out the Land*, pp. 34–61. The stress here on the differences between slave and nonslave colonies is, however, my interpretation.

[72] A similar argument could be made for Quakers where the persecution of the 1680s was never repeated (Dunn, *Sugar and Slaves*, 103–6). What is lacking in their case, however, is a differential in the colonial and metropolitan environments. In fact Quakers quickly came to do very well indeed on both sides of the Atlantic.

[73] See the sections on naturalization in Jamaica and Virginia in *An Abridgement of the laws in Force and Use in Her Majesty's Plantations* (London, 1704), pp. 42, 121.

not just from England and Scotland but any European port. "Jews, cripples and children under 11 years of age" were specifically excluded, and, among provenance areas, Ireland was conspicuously not mentioned.[74]

For English relations with non-English of all types, but especially with Irish and Jews, Edmund S. Morgan's well-known argument for Virginia might be inverted. Morgan argued that planters resorted to slaves in the second half of the seventeenth century in part as a device to keep unruly and propertyless whites under control – or at least to provide a basis for bonding between elite and lower-class whites. Rather, the present discussion suggests that increased reliance on slaves resulted in the European inhabitants stressing what the Europeans had in common with each other. The end result, that of a large divide between peoples of European and African descent, is the same as in Morgan's interpretation of Virginian history, but the starting point is the need for African slavery, not the need for social control of one group of whites by another. In the shifting cosmopolitan environment of the early modern Atlantic world, expanding slave societies required not only a continuous supply of new slaves but also an ability on the part of slave owners to absorb new elements into their own ranks, not all of whom, as the southern colonies demonstrate, needed to be owners of slaves. In the Caribbean it was not only the slave population that could not reproduce itself: planters, though for different reasons, also had great difficulty in maintaining their numbers through natural increase. Planter groups that lacked demographic stability, or at least could not maintain the bonds that held these new elements together (as happened in St. Domingue after the French Revolution) collapsed.[75]

The strong pressures on descendants of both Africans and Europeans to search for and stress common bonds with others on the same side of the slave-free divide went further and fastest in the Americas. African nationalities sought out their own kind on seventeenth-century sugar plantations when establishing personal relationships and celebrating the rituals of life, sometimes with the help of slave owners.[76] Even in the earliest days there were no counterparts to grommettoes or guardians in the plantation Americas whose sole function was to prevent rebellion among those of different ethnicity from themselves. Much less were there recorded instances of slaves of one ethnic group coming to the aid of their owner against another.[77] For Ligon, who

---

[74] Act 9, 1693, *ibid.*, 162–4.

[75] Morgan, *American Slavery; American Freedom*; for the large influx of new slave owners (and nonslave owners) into St. Domingue between 1763 and 1789, and the impact of this after 1789 see Stein, "The Free Men of Colour," 15–28.

[76] Thornton, *Africa and Africans*, 197–201, especially the discussion of marriage on the Remire estate in Cayenne in the late 1680s.

[77] There is the widely cited reference of a Jamaican official to the help the English were getting from "negroes" (maroons) in tracking down escaped slaves: "The enemy in our bowels to whom our lives have been a prey, and many men have been

observed the earliest English plantations, a work force of several nations was potentially troublesome. One estate of two hundred slaves was considered well run, "as there are no mutinies amongst them, yet of several nations."[78] Nevertheless, the rebellions and conspiracies in Barbados later in the seventeenth century show little sign of internecine strife. The Coromantines (from the Gold Coast), most of whom presumably had been brought over as guardians on slave ships, had a prominent role in the Barbados slave conspiracy of 1675, but they were neither acting alone nor thwarted by non-Coromantines. The conspiracy was described as having "spread over most of the plantations" and was "a damnable design of the negroes to destroy them all."[79] The better known and documented slave conspiracy of 1692 contains no hint of ethnic divisions.[80] In Jamaica, an open land frontier ensured a greater frequency of armed resistance and escape. There is almost a consensus among scholars that slaves from the Gold Coast were overrepresented among the rebels, but seventeenth-century documents on Jamaican revolts contain almost no references to the African origins of rebels and none at all to inter-ethnic strife. As Gold Coast slaves were overrepresented among the early Barbados and Jamaican slave populations, Coromantines might have a larger place in the records on rebellions for the simple reason that they had a larger place in islands' slave populations.[81] Maroon communities, seen by some scholars as the ultimate statement of black solidarity against whites, did on occasion organize themselves around concepts of African nationhood. Acceptance of newcomers into such communities, however, had much more to do with geopolitical realities and the survival of the community than with the African origins of newly escaped slaves, and in the Jamaican case, division between Spanish- and English-speaking maroons was more important than ethnic divisions among African.[82]

subjected to their mercy (I mean the negroes) are now become our bloodhounds, and we are daily making depredations on them, and they are in our behalf more violent and fierce against their fellows than we can possibly be" (CSPCS, 4:345). But this somewhat cryptic comment contains no reference to ethnicity and is dated, significantly, May 1660, shortly after the English conquest and long before the island had become developed.

[78] Ligon, *True and Exact History*, p. 55.

[79] Sir John Atkins, Oct. 3, 1675, CSPCS, 9:294.

[80] Dunn, *Sugar and Slaves*, 258. For a full account see CO1/28, pp. 200–5.

[81] See CSPCS, 1685–88, docs. 299, 311, 330, 339, 445, 560, 623, 869, 883, 965, 1,286; and *ibid.*, 1689–92, doc. 1,041. References to the prominent role of Gold Coast slaves in slave resistance all appear to come from the eighteenth century, even though they refer in some cases to events in the previous century.

[82] Orlando Patterson, *The Sociology of Slavery: An Analysis of the Origins, Development and Structure of Negro Slave Society in Jamaica* (London, 1967), pp. 267–8; idem, "Slavery and Slave Revolts: A Sociohistorical Analysis of the First Maroon War," in Richard Price (ed.), *Maroon Societies: Rebel Slave Communities in the Americas*, second ed. (Baltimore, 1979), pp. 254–9; Michael

In the rapidly expanding early modern English Caribbean, experienced slave purchasers were as aware of differences among peoples from the various African regions, broadly defined, as they were of differences among Irish, Jews, French, and Spanish. Plantation profits depended on an awareness of cultural differences. Diet, language, knowledge of crops, and perhaps too, in the very earliest period, "the animosities (of) their own country" became elements in the decisions of owners for the very reason that they were elements in the way that slaves defined themselves. While the planters' basic requirement was slave labor from anywhere in Africa, no one can read the transatlantic correspondence of the early modern slave systems without recognizing the importance of African nationhood in the shaping of the plantation regimes. If the grometto and guardian activity is a guide, these differences were important to Europeans precisely because they were important to Africans.

No more than Europeans did peoples of African descent come to the Americas as random units of labor. The slave trade established transatlantic connections with patterns that were clearly discernible and have some intriguing parallels, as well as contrasts, with those of European migration. Cultural historians have tended to treat African and European movements across the Atlantic in isolation from each other. Consider the historiography: scholars have argued for the importance of the New World environment over Old World identities, or vice versa, *within* the African or European communities often without recognizing the parallels. According to Jack Greene, the environment in the Americas was the overwhelming determinant of New World Euro-American culture. For David Hackett Fischer, on the other hand, the background of the European (in his case British) settlers explains all that is culturally significant.[83] An almost identical split occurs among those interested in Afro-American cultures, a division that goes back to the work of Herskovits[84] and is made sharper by the wrenching impact of enslavement and the trauma of the middle passage. New data on Africans crossing the Atlantic have raised the prospect of considering European and African migration together.

Table 9-1 shows the African coastal origins of 192,000 Africans arriving in six regions of the British Americas between 1658 and 1713. For all of these (except Barbados) the dates cover the inception of the slave system. Scholars today see the experience of enslavement, movement to the African coast, assembly there and the subsequent voyage with peoples of

Craton, *Testing the Chains: Resistance to Slavery in the British West Indies* (Ithaca, 1982), pp. 74–80.

[83] Jack P. Greene, *Pursuits of Happiness: The Social Development of Early Modern British Colonies and the Formation of American Culture* (Chapel Hill, N.C., 1988), especially pp. 170–206; Fischer, *Albion's Seed.*

[84] Melville J Herskovits, "A Preliminary Consideration of the Culture Areas of Africa," *American Anthropologist,* 26(1924):50–63; idem, *The Myth of the Negro Past* (New York, 1941), especially, pp. 54–85.

Table 9-1. *Percentage Distribution of the African Regional Origins of Slaves Arriving in Major British Colonies, 1658–1713**

	Chesapeake	Barbados	Jamaica	Antigua	Montserrat	Nevis
Senegambia	34.2	5.3	5.4	2.5	21.8	8.9
S. Leone	0	0.8	0.5	3.0	0	5.0
Windward C.	0	0.2	0.4	0	0	2.9
Gold Coast	16.5	39.6	36.0	44.8	37.8	32.1
B of Benin	4.0	25.7	26.0	13.9	8.1	12.0
B of Biafra	44.0	13.4	11.5	32.3	12.6	24.7
WC Africa	1.2	10.2	20.1	3.6	0	13.1
SE Africa	0	4.8	0.2	0	19.7	1.4
N of slaves	7,795	85,995	72,998	8,926	2,037	14,040

*Columns 1 to 6 sum to 100.
Source: TSTD; Eltis, "Volume and Direction."

different nations on a ship that had already called at several points on the African coast to pick up slaves, as highly destructive of African influences on African-American communities. For Mintz and Price slaves on the middle passage were a "crowd" of disparate cultures rather than a grouping in any cultural sense.[85] The key elements in African-American culture were necessarily forged in the New World and contained components that were not originally African. Table 9-1 suggests that in the early British Americas, at least, this picture may be overdrawn. In terms of coastline geography a large degree of homogeneity in provenance zones existed. Nearly four-fifths of the slaves arriving in Barbados, the principal market for slaves in this period, and three-quarters of those coming to Jamaica, the second most important British market, came from the adjacent African regions of the Gold and Slave Coasts and the Bight of Biafra. Except for Angola, which contributed one-fifth of Jamaican arrivals and about which more later, no other African region from the very large region spanning Senegambia in the north to southeast Africa was really significant. Within the dominant region, the adjacent Gold Coast and Slave Coast alone accounted for two-thirds of Barbados arrivals and 62 percent of their Jamaican counterparts.

[85] Sidney Mintz and Richard Price, *An Anthropological Approach to Afro-American Past: A Caribbean Perspective* (Philadelphia, 1976), pp. 3–26. Most recently, see Morgan, "Cultural Implications of the Slave Trade," essentially in support of Mintz and Price, and Paul E. Lovejoy, "The Identifications of Africans in the African Diaspora" in Paul E. Lovejoy (ed.), *Constructions of Identity: African Communities in the Shadow of Slavery* (forthcoming), who effectively aligns himself with the David Hackett Fischer approach to Old World influences on the New.

The Gold Coast-Slave Coast dominance was even greater than Table 9-1 suggests. Chapter 8 established the importance of both Jamaica and Barbados as slave entrepots for the Spanish Americas. While precise figures for the African origins of those sent on to Vera Cruz, Portobello, and other ports from the British islands do not exist, there is abundant evidence that Africans from Upper Guinea, the Bight of Biafra, and Angola were overrepresented in this intra-American trade. In the 1660s, the Company of Royal Adventurers designated slaves from the Bight of Biafra for the Spanish market.[86] Jamaican planters sell to the Spanish "those negroes they find less usefull in their [own] plantations," stated the RAC in 1683.[87] Shortly after, their Jamaican agent sold a complete shipment from the Gambia to the Spanish and that "in doeing soo wee shall not much Dissatisfy the Countrey [that is, the English planters in Jamaica] who have noe esteeme for those sorts of negroes."[88] When the Portobello market was glutted in 1686, the RAC factor in Jamaica told the company to stop sending slaves from the Gambia because there was no other market for them.[89] The Royal African Company noted that "Angola, Gambia & Bite Negroes are not acceptable to our Planters [in Jamaica], So shall henceforward Supply you wth Negroes from ye Gold Coast & Wedah." However, the letter continued, they expected a renewed surge in "trade wth the Spanish and that those Negroes [Angola, Gambia, and Bight] will then turn to account."[90] The RAC was just one of many Jamaican-based sellers of slaves, but for every slave from the Gold and Slave Coasts it sold to the Spanish at Jamaica, there were six or more from other regions, especially Angola.[91] On Jamaica plantations at least, the estimate of two-thirds of all slaves coming from the Gold Coast-Slave Coast regions is very much a lower-bound figure, with the true figure perhaps in excess of 80 percent.

For Barbados, there is a sense of a policy change or even a learning curve. In the 1640s, Ligon's oft-quoted remark that "some ... (slaves) ... are fetched

[86]   "A Brief Narrative of the Trade and Present Condition of the Company ... ," CO1/19, f. 7v, n.d., but c. 1665.
[87]   "Some reasons ... offered to the ... Privy Councill of the Committee for Trade and Plantacons ... Why the late law ... in Jamaica setting the price of negroes at £18 per head Should not passe ...." Oct. 24, 1683, T70/169, f. 5.
[88]   Molesworth, Penhallow, and Riding to RAC, April 7, 1684, T70/16, f. 80.
[89]   *Ibid.*, July 5, 1686, T70/12, p. 73.
[90]   RAC to Charles Chaplin, Jamaica, February 23, 1703, T70/58, f. 28.
[91]   See the *Mediterranean* (voyage id, 14,909) and *Warrington* (voyage id 14,906), both from Angola whose 850 slaves were all sold to the Spanish (Walter Ruding, July 27, 1691, T70/17, f. 26), as well as the *Good Hope* (voyage id 9,668) and *Friend's Adventure* in the 1680s (voyage ids, 9,667, 9,680, 9,824). See Molesworth and Penhallow to RAC, Jan. 1685 (?), T70/16. f. 43, and Molesworth, Penhallow, and Riding to RAC, March 6, 1686, T70/12, p. 71. Calabar slaves from the *Expedition* were dealt with likewise (voyage id, 9,844. See *ibid.*). For a sale (or at least an expected sale) from the Gold and Slave Coasts see Ruding to RAC, March 31, 1691, T70/11, p. 85.

from Guinny, and Binny (Gold Coast to Bight of Biafra), some from Cutchew (Cacheo in Upper Guinea), some from Angola, and some from the River Gambia," suggests an almost randomised pattern of provenance.[92] An examination of the African regions of purchase by British slave ships before 1666 confirms Ligon's observation. Only 37.8 percent of British-purchased slaves are from the Gold and Slave Coasts compared to 39.3 percent from the Bight of Biafra, 12 percent from Angola and southeast Africa, and 11 percent from upper Guinea.[93] This is quite a different pattern from what held for the rest of the seventeenth century shown in Table 9-1 when the English acquired the great bulk of their early plantation labor force. "I have observed," wrote the owner of Drax Hall and Hope plantations to his overseer in the early 1690s, "that the Cormantine or Gold Coast Negros have always stood and prov'd best ... therefore you will do well to buy of that nation." In the same document he also ordered the construction of separate "negro housing ... for the better acomodation of Papa and Gambo Negros."[94] If, indeed, separate housing was required at this stage, then there was a clear additional cost associated with buying "of several nations" to use Ligon's phrase. Coupled with the quantitative evidence, such preferences for Gold and (also Slave) Coast slaves suggest a move toward a much less randomised approach to African regions on the part of English planters after their initial exposure to the trade.

The pattern of heavy Gold/Slave Coasts dominance is less pronounced in the smaller British-American markets. In all but the minor sugar island of Montserrat, however, a similar pattern of dominance by only two of the eight major African regions is apparent. In all cases, moreover, one of the dominant regions was the Bight of Biafra, slaves from which "were not highly esteemed" in the two larger markets of Jamaica and Barbados. The second dominant provenance zone for the smaller British markets was the Gold Coast. For Antigua and Nevis, the Gold Coast and the Bight of Biafra together accounted for 78 and 57 percent, respectively, of all slaves. In the Chesapeake, however, the two dominant African regions were Senegambia (the only slave colony in the British Americas where this region was prominent) and the Bight of Biafra, which together supplied almost four of every five of all arrivals. Planters in the Leewards had the same preferences as

---

[92] Ligon, *True and Exact History,* p. 47.

[93] TSTD. Note that this sample is for English slave ships, whereas Table 9-1 is based on slave ships arriving in the English Americas. The reason for changing the basis of the sample is that many early English slavers were recorded as going to Africa but left no further record of their voyage. As the English supplied only the English Americas with slaves before 1666, it is reasonable to compare this sample directly with the more rigorously defined sample used in Table 9-1.

[94] "Instructions which I would have observed by Mr Richard Harwood in the Mannagement of my plantation ....' n.d., but probably 1670s, Rawlinson, A.348, pp. 4, 23.

those in Barbados and were prepared to pay a premium to realize those preferences, but usually the premium was not sufficient to outbid the Barbados and Jamaica planters.[95]

The significance of these findings becomes greater if, first, the coastal patterns of trade on the African coast and second, the demographic structure of the coerced migrant flow are considered. Because of the strongly differentiated regional preferences for merchandise along the African coast, ships leaving on a slave voyage would normally trade in only a single region, though occasionally at several ports in that region. The *Transatlantic Slave Trade Database* contains information on the African coastal origins of 15,548 voyages, between 40 and 50 percent of all the slaving voyages made. Only 1,785 of these, or 11.5 percent, are recorded as trading at two or more places, and only 812 voyages, or 5.2 percent, traded at another place of trade *outside* the region in which the first trade occurred. Gold Coast ships figure disproportionately among these interregional traders, but on average they obtained a small minority—twenty percent—of their slaves at one of the two regions at which they traded. Table 9-1 thus provides a reasonably accurate picture of the regions where slave ships obtained their slaves.

Further, the distribution of actual embarkation points, as opposed to regions, was limited. Of the nearly 90 percent of slave ships that obtained their slaves at only one port, most obtained them at only a handful of different ports. Table 9-2 gives some indication of the extreme geographic concentration of the African end of the slave trade. Many embarkation points are known only through cryptic references made after the vessel reached the Americas: "Bite" negroes on board (for slaves from the Bight of Biafra) or "arrived from the Gold Coast." But for the 556 slave voyages to the British Americas for which specific embarkation points have survived, an astonishing 86 percent sailed from only six African ports. Of course these points must be regarded as the mouths of funnels for slaves collected from a wide range of coast and sometimes taken by ship or, more commonly, canoe to the transatlantic embarkation point; yet the fact remains that there were far fewer African points of embarkation at this time than there were ports of departure in Europe or ports of disembarkation in the Americas. Thus

---

[95] Clement Tudway and Edward Parsons, Antigua to RAC, June 11, 1687, T70/12, p. 164 noted a 12 percent premium for slaves from the Gold Coast. See also John Huffam, Nevis, May 25, 1710, T70/8, f. 54. Philip Brome, Nevis to RAC, July 28, 1698, *ibid.*, p. 142 observed that Nevis was "not in the condicion of Jamaica and other monyed islands" in that he (Brome) "was forced to give time" (credit to the planters) to sell the Gold Coast slaves from the *Sally Rose* (voyage id 9,723). Slaves from the Gambia that would not sell well in Barbados were sent on to Nevis and other Leewards for sale. On this see Bate and Stewart, Barbados, Oct. 12, 1708, T70/8, f. 41. For St. Kitts see John Huffam, December 3, 1711, T70/8, f. 60.

Table 9-2. *Principal Points of African Embarkation of Slave Vessels Arriving in the British Americas, 1658–1713, in Ascending Order of Importance*

Embarkation point	Number of vessels with known embarkation point	Percentage of vessels with known embarkation point
Cape Coast Castle	52	10
New Calabar	55	10
Offrah	70	14
Old Calabar	80	15
Gambia River*	85	16
Whydah	134	24
All known points**	556	100

Notes: *Ships leaving the Gambia carried fewer slaves on average than those leaving other ports. **Excludes voyages for which the region of embarkation was known, but not the port.
Source: TSTD.

Offra in Ardrah, then Whydah, dominated the Slave Coast; Cape Coast Castle, the Gold Coast; and Old and New Calabar, the Bight of Biafra.[96] The Gold Coast had the widest range of embarkation points of any region with Anishan, Anamaboe, Agga, Tantumquery, Wyamba, Accra, and Alampo all supplying slaves directly to transatlantic slave ships. More slaves left from Cape Coast Castle than from all these Gold Coast "outfactories" combined, but many of them had reached the castle via the smaller factories. Accra probably supplied greater numbers than any of the outports in the

---

[96] There appears to be some bias in the sources for Bight of Biafra ports at least as far as Bonny was concerned. Bonny was clearly important in the late seventeenth century. In 1701, a nephew of the king of Bonny visited London (RAC to Great King of Bandie, Sept. 15, 1702, T70/51, f. 150), and the separate traders of London were on intimate terms with the rulling elite of the port (Donnan, *Documents Illustrative*, 4:72–81). The port is of minor seventeenth-century importance in the *TSTD*, however. It seems likely first that Portuguese and Dutch slave ships were more common than English ships at this time (*ibid.*, 74), and second that ships arriving in the Americas from Bonny were described as being from Old Calabar. See for example the *Bridgewater* (voyage id, 14,995), which was reported in Jamaica as being from Old Calabar (T70/950, ff. 71–2), but was the ship that brought the nephew of the king of Bonny to England. *Bight* and *Bonny* may have been synonyms to some extent. The geographic concentration in the Bight of Biafra may thus be somewhat less than the data in Table 9-2 suggest, but it is also clear that there was almost no slaving activity of any kind at this time in the Bight of Biafra outside the three ports of Old and New Calabar and Bonny.

last twenty years of the seventeenth century.[97] All these subsidiary points of embarkation lay east of Cape Coast Castle or on the part of the Gold Coast closest to the Slave Coast. It thus becomes clear that nearly two out of every three slaves arriving at the major slave markets of the early British Americas – Barbados and Jamaica – came from a stretch of African coast between Cape Coast Castle to the west and Whydah to the east that was only 200 miles long. In the seventeenth-century English Caribbean, Bristol and London were only slightly more important to the servant trade than were Cape Coast Castle and Whydah to the slave trade. It is also important to note here that the English drew their guardian slaves used to control slaves from the Slave Coast, from points windward, or east, of Cape Coast – *outside* the region defined earlier.

What of the age and sex of Africans carried to the Americas at this time and why should it matter? To answer the second question first, generally the influence that any emigrant society has on its immigrant counterpart depends on the age and sex of the migrants. If the latter are all male or all female, then any impact on the receiving society will likely be weaker. As noted earlier, of the thousands of almost exclusively male Chinese who entered Cuba and Peru as contract laborers in the nineteenth century and the millions of predominantly female Africans who crossed the Sahara as slaves, there is now little trace. Tables 9-3 and 9-4 provide breakdowns of male and child proportions of the slaves who arrived in the early English Americas broken down by African region of provenance. The marked differences among African regions in the composition of their coerced emigrants discussed in Chapter 4 must have had profound effects on the way African Americans came to define themselves in the early British Americas. The numerically dominant provenance zones of the Gold and Slave Coasts also had relatively high proportions of females among the slaves leaving their shores – more than 40 percent as against less than 25 percent from Senegambia, an important area for the Chesapeake and to a lesser degree Montserrat. Of the other secondary areas at this time, Angola had much higher proportions of children among their captives than other regions. Women made up the greatest share of migrants from the Bight of Biafra but as noted the region was numerically important only in the Chesapeake and Antigua at this time.

---

[97] For slaves from the Gold Coast's "outfactories" and the eastern imbalance of slave numbers, see the numerous references in Rawlinson, c. 745 and c. 746, and the discussion by Robin Law, "The Royal African Company of England in West Africa, 1681–99" in Robin Law (ed.), *Source Material for Studying the Slave Trade and the African Diaspora: Papers from a Conference at the Centre of Commonwealth Studies, University of Stirling, April 1996* (Stirling, 1997), pp. 10–11. For the importance of Cape Coast Castle see John Brown, Feb. 11, 1704, T70/13, f. 61, and Dalby Thomas, Nov. 16, 1704, T70/28, f. 49, though neither of these assessments makes allowance for the slaves carried to Cape Coast from the outfactories.

Table 9-3. *Percentages of Male Slaves Arriving in Major British Colonies, from Select Coastal Regions of Africa, 1658–1713*

	Chesapeake	Barbados	Jamaica	Antigua	Montserrat	Nevis	All regions
Senegambia	79.3	70.0	78.1	78.0	90.8	74.6	76.2
S. Leone	—	80.1	—	75.3	—	73.3	75.7
Gold Coast	50.2	58.7	58.0	55.5	51.9	57.2	58.0
B of Benin	—	62.5	61.7	64.6	—	59.4	62.0
B of Biafra	62.2	47.8	51.2	47.7	49.6	47.7	49.3
WC Africa	—	62.2	60.9	50.0	—	52.9	60.5
Weighted mean (all regions)*	66.0	59.2	59.8	55.3	59.0	58.4	
Number of slaves	1,435	37,361	29,160	4,414	748	8,765	81,883

*Weights for weighted mean set according to the regional shares shown in Table 9-1. Note that no age and sex data exist for the Windward Coast and Southeast Africa for this period. In calculating weighted means the male ratio for Windward Coast was set equal to the ratio for Sierra Leone and that for Southeast Africa was set equal to the ratio for all regions combined. *Source: TSTD.*

Table 9-4. *Percentages of Children Arriving in Major British Colonies, from Select Coastal Regions of Africa, 1658–1713*

	Chesapeake	Barbados	Jamaica	Antigua	Montserrat	Nevis	All regions
Senegambia	4.5	6.1	7.3	7.1	1.2	5.2	5.9
S. Leone	—	8.2	—	0	—	4.6	5.0
Gold Coast	4.0	12.2	11.7	18.9	34.7	13.3	12.7
B of Benin	—	14.8	14.9	15.3	—	12.4	14.7
B of Biafra	7.1	8.8	14.0	11.2	8.6	10.3	11.2
WC Africa	—	19.5	22.1	19.6	—	25.7	21.5
Weighted mean (all regions)*	6.2	12.7	14.6	15.1	15.7	12.8	
Number of slaves	1,202	36,674	28,146	4,189	748	8,765	79,724

*Weights for weighted mean set according to the regional shares shown in Table 9-1. Note that no age and sex data exist for the Windward Coast and Southeast Africa for this period. In calculating weighted means the Windward Coast was set equal to the ratio for Sierra Leone and Southeast Africa was set equal to the ratio for all regions combined. *Source: TSTD.*

Thus far the analysis suggests two important conclusions, each of which calls into question the "crowd" consensus of the impact of the African slave trade. The first is that the early British Americas were supplied from a small number of African embarkation points – most of them located on a two-hundred-mile range of coast. Second, the age and sex mix of coerced migrants that left this littoral was such that, to the extent that family life was possible on the early sugar estates, there was more potential for it among migrants from the western Gold Coast/eastern Slave Coast than from other African regions or indeed among English indentured servants.

As with other aspects of the slave trade – the prices, age, and sex of slaves, for example – the geographic concentration noted here emerged from interaction between Africa and the Americas. By the last third of the seventeenth century the first preference of planters was for slaves from the Gold Coast. Throughout the early English Americas, planters would have been happy to have only Coromantines as they were called. "Gold Coast negroes," stated a factor in the West Indies, "are deare bought ... and allways the best in Esteem in all the Ilelands."[98] "We observe what you writt that Angola, Gambia & Bite Negroes are not acceptable to our Planters," wrote the company to its factor in Jamaica, "[s]o shall henceforward Supply you wth Negroes from ye Gold Coast & Wedah but hope the force wee have in your parts will be a Means to open the trade wth the Spanish and that those Negroes (from outside the Gold Coast/Whydah regions) will then turn to account."[99] From Barbados, where a leading planter had expressed a strong preference for Coromantines as early as the 1670s, the factor complained that "few people that would give good prices and make quick pay would come to buy Ardra and Gambia negroes of us while Cap[tain] Nurse had so many ... Gold Coast Negroes aboard him."[100] Slaves from the Slave Coast were thus a second choice, one made necessary by the short supply of those from the Gold Coast, which "sold for 3£ or 4£ a head more than the Whidaw, or as they call them Papa Negroes."[101] Such preferences continued through the eighteenth century long after other regions of Africa had displaced the Gold/Slave Coasts as the major provenance zones.[102] There was no indication here of buying from different regions for security reasons, and it was possible that maximising plantation output in these early days hinged on buying people of similar rather than different backgrounds to work together.

---

[98] Urban Hall, to Nath. Samson, Jan. 23, 1700, T70/57, f. 152.
[99] RAC to Chas Chaplin, Jamaica, Feb. 23, 1703, T70/58, f. 28.
[100] Edwin Steed and Stephen Gascoigne to RAC, March 19, 1683, T70/16. See also Peter Beckford and Lewis Galdy, Nov. 10, 1707, T70/8, f. 28; John Huffam to RAC, May 25, 1710, T70/8, f. 54; Churchill, *A Collection of Voyages*, 6:230. For the planter's comment see Jerome S. Handler, "An African-Type Healer/Diviner and His Grave Goods: A Burial from a Planatation Slave Cemetery in Barbados, West Indies," *International Journal of Historical Archaeology*, 1(1997):91–130.
[101] Churchill, *A Collection Voyages*, p. 230.
[102] Handler and Lange, *Plantation Slavery in Barbados*, 26.

Identifying the core African coastline on which Barbados and Jamaica drew and throwing light on the age and sex of those leaving that coast still do not tell us who the slaves were. The cultural identities of those leaving Africa in the second half of the seventeenth century are difficult to track, but the ultimate limits of the slave-supplying hinterland of this zone are geographic and economic. On the eastern fringe, there were various Yoruba-speaking societies and beyond that a slave supply system centered on Calabar and other Bight of Biafran outlets. There is simply no trace of any Yoruba culture in seventeenth-century Barbados and Jamaica (whether Lucumi or any other subgroup), a culture that, in the broad spectrum of Old World influences on the New, particularly in nineteenth-century Cuba and Bahia, has had an impact out of all proportion to its relative demographic weight, and might be expected to manifest itself if present.[103] There is some evidence of Lucumi peoples in seventeenth-century Peru and the French West Indies, but the proportions (as well as the samples) are small, and hard evidence of Yoruba slaves passing through Slave Coast outlets is mostly confined to the period before 1660 and after 1713.[104]

The gold-producing areas beginning with the Pra and Birim Rivers defined the eastern limit of this region. Here, gold production and associated forest-clearing activities, both carried out by slaves, made this western part of the Gold Coast more likely to import than to export slaves – gold production probably peaking at the end of the seventeenth century. This, of course, helps explain why it was that Gold Coast slaves entering the Atlantic trade came from eastern parts of the region, as well as identifying clearly the difference for seventeenth-century Europeans between Windward cargoes (that is, destined for the coast west of the major forts and intended for gold) and Leeward (that is east of Cape Coast Castle and intended for slaves).[105] The northern limit of slave provenance for the Gold/Slave Coast region is less certain. Thinning population densities on the Savanna and a growing Islamic influence defined the ultimate limits, but the low prices that held in the second half of the seventeenth century (probably the lowest in real terms of the whole transatlantic slave trade era) made a long-distance slave

[103] Eltis, Richardson, and Behrendt, "The Structure of the Transatlantic Slave Trade.

[104] Law, *Slave Coast*, 188–91; idem, "Ethnicity and the Slave Trade: 'Lucumi' and 'Nago' as ethnyms in West Africa," *History in Africa*, 24(1997):205–19. There is also the more general point that, for whatever reason, slave purchasers in the Spanish Americas, from seventeenth-century New Spain to nineteenth-century Cuba, were less concerned with regional preferences than were their counterparts in other jurisdictions in the Americas. We would therefore expect a greater mix of African peoples in the Spanish areas.

[105] Ray A. Kea, *Settlements, Trade and Politics in the Seventeenth Century Gold Coast* (Baltimore, Md. 1982), 33, 197–205; Ivor Wilks, "Land, Labor, Capital, and the Forest Kingdom of Asante: A Model of Early Change," in J. Friedman and M. J. Rowlands (eds.), *The Evolution of Social Systems* (London, 1997), pp. 517–21.

trade in the interior unlikely. Moreover, all of the heavily represented groups mentioned in a recent review of the peoples entering the Atlantic trade at this period lived within 150 miles of the coast.[106] Two out of every three slaves therefore were drawn from a region bounded by Yorubaland in the east, gold production in the west, and a line drawn parallel to, and 150 miles from, the coast in the north. This area was smaller than England, and much smaller than the low German linguistic region from St. Petersburg to Dunkirk that allowed soldiers from East Prussia serving on the Western Front in 1914–18 to make themselves understood in Flanders.[107]

In what sense was the Gold/Slave Coast region politically, culturally, or linguistically unified? Or as John Thornton has asked in a wider context, how successful were peoples from the region likely to be in interacting with each other given the pressure of forcible expulsion and a transatlantic relocation?[108] Politically, as in mainland Europe, there was no unity. States in the territorial sense existed, but they were numerous and while not unstable, even during the short rise to preeminence of the British Americas, they were liable to adjust boundaries.[109]

Language provided a better foundation for a sense of shared identity with the major division being set by the Volta River. Those to the east spoke Aja; those to the west, Adangme, an Akan language. Scholars disagree on the compatibility of the two. For Thornton, the similarities were such that "multilingualism was not particularly difficult." Differences between peoples on either side of the Volta were not likely greater than those among the northern French, Flemings, Dutch, and Germans on either side of the lower Rhine. Robin Law has argued that when Akwamu conquests west of the Volta created refugee immigrant communities east of the river around 1680, linguistic integration was far from instantaneous.[110] However, the most detailed study of changes in ethnicity in early modern West Africa is for precisely one of these communities – the Gold Coast Adangme who moved into the Keta lagoon area of the upper Slave Coast. Here, the dividing line between insider and outsider (a line of constructed ethnicity) came to be defined not in terms of indigenous and refugee populations but rather grouped together host populations and early immigrants on the one hand, against later immigrants (also Adangme speakers) on the other, the latter remaining outsiders for several more decades.[111] More generally, inland lagoons and rivers facilitated extensive economic exchange in the area, with trade in basic food and clothing predating a significant transatlantic slave

---

106   Law, *Slave Coast*, 188–91.
107   I would like to thank Pieter Emmer for drawing this parallel to my attention.
108   Thornton, *Africa and Africans*, 184.
109   Law, *The Kingdom of Allada*, 29–62.
110   Law, *Slave Coast*, 22–24; Thornton, *Africa and Africans*, 184–92.
111   Greene, *Gender, Ethnicity and Social Change*, 24–8, 47.

trade. Awareness of different groups and what they contributed to and had in common with one's own life would have been widespread.

At the same time that the English were expanding their trade in slaves, they were also shipping large, if at this stage somewhat diminishing, numbers of Europeans across the Atlantic. Indeed, as we have seen, to some degree the two migrant streams were substitutes for each other (see Map 8 in the map section following appendices). One was forced; the other came of its own volition. One shared culture, language, a system of government, and the possibility of advancement with an elite that controlled the colonised territory; the other could expect nothing but a life of hard labor and attenuated self-possession. But having recognized the obvious differences, a search for similarities may be productive.

Indentured servants also found themselves thrown together for an Atlantic crossing, and their experiences had something in common with slaves. Ships full of servants left from a small number of ports, and, while detours to Ireland to complete a cargo were not uncommon, most ships sailed direct to the Americas from London or Bristol or whatever their first port of embarkation might be. As in the slave trade to the early English Caribbean, servants would be separated from family members and might mix, especially after arrival, with other servants born far away in London or Bristol and who spoke a dialect that would be hard to grasp initially. A core or numerically dominant culture was a salient feature of both migrant flows. As noted, perhaps two-thirds of the servants and free migrants, too, arriving in the English Caribbean began their journey in the London area.[112] Of course, the concept of a "folkway" in the Fischer sense from a central place such as London is questionable in that, as the largest city in the Atlantic world, it was itself made up of migrants and spawned the phrase "the great wen" for its capacity to consume people. But it was, at least, overwhelmingly English. The core culture was surrounded by a number of smaller groups – Irish, Scots, and Jews. In the early eighteenth century, in part as a function of Marlborough's military campaigns, came the first of a major stream of German servants, almost all of whom went to mainland North America.[113]

Seventeenth-century Barbados and Jamaica thus had two core cultures, the one, southern English, the other, Akan/Aja. In one way, the cultural connections between Africa and Barbados/Jamaica were likely to have been stronger than their English counterparts. As already noted, over three-quarters of indentured servants were male, a ratio that increased after 1700. By contrast,

[112] Burnard, "The Composition of Jamaica's White Population"; the records of indentures are better for Bristol than for London, but no one maintains that Bristol was the leading port of departure for servants.

[113] Walter A. Knittle, *Early Eighteenth Century Palatine Emigration* (Philadelphia, 1937); Farley Grubb, "German Immigration to Pennsylvania, 1709–1820," *Journal of Interdisciplinary History* 20(1990):417–36.

more than two out of five arrivals from Africa were female. More broadly, perhaps four out of every five females who crossed the Atlantic before 1800 were African, not European. In the Caribbean, at least (with the possible exception of Barbados), neither white nor black populations were reproducing themselves. While hard information on seventeenth-century population pyramids is scarce, it is probable that with the exception of Barbados and possibly Irish-dominated Montserrat, none of the islands approached a balanced sex ratio for their white populations.[114] The prospect of early death was a constant threat to family life, black and white. Paradoxically the relatively large presence of women among arrivals from Africa might have meant that family formation (and all the cultural ramifications of this) on the part of those born in the Old World was actually easier among the black community than in many early white settlements. In Jamaica in 1661, for example, just as slave ships were delivering more males than females to the island there were six men for every woman in the white population.[115] Moreover, servants worked for the time of their contracts and then left the Caribbean in large numbers, further reducing the prospect of family formation. Slaves had no such choice.

African arrivals in the early English Americas, certainly the core islands of Barbados and Jamaica, were thus no more diverse than their counterparts from Europe, and they included many more females. It will never be possible to reconstruct African-American cultures for the early eighteenth-century Caribbean. Like archaeologists, all we can perceive at this stage are a few demographic foundations upon which that culture rested. To these may be added artifacts from grave sites and occasional references from travellers and officials that allow us to say categorically that prior to the nineteenth century slaves had control over their burial practices and probably many other of the central rituals of life.[116] In other words, a culture separate from whites and with a large African component must have existed. For its English counterpart we can see these same foundations and more of the original superstructure besides. Unlike English indentured servants, African slaves had nothing in common with the landowners and state officials who shaped the English Americas. The surviving remains, however, suggest the strong

---

[114] Akenson, *If the Irish Ran the World*, 115–16, 236–7.
[115] For the white population see CSPCS, 5:65. For slaves, the ledger book T70/599 records the sex of 1,496 arrivals in Jamaica between 1662 and 1665, from which a male ratio of 0.496 is calculated. Of course, the impact of immigration however defined, depended heavily on the size and structure of the host population. The populations of many settlements in the New World became self-sustaining eventually, and greatly increased size was associated with the evolution of more normal population pyramids and reduced migrant influence. But this was a slow process in the Caribbean. The origins and demographic structure of in-migration thus had a powerful impact on receiving societies.
[116] Handler and Lange, *Plantation Slavery in Barbados*, 171–215; Handler, "An African-Type Healer/Diviner," p. 120.

probability that conceptions of Africanness (or separateness from Europeans) must have contained fundamental and dominant Akan/Aja components. In Jamaica and Barbados in 1713 African slaves must have been as distinctively Akan/Aja as the European settlers were distinctively English.

However, just as the English planter class became more diverse, so too did the Africans laboring in the fields. After 1713, first, the Bight of Biafra took over from Akan/Aja region and then was itself replaced, though less completely, by Angola. But the process was sequential, gradual, and quite different from some other regions in the Americas, notably Cuba and Bahia. In Cuba, there was no dominant African group; in Bahia, the dominant group remained the same from one half-century to another, though in both Bahia and Cuba whites were far more numerous than in the Caribbean. Among whites, Spanish, French, and Dutch planters fell into the British orbit after 1750 and were successfully absorbed. Planters in Barbados and Jamaica, of course, remained predominantly English. In the course of a century and a half, the essential division in the Caribbean (St. Domingue in the two decades before 1792 notwithstanding) came to be just black and white. The two groups had become more homogeneous within themselves and more exclusive toward the other. Ethnicity had come to be defined almost entirely in terms of skin color.

From a transatlantic perspective, there were by the mid-eighteenth century two European conceptions of the insider/outsider division and a third, slightly different African version. Among those of European descent in the slaveholding Americas, the move to a more inclusive conception – one at least that might include blacks, as opposed to different kinds of whites – had come to a complete halt. Divisions between Europeans had lessened, but the experience of slavery made the divide with those descended from Africans close to absolute. In Europe itself the slow move to more inclusive definitions – specifically including non-Europeans – continued, generating in the long run a movement to abolish the slave systems of the Americas. For Africans, and more especially for those of African descent in the Americas, a conception of separateness from whites was inevitable, given the power relations on plantations and slave ships. Africans on both sides of the Atlantic displayed an increased willingness to downplay national differences. This is somewhat earlier than Michael Gomez has argued for in the case of slaves in the Old South.[117] This is not to argue that national differences among either Europeans or Africans ever disappeared. Ethnocentrism, however, was recast (or perhaps recaste) along lines of skin color, although the elements of such a division were already part of European, and especially English, identities, before the appearance of the first slave colonies in the Americas.

[117] Michael Gomez, *Exchanging Our Country Marks: The Transformation of African Identities in the Colonial and Antebellum South* (Chapel Hill, N.C., 1998), especially pp. 154–85.

10

Europe and the Atlantic Slave Systems

FOR NEARLY FOUR centuries, two increasingly different labor systems evolved on opposite sides of the Atlantic. Chapters 1 and 2 argued that, at least as they appeared in the second half of the seventeenth century, the systems grew from the same European roots, even though interactions among peoples from all parts of the Atlantic world, especially Africa decided central issues of their geographical location and who participated in them. But the earlier chapters did not address the issue of why, in the very long run if slavery and freedom had the same origins, one survived and the other withered. It is time to return to the longer view and explore how the systems of slavery and free labor affected and sustained each other in the European-dominated Atlantic world, especially after 1700. The issue has both an economic and an ideological side.

Historians have paid most attention to the material links between European slave and non-slave sectors that straddled the Atlantic. The rapid economic growth of both slave and non-slave sectors in the European Atlantic world, especially the northwest European Atlantic world, derived ultimately from the same intra-European demographic patterns, social structures, resource mobility, market values, and market institutions that placed Europe technologically and perhaps materially ahead of the rest of the world at the outset of European expansion. Initially, capital and labor flowed to the tropical Americas from Europe, presumably because the productivity of both was higher there than in Europe. The motivations behind such movements and the institutions that facilitated them were no different from those that marked similar shifts within Europe. Status and success or failure would be measured by the same standards in slave and nonslave societies. Richard Ligon and Père Labat, like most European observers visiting the Caribbean, found themselves in an alien world, but apart from the physical environment and the terms on which labor was used, it was an European milieu, despite the heavy African presence. European visitors could observe far more that was familiar and blend more easily into the society they found than could the several emissaries and children of African rulers who went to Europe via the West Indies in the slave-trade era to represent the interests of African slave dealers.

The plantation complex was nevertheless more than just the creation of merchants, plantation owners, and, less precisely, early modern capital, on which much of the literature dwells. In fact, the slave systems and what is perceived as their worst aspect, the transatlantic slave trade, were shaped as much by European consumers, African enslavers, and, as we saw in Chapter 7, African slaves themselves. European consumers demanded the cheapest possible sugar, tobacco, and cotton, and for most of this period cared little for how they were produced. From the sixteenth to the nineteenth centuries the price of sugar fell so much that the product moved out of the medicinal and luxury category to become a common grocery item and, indeed, given its role as an additive, a basic foodstuff. Tobacco and cotton followed analogous paths. Given the widespread demand for these products, those promoting the slave system included almost all living in western Europe, particularly the sweet-toothed British.

It has become commonplace to point to intensifying exploitation of both domestic workers and colonial slaves brought about by the changes that reached a crescendo with the Industrial Revolution. The fact that consumers of plantation products in Europe helped create the slave systems has received less attention. Yet if the ordinary European and, more particularly, the English (for centuries, by far the largest consumers of sugar in the world) had eschewed sugar or attempted to impose a moral economy that did not allow for the consumption (and thus production) of slave-grown sugar, the slave trade would not have existed. The English rioted against engrossers and middlemen generally who were thought to raise the price of comestibles, especially bread.[1] Eventually they rose in condemnation of slavery, but only after three centuries. One of the largest riots in eighteenth-century England occurred in Liverpool in 1774 when sailors gutted slave ships and turned ships' guns on the city houses of slave-ship owners. The seamen were not expressing outrage at the slave trade, however, but rather their unhappiness at wages – the share of the income they received from the slave trade.[2] Resistance by ordinary Europeans in the form of support for abolition undoubtedly helped end the slave systems, but what needs more attention is the lack of resistance (indeed, the active support) of those same ordinary Europeans that allowed the inception and continuation of slavery and the slave trade for more than three centuries.

---

[1] For the classic statement see Edward P. Thompson, "The Moral Economy of the English Crowd in the Eighteenth Century," *Past and Present*, 50(1971):76–123.

[2] Gomer Williams, *History of the Liverpool Privateers* (London, 1897), pp. 555–60. I would like to thank Steve Behrendt for this reference.

European waged labor and slave systems may have become more different from each other between the seventeenth and nineteenth centuries but they nevertheless continued to reinforce each other. Among the strongest (and most ironic) ties between the slave and non-slave systems of the European Atlantic are those suggested by a closer look at the "modernisation" process in England. As noted in Chapter 2, early English transatlantic migration was intimately connected with this process, the focal point of which was the creation of a modern labor force. English pamphlet literature circulating among the elite moved away from stressing low wages and draconian social legislation and toward the advantages of high wages in creating both enhanced worker productivity and a market for goods. Among the goods that European workers wanted were, of course, sugar, alcohol, tobacco, and, eventually, cotton goods, all of which meant slavery. Arguments stressing the advantages of high wages, some of which were used to purchase tropical produce, appear in Britain in the later seventeenth century just as transatlantic labor markets tightened.[3]

But slavery contributed in a less obvious way to these high wages. The Americas and Africa affected the English labor market by providing an alternative source of demand for labor-intensive manufactured goods. Both the Americas and Africa helped create markets both separate from Europe and with less likelihood of sudden imposition of tariff restrictions. International trade was certainly more important to the English in 1800 than in 1660. But the strongest growth between these two dates was in trade with the long-distance markets of Asia and the Americas, and in reexports of the products of these regions to the continent of Europe. Most long-distance markets afforded some protection for English goods. Transportation costs certainly acted like a tariff barrier, but at least it was a tariff barrier less susceptible to sudden changes than its man-made counterpart. It also tended to fall over the long term as transportation costs declined.[4] More important,

[3] A. W. Coats, "Changing Attitudes to Labour in the Mid-Eighteenth Century," *Economic History Review*, 11(1958–59):35–51; Engerman, "Coerced and Free Labor"; Jan de Vries, "Between Purchasing Power and the World of Goods: Understanding the Household Economy in Early Modern Europe," in Brewer and Porter (eds.), *Consumption and the World of Goods*, pp. 85–132.

[4] Anon, *Popery and Tyranny: or, the present state of France in relation to its government, trade, manners of the people, and nature of the countrey*, London, 1679, complained at the various subsidies and state aid to business provided by the French king. The latter was endeavoring "to make his subjects sole merchants of all Trades, as well imported as exported, and not only by the Priviledges already mentioned . . . , but also by putting all manner of Discouragements upon all Foreign Factories and Merchants by Difficulty in their Dispatches, delayes in point of Justice, subjecting them to Foreign Duties and Seizures, not suffering them to be factors to the French or any other Nation but their own, and in case of Death to have their Estates seized as Aliens, and the countenance and conceiving the French have as to all Duty when employ'd in the service of Foreigners" (p. 13).

the traditional, highly competitive continental markets for English products grew slowly, lagging behind both total trade and national income in growth, though Europe continued to comprise the largest single market for manufactured exports. In 1640, close to 90 percent of exports from London comprised manufactured goods to Europe; in the mid-1660s, the equivalent ratio was 76 percent, and in 1700, 69 percent. The major decline came after 1700. By 1785, if we take exports from Great Britain as the base instead of exports from London, manufactured goods to Europe accounted for just 28 percent of the total. Relative to national income, the figures are equally suggestive. In 1700 European purchases of English manufactured goods may be estimated at 5.2 percent of English national income; in 1785, only 2.3 percent, though of course the growth in absolute terms of all these markets was considerable.[5]

The importance of the rise of colonial markets for English wages is that as long as the continent of Europe was the market for English manufacturers, other things being equal, low wages were essential. As this market became less important so would the preoccupation with a low-wage economy. The slave system of the Americas provided a more secure market for English manufactures than did continental Europe. Thus the strong growth of the slave-based Atlantic system after the Restoration removed some of the urgent need to keep domestic wages as low as those in mainland Europe. The coincidence of this with the changing ideal in eighteenth-century pamphlets from a low- to a high-wage economy, attributed to a change in leisure preferences among English workers and improved productivity, is striking. In effect, the gradual change in the direction of English exports – from exclusive dependence on highly competitive European continental markets to the more protected environment of the British Americas and British East India markets – provided an additional stimulus to this acceptance of a high-wage economy. But there were also countervailing effects. As noted in Chapter 2, more than three hundred thousand English came to the Americas in the second half of the seventeenth century and about the same number of Africans (allowing for mortality) arrived in English territory in the Americas. Without

For the importance of protected transatlantic markets to English manufacturers see Davis, "English Foreign Trade, 1660–1700," 153.

[5] London exports calculated from Fisher, "London's Export Trade," and Davis, "English Foreign Trade, 1660–1700," pp. 163–6; London and English manufactured exports to Europe for 1699–1701 are calculated from Davis. For 1784–86 see idem, *The Industrial Revolution and British Overseas Trade* (Leicester, 1979), Table 38. Reexports are excluded as are all trade data for the 1790s and early 1800s because of the distorting effect of war. National income data for 1700 and 1785 were interpolated from the Gregory King and Joseph Massie estimates as revised in Lindert and Williamson, "Revising England's Social Tables, 1688–1913." For 1785, the Lindert and Williamson estimate for 1801/3 was adjusted using the rate of growth estimates for 1780–1801 in N.F.R. Crafts, *British Economic Growth During the Industrial Revolution* (Oxford, 1985), pp. 9–47.

African slaves, wages in the colonies would have been higher and even more English would have emigrated, putting upward pressure on domestic wages. Given the relatively small importance of transoceanic trade when measured against the domestic economy, discussed further later, none of these effects could have been large.[6]

Yet small though the effect may have been, it is hard to avoid the conclusion that it was not just the European and African slave merchants that helped ensure Africans would become slaves in the Americas; it was also the aspirations of European workers. Workers turned away from transatlantic migration in increasing numbers after 1660 as wages rose, thus ensuring increased demand for African labor. Their demand for cheap plantation produce was part of a gradual, secular rise in well-being that occurred in the second half of the seventeenth century, at least in the English case, and then later elsewhere in Europe. This was accentuated by changing values on the part of the worker as plantation produce formed a part (albeit small) of the goods that the "modernised" worker was now beginning to demand, as well as by the associated willingness to respond to higher wages on the part of more English and, later, European workers. Given the European taboo against European slaves, modernisation of the English work force thus meant more slavery in the Americas for Africans.

Less is known about the aspirations of seventeenth-century Africans. An analogous process of seeking to acquire more material objects, termed a "first consumer revolution," has been observed among indigenous populations as they came into initial contact with European goods. But the additional effort required for Amerindians and Africans to obtain such items was devoted to the acquisition of commodities (or in the African case, slaves) for trade rather than into a formal labor market. No more than Europeans would Africans and Amerindians work voluntarily in mines and sugar plantations in gang labor conditions, though unlike Europeans many of them were not given the choice.[7] The scarcity of voluntary migration from Africa to the Americas meant that Europeans rarely saw free Africans, but such scarcity also reflected the relative land abundance in Africa, which removed the incentive for voluntary African migration. Low population densities in Africa have also been seen as a reason for the stress in many African cultures on acquiring people as opposed to land.[8] It is of note that when Africans and those of African descent in the Americas eventually obtained an element of choice

---

[6] If all Africans had been replaced by English, three hundred thousand extra emigrants from England, 1650 to 1700, or about six thousand per year, would have constituted about a quarter of one percent of the English labor force in this period.

[7] James Axtell, *Beyond 1492: Encounters in Colonial North America* (New York, 1992), pp. 125–51, especially, 128–9; Thornton, *Africa and Africans*, 43–71.

[8] See Thornton, *Africa and Africans*, especially pp. 72–97; Kopytoff and Miers, "African Slavery as an Institution of Marginality," in idem (eds.), *Slavery in Africa*, pp. 3–76.

over their lives at emancipation, those able to do so left the plantations in search of land – a goal, in fact, of English workers between the seventeenth century and nineteenth century. Nevertheless it would be surprising, given the very different cultural backgrounds of seventeenth-century Africans and Europeans, if the aspirations of the two groups were the same. But because those who became slaves did not have choices, Africans affected the Atlantic world chiefly through their labor and, as seen in Chapter 7, their resistance.

How important were the slave systems of the Americas to Europeans in more conventional terms, for example as markets for European goods, as suppliers of raw materials, as generators of profits, and, more generally, as a share of British national income? Generally, if we rely on the evidence of the historical actors involved in any trade, or modern historical specialists who study it, the industry in question appears very important indeed. Arguments tend to be in terms of its indispensability, with the absence or decline of the particular activity seen as having disastrous implications for the well-being of the country as a whole. In 1625, in an early environmental twist to the concept, the "rapidly disappearing" forests of North America were cited as the beginning of the end of British naval strength.[9] In 1774, an agent of the Russian Company told Parliament that in the absence of trade with Russia "our navy, our commerce, our agriculture are at an end."[10] About the same time, exploitation of India, specifically, the drain of bullion to Britain, has been cited as the key contribution to the pool of savings that made the industrial revolution possible. But it is the West Indies that has figured most heavily in assessments of the importance of the colonies to the European metropoles, on the part of both scholars in the second half of the twentieth century and interest groups during the slavery era. In 1655, the planters of Barbados pressed for the removal of duties on sugar and other plantation goods they produced on the grounds of the great contribution they and "twenty thousand Negroes" made to the "National Stock," and in the process provided an estimate of the value of their activities broadly consistent with the discussion in Chapter 8.[11] In 1670, in a pamphlet arguing for lower sugar duties, an author wrote that without trade with the plantations, "this Nation must have totally sunck."[12] At this point, the settlements in the Americas could not have been producing in total more than half of one percent of English national product and would have had a lower proportion again in 1655.

Quite apart from the natural tendency of merchants and specializing historians alike to exaggerate the importance of what they are doing, the dramatic

---

[9] Eburne, *Plaine Pathway to Plantations*, 22.
[10] Cited in Immanuel Wallerstein, *The Modern World System III: The Second Era of the Capitalist World-Economy 1730–1840s* (New York, 1989), p. 142, n. 62.
[11] Add ms, 11, 411, f. 9.
[12] *The State of the Case for the Sugar Plantations*, Rawlinson manuscript, A. 478, f. 48.

expansion of the English Caribbean suggests the need for an assessment of the significance of the West Indies to the British economy which, for the second half of the seventeenth century, effectively meant Barbados. John Stuart Mill stated that the West Indies were so closely integrated with the English economy that trade with the islands "is ... hardly to be considered as external trade but more resembles the traffic between town and country, and is amenable to the principles of home trade."[13]

With this as a cue, it may be useful to ignore, for the moment, the separateness, both geographic and conceptual, of the West Indies and treat the Caribbean as part of British economy. In 1700, the population of Barbados was about that of a small prosperous English county or a larger town.[14] In England a county of this scale would have grown wheat and other produce to sell in market towns. From Barbados, no crop grown in England could have borne the cost of transportation across an ocean and no comparable market existed in the Americas at this time. The ability of the island to maintain trading links with an English (and North American mainland) economy thousands of miles away hinged on two factors. The first was transatlantic shipping technology; the second was the related issue of being able to carry over and coerce peoples from another continent with an intensity that would have been out of the question if the only source of labor had been England itself. These were high-cost activities, and most of the high value to weight that sugar commanded at this time (relative to, say, wheat) went to pay for the cost of transporting first, Africans to the Caribbean, and second, sugar from the Caribbean to Europe. Any additional or excess profit was probably offset by the cost of defending this new English territory, which was many times higher than would have been the case if it had formed part of the British Isles. Thus, while the Caribbean economy grew strongly in the ensuing century, before 1700, Barbados, and by implication the Chesapeake, were the economic counterparts of perhaps an additional Rutland with, say, coal reserves, or more appropriately for the Chesapeake, given population densities, Westmorland. This was enough, however, to make them far more significant than any other region of the Americas. The English who went forth and multiplied (temporarily in Barbados and eventually in the Chesapeake) would probably not have been unemployed if they had stayed at home, though they may have been less productive. The Africans who were forced to relocate, on the other hand, were from an imperial perspective, an increment, or pure gain. But sailing the Atlantic was not costless. For the English who stayed behind, the Americas in the seventeenth century meant a very few more wealthy individuals in an already unequal society, marginally cheaper sugar and tobacco – items

[13] Mill, *Principles of Political Economy with Some of their Applications to Social Philosophy*, 2 vols. (London, 1895), 2:256–7.
[14] For the evidence and calculations to support the assessments in this paragraph, see Eltis, "Total Product of Barbados."

claiming a tiny share of a household budget in the seventeenth century – and a few thousand extra jobs and the ships to provide them in long-distance trade.

The dramatic expansion of the slave system continued long after 1700 but so too did the British economy. Did the relative position of the Caribbean change? The usual approach to this question is to compare the sugar sector in 1700 with the sugar sector at some later date. The years 1775, 1783, 1800, and 1850 are commonly used benchmarks, and the expansion of slave-grown sugar in the Americas (and the slave trade from Africa, which lay behind such expansion) in any of the periods suggested by these benchmarks was very strong. For many scholars such growth makes a prima facie case for exploring potential impacts on the economic activity in any European mother country. No scholarly issue should be left prima facie, however. If we compare British slave trade and plantation sectors with those of other European nations and in addition set British sugar against a backdrop of some other well-known British industries, then the importance and certainly the uniqueness of British sugar production fades considerably.

On the first of these, it is now clear that whatever the morality of the business in the eyes of abolitionists and later observers, the slave trade formed such a tiny share of the Atlantic trade of any European power that, even assuming the resources employed in the slave trade could not have been employed elsewhere, its contribution to the economic growth of any European power was trivial. The largest number of slave ships to leave Britain in any five-year period was in 1798–1802, long after the beginning of the structural changes in the British economy that might be termed industrialization. The busiest single year was 1792 when 204 vessels comprising 38,099 tons of shipping, or about four slave ships each week on average, left England to carry slaves from Africa to the Americas. Each voyage lasted just over a year. In 1792, there were 14,334 vessels registered in Britain totaling 1.44 million tons.[15] The slave trade thus accounted for less than 1.5 percent of British ships, and much less than 3 percent of British shipping tonnage. Ratios of cargoes carried and freight earned would be in the same range, and of course, as a share of any measure of all British economic activity, including profits, as opposed to just shipping, the shares are so small as to be meaningless. Moreover, if such a trace amount of economic activity could contribute significantly to industrialization, then we might expect the first industrial economy to have been Portugal, not Britain. Though Portugal had less than one-third the population of the British in the late eighteenth century and a national income that was no doubt lower than one-third the British level, the country's nationals nevertheless managed to carry 40 percent more slaves across the Atlantic than did the British. While the British outperformed the Portuguese as slave traders in the long eighteenth century, the relative size of

---

[15] Slave trade data computed from *TSTD*. General shipping data are from Mitchell, *British Historical Statistics*, 539.

their two economies (even if we include Brazil) always meant that the slave trade was far more important to the Portuguese than to the British.[16]

The trigger to metropolitan economic development that has emerged in the literature in the last two decades, however, is seen as the slave system, rather than the slave trade per se, upon which Eric Williams placed such stress.[17] But here too, from an international perspective, there is no systematic connection between the size of the plantation system – defined in either absolute or relative terms – and the development of the metropolitan society that spawned it. Despite the impressive performance of the British Caribbean in the seventeenth and early eighteenth centuries, the French plantation sector expanded much more rapidly than did its British competitor after 1714. By 1770, the French Caribbean was producing 17 percent more sugar, nine times more coffee, and thirty times more indigo than its British counterpart. Overall, as contemporaries fully appreciated, the French Caribbean produced 43 percent more crops by value than did the British just before the American Revolution.[18] Between 1770 and 1791 the phenomenal expansion of St. Domingue ensured that the French planter and slave increased their lead over the British. The British Caribbean, which had continued to grow in absolute terms after 1770, though more slowly than the French, surpassed the French once more after the St. Domingue revolution effectively removed French competition. Yet British abolition mean that by 1850 other areas had nevertheless overtaken the British. By 1850, slave-grown sugar from Cuba and Brazil, cotton from the U.S. South, and coffee from south-central Brazil were all much greater in both volume and value than the British plantation system had ever produced. Indeed, from the broad perspective, British domination of the American plantation sector was limited to 1665–1730 and 1792–1820. No one attributes French industrialization to the French plantation sector nor looks for links between the economic development of Iberia, or Brazil, and the Brazilian slave system. Such international comparisons make it difficult to understand why the scholarly effort devoted to establishing causal links between slavery and industrialization continues to focus on Britain.

[16] David Eltis, Stephen D. Behrendt, and David Richardson, "The Volume of the Transatlantic Slave Trade: A Reassessment with Particular Reference to the Portuguese Contribution" (Unpublished paper, 1998).

[17] Williams, *Capitalism and Slavery* (London, 1944). For examples of recent restatements of Williams' thesis on the contribution of slavery to industrialization see William A. Darity, "British Industry and the West Indies Plantations" and Ronald Bailey, "The Slave(ry) Trade and the Development of Capitalism in the United States: The Textile Industry in New England," both in Joseph E. Inikori and Stanley L. Engerman (eds.), *The Atlantic Slave Trade: Effects on Economies, Societies, and Peoples in Africa, the Americas, and Europe* (Durham, 1992), pp. 205–79.

[18] Eltis, "The Slave Economies of the Caribbean," Table 1. The inclusion of Virginia and South Carolina would close the British-French gap somewhat but would not come close to eliminating it.

The French economy was of course much larger than the British throughout the eighteenth century and therefore arguably was less sensitive to the impact of any one sector, however dynamic. But if we switch from absolute to relative assessments of the impact of slavery on European economies, there are still better candidates than the English for industrial development. In relative terms, the Brazilian slave system (before the 1790s, sugar and gold sectors specifically) always comprised a far larger share of a Portuguese-Brazilian transatlantic economic system than did Caribbean sugar in any British equivalent. In the mid-nineteenth century, any reasonable estimates of the value of sugar produced, goods imported, or profits earned in Cuba must form a far larger share of Spanish national income than did their counterparts in the eighteenth-century British Caribbean colonies when set against British national income of the day.[19] For neither the Spanish nor the Portuguese was there a take-off into permanent and long-run industrial growth.

The heart of the case for a causal linking of the slave systems of the Americas with accelerated European growth lies in, first, the supposedly higher profits that the systems generated – higher, that is, than could be obtained in the domestic European sector[20] – and second, in the strong linkages with the rest of the British economy that are estimated to have existed for the sugar sector. The argument for this last effect is based partly on the size of the sugar sector by the second half of the eighteenth century and partly on the demand for British goods that the sector generated.[21] A new perspective on some of these arguments is possible if the sugar sector is assumed to have been part of the British domestic economy in line with Mill's argument. This assumption allows a comparison of the sugar sector's value added (the difference between what the industry paid for inputs and the revenue it received for its outputs) or contribution to national income with those of some other British industries. Table 10-1 presents some rough estimates for seven well-known British industries at the beginning of the nineteenth century and compares them with equivalent data for sugar. It makes the comparison when the British slave trade and sugar sector were close to their respective peaks. The industries have been selected partly on the basis of data availability but

[19] *Ibid*; Table 2. Idem, *Economic Growth*, Chapter 1. Some might counter that in the nineteenth century the effective metropolitan centre for Cuba was the United States rather than Spain. But there can be little doubt that more rapid growth in the United States was well established before the United States came to occupy this role in the Spanish colony.

[20] The clearest statement of this position is Barbara Solow, "Caribbean Slavery and British Growth: The Eric Williams Hypothesis," *Journal of Developmental Economics*, 17(1985):99–115.

[21] For the best exposition of this impact see David Richardson, "The Slave Trade, Sugar, and British Economic Growth, 1748–1776," in Solow and Engerman (eds.), *British Capitalism and Caribbean Slavery*, 103–33. In staples thesis parlance these are the product of backward and final demand linkages.

Table 10.1. *Value Added in Millions £s (current) and Labor Forces of Select Industries of the United Kingdom and British Caribbean in 1805*

	Value of output	Value of inputs	Value added	Labor force
Iron (wide definition)	16.2	1.5	14.7	n.a.
Woollen textiles	22.0	9.2	12.6	n.a.
Cotton textiles	18.0	7.5	10.5	274
Sheep farming*	7.8	<0.2	c.7.6	n.a
Caribbean sugar**	5.97	c.0.5	5.47	176
Coal	5.11	0.49	4.62	70
Linen textiles***	7.2	2.9	4.3	n.a.
Paper	1.65	0.83	0.83	6

Notes: *1800 **1800–1804 ***1803

Sources: Sheep farming: Wool output in 1800 from Robert Allen, "Agriculture During the Revolution," in Roderick Floud and Donald McCloskey (eds.), *The Economic History of Britain Since 1700*, 3 vols. (Cambridge, 1994), 1:102. Wool prices from Brian R. Mitchell, *British Historical Statistics*, second edition (Cambridge, 1988), p. 766 (for 1801). Mutton carcasses and prices from B. A. Holderness, "Prices, Productivity and Output," in Joan Thirsk (series ed.), *The Agrarian History of England and Wales*. (Cambridge, 1989), vol. 6, G. E. Mingay (ed.), *1750–1850*, pp. 110, 155, 171–4.

Sugar: Includes rum and molasses. Sugar values from Barry W. Higman, *Slave Population and Economy in Jamaica, 1807–1834* (Cambridge, 1976), p. 213. Values converted to pounds sterling, adjusted for rum and molasses output (26 percent of sugar output), and expressed in terms of sugar prices in Jamaica which averaged 57.2 percent of London prices, 1800–1804 (David Beck Ryden, "Does Decline Make Sense?" [paper presented to the Social Science History Association Meetings in Washington, November, 1997]. According to Seymour Drescher (*Econocide: British Slavery in the Era of Abolition* [Pittsburgh, 1977]), pp. 79, 80), Jamaica produced 52 percent of all British Caribbean sugar, 1801–1805. Total for Caribbean derived accordingly. Estimates of the labor force in sugar are derived from Barry W. Higman, *Slave Population of the British Caribbean* (Baltimore, 1984), which gives 56.8% of the slave labor force on sugar estates in 1810 and 60.1% in 1820. Ratio for 1800–1804 taken as 55%. The slave population was 765,350 in 1810 which, after allowing for slave arrivals (calculated at 180.7 thousand 1801–1807 from the *TSTD*) and net natural decreases, suggests a slave population of about 700,000 in 1800. Further adjustments made for age and sex structure of the sugar estate population and for nonsugar activities (domestic service, provision growing, etc.) on those estates. Worksheets available from the author.

Coal: Michael W. Flinn, *History of the British Coal Industry*, 4 vols (Oxford, 1984), 2: *1700–1830: The Industrial Revolution*, pp. 292–3, 365, 451; Mitchell, *British Historical Statistics*, 252.

Paper: Calculated from D. C. Coleman, *The British Paper Industry, 1495–1860: A Study in Industrial Growth* (Oxford, 1958), pp. 88, 105, 169, 203, 289, 346.

All others: Phyllis Deane and W. A. Cole, *British Economic Growth, 1688–1959* (Cambridge, 1969), pp. 204, 212, 223.

also because of their representativeness. Four industries larger than sugar are included: iron, widely defined to include ore mining and metal trades, two textile industries and sheep farming, and three that, during the early phases of industrialization, were smaller, coal, linen, and paper.

Table 10-1 indicates that the business of producing muscovado sugar was one of the larger economic activities in the British economy broadly defined. Its growth during nearly two centuries after 1640, thousands of miles distant from its main markets, was extremely impressive. By the early nineteenth century the industry was producing more than the British coal industry, though this situation would not last for much longer. During this period, and for long after, the British consumed more sugar than any other peoples in the world and managed at the same time (in 1801) to reexport about 20 percent of what they brought into the country. Yet sugar claimed a tiny part of the British consumers' budget, and the production of many other food staples (not included in Table 10-1) generated economic activities that had far larger net outputs and much stronger economic linkages than did the Caribbean sugar sector. Within agriculture alone, wheat and cattle farming were more important than either sheep farming or sugar, shown in Table 10-1, and barley, hops, and brewing together probably had higher value added than sugar. Outside agriculture, and indeed outside the flagship manufacturing industries, there was a range of construction and service activities the value of whose output rivaled that of sugar. The English shipping industry, for example, probably had a larger work force and higher revenues than the sugar sector.[22] The size and complexity of the British economy at the outset of the nineteenth century suggest the insignificance, not the importance, of sugar. Indeed, the growth of no complex economy anywhere can hinge on the fortunes of a single industry.[23]

In both economic and demographic terms and in common with every other slave system in the Americas, the British Caribbean colonies certainly increased in size relative to the British economy between 1700 and 1800. But such relative growth was small compared to, say, the growth of Cuba to the Spanish economy between 1790 and 1860. To return to the John Stuart Mill analogy, if in 1700 the British Caribbean colonies were together equivalent to one of the smaller counties, by 1801 they had grown to be on par with one of the larger English counties. With an estimated population of 760,000 in 1801, the British Caribbean was smaller than Middlesex or Yorkshire but still larger than Lancashire at this point.[24] In terms of the Celtic fringe, the

[22] There were nearly 1.8 million tons of shipping registered in 1801. If one crew was required for every ten tons such shipping would have employed 180,000 seamen.

[23] Robert W. Fogel, *Railroads and American Economic Growth: Essays in Econometric History* (Baltimore, Md., 1964), 234–7.

[24] Population projected backwards from 1807 estimate of Higman *(Slave Populations*, 417) on basis of slave arrivals in the British Caribbean, 1802–7 from

Caribbean had a smaller population and probably total product, too, than Ulster, in which was located over four-fifths of the prosperous Irish linen industry, and the much larger Scotland.[25] Neither of these Celtic areas have formed part of attempts to explain the development of the overall British economy. If it is not difficult to envision industrialization in England and Wales if Scotland or Ulster had remained outside the British orbit, why is it so difficult to imagine industrialization if Columbus had sailed in 1792 instead of 1492?

But was there anything exceptional about the production of sugar that gave it a special role in stimulating economic development? Was it in any sense what used to be called a strategic industry? Compared to most industries, including those listed in Table 10-1, it provided relatively small inputs to other industries. The sugar-refining industry must have been somewhat smaller than the paper-manufacturing industry shown in Table 10-1. Compared to iron or coal or even textiles, sugar was not a large intermediate product. The sugar sector did make possible the purchase of a wide range of consumer products in the Caribbean and England on the part of absentee owners, but then so did all the other industries in Table 10-1. The key point to remember here, however, is that, unlike all other domestic activities, the products entering the sugar sector were recorded in British trade statistics for the simple reason that the industry was located in the Caribbean. Products bought by sugar plantations therefore have a much higher profile for historians than do products bought by owners and workers in, say, textile mills or on sheep farms. If records had survived of consumer and capital goods entering all English agricultural and industrial sectors the way they have survived for the slave trade and the Caribbean, the sugar sector would probably not be regarded by anyone as an industry with a vital role in economic development. The important point is that sugar was just one of hundreds of industries in an economy that was already complex. Sugar was one of the larger industries, but its linkages with the rest of the economy and thus its role as an engine of economic growth compare poorly with textiles, coal, iron ore, and those British agricultural activities that provided inputs into significant manufacturing activities or cheaper food for urban workers.

Even if we grant sugar a key role in economic development, it is not at all clear that sugar was exactly coterminous with slavery. Much recent literature on the early modern Atlantic world has implied that without the African slave trade there would have been no, or at least very few, plantations operating in the Americas and a greatly reduced level of transatlantic commerce. Of the superior efficiency of African slave labor for sugar and other plantation

---

TSTD. Slave population assumed to have been 88 percent of total population in 1801. For populations of English counties in 1801 see Schofield and Wrigley, *Population History*, 622.

[25] Population of Ulster was 1.1 million in 1821 (earliest year for which data are available), that of Scotland, 1.6 million (in 1801).

produce there can be no doubt. Yet to assume that in its absence there would have been nothing but subsistence agriculture in the Americas is unrealistic. As we have seen, the dichotomy between free and slave labor was not as sharp for the seventeenth-century English as it became later. Coerced labor came in many forms, and while there are no instances of any groups reducing people in their own societies to outright chattel slavery, some form of coerced labor, either of their own people or of others was entirely possible in the absence of Africans. Sixteenth-century Iberians exported many commodities from the Americas, including sugar, using forced, but not initially African labor. For early modern consumers, the absence of African slavery would have meant more expensive sugar until the beginning of the nineteenth century and the more rapid (and possibly earlier) development of beet sugar. Any estimate of the impact on consumption of using non-slave labor for the production of sugar, or, more widely, the general development of the English economy, hinges on technical considerations that cannot be addressed here. But only some rather improbable assumptions would support an assessment of no production of sugar, and later cotton, in the Americas.

Table 10-1 provides no indication of profits, which in the case of the slave trade and sugar are sometimes seen as making the vital contribution to the pool of savings funding the British industrial revolution. However, there must have been at least fifty industries with the potential to produce gross profits equal to or similar to sugar and hundreds more that could have done so in combination with related activities. Under the most extreme (and improbable) assumptions, sugar could have generated savings equivalent to 5 percent or more of the gross fixed capital formation. Barbara Solow has pointed out that profits from the slave trade alone could have formed "one half of 1 percent of national income, nearly 8 percent of total investment, and 39 percent of commercial and industrial investment." Such ratios she rightly describes as "enormous."[26] But what was true for the slave trade or sugar was also the case for a wide range of other economic activities in early industrial Britain, both at home and abroad – under the same extreme assumptions.[27] Banking, insurance, horse-breeding, canals, hospitality, construction, wheat farming, fishing, and the manufacture of wooden implements are just a few randomly selected candidates to add to most of the industries in Table 10-1. In terms of gross profits, it is not at all clear why slave trading or the larger sugar business should be singled out, once we set aside the comments of interested observers of the time and the historians who quote them without recognizing that other industries had similar spokespersons.

But were sugar profits higher than elsewhere? Many British owners of sugar estates had the option of investing in a range of British agricultural

---

[26] Stanley L. Engerman, "The Slave Trade and British Capital Formation in the Eighteenth Century: A Comment on the Williams Thesis," *Business History Review*, 46(1972):430–43.

[27] Solow, "Caribbean Slavery and British Growth," 105–6.

activities, as well as coal, iron, and the burgeoning transportation structure, to mention just a few opportunities of which landed aristocrats availed themselves. If the rate of return had been higher for Caribbean sugar than for these other activities, it would have been extremely easy for them to switch the direction of the flow of their funds, and, in the process, have the unintended impact of keeping the rate of return similar across these disparate industries.[28] But even if this equilibrium-inducing process had not occurred, sugar formed such a tiny part of the overall British transatlantic economy that the rate of additional return from sugar production would have had to have been much higher than for non-sugar activities for many years, to have made a difference to the pool of British savings available for investment purposes. But the basic point remains that if returns were so much higher, why would investors have bothered with textile factories, canals, and coal mines when they could make so much more in sugar?

Caribbean plantations needed British savings far more than the reverse. In short, would the British have found it possible to fund government war-induced debt, or build canals or textile mills, or feed a rapidly growing population in the absence of Africa and the Americas? Probably, yes. Would there have been a slave trade and capital-intensive plantations in the Americas without the credit and mortgage financing that flowed out from the European metropolitan centers and made long-distance labor flows possible?[29] Certainly not, though as noted earlier, Caribbean sugar (along with most other early modern industry) eventually generated most of the capital it needed.

If sugar and the slave trade were such small parts of the overall picture and a smaller non-slave plantation sector or substitute forms of coerced labor are conceivable, then the strongest and most interesting influence of race-based slavery in the Americas on Europe, as well as vice versa, may not have been economic at all, but rather ideological. In effect, the growth of the slave system in the second half of the seventeenth century well outside England itself (if not outside English jurisdiction) allowed the full celebration of English liberties; English commentators did not have to cope with the dilemma of free labor in a land-abundant environment until the British abolished slavery in their own part of the Americas in the nineteenth century.[30] In the

---

[28] "The rate of profit in the colonies will be regulated by English profits: the expectation of profit must be about the same as in England, with the addition of compensation for the disadvantages attending the more distant and hazardous employment ..." (Mill, *Principles of Political Economy*, 257).

[29] See the discussion of these issues in Stanley L. Engerman, "The Atlantic Economy of the Eighteenth Century: Some Speculations on Economic Development in Britain, America, Africa and Elsewhere," *Journal of European Economic History*, 24(1995):146–57.

[30] Perhaps this is why the ideological tensions between slavery and freedom in Revolutionary America have received more attention than the same phenomenon in late-seventeenth-century England. For John Locke's association with the slave

long run, shifts in worker attitudes toward consumption served to make slave and wage systems incompatible and helped destroy the former. By the late eighteenth century, waged workers worked longer and harder in order to consume. Higher productivity and the emergence of an industrial sector were associated with the emergence of a free labor force in the modern sense where employers no longer held property rights in the employed and where the two groups were considered legal (as opposed to material) equals. If, as argued in Chapter 1, possessive individualism and the market system seemed equally compatible with waged and slave labor before, say, 1750, they appeared ideologically much closer to the waged than to the slave systems by the nineteenth century.[31] But the divergence of slavery from the freer labor of Europe was a result of movement on the part of both systems. By the late eighteenth century the European world attempted to impose only one labor system – the waged – on the non-European world, instead of two. Where this strategy failed or at least took many years to have an impact, such as, for example, northern Nigeria, the explanation was not usually hypocrisy or lack of resolve but lack of power in the face of local realities – the same factors that diverted the plantation complex to the Americas in the early modern era.[32]

In summary, freedom as it developed in Europe first made possible the slavery of the Americas and then brought about its abolition. The argument here has focussed on the links between freedom in Europe and slavery in the Americas. Specifically, the conditions – mainly environmental – that made Europe different from the rest of the world also created a social structure where the extremes of slavery and freedom were possible. It also stresses the significance of slavery being confined to those of African descent and downplays the European awareness of the slave-free paradox (as opposed to a consciousness of their own liberty, at least in the English case) prior

trade and the governance of slave colonies see Anthony Pagden, "The Struggle for Legitimacy and the Image of Empire in the Atlantic to c. 1700," in *The Oxford History of the British Empire*, 4 vols. (Oxford, 1998–), Vol. 1, Nicholas Canny (ed.), *The Origins of Empire: British Overseas Enterprise to the Close of the Seventeenth Century*, p. 42.

[31] Steinfeld (*The Invention of Free Labor*, pp. 138–72) argues that antislavery and a rising awareness of slavery helped create the modern concept of a free labor force. This was undoubtedly true, but the countereffect, that the changing nature and apparent success of free labor (free in the modern sense) helped create and shape antislavery, seems on balance to have been more important. Antislavery in Steinfeld's argument appears as deus ex machina. For possessive individualism see Macpherson, *Possessive Individualism*.

[32] Howard Temperley, "Capitalism, Slavery and Ideology," *Past and Present*, 75(1977):94–118 and "Anti-Slavery as a Form of Cultural Imperialism," in Christine Bolt and Seymour Drescher (eds.), *Anti-Slavery, Religion and Reform: Essays in Memory of Roger Anstey* (Folkestone, Kent, 1980), pp. 336–50; Eltis, *Economic Growth*, 17–28.

to the late eighteenth century. Slavery was associated with very high land-labor ratios (the Nieboer-Domar hypothesis) prevalent in the early modern Americas, but the slaves themselves were normally drawn from outside the community or kin group. This held for Europeans, indigenous Americans, and Africans alike. Of course, while European conceptions of freedom made slavery possible, they also in the end ensured its demise.

The central development shaping western plantation slavery from the sixteenth century onward was the extension of European attitudes to the non-European world. If, by the sixteenth century it had become unacceptable for Europeans to enslave other Europeans, by the end of the nineteenth century it was unacceptable to enslave anyone. Put in relative perspective, before the eighteenth century Europeans, in common with most peoples in the world, were unable to include those beyond the oceans in their conception of the social contract.[33] Unlike most other peoples in the world, Europeans had the power to impose their version of that contract on others, which for three centuries meant African slavery.[34]

The emphasis here on what is ultimately a non-economic argument allows a reevaluation of the work of other scholars who have addressed the slave-free dichotomy. Generally, the position advanced here finds little echo in the historiography. The tensions posed by slavery in the Americas came to be recognized in the late eighteenth and nineteenth centuries. Given the not co-incidental growth of abolitionism, the initial response to this recognition was to demonize slaveowners and slave traders, and see slavery as aberrant and certainly temporary. The conception of slavery as a "peculiar institution" was born in the abolitionist era. The Aristotelian view that some peoples were slaves by nature to which Las Casas subscribed came to be tempered by the idea that slavery was one stage through which all "uncivilized" peoples

---

[33] Drescher, *Capitalism and Anti-Slavery*, 1–24. There is a striking complementarity between the shift in English perceptions outlined by Drescher and the market-driven emergence of humanitarianism that Haskell argues for in "Capitalism and the Origins of the Humanitarian Sensibility."

[34] A somewhat attenuated version of the same process might be seen in Japan, the non-European society with the most western family and social structure before the twentieth century. Slaves in Japan were overwhelmingly Japanese (drawn from criminals and the poor) before the modern period (Patterson, *Slavery and Social Death*, 127). In the nineteenth and twentieth centuries the Japanese increasingly drew on foreign sources for slaves though the numbers were much lower than those carried across the Atlantic. Both before and after Japan imposed the abolition of slavery on Korea in 1910, Korea had come to be the major source of forced laborers taken to Japan. The absorption of foreigners into the Japanese view of the social contract – a process some would argue that is not yet complete – might account for the gradual disappearance of coercion of foreigners, though in this case there are extraneous geopolitical developments to be reckoned with in the form of world wars (Mikiso Hane, *Peasants, Rebels and Outcasts: The Underside of Modern Japan* (New York, 1982), 236–7).

progressed toward a measure of freedom.[35] But in this form, as the influence of Ulrich Bonnell Phillips suggests, it remained widely held into the twentieth century. If slavery was a temporary condition and all peoples were potentially equal, then it might be assumed that the paradox of the extremes of slavery and freedom appearing in the Western world would be a temporary phenomenon.

From the mid-twentieth century the literature lurched toward explanations in terms of the economic self-interest of Europeans. For world-systems' scholars, slavery is associated with an early phase of European capitalism called mercantile or merchant as opposed to a later version termed industrial capital. Slavery and the slave trade have a central role in the growth of the former and therefore flourish with merchant capitalism but are incompatible with the latter and go into decline when industrial capitalism becomes dominant. But even when the former is in the ascendant, slavery is profitable only in the Americas, or periphery. In the metropolitan center of the European world system, it is always more profitable to use free labor. The pattern of slave-free use is thus explained by the self-interest of European capitalists.

The absoluteness of the barrier that prevented Europeans from becoming slaves suggests that the world-systems model in which European capitalists organized coerced labor on the periphery and free labor in the core economies is at least incomplete. We should have expected some Europeans – the prisoners of war, felons, and displaced Irish who were forced to the colonies – to have been slaves. Yet Portuguese degradados in Angola, Brazil, and Goa, French convicts sent to Louisiana and Canada, their Spanish counterparts who built the Havana fortifications, and the thousands of Cromwellian prisoners were never chattels and were always subject to "Christian usage."[36] More fundamentally the ethnic barriers, like the gender barriers that barred European women from skilled manual occupations, lead us to question all explanations of European expansion that hinge on unrestrained mercantile and mercantilist capitalism. If, as seems likely, European slaves would have been available more cheaply than Africans (as providing women with

---

[35] As Seymour Drescher has pointed out (*Capitalism and Antislavery*, 18–20, and "The Ending of the Slave Trade and the Evolution of European Scientific Racism," *Social Science History*, 14(1990):415–50), both the proslavery and antislavery campaigns in England in the late eighteenth and early nineteenth centuries were relatively free of the biological racism that became prevalent in the mid-nineteenth century. Prior to the 1820s the abolitionist literature conveyed a strong sense that any cultural differences between European and Africans were to be explained by the ravages of the slave trade. Yet there is also a sense that Africans were at an earlier stage of development than Europeans – most clearly expressed in Henry Brougham's *An Enquiry into the Colonial Policy of the European Powers* (Edinburgh, 1803), II, 507–18, which embodied the stages model of human development popular in the eighteenth century.

[36] Coates, "Exiles and Orphans," 1–31; Choquette, *Frenchmen into Peasants*, 273–7; "Order of the Council of State ... ," Sept. 10, 1651, CSPCS, 1:360.

skills would have reduced the cost of skilled labor), then European merchants could not have been both profit maximizers and prejudiced (or outright racist and sexist) at the same time. Between 1500 and 1750, and no doubt beyond, European economic behavior was subordinated to major non-economic influences. At least the image of naked predatory capitalism that dominates the current historiography of early European expansion requires some modification. Indeed, a more pecuniary or profit-maximising or "capitalist" attitude would have meant less African slavery (and greater equality for females) in the Americas.

An alternative method of dealing with the parallel evolution of more extreme forms of freedom and coercion – which also relies on the self-interest of European capitalists – rests on the argument that there was little substantive difference between waged workers and slaves. If the freedom of the waged labor market was at root a freedom to starve, freedom was therefore largely illusory. Slavery in the colonies and wage labor at home appear as two different methods of coercing workers and, as some English radicals argued in the early nineteenth century, the difference between the two was small. Abolition of slavery, when it eventually occurred, simply imposed a new form of coercion on the ex-slaves, and both the rise of slavery and its abolition thereby become less in need of an explanation. Much recent work on the post-emancipation Caribbean is consistent with this approach. From such a perspective, the economic elite, especially in northwestern Europe, used different methods to reduce the economic independence of non-elites in Europe on the one hand and in the Americas on the other. By the nineteenth century it had become necessary to rely on wage labor, effectively if indirectly controlled, in all parts of the Atlantic world. Once more, the tension between Western freedom and Western slavery is reduced once we understand the true interests of European capitalists and the strategies they adopted. Variants of this draw on Gramsci, wherein slavery, or perhaps the abolition of slavery as espoused by the elite, becomes a way of legitimising the ruling classes and making the conditions of European workers seem acceptable by comparison with those of slaves.[37]

Yet the self-interest of capitalists or indeed economic motivations in general seem, by themselves, to provide an unpromising route to understanding or setting aside the paradox. Slavery was certainly an economic system offering costs well below those possible using waged labor. But if the system was so effective, why was it confined so absolutely to non-Europeans? As for the contrast (or rather lack of) between free and slave labor – there never seems to have been the slightest doubt on the distinction among slaves and free laborers, both before and after abolition, nor any hesitation in the

[37] See most recently the essays by Nigel Bolland, Lucia Lamounier, and Mary Turner in Turner (ed.), *From Chattel Slaves to Wage Slaves*.

former to achieve non-slave status, however defined and hedged – at least in the European-dominated world. Having experienced slavery, Frederick Douglass was particularly sensitive to the differences between slave and non-slave labor. To underline the peculiar awfulness of the former, he several times informed crowds he was addressing that a job vacancy had been created by his escape from slavery and that free laborers could offer their services as slaves to fill it.[38]

The various attempts to deal with the paradox – best embodied perhaps in the work of David Brion Davis, Seymour Drescher, Edmund S. Morgan, and Orlando Patterson – have tended to explore the paradox rather than attempted to resolve it in terms of class or economic interests. The cultural evolution and economic growth of the West that have shaped the modern world embody a tension between coercion and freedom of choice that may be elaborated or understood, but not reduced, dismissed, or readily explained. For Patterson, the tension long predates European overseas expansion. Freedom as a social value could not exist without slavery in the sense that in all societies what is marginal defines what is central. The conception of freedom as autonomy from personal and social obligations was perhaps possible only if an antithetical slave status defined as total dependence on another also existed. Sparta, with helots rather than pure chattel slaves, had narrower concepts of individual freedom than Athens, where slavery was extensive and closed and where the lack of rights of slaves was frequently set against the rights of adult male citizens. Both here and in Rome the appearance of full chattel slavery was associated with the disappearance of any status intermediate to the slave-free polarity – a situation with some analogies to the early modern European Atlantic world.[39]

In seventeenth-century England, the term *slavery* was applied to many situations of perceived injustice, and it already represented something devalued. The implication, clearly, was that Englishmen should be free from such restraints. Historians of North America have developed variants of this relationship to explain social cohesiveness and the ability of slaveholders to espouse an ideology in which the right of peoples to be free from oppression had a central place – "peoples" and "social cohesiveness" being for those of European descent.[40] On the other hand, historians also see a dramatic reversal in this mutually sustaining relationship helping to overthrow the slave system from the end of the eighteenth century. In the era since slavery disappeared from the Americas, western concepts of freedom have tended

---

[38] David R. Roediger, "Race, Labor and Gender in the Languages of Antebellum Social Protest," in Engerman, *Terms of Labor*, 170–9.

[39] T. E. J. Wiedmann, *Slavery* (Oxford, 1987), pp. 3–6.

[40] Morgan, *American Slavery; American Freedom*, 338–87; Duncan J. MacCleod, *Slavery, Race and the American Revolution* (Cambridge, 1974), pp. 62–108, 183–4.

instead to be defined in terms of what is perceived as a lack of freedom in non-western societies, particularly the Soviet-dominated world for most of this century.[41]

Yet before the eighteenth century, these associations seem, if not invalid, somewhat overdrawn. Personal freedom in the seventeenth-century Netherlands appears much more rooted in the social structure, religion, and immigration trends of the Low countries than in the coercive activities of a few thousand Dutchmen in Asia. The Dutch did not even enter the Atlantic slave trade until the 1630s and compared to the Portuguese and the English they remained of marginal importance until well after 1660. Likewise it would be difficult to attempt to link any of the political or religious upheavals of England in the 1640s and 1650s to a nascent slave system on one small island over 4,000 miles away, involving at most thirty thousand people in 1650, less than half of whom were slaves. Even at the time of the English Revolution, the English slave system in the Americas was of trivial importance compared to the domestic economy and society. It did not occupy a large part of the domestic consciousness.[42] In no sense did the English or Dutch live with slaves as did their counterparts in ancient Greece and Rome. In the English case, the Irish would seem more promising territory for this type of analysis, but while the Irish were conquered, expropriated, and absorbed into the English economy as thoroughly as any Mediterranean peoples into, say, the Roman Empire, they were never enslaved nor even reduced to serfdom.

After 1700 the slave empires of the Americas were of larger significance to Europe in all senses, but the rise of movements to abolish slavery in the 1780s makes it hard to evaluate the impact of slavery on freedom and vice versa. Abolition may have helped validate waged labor systems in Europe and reinforce the position of political and economic elites, but the fact remains that the slave systems themselves were abolished in the process. Moreover, in ideological terms, surely the employers of labor in England would have found it more useful to have slavery in the colonies continue rather than come to an end. Slavery would have acted as a continuing reminder to free laborers of how much worse their predicament might be and, indeed, as the mining serfs in seventeenth-century Scotland discovered, might become. In any event, in the post-1700 world, it seems that Europeans, especially the English, rather quickly outgrew any need for slavery to define concepts of freedom for themselves even supposing that they had once felt such a need.

The work of Drescher, Patterson, Davis, and Morgan has moved beyond explanations rooted in the self-interest of a European elite but, with the

[41] Davis, *Slavery and Human Progress*, 279–320.

[42] As a test of this see the sections on "Slavery" and "Colonies" in the index and catalogue of the *Goldsmith's-Kress Library of Economic Literature: A Consolidated Guide*, 4 vols. (Woodbridge, Conn; 1976–77). Before the mid-eighteenth century the coverage of either topic can only be described as thin.

exception of Drescher, each of these scholars, in different ways, makes freedom in the Western world dependent to some degree on the slave systems that western Europe also developed. To these might be added the work of Robert Steinfeld on the demise of indentured servitude and the emergence of modern conceptions of free labor. For Steinfeld, the indenture contract could not survive a nineteenth-century world that had come to see slavery as immoral, at least in the United States.[43] Indentured servitude had just too many elements that parallelled slavery. The argument throughout the present work by contrast is the reverse of these positions: the rise of slavery in the Americas was dependent on the nature of freedom in western Europe.

While abolition is not a major concern here, it is also possible that the more often coercion is seen to be unconscionable for people like oneself and appropriate for others, the more likely that coercion for anyone will eventually be questioned. Awareness of the insider-outsider divide was tantamount to the ending of the slave system. In 1784 Necker, in France, reflected educated European opinion in condemning the trade, but he also found action by any single nation alone impossible to contemplate.[44] A few years later, the line was crossed when Charles James Fox posed a question in the House of Commons that he described as "the foundation of the whole business." How would members of Parliament react, he asked, if "a Bristol ship were to go to any part of France ... and the democrats (there) were to sell the aristocrats, or vice versa, to be carried off to Jamaica ... to be sold for slaves?"[45] After this point the number of slaves in Brazil would increase by half, those in the U.S. south would quintuple, and those in Cuba would increase eightfold. Nevertheless, when set against the backdrop of western thought, the very posing of the question – and this is the earliest documented example by someone close to power – meant that the issue was not now *whether* the system would end but rather *when*. To return to where this book began, abolition – the idea that no one should be a slave – was as quintessentially and uniquely western a concept as was gang labor on a Caribbean sugar estate.

The evidence discussed here thus suggests that whatever the powerful validating influences of American slave systems on concepts of freedom and, more specifically waged labor systems, of the north Atlantic, the influence of free over slave systems of the early modern world was greater than any reverse effect. There is no suggestion in any European country of a bargain between workers and ruling elite to reserve slavery for Africans and Amerindians and to guarantee at the same time wider freedoms for non-elite

---

[43] Steinfeld, *Invention of Free Labor*, 163–72.
[44] *De l' administration des finances de la France* cited in Olivier Pétré-Grenouilleau, *Les Traites des Noirs* (Paris, 1997), pp. 64–5.
[45] *Parliamentary Debates*, 1792, XXIX, 1122.

Europeans.[46] The real possibility of enslaving other Europeans appeared to lie beyond the serious intent of any European class or nation even before the onset of the early modern period. Slavery in the Americas was created by the freedom that Europeans had to develop resources in Africa and the Americas without the restrictions of social structures and values that held in the non-European world – the same factors that underlay the rise of waged labor systems. In stark contrast to classical times, however, this freedom of the individual against the group did not include the right to enslave other Europeans. European conceptions of the other ensured that only non-Europeans could be slaves.

---

[46] Patterson argues for an implicit bargain in Solonic Greece between slave owners and non-slaves. The latter tolerated the manumission of slaves (which was a way reinforcing the slave system) because non-slaves were assured of a measure of personal and civic freedom (*Freedom*, 64–81). There are parallels here with Edmund Morgan's argument for an implicit alliance between rich and poor whites in Virginia against African slaves, though the Greek case appears to lack the ethnic element (*American Slavery American Freedom*, 295–337).

Epilogue on Abolition

THE FIRST STEP PERHAPS was the idea that the enslavement of Europeans anywhere in the world was a wrong that needed to be righted. The belief that members of one's own community were not appropriate subjects for enslavement was not confined to Europe. Roman, Greek, Islamic, and indeed all other societies developed similar attitudes. But Europeans began to back this up with substantial resources during the early modern period. As noted in Chapter 3, Spanish and Portuguese religious orders began working for the release of captives in the sixteenth century – the first such efforts on a large scale. Further north almost every coastal town in the Netherlands had a slave fund for redeeming Dutch sailors from the galleys of the Barbary states by the seventeenth century.[1] European seafaring states signed a series of treaties with North African powers and the Ottoman Turks to safeguard ships and crew from capture and enslavement. Most provided for the issuing of safe-conduct passes to merchant ships.[2] The irony that among the main beneficiaries of such arrangements were Dutch and English slave traders on their way to Africa appears to have escaped historians and then contemporaries, among them the Earl of Inchquin, who was held captive in Algiers before becoming governor of the slave colony of Jamaica. When the passes proved ineffective and seamen were captured and enslaved, petitions to the British government seeking their release demanded action in the cause of "Christian charity and humanity" – long before abolitionists began to invoke similar principles.[3] Indeed, the Lady Mico trust, used in the

---

[1] Personal communication from Pieter C. Emmer.
[2] Richardson, *Mediterranean Passes*. Among the first duties of ships commissioned by the early American Republic at the end of the eighteenth century was protection of U.S. shipping against the Barbary pirates.
[3] James Kirkwood to Secretary of State, June 6, 1709, CO 388/12, K25.

nineteenth century to fund education in the British West Indies in the aftermath of slavery, was first established in 1670 to redeem Christians from North Africa. Like Samuell Pepys, and presumably the Earl of Inchquin, the early Mico Trustees could see the suffering of Europeans in the Barbary states but not of Africans in America.[4] The relevant question is at what point did "Christian charity and humanity" come to encompass those of African descent for enough people to make a difference?

The gradual removal of the barriers that kept non-Europeans from insider status was a slow process, and as the modern world suggests, easily capable of reverse.[5] As noted earlier, it was extended partially to American aboriginals before Africans and perhaps to non-Europeans living in Europe before their overseas counterparts. It can be traced in intellectual developments. While no major thinker after Locke was able to defend the practise of enslaving those outside the social contract, the ambivalence of the Enlightenment on the issue of slavery for non-Europeans is clear.[6] It can also be traced at the level of personal experience in both the Anglo-Saxon and the Hispanic Atlantic, where proximity to the exploitation could, for a minority, breed sensitivity as well as indifference.[7] It is possible that among the European working class, the first abolitionists, or at least those who were prepared to identify with blacks, were seamen rather than industrial artisans.[8] Certainly the European country with the most successful slave trade and, for a time,

---

4 Frank Cundall, *The Mico College, Jamaica* (Kingston, 1914), 7–9. Samuell Pepys' comments on the European slaves held by the Barbary states are in his diaries dated January 8 and November 28, 1661.
5 Philip D. Morgan argues that white attitudes toward blacks hardened over the colonial period. In the sense that Chapter 9 has argued – that skin color and "Europeanness" became increasingly important in the way people identified themselves – this is undoubtedly true. However, this does not explain the emancipation issue that arose in the northern states during and after the Revolution or changing white attitudes to blacks in the abolition movement in the wider Atlantic region in the eighteenth century ("British Encounters with Africans and African-Americans, circa 1600–1780," Bernard Bailyn and Philip D. Morgan (eds.), *Strangers within the Realm; Cultural Margins of the First British Empire* [Chapel Hill, N.C., 1991], 157–219).
6 Davis, *The Problem of Slavery in Western Culture*, 137–9, 319–479; idem, *Slavery and Human Progress*, 107–16, 154–8. Also see the discussion of Montesquieu in Seymour Drescher, "Capitalism and Abolition: Values and Forces in Britain, 1783–1814," Roger Anstey and P. E. H. Hair (eds.), *Liverpool, the African Slave Trade, and Abolition* (Liverpool 1976), 182. It would seem that for Locke the universe of the social contract was not the state but rather the European nation state.
7 John Newton and Alexander Falconbridge are among the better known slave-ship officers who turned against the trade.
8 Peter Linebaugh and Marcus Rediker, "The Many Headed Hydra: Sailors, Slaves and the Atlantic Working Class in the Eighteenth Century," *Journal of Historical Sociology* 3(1990):225–51. For the wide range of attitudes of Europeans and Africans toward each other see Morgan, "British Encounters with Africans and African-Americans," 157–219.

the richest slave colonies was the center of the strongest abolition movement and the leader of world abolitionism. English citizens moreover had an extraordinary proclivity to migrate, most of them before 1800 going to plantation regions forming part of the most integrated of all eighteenth-century colonial systems. As noted earlier, "communication and community" across the English Atlantic attained a depth, richness, and reliability of contact unrivalled among European powers and quite unprecedented in the history of long-distance migration.[9] Such characteristics have clear implications for metropolitan awareness of events "beyond the line."

The Netherlands, by contrast, despite its early commitment to social and economic freedom, was among the last to take action and did not experience mass antislavery of any kind. Also by contrast it was without a slave trade fleet after the 1780s; the slave sectors of its empire were not only small but also of declining significance from the late eighteenth century. More important, low Dutch migration and a failure to keep pace with English Atlantic trade in the two centuries before 1800 meant that Dutch transatlantic networks and contacts with non-Europeans were simply many times less frequent and dense. Even if we allow for the Dutch East Indies, intercourse between England and the transoceanic world would have been much more likely to have created an awareness of the association of the consumption of sugar with the enslavement of Africans, and eventually abolitionism. The English had far more settlement colonies than the Dutch and, as mentioned, a much stronger transatlantic community. This is not the place to reassess the origins of abolitionism. The intention is to suggest only that the key counterpoint is not slavery and abolition but rather the enslavement of non-Europeans and abolition.[10]

These arguments have some interesting implications. One is that Europeans, and more particularly the English, failed to take advantage of two rather large economic opportunities. If they had emulated the sixteenth-century Russian aristocracy, created some ideological distance between the masses and themselves, and enslaved some elements of their own society, lower labor costs would have ensured faster development of the Americas and higher exports and income levels on both sides of the Atlantic. For those who see European, in particular English, economic power built on overseas colonies, it might be argued that for the underpopulated tropical Americas at least, exploitation of the periphery and the transfer of surplus to the core would have been far more rapid with white slave labor. A second failure

---

[9] Steele, *English Atlantic, 1675–1740.*
[10] For the recent literature and a judicious discussion of the roots of antislavery in the English context see David Turley, *The Culture of English Anti-Slavery, 1780–1860* (London, 1991), 1–46, 227–36. For the decline of Dutch slavery in the East Indies, where it might be noted that the institution was not related to export production, see Abeyasekere, "Slaves in Batavia: Insights from a Slave Register," 286–314, especially, 308–10.

to maximise an economic advantage was that Europeans gradually widened their perception of what constituted an insider from the late eighteenth century to include transoceanic peoples. This in effect brought a very profitable institution to an end. The first "missed opportunity" helped create the Atlantic slave trade from Africa; the second one ended not only the slave trade but slavery in the Americas as well. The broadest implication, however, is not just that economic interpretations of the rise and fall of African slavery in the Americas have shortcomings, but that in the end any economic interpretation of history risks insufficient probing of the behaviour of people. At the very least, it will run the risk of missing the cultural parameters within which economic decisions are made.

Appendix A

The Age and Sex of Africans in the Transatlantic Slave Trade, 1663–1713

Sex and age characteristics exist for 111,323 Africans carried across the Atlantic or close to more than one-tenth of all Africans who left for the Americas on British ships between 1663 and 1714. Traders took these slaves from every major African region involved in the traffic at this time, except for southeast Africa, and carried them to mainly Caribbean destinations on a total of 432 ships – 361 operating from English ports, 46 from Dutch, 22 from Danish, and 3 from French. The sample is thus large and well distributed. The major bias is the lack of observations for Brazil and the fact that the English slave trader and the English Caribbean are overrepresented. However, it is likely that the English carried more slaves than all other nationalities combined in these years and that the English Americas absorbed more slaves than all other transatlantic regions. Mean number of Africans per ship in the sample is 257.7 (s.d. = 152.3).[1]

Three preliminary comments are called for. The counts of men, women, and children or males and females included in the sample were sometimes

[1] Compared to the sample of slaves carried by Royal African Company ships used by Galenson in *Traders, Planters and Slaves*, the data from *TSTD* used here include additional company records, Africans who died before reaching the Americas, and Africans carried by the Dutch, Danish, and French. Galenson's sample was for 74,614 individuals for the period 1673–1725 or 69,783 for the period covered by the present data set. Joseph Inikori has added records of 7,882 slaves to Galenson's data, from the account books of the Company of Royal Adventure for the 1660s ("Export versus Domestic Demand," 131). The present sample includes the Galenson/Inikori sources and adds others. It is almost 50 percent larger and, unlike Galenson/Inikori, incorporates data on African points of departure for most of the records, as well as some entry points in the Americas beyond the English colonies. Most of the data used here were incorporated into two wider ranging studies of this topic co-authored with Stanley L. Engerman: "Was the Slave Trade Dominated by Men?" and "Sex and Age Ratios in the Transatlantic Slave Trade."

made before the ship began its journey, sometimes at the point of arrival or point of sale, and sometimes at all three locations. The possibility arises that mortality between these points was age- or sex-specific and that demographic ratios on board ships leaving Africa would not be the same as on those arriving or sold in the Americas.[2] However, tests of the sample showed no systematic fluctuations in the sex and age patterns of shipboard mortality. Generally, the data used here are those from the American end of the voyage. African data are used only when American data have not survived.

A second issue is multiple points of embarkation and disembarkation. Ships often called at more than one location to obtain slaves and sold their purchases at more than one port in the Americas. This problem is somewhat reduced by the large size of the geographic zones used in the analysis, but where ships clearly traded across zones (as for example between the Gold Coast and the Slave Coast), the record has been assigned to the zone from which the ship took (or sold) the largest number of Africans or, in seven cases where approximately equal numbers were associated with two ports, a separate voyage entry was made for each group carried.

A third issue is the appropriate unit of analysis. Should this be the ship – or more specifically the group of Africans carried in each ship – or should it be the total number of persons in the year in which Africans departed or arrived? The first is useful for examining the familiar issue of African versus non-African influences over the trade; the second is appropriate for discussing some demographic and economic aspects of the trade. As the second formed the basis of Galenson's study and much of the novelty of the current data lies in the African origins of the slave ship (thus allowing some assessment of African influences), most of the present analysis will use a ship-based approach. However, the number of Africans carried in each ship varied substanitally, and in order to ensure that small ships or part-loadings do not carry as much weight in the analysis as their larger counterparts, a weighting system is employed based on the mean number of Africans carried per ship.

We turn first to preliminary breakdowns by regions of departure and arrival for the whole fifty-two-year period. Tables A-1 and 4-4 distribute basic demographic categories by major African and American regions involved in the trade. On the American side, shown in Table A-1, the regions are well known, but we should note here that Dutch slave ships went to two distinct markets – plantations in Berbice, Demerara, and Surinam on the one hand and the entrepot islands of Curacao and St. Eustatius on the other. The entrepot islands supplied Spanish America, a destination that required a further long-distance journey. As shipping costs did influence the demographic

---

[2] See Johannes Postma, "Mortality in the Dutch Slave Trade, 1675–1795," in Gemery and Hogendorn, *The Uncommon Market*, 254–6, for this phenomenon in the Dutch slave trade.

Table A-1. *Percentages of African Males, Women, Men, Girls, and Boys Carried to the Americas, 1663–1714, by American Region of Disembarkation (sample size in parentheses)*

	Males	Women	Men	Girls	Boys
Jamaica	60.2 (28,477)	35.6 (28,052)*	51.1	4.3	9.0
Barbados	60.5 (41,486)	36.0 (40,799)	50.6	4.0	9.4
Leeward Island	57.6 (14,363)	38.2 (14,138)	48.8	4.3	8.8
Dutch S. America	63.4 (4,992)	32.0 (2,618)	51.7	3.5	12.8
Danish Islands	68.2 (4,351)	27.4 (4,351)	54.5	4.4	13.7
Spanish America/ Chesapeake**	68.5 (14,750)	29.9 (12,605)	59.1	2.6	8.5
Americas***	61.5 (111,323)	34.9 (104,151)	51.8	4.0	9.4

*Women, Men, Boys, Girls drawn from same sample. Males includes some individuals identified by sex only.   **Includes slaves carried to Dutch Islands, but intended for the Spanish Americas. ***Includes some going to unidentified American regions.
Source: TSTD.

structure of the trade, the Dutch sample is divided into two in the present analysis and labelled Dutch South America and Spanish America, the latter used in place of Dutch Caribbean. Further, there are seven ships in the current data set recorded as disembarking in Virginia, which comprised a second longer-distanced market. Indeed not only did the Spanish and Chesapeake regions have distance from Africa in common, they were also similar in that neither produced sugar for export. They are in fact the only non-sugar regions in the sample. Accordingly Virginia and the Dutch Spanish American sample are grouped together for present purposes. The African breakdowns are described in Chapter 4.

Tables A-1 and 4-4 show some large differences among regions on both sides of the Atlantic, but those for women and boys seem to be greater than for the other demographic categories. Overall, the regional differences appear greater for Africa, shown in Table 4-4, than for the Americas in Table A-1. The proportion of children leaving the west-central Africa region, for example, was more than three times greater than among slaves leaving Senegambia and Sierra Leone (Upper Guinea). Almost double the proportion of women left the Gold Coast and the Bight of Biafra as left Upper Guinea, while the proportion of men leaving this latter region was two-thirds greater

Table A-2. *Regression Based Anova of Ratios of Men, Women, Boys, and Girls on Slave Ships from Major African Regions of Embarkation*

	Coefficient	*t*-stat	Coefficient	*t*-stat
(a) Men ($R2 = 0.31$)			(b) Women ($R2 = 0.33$)	
Upper Guinea	.2582	10.7	−.1661	−8.3
Bight of Benin	.0784	5.3	−.0460	−3.8
Bight of Biafra	−.0365	−1.9	.0700	4.3
West-Central Africa	.0349	1.8	−.1074	−6.8
Intercept	.4580	38.7	.3923	39.7
(c) Boys ($R2 = 0.22$)			(d) Girls ($R2 = 0.14$)	
Upper Guinea	−.0622	2.9	−.0298	−4.6
Bight of Benin	−.0230	−4.8	−.0095	−2.4
Bight of Biafra	−.0253	−2.4	−.0081	−1.5
West-Central Africa	.0554	5.4	−.0173	3.3
Intercept	.1040	16.2	.0457	14.2
n = 390				

Reference variable (intercept) for each equation is the Gold Coast.

than from the Bight of Biafra. There are no differences between American regions that match the scale of these.

Were such variation that show up in Tables A-1 and 4-4 systematic rather than random? Table A-2 and A-3 show the results of an ordinary least-square-regression-based analysis of variance with in each case one major region omitted, the Gold Coast for Africa in Table A-2 and Barbados for the American equations in Table A-3. The unit of analysis here is the voyage or slaving expedition, and no attempt is made to take time, or indeed any other variable, into account. A separate equation was estimated for men, women, boys, and girls. The *t*-statistics in the tables suggest differences significant at the 5 percent level on both sides of the Atlantic (a *t*-statistic of 2.0 or over indicates that there is only a 5 percent or less probability of the observed difference being random). Compared to the Gold Coast, Upper Guinea and the Bight of Benin saw a larger share of men taken to the Americas, and the Bight of Biafra a smaller share. Women were almost as common as men on ships leaving the Bight of Biafra, but among those leaving Upper Guinea and west-central Africa the proportion of women was only half the Bight of Biafra ratio. As this suggests, proportions of both girls and boys were much larger on ships from west-central Africa and smaller in the Bight of Benin and Upper Guinea.

On the American side, the Spanish Americas and Virginia category had above-average ratios of men and a smaller proportion of girls compared to Barbados. The Danish islands received larger shares of women and boys, but in general there were few statistically significant differences among the main sugar plantation regions of Dutch South America, Barbados, Jamaica,

Table A-3. *Regression Based Anova of Ratios of Men, Women, Boys, and Girls on Slave Ships Arriving in Major American Regions of Disembarkation*

	Coefficient	*t*-statistic	Coefficient	*t*-statistic
(a) Men ($R^2 = 0.05$)			(b) Women ($R^2 = 0.05$)	
Danish Islands	.0386	1.2	−.0861	−3.1
Dutch South America	.0105	0.3	.0400	1.1
Spanish Amer/Virginia	.0843	4.0	−.0615	−3.5
Leeward Islands	−.0182	−0.9	.0214	1.3
Jamaica	.0049	0.3	−.0037	−0.3
Intercept	.5063	49.4	.3600	41.7
(c) Boys ($R^2 = 0.03$)			(d) Girls ($R^2 = 0.02$)	
Danish Islands	.0434	2.5	.0041	0.5
Dutch South America	.0344	1.6	−.0049	−0.5
Spanish Amer/Virginia	−.0087	−0.8	−.0141	−2.7
Leeward Islands	−.0058	−0.6	.0026	0.5
Jamaica	−.0038	−0.5	.0026	0.7
Intercept	.0936	17.6	.0401	16.1
n = 425				

Reference variable or intercept for each equation is Barbados.

and the Leeward Islands. Both the number of regions showing significant differences and the significance levels themselves tended to be smaller on the American side than on the African.

A fuller analysis is possible by including the regions of embarkation and disembarkation in the same equation (instead of separately as in Tables A-1 and 4-4) as well as a number of dummy variables that attempt to take into account crop types, particular characteristics of African regions, and war. In addition, a time trend variable is added with *t* set at the year in which the observation occurred.

The major export crop grown in the Americas at this time was sugar. Regional specialization in sugar production occurred at different times in the Americas. Some scholars have argued that planters required more men or males during the early development of a sugar-growing area because of the heavy work requirements of clearing land and planting cane for the first time. Areas experiencing rapid expansion of sugar production before 1714 are taken as Jamaica, the Danish Island, Dutch South America, the Leewards, and Barbados before 1670.[3] For these regions and periods the sugar dummy variable is set at 1. For the Spanish America/Virginia category and Barbados

---

[3] Evidence presented elsewhere suggests that, while all Barbados land had been taken up by 1663, the year of the first observation in the present set, sugar exports were expanding in the 1660s.

after 1670, this variable is set at 0. The binary variable for war is set at 1 for the years 1665 to 1668 (the period of hostilities in the second Dutch War), 1672 and 1673, 1689 to 1697, and 1702 to 1713, the last two reflecting the years of general European conflict. All other years are set at 0. It would be desirable to add a slave price variable for the Americas, for Africa, or for both regions. Slave price in the Americas was a key variable in Galenson's analysis. However, Galenson collected his data on an annual basis, whereas the present sample is organised on a voyage-unit basis. Linkage of the two data sets – and perhaps an increase in the explanatory power of the estimating equations – is a future project.

Table A-4 presents the estimating equations for each of the four demographic categories. Overall the R2s are modest, ranging from .27 to .45, but given the absence of any variables that directly reflect costs, prices, and the total volume of the trade, this explanatory power is not unimpressive. More important the equations serve to isolate certain factors that have received attention in the literature and allow closer study of regional factors.

It is immediately apparent from the table that the differences among African regions are more numerous, larger, and have greater statistical significance than do those of the Americas. Among the five American regions for each of the four demographic categories (a total of twenty variables) only five show differences significant at the 5 percent level. Markets further away from Africa (the Spanish and English mainland) took more men and fewer women and girls proportionately than did other regions, and the Danish Islands took fewer women and more boys. The coefficients among African regions, however, are much wider with negative and positive signs in each of the four equations and thirteen of the sixteen coefficients significantly different at the 5 percent level. Putting regions of origin and destination together in the same equation and adding three other binary variables had the effect of reducing the number of regions in the Americas that were significantly different from reference variable and, on average, reduced the t-statistic. For African regions, on the other hand, this same procedure had much less impact, serving in the main to reduce slightly average t-statistics.

After controlling for region of disembarkation, time, crop type, and war, the distinctiveness of African regions from each other is even more striking. Among the non-geographic variables there are some interesting counterintuitive results. Expanding sugar production was associated with fewer men and more children. The share of boys in new sugar regions was 5 percentage points higher than in established or non-sugar regions. The coefficient for girls in new sugar regions was also positive though non-significant. The best explanation is that the demand for labor was at root undifferentiated. More formally, the demand for slaves of a particular gender and age was far more elastic than the demand for slaves as a whole. The seventeenth century saw the transition of sugar from a medicinal to a consumer product with a

Table A-4. *Explaining Ratios of Men, Women, Boys, and Girls among Africans on Board Slave Ships, 1663–1714: Results of Ordinary Least Squares Regression*

	Coefficient	*t*-statistic	Coefficient	*t*-statistic
(a) Men ($R_2 = 0.40$)			(b) Women ($R_2 = 0.45$)	
Upper Guinea	.1834	8.3	−.1230	−7.3
Gold Coast	−.0713	−4.9	.0480	4.1
Bight of Biafra	−.0946	−4.8	.0781	5.0
West-Central Africa	−.0564	−3.2	−.0675	−4.8
Barbados	−.0389	−1.2	−.0232	−0.9
Danish Islands	.0101	0.3	.0272	0.8
Spanish Amer/Virginia	.0423	1.2	−.0253	−0.9
Dutch South America	.0653	1.8	.0169	0.6
Jamaica	.0187	1.0	−.0273	−1.9
Wartime	.0479	3.3	−.0456	−3.9
Time trend	−.0001	−1.0	−.0016	−2.6
New sugar region	−.0586	−1.9	.0033	−0.1
Intercept	.5688	12.0	.4365	11.4
(c) Boys ($R_2 = 0.30$)			(d) Girls ($R_2 = 0.27$)	
Upper Guinea	−.0344	−2.9	−.0197	−3.3
Gold Coast	.0173	2.2	.0060	1.5
Bight of Biafra	.0101	0.9	.0064	1.2
West-Central Africa	.0898	9.5	.0341	7.3
Barbados	−.0554	3.1	.0068	0.8
Danish Islands	−.0335	−1.5	−.0038	−0.4
Spanish Amer/Virginia	.0096	0.5	−.0026	−2.9
Dutch South America	−.0200	−1.0	−.0287	−2.9
Jamaica	.0060	0.6	.0027	0.6
Wartime	.0060	0.8	−.0081	−2.1
Time trend	.0015	3.8	.0001	4.0
New sugar region	.0492	3.0	.0061	0.8
Intercept	−.0183	−0.7	.0130	1.0
n = 366				

The omitted variables in each equation are the Bight of Benin and Leeward Islands.

resulting massive expansion in the market. As new sugar regions came on stream the demand for slaves increased faster than the supply and the price of slaves increased. This in turn made it profitable to carry children across the Atlantic in increasing numbers, as Galenson has outlined. Thus the relative share of boys and girls to men and women increased. This is also the basic explanation behind the rising time trend for both boys and girls and the declining trend for women. Over the half-century covered here, the share of men and women in the traffic declined by 0.16 of a percentage point in each year, and the share of boys and girls increased accordingly. The men's time trend coefficient is negative though non-significant.

The binary variable for war generates slightly more problematic results. The results here provide partial support for this connection in that war was associated with an increase of nearly 5 percentage points in the proportion of men carried. While the coefficient for the child ratio was negatively signed, it was also non-significant. However, the ratio of women also decreased, despite the fact that women were more highly valued than children of either sex and indeed cost only slightly less than men in the Americas. Although further formal analysis is not possible at this stage, a more general discussion of the factors that might be behind these patterns is found in Chapter 4.

Appendix B

Slave-Price Appendix

For the Americas, Galenson's series for Barbados, 1673 to 1711, is accepted without adjustment (no data for 1685).[1] For 1663 and 1664, Galenson's unweighted mean prices for men, women, and boys are converted into a composite price for the average slave by calculating a weighted mean – the weights being set at the ratios of 4,393 men, women, and boys disembarked in Barbados in these years and contained in a separate data set.[2] The ratios for 1663 are: men 0.422, women, 0.470, boys, .071, girls, 0.038; for 1664, they are 0.467, 0.443, 0.062, 0.028, respectively. The price of girls, not supplied by Galenson, is set equal to the price for boys. This procedure yields £13.89 sterling as the average slave price in Barbados for 1663 and £14.58 for 1664.

For Africa, the slave price series is derived from a register of merchandise sent to Africa compiled by a committee of the governing body of the Royal African Company, the Court of Assistants. This is contained in T70, volume 1222, and has been supplemented from other RAC sources. The registers typically provide a list of merchandise and an estimate of the number of slaves or quantities of other produce the merchandise would buy. The committee provided no breakdowns of sex and age of the slaves they expected to get. However, there were few children in these early years of the English slave trade; it was understood that while captains would seek men, they would end up taking almost as many women. In any event the difference in the price of men and women on the African coast was not great. Details of the merchandise carried by 338 ships have survived, and as these ships were relatively large, they accounted for at least one-quarter of all merchandise carried to Africa by the English in this era and probably between 10 and 15 percent of all merchandise that arrived in Africa from any Atlantic source.

[1] Galenson, *Traders, Planters and Slaves*, 65.
[2] *Ibid*, 67.

Twenty-six of the 338 ships carried cargoes for produce only, and almost all of these returned directly to England.[3]

The great advantage of the RAC data for present purposes is that the merchandise proposed for each trading expedition was always assigned to a specific part of the African coast. Thus ships sailing to Africa had a target region of trade set by the company as well as an estimate of how many slaves could be obtained in that trade.[4] Indeed the preferences of Africans varied so greatly over the thousands of miles of coastline (as we might expect) that a cargo of trade goods for, say, Old Calabar in the Bight of Biafra would scarcely sell at all in Angola to the south or the slave coast to the west. Cross referencing of the cargo data with the separate data set of completed slave-ship voyages suggests that almost all the cargoes proposed for a region in the RAC's cargo books were in fact traded in that region. However, not all the merchandise proposed was actually shipped and not all that was shipped was actually traded.[5] The information available to the committee in London was very good, but there were inevitable misjudgments of prices and shifting tastes in markets several thousand miles distant. The committee's estimate of prices is thus not to be confused with prices at the point of exchange. Nevertheless these data may be judged adequate for estimating trends over time and regional differentials, as well as providing a rough basis for comparison with prices in the Americas.

An RAC ship heading for the America via Africa would sometimes carry just one cargo, but the norm was a combination of two or more of the following: a cargo for slaves, a Windward cargo (for gold along the coast west of Cape Coast Castle), a castle cargo (for Cape Coast Castle itself), and a cargo for ivory.[6] There are four grain coast cargoes in the committee's

---

3   "Merchandise exported to Africa by the English African Companies, 1662–1703."
    Three of the cargoes listed in T70/1222 and one from a companion volume,
    T70/1223, all intended for the Slave Coast region, have been analysed recently
    in Law, *Slave Coast of West Africa*. In addition Philip Curtin analysed forty-four
    cargoes sent to the Gambia in the 1680s using one of the Gambia account books,
    T70/546. See Curtin, *Economic Change in Pre-Colonial Africa*, 86–7, and ff. Sum-
    maries of cargoes carried to Africa by ships of the Royal African Company may be
    found in Davies, *Royal African Company*, especially pp. 350–7. These summaries
    have been widely cited in the literature. The present data set is analogous to an
    itemised version of Davies' summaries with data on type of cargoes and African
    destination added.

4   In the 10 percent or so of cases where the nature of the return cargo is not stated,
    inferences are often justified. Thus there was no evidence of produce leaving the
    Slave Coast and very little leaving west-central Africa and the Bight of Biafra.

5   The separate slave-ship data set for this period (*TSTD*) shows that 202 slave ships
    sailing between 1663 and 1713 obtained on average 92 percent of their intended
    numbers of slaves.

6   The RAC defined the Windward Coast as stretching between Cape Mount and
    Cape Three Points (T70/61, f. 3), but the phrase was normally used in the sense of

register of cargoes intended mainly for malaguetta pepper. Late in the period when RAC ships took slaves from windward of Cape Coast Castle (not to be confused with the Windward Coast), the cargo to be exchanged for them was always listed separately from other merchandise. Ships sailing for produce only, generally smaller than their slaving counterparts, would usually carry just one cargo, though if intended for "north" Guinea it might have more: Sherboro, Sierra Leone, and the Gambia proper differed from each other in their preferences for merchandise. The unit of record in the data set is thus cargo rather than ship, but in almost all cases the ship in which the goods were to be carried is clearly identified.[7] Of the total value of £1.042 million pounds sterling in constant values using the Schumpeter index, £325,404 was labelled for slaves, £331,615 was sent for produce, £228,474 was described as Castle cargo, and £156,516 was entered without designation in the cargo books. For this last category, however, there can be little doubt that the committee had a definite purpose in mind – a record of it has simply not survived. The RAC intended to obtain a total of 85,437 slaves with the part of this merchandise that was designed for slaves. This amounts to almost one-third of all the slaves the English as a whole (and not just the RAC) carried off from Africa at this time.[8] Table B-1 shows the expected prices of 73,525 of these slaves from the four busiest trading zones

windward of Cape Coast Castle. The RAC instructions to the captains used Wind-ward in the latter sense and, consistent with this, there is no doubt that the Wind-ward cargoes were disposed of in large part on the Gold Coast before the ship reached Cape Coast Castle. This was a major source of irritation between the agent at the Castle and the London officials. Davies, however, assumes that Windward and Gold Coasts did not overlap (*Royal African Company*, 222–8). The letters from the company agent at Cape Coast Castle (in the T70 series) and between the chief agent and the outlying forts and factories on the Gold Coast (Rawlin-son manuscript c. 745–7) indicate that ships acquired very few slaves with their Windward cargoes.

[7]   Some of the cargoes were grouped together in the register, though this always seems to have been clearly indicated when it happened. Allowance for this grouping suggests that data set contains 585 cargo equivalencies.

[8]   For a few cargoes, values of merchandise are not supplied. These have been inferred on the basis of average values of the same period computed from cargoes of known values. There are also a few cases where the cargo was clearly intended for slaves but the number of slaves was omitted. Again this information has been inferred from those cargoes for which the data were complete. The Schumpeter price index used to convert current to constant values is neither weighted nor broadly based. On balance, however, the advantages of using it seem to outweigh the drawbacks. The cargo lists contain several items included in the index, the major omissions being East Indian textiles, iron bars, and cowries. Schumpeter presented two indexes, and I have used a simple unweighted average of the two. For the two cargoes that fall outside the 1663–97 period, one for 1698 and one for 1703, I bridged the Schumpeter with the Schumpeter-Gilboy indexes (Mitchell, *British Historical Statistics*, second edition, 720).

Table B-1. *Prices of Slaves Expected to be Paid by the Royal African Company, 1663–1698, Year by African Region of Embarkation in Current Pounds Sterling (number of slaves expected to be purchased in parentheses)*

	Gold Coast		Bight of Benin		Bight of Biafra		West-Central Africa		All regions combined (weighted)*
1663	4.14	(340)	3.56	(1,200)	3.39	(3,255)			3.44
1664			4.99	(3,500)	3.72	(4,720)	3.68	(360)	4.06
1665					3.45	(1,920)			3.63
1674			2.33	(1,062)	3.72	(430)			3.46
1675			2.22	(745)	3.08	(1,255)			3.97
1676	2.94	(430)	2.08		2.86	(920)	3.36	(780)	2.67
1677			2.29		3.14	(1,180)	4.30	(300)	3.04
1678	3.64	(220)	1.77		2.43	(1,270)	3.07	(980)	2.31
1679	3.01	(200)	2.17	(2,000)	2.47	(1,835)	4.13	(500)	2.65
1680	3.04	(560)	2.35		2.29	(1,360)	3.61	(2,380)	2.54
1681	2.56	(980)	2.82	(1,360)	2.20	(2,180)	3.94	(980)	2.96
1682	2.44	(380)	2.78	(1,350)	3.26	(1,000)	4.26	(1,260)	3.27
1683			3.90	(2,270)	3.02	(510)	4.23	(1,380)	3.78
1685			3.05	(3,338)	2.98	(1,120)	4.52	(1,780)	3.41
1686			2.92	(2,960)	3.06	(1,060)	3.94	(2,280)	3.21
1687	3.59	(350)	2.88	(1,610)	2.63	(200)	3.98	(320)	3.10
1688	3.23	(340)	2.98	(1,700)	3.00	(730)	3.42	(400)	3.10
1689	3.49	(500)	3.26	(1,030)					3.49
1691			3.20	(1,300)			6.61	(420)	4.15
1693			4.00	(3,800)	3.04	(340)	5.39	(500)	4.22
1694			3.42	(1,150)	3.22	(340)			4.16
1696			4.08	(1,830)					4.90
1697			3.85	(525)					4.62
1698			4.54	(550)					5.45
1703			5.49	(400)					
1707			6.24	(1,051)					
1663 –1701	3.96	(4,300)	3.36	(34,731)	3.07	(25,625)	4.04	(14,620)	

*Weights used in the calculation of the last column are the proportions of slaves carried from each region taken from the *TSTD*.

in Africa. The Bight of Benin (effectively the Slave Coast) was to account for 33,280 of these; 25,625 were intended from the Bight of Biafra, 14,620 from west-central Africa, and 4,300 from the Gold Coast.

The four slave price series in Table B-1 are for each of these regions, the Gold and Slave Coasts, the Bight of Biafra, and west-central Africa, respectively, as calculated from merchandise values. The values are in current prices. Numbers of slaves expected to be obtained are shown in parentheses.

For those cells without an attendant parenthetical number, the slave price is an interpolation derived from the surrounding data. It should be noted that for many years for which interpolations are calculated, especially for west-central Africa in the 1690s, very few slaves were actually traded by the RAC – the reason in fact why data on prices have not survived. The last column in the table is a weighted mean of slave prices with the weights set according to the decadal proportions of slaves that the English took from each of the three regions in the table. These regions together accounted for about 80 percent of all slaves taken from Africa by the English between 1663 and 1700. The Upper Guinea region, or more specifically the Gambia, as well as the Gold Coast does not yield sufficiently good data to support an annual time series, and these regions are not included in the weighted mean. As prices in these regions would tend to be somewhat higher than elsewhere (perhaps 20 percent or so on average), their omission imparts a downward bias to the series in Table B-1. The means for each region calculated for the whole period 1663–98 at the foot of the table are weighted according to the number of slaves in parentheses.

Finally, for west-central Africa, it might be useful to note an alternative series derived from Portuguese sources. Prices for prime slaves in Luanda, south of the ports at which the RAC traded, are reported at £5.9 in the 1680s and £6.2 in the 1700s.[9] In a separate series, slave prices in milreis are reported unchanged between 1650 and 1700. Neither pound sterling nor milreis series, it is worth noting, are highly inconsistent with the estimates in Table B-1.[10] The annual average during the 1680s for RAC slaves was £4.2, but this was for all slaves traded, not just prime males. In addition, a good part of the costs of assembling slaves into a group that could be put on board a ship may have been absorbed in the Luanda price. There were far more shore establishments at Luanda than at Cabenda or Malimbo where the RAC traded.

---

[9] Joseph C. Miller, "Slave Prices in the Portuguese Southern Atlantic, 1600–1830," in Lovejoy (ed.), *Africans in Bondage*, 67. The prices quoted here seem to be expressed in terms of the value in Lisbon of goods traded for slaves (*ibid*, pp. 54–5). This is similar in concept to the valuation used by the RAC.
[10] *Ibid*, 63.

Appendix C

Merchandise Imported to West Africa, 1662–1713

The basic source for African imports used here is an invoice book of cargoes carried to Africa on the vessels of the Royal Company of Adventurers and its successor organization, the Royal African Company. This is the same source and database used for the slave price data.[1] All these ships departed from London. A description of the data set is included below in the sources. A summary of the cargoes in constant pounds broken down by African region of embarkation is shown in Table C-1.

This summary does not reflect all merchandise arriving in Africa from the Atlantic world, nor even all the merchandise carried by the vessels of these companies. Between 1666 and 1713, records exist of nearly two hundred ships that sailed to Africa from the Caribbean rather than from Europe and many of them belonged to the Royal African Company. Almost all these ships carried rum, most of them from Barbados. Out of every ten ships, about seven went to the Gold Coast, two to the Gambia, and one to the Slave Coast, though in the latter case the rum was probably disembarked at Cape Coast Castle on the Gold Coast, before the ship proceeded to Whydah for slaves.[2] The trade began in the late 1670s, with about two ships a year involved on average to 1698. Thereafter the volume quadrupled to ten ships a year. Each ship arrived with perhaps 6,700 gallons of rum suggesting 1.3 million gallons imported over thirty-three years, four-fifths of it to the Gold

---

[1] "Merchandise exported to Africa by the English African Companies, 1662–1703."
[2] All these data are from the *TSTD*. Ninety of the two hundred ships have an African place of trade identified. Of these sixty-three traded on the Gold Coast, seventeen in the Gambia, and eight at Whydah, though it seems likely that most of this last group sailed to Whydah after disembarking their rum at Cape Coast Castle.

Table C-1. *Merchandise Shipped to West Africa by the English African Companies, 1662–1703, by Type of Product and African Region of Import (in thousands of constant pounds sterling, base year = 1697 (Schumpeter index); column ratios in parentheses)*

	Upper Guinea	Gold Coast	Slave Coast	Bight of Biafra	West-Central Africa	Total*
Textiles	5.8 (.12)	331.2 (.77)	23.4 (.27)	1.8 (.01)	33.6 (.54)	398.0 (.55)
Metals	12.6 (.27)	27.2 (.06)	7.3 (.08)	72.2 (.80)	7.7 (.12)	127.0 (.18)
Cowries	0.4 (.01)	3.9 (.01)	38.3 (.44)	0.8 (.01)	0	43.4 (.06)
Personal Decorator Items	12.7 (.27)	4.6 (.01)	6.7 (.08)	13.0 (.14)	0.9 (.01)	38.0 (.06)
Containers	2.5 (.05)	10.0 (.02)	3.6 (.04)	1.3 (.01)	10.5 (.17)	28.1 (.04)
Guns and Gunpowder	1.4 (.03)	20.0 (.05)	1.2 (.01)	0.2 (.01)	3.4 (.06)	26.6 (.04)
Spirits	3.8 (.08)	8.9 (.02)	1.2 (.01)	0	0.6 (.01)	14.6 (.02)
Luxury Goods	0.9 (.02)	6.4 (.01)	0.4 (.01)	0	2.9 (.05)	10.6 (.01)
Misc. Items	7.3 (.15)	16.0 (.03)	5.7 (.07)	0.7 (.01)	2.2 (.04)	32.0 (.05)
Total	47.4 (1.0)	428.2 (1.0)	87.8 (1.0)	90.0 (1.0)	61.8 (1.0)	718.3 (1.0)

Notes: *Includes four cargoes for the Windward Coast for which breakdowns are not presented here.
Source: Computed from T70/1222 and 1223.

Coast.[3] At an average price of 1.22 shillings per gallon in Barbados,[4] this rum was worth about £82,000 in current values.

There is no record of New England ships – so common later in the eighteenth century – selling rum in West Africa at this time. There was, however, another source of alcoholic beverages. Portuguese ships sailing from Bahia

[3] A sample of eleven ships between 1683 and 1712 gleaned from the T70 series, vols. 2–20, carried a mean cargo of 6,670 gallons delivered. Leakage between the Caribbean and Africa was about 20 percent of the invoice quantity.

[4] Computed from McCusker, *Rum and the American Revolution*, 114–15. No attempt is made here to calculate annual values, partly because of the roughness of the calculation. It might be noted that fluctuations in the annual average price of rum were not very great at this time.

carried rum (actually, cachaca) as well as tobacco, though there seems little doubt that tobacco was by far the dominant commodity in the Bahia–Slave Coast trade.[5] Records exist of 463 ships leaving Bahia for West Africa between 1680 and 1713. If we assume that these Portuguese tobacco ships carried one-fifth of the rum of British Caribbean vessels, then they would have brought 620,000 gallons to West Africa – about half of the quantity on British Caribbean vessels. Dutch and French ships brought small quantities of brandy (three times the price of rum), which may be ignored. On these assumptions, West Africa absorbed at least two million gallons of alcohol between 1680 and 1713 or about 60,000 gallons a year, two-thirds of it sold on the Gold Coast. The large increase in the slave trade after 1697 suggests that the annual average of alcohol imported would have been greater after 1697 than before. The total value of this alcohol (assuming Brazilian and Caribbean rum was similarly priced and counting both together) would have been £120,000.

[5] For Portuguese rum see RAC to Humfries, Wright, and Boylston, May 3, 1687, T70/50, f. 37; Humphries, Wight, and Elwes to RAC, November 19, 1689, T70/11, p. 38; Frances Smith, Dixove Fort to RAC, December 11, 1692, Rawlinson manuscripts, c. 747, f. 321; Capt. Richard Willis, Whydah, to RAC, July 27, 1704, T70/14, f. 54.

Appendix D

Valuations of Produce Exports from the Leeward Islands in 1700

Valuations of exports from Barbados and Jamaica for selected years, 1664–1701, are presented elsewhere.[1] Data, and indeed records generally, are less abundant for the English Leeward Islands. There are few counterparts in the Leewards to the naval officer's reports that allow us to derive valuations of produce in the major English islands. Summaries of reports for the Leewards have survived from which John McCusker derived estimates of sugar exports and production for individual islands, but these do not lend themselves to estimates of values of overall trade.[2]

Limitations on data availability restrict the estimates to the year 1700. McCusker's figures for sugar volumes are accepted here as the starting point, and valuations of sugar are derived by multiplying these volumes by the price for 1700 extracted from McCusker's time series on sugar prices. The question is, what was the volume and price of sugar by-products that were exported, as well as their non-sugar counterparts? The answers offered here come from two sources. The first are the fragmentary returns of produce entered for export that have survived for what were the three major Leewards at this period, Antigua, Nevis, and Montserrat. For Antigua there are detailed reports for May 27 to September 1704, December 25, 1705 to June 26, 1706, September 25, 1707 to March 25, 1708, and June 25 to September 25, 1708. For Nevis, the extant naval officer's returns are for August 29, 1683 to August 25, 1684, November 4, 1685 to August 8, 1687, and January 12, 1704 to December 25, 1705. For Montserrat, the returns are for July 12, 1704 to May 12, 1705. None of these reports are for the same years for which there are reasonable data for Barbados and Jamaica (1698–1701), and none of them provide a continuous run for all the Leewards together. As a consequence, instead of extracting volumes of exports directly from

---

[1] Eltis, "New Estimates of Exports."
[2] McCusker, *Rum and the American Revolution*, 180, 187, 171, 193, 1143.

Table D-1. *Values of Sugar and Nonsugar Products Exported from the Leeward Islands for Selected Years, 1683–1709, Expressed in Terms of Millions of Pounds of Sugar (Non-sugar items converted to sugar equivalencies)**

	Sugar	Molasses	Rum	All Other	Total
Antigua	22.65	2.09	1.23	1.52	27.49
Montserrat	5.21	0.01	0	0.02	5.23
Nevis	31.20	0.13	0	0.10	31.43
Total	59.05	2.23	1.23	1.64	64.15

*Years for each island vary, see text.
Sources: Quantities of produce calculated from Co157/1. Conversion ratios to sugar equivalencies of nonsugar products calculated from the Barbados Customs books for 1664–67.

these returns, I have elected to use them to calculate the proportions of total exports accounted for by muscovado sugar, rum, molasses, and all nonsugar products combined. I then apply the resulting ratios to McCusker's estimates of muscovado sugar exports for 1700 to derive estimates of rum, molasses, and non-sugar products for 1700.

The second source used here provides a means of valuing multitudes of products other than muscovado sugar that are included in the naval officer's returns. Valuation is necessary for the simple reason that the naval officer provided only quantities of produce, not values, and any comparison of sugar and non-sugar items carried from the islands hinges on such valuation. This second source is the Barbados customs books for the mid-1660s, which provide sugar equivalencies for a wide range of Caribbean produce.[3] The first step in putting a value on non-sugar produce is to convert the quantities of rum, molasses, cotton, tobacco, ginger, indigo, and various log-woods, especially lignum vitae, cocoa, pimento, etc., provided by the naval officer's reports into their pounds of sugar equivalencies.[4] Clearly, the relative values of these items may have changed in the one-third of a century after 1667. But changes of non-sugar items as a whole, in other words net changes, would be less likely to shift, and our chief interest here is in non-sugar as a group of products. It should also be noted that this group formed less than 10 percent of overall exports from any island, and the quantities listed are in most cases small, if not trivial. Thus any errors are

[3] A few items are not to be found in the Barbados custom books, but the quantities of these items are very small, and rather than attempt a conversion I have simply added 1 percentage point of value to the non-sugar category to make allowance for them.
[4] For sugar equivalencies see Eltis, "New Estimates of Exports," 638.

Table D-2. *Sugar and Nonsugar Products Exported from the Leeward Islands for Selected Years, 1683–1709* Expressed as Shares of All Products Exported*

	Sugar	Molasses	Rum	All Other	Total
Antigua	0.824	0.076	0.045	0.055	1.0
Montserrat	0.996	0.001	0	0.003	1.0
Nevis	0.992	0.004	0	0.003	1.0
Total	0.921	0.035	0.019	0.026	1.0

*Years for each island vary, see text.
Sources: Calculated from Table D-1.

Table D-3. *Estimates of Current Values of Exports from Antigua, Montserrat, Nevis, and St. Kitts in 1700 in Thousands of Pounds Sterling (current values)*

	Sugar	Molasses	Rum	All Other	Total
Antigua	88.0	8.1	4.8	5.9	106.8
Montserrat	31.6	0	0	0.1	31.7
Nevis	85.4	0.3	0	0.3	86.0
St. Kitts*	15.9	0.6	0.3	0.5	17.3
Leeward Is	220.8	9.1	5.2	6.7	241.8

Notes: *ratios to derive the St. Kitts' figures are taken from row 4 of Table D-2.
Sources: Column 1: Calculated from quantities of sugar and prices of sugar in McCusker, *Rum and the American Revolution*, 180, 187, 171, 193, 1143. The London sugar price on p. 1143 is multiplied by 0.678 to reflect approximate fob values in the Caribbean.
Column 5: Column 1 divided by the equivalent cell in Column 1 of Table D-2.
Columns 2–4: Column 5 multiplied by the equivalent cell in Table D-2.

not likely to be of large consequence. Table D-1 shows the results of this procedure.

The third step in deriving valuations is the calculation of the shares of total produce accounted for by each major product category. Table D-2 shows row percentages derived from Table D-1, in effect the relative importance of each product category for the three major Leewards. To derive estimates of value for 1700 the ratios from Table D-2 are applied to the product of McCusker's estimates of the total quantity of sugar exported in that year and the price of sugar in 1700. There is an estimate of sugar exports from St. Kitts for 1700, but no information on non-sugar produce from the naval officer's lists. As a consequence the ratios for the Leewards as a whole (row 5 of Table D-2) are used as a proxy. In any event St. Kitts at this time was exporting far less than the other Leeward Islands. Finally the sugar quantities and sugar equivalencies (for nonsugar items) for each island are converted to pounds sterling by means of the average London price of sugar for the year 1700. To derive approximate fob values in the Caribbean, however, this price requires adjusting downward. Consistent with discussion in an earlier publication, Caribbean prices are taken as 0.678 of London prices.[5]

5   *Ibid.*, pp. 638–41.

Map 1 Regions of the Atlantic Involved in the Early Modern Slave Trade

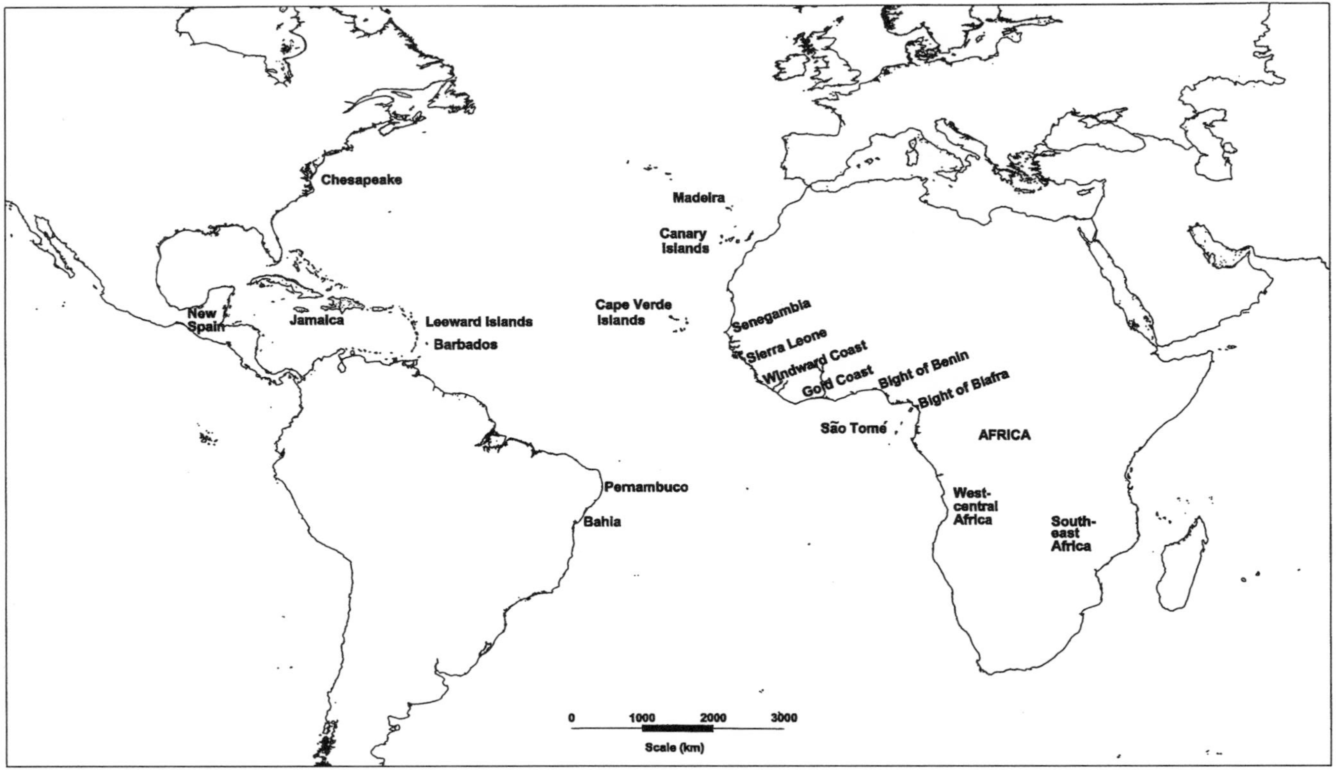

Chesapeake

Madeira

Canary
Islands

Leeward Islands
Barbados

Cape Verde
Islands

Senegambia

Sierra Leone
Windward Coast
Gold Coast
Bight of Benin
Bight of Biafra

AFRICA

São Tomé

West-
central
Africa

South-
east
Africa

New
Spain
Jamaica

Pernambuco
Bahia

Scale (km)

0   1000   2000   3000

307

Map 2 Senegambia

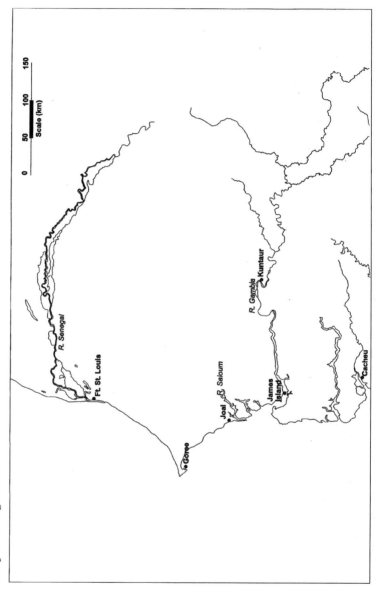

Map 3 Gold Coast

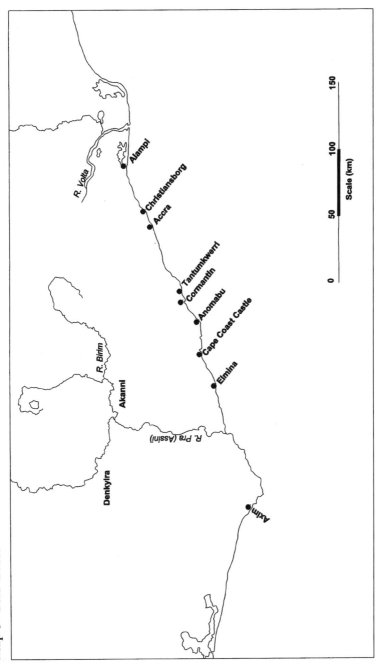

Map 4 Bight of Benin

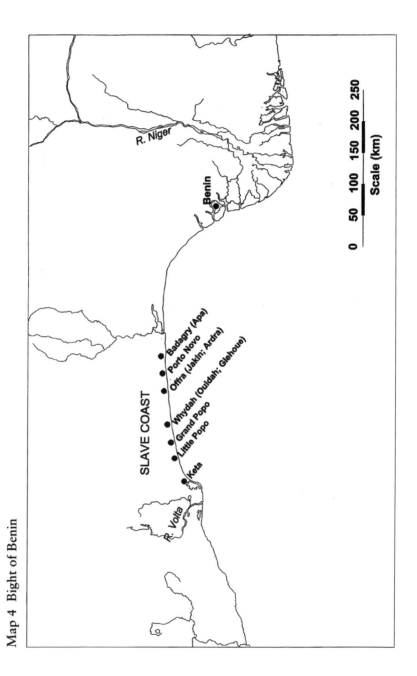

Map 5 Bight of Biafra

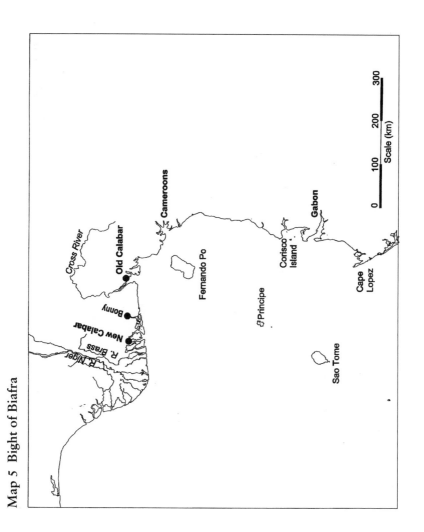

Cross River

Old Calabar

Cameroons

Bonny

New Calabar

R. Brass

R. Niger

Fernando Po

βPríncipe

Corisco
Island

Gabon

Sao Tome

Cape
Lopez

0   100   200   300
Scale (km)

Map 6 West-central Africa

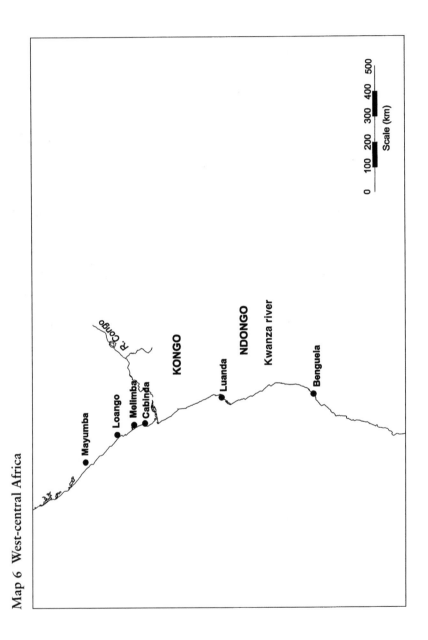

Map 7 Caribbean

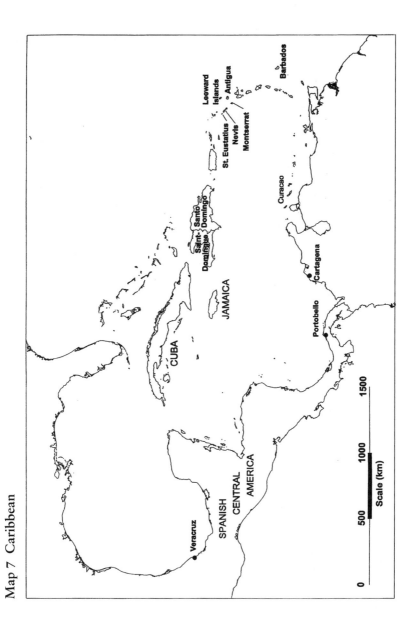

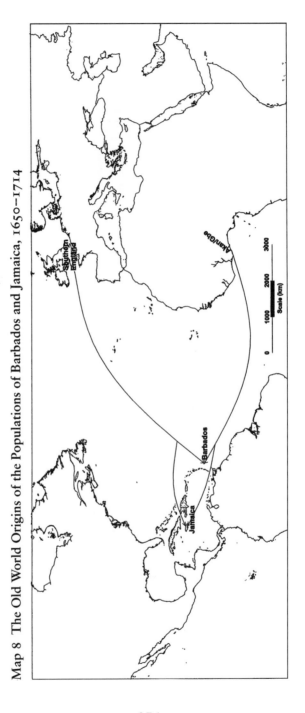

Map 8 The Old World Origins of the Populations of Barbados and Jamaica, 1650–1714

Sources

1. Voyages in the Slave Trade

DATA FOR THE SLAVE TRADE taken from David Eltis, Stephen D. Behrendt, David Richardson, and Herbert S. Klein, *The Trans-Atlantic Slave Trade: A Database on CD-ROM* (Cambridge, 1999). The introduction to and list of sources for this publication describe the composition and provenance of the set. The set includes 27,233 voyages that sailed between 1527 and 1866. Voyage numbers from this set are included in the footnotes of the present work.

2. Slave-ship Revolts

David Eltis, Stephen D. Behrendt, and David Richardson, "Revolts on Board Slave Ships: A Database" (Unpublished, 1998). Contains 448 cases of slave revolts and attacks on slave ships or the boats of slave ships and 124 variables enumerating various aspects of shipboard violence between Africans and Europeans and its outcome.

3. Migrants from England

David Eltis and Ingrid Stott, "Coldham's Emigrants from England, 1640–1699: A Database" (Unpublished, 1994). Contains 32,703 records of individual migrants and 14 variables, covering the period 1640 to 1699. Extracted from Peter Wilson Coldham, *The Complete Book of Emigrants, 1607–1660* (Baltimore, Md., 1988), and idem, *The Complete Book of Emigrants, 1661–1699* (Baltimore, Md., 1990).

4. Merchandise

"Merchandise Exported to Africa by the English African Companies, 1662–1703." Extracted from "Register of calculations of the Charges of Shippes and Cargoes reported by the Committee of the Court of Assistants," T70/1222. This has been supplemented by summaries of cargoes taken from T70/50, ff. 143; /61, ff. 165–6; /169, f. 135; and /175, f. 158, and T70/1223. The data set comprises 569 separate cargoes itemised by type of product. It includes both physical quantities and values. The total value of all merchandise in the data set is 1.042 million pounds sterling in constant values using the Schumpeter index, which has a base year of 1697.

5. Servants

David Eltis and Kelly Dunn, "Servants and Passengers arriving at Barbados and Jamaica, 1678–1699." Extracted from the naval office shipping lists. This is a voyage-based database of all vessels entering Jamaica and Barbados carrying servants. It includes information on the number of servants carried and the characteristics of the vessel.

Unpublished Documents

British Public Record Office

Treasury Papers
T11, volume 13.
T70, volumes 1–28, 40, 41, 44, 45, 50–4, 57–59, 61–4, 66, 68–76, 100, 101, 134, 138, 164, 169, 170, 175, 269, 309, 544–46, 599–600, 635, 646, 829, 830, 869–70, 909–25, 936–69, 1193, 1205, 1213, 1216, 1222–5, 1433, 1438, 1575.

Colonial Office Papers
CO1, volumes 9, 12, 14, 16–25, 31, 33, 34, 43, 44.
CO5, volumes 1, 1320.
CO28, volume 1.
CO29, volume 1.
CO31, volumes 1–3
CO33, volumes 13–15.
CO142, volumes 13, 14.
CO152, volumes 13, 19.
CO157, volume 1.
CO268, volume 1.
CO324, volume 1.
CO386, volume 91.
CO388, volumes 1–3, 8, 10–15, 18, 25.
CO389, volumes 1, 2, 15.
CO390, volumes 6, 12.
"Minutes of the Council of Barbados, Vol. 1, 1654–8, from the Original in Barbados," type-script.
"Minutes of the Council of Barbados, Vol. 2, 1658–62, from the Original in Barbados," type-script.

Bodleian Library, Oxford University
Clarendon manuscripts, vols. 53–5.
Early English History Manuscripts. B. 122.
"A Coppie Journal of Entries made In the Custome House of Barbados Beginning August the 10th, 1664 and ending August the 10th 1665."
Rawlinson manuscripts, A60, A312, A328, A348, A478, C745–7, D924.

British Library, Additional Manuscripts
2395 Egerton manuscripts.
3984, Sloan manuscripts.
11, 410–11, Letter books of Thomas Povey, 1655–60.
19, 560, Le Sieur des Marchais, "Journal de Navigation du Voyage de la Coste de Guinée …" from January 1704 to January 1706.
22, 676, Long manuscripts.
25495–8, South Sea Company, Papers, Minutes and Correspondence
30, 567, "Tartre et autres memoires touchant les commerce de mer et compagnies pour le traffic, faites ètranger; 1588–1604."
39, 946, "Narrative of Voyages to the Guinea Coast and the West Indies, 1714–1716."

House of Lords Record Office
Lloyds' Lists, 1702–4.

Hispanic Society of America, New York

"A Coppie Journal of Entries made In the Custome House of Barbados," Beginning August 11, 1665 to April 22, 1667.

Magdalene College, Library, Cambridge University "Capt. Robert Holms his Journalls of Two Voyages into Guynea ... in the Years 1660/61 and 1663/64."

Printed Documents and Contemporary Sources

Anon. *An Abridgement of the laws in Force and use in Her Majesty's Plantations.* London, 1704.

Anon. *Popery and Tyranny: or, the present state of France in relation to its government, trade, manners of the people, and nature of the countrey.* London, 1679.

Anon. *The Interest of the Nation as it Respects all the Sugar-Plantations Abroad and Refining of Sugars at Home.* London, 1691.

Bartlett, John Russell, ed. *Records of the Colony Rhode Island and Providence.* 4 vols., Newport, 1856–65.

Bosman. *A New and Accurate Description of the Coast of Guinea.* London, 1705, repr. 1967.

Brougham, Henry. *An Inquiry into the Colonial Policy of the European Powers, 2 vols.* Edinburgh, 1803.

Burton, Thomas. *Diary of Thomas Burton, esq. Member in the Parliaments of Oliver and Richard Cromwell, From 1656 to 1659.* 4 vols. London, 1828.

Chamberlayne, Edward. *Angliae Notitia or the Present State of England: Together with Divers Reflections on the Antient State thereof.* Sixth edition. London, 1672.

Child, Josiah. *A New Discourse of Trade.* London, 1679.

Churchill, Awnsham and John Churchill. *A Collection of Voyages and Travels.* 6 vols. London, 1744–6.

Crow, Hugh. *Memoirs of the Late Hugh Captain Hugh Crow of Liverpool.* London, 1830.

Eburne, Richard. *Plaine Pathway to Plantations: that is A discourse in generall concerning the plantation of our English People in other Countries.* London, 1624.

Firmin, T. *Some Proposals for the imploying of the poor especially in and about the city of London.* London, 1678.

Foyle, Oxenbridge and Marcellus Rivers. *England's Slavery, or Barbados Merchandize; Represented in a Petition to the High and Honourable Court of Parliament.* London, 1659.

Gentleman's Magazine. 43(1773).

Haines, Richard. *Provision for the Poor: or Reasons for the erecting of a working-hospital in every county ... Linnen Manufactory.* London, 1678.

Hair, Paul, ed. *Barbot on Guinea: The Writings of Jean Barbot on Africa.* London, 1992.

Historical Manuscripts' Commission. *The Manuscripts of the Duke of Portland.* 2 vols. London, 1893.

Jeaffreson, John C. *A Young Squire of the Seventeenth Century: Papers of Christopher Jeaffreson.* 2 vols. London, 1878.

Ligon, Richard. *True and Exact History of the Island of Barbados.* London, 1657.

Lyttleton, Edward. *The Groans of the Plantations.* London, 1689.

Massie, Joseph. *A State of the British Sugar Colony Trade.* London, 1759.

Meriton, George. *A Guide for constables, churchwardens, overseers of the poor.* London, 1669.

Moore, Francis. *Travels into the Inland Parts of Africa.* London, 1738.

North, Dudley. *Observations and Advices Oeconomical.* London, 1669.

O'Callaghan, E.B., ed. *Documents Relative to the Colonial History of New York.* Vol. 10. New York, 1853–7.

Oldmixon, John. *The British Empire in America.* 2 vols. London, 1741.

Pommegorge, Pruneau de. *Description de la 'Nigritie.'* Paris, 1789.

"Records of the Vestry of St. Michael." *Journal of the Barbados Museum and Historical Society* 15(1948):19–27, 98–104.

Sainsbury, W. Noel, ed. *Calendar of State Papers, Colonial Series.* Vols. 1–10. London, 1860–78.

Thomas, Dalby. *An Historical Account of the Rise and Growth of the West India Colonies.* London, 1690.

Turnbull, David. *Travels in the West. Cuba: with Notices of Porto Rico and the Slave Trade.* London, 1840.

Winstanley, Gerard. *The law of freedom in a platform ... Wherein is declared, what is kingly government and what is commonwealth's government.* London, 1652.

Secondary Sources

Abeyasekere, S. "Slaves in Batavia: Insights from a Slave Register." In *Slaves, Bondage, and Dependency in South-East Asia*, ed. Anthony Reid. St. Lucia, Queensland, 1983.

Akenson, Donald Harman. *If the Irish Ran the World: Montserrat, 1630–1730.* Montreal, 1997.

Allen, Robert. "Agriculture During the Industrial Revolution." In *The Economic History of Britain Since 1700*, eds. Roderick Floud and Donald McCloskey 1. Cambridge, 1994.

Altes, J. Korthals. *Sir Cornelius Vermuyden.* London, 1925.

Altman, Ida. "Moving Around and on: Spanish Emigration in the Sixteenth Century." In *Migrations, Migration History: Old Paradigms and New Perspectives*, eds. Jan Lucassen and Leo Lucassen, 253–69. Bern, 1987.

Altman, Ida. *Emigrants & Society: Extremadura and Spanish America in the Sixteenth Century.* Los Angeles, 1989.

Altman, Ida. "New World in the Old: Local Society and Spanish Emigration to the Indies." In *'To Make America': European Emigration in the Early Modern Period*, eds. Ida Altman and James Horn. Berkeley, 1991.

Amadiume, Ifi. "Female Husbands in Southern Bantu Society." In *Sexual Stratifications: A Cross Cultural View*, ed. A. Schlegel. New York, 1977.

Anderson, Virginia DeJohn. *New England's Generation: The Great Migration and the Formation of Society and Culture in the Seventeenth Century.* Cambridge, 1991.

Ankerloo, Bengt. "Agriculture and Women's Work: The Direction of Change in the West, 1700–1900." *Journal of Family History* 4(1979):11–20.

Appleby, John C. "A Guinea Venture, c. 1657: A Note on the Early English Slave Trade." *Mariner's Mirror* 79(1993):84–7.

Appleby, Joyce Oldham. *Economic Thought and Ideology in Seventeenth Century England.* Princeton, N.J., 1978.

Ashcraft-Eason, Lillian. "She 'Voluntarily Hath Come to ... [The Georgia] Province': A Gambian-Woman Slave Trader Among the Enslaved." In *Constructions of Identity: African Communities in the Shadow of Slavery*, ed. Paul Lovejoy forthcoming.

Attman, Artur. *American Bullion in the European World Trade, 1600–1800.* Translated by Eva and Allan Green. Goteborg, 1986.

Austen, Ralph. "The Trans-Saharan Slave Trade: A Tentative Census." In *The Uncommon Market: Essays in the Economic History of the Transatlantic Slave Trade*, eds. Henry A. Gemery and Jan S. Hogendorn. New York, 1979.

Axtell, James. *Beyond 1492: Encounters in Colonial North America.* New York, 1992.

Bachman, Van Cleaf. *Peltries or Plantations: The Economic Policies of the Dutch West India Company in New Netherland, 1623–1639.* Baltimore, Md., 1969.

Baesjou, R. and P. C. Emmer. "The Dutch in West Africa: Shipping Factories and Colonisation, 1800–1870." In *Shipping, Factories and Colonization*, eds. J. Everaert and J. Parmentier. Brussels, 1996.

Bailey, Ronald. "The Slave(ry) Trade and the Development of Capitalism in the United States: The Textile Industry in New England." In *The Atlantic Slave Trade: Effects on Economies, Societies, and Peoples in Africa, the Americas, and Europe*, eds. Joseph Inikori and Stanley L. Engerman. Durham, 1992.

Bailyn, Bernard. *New England Merchants in the Seventeenth Century.* Cambridge, Mass., 1955.

Bailyn, Bernard. *Voyagers to the West: A Passage in the Peopling of America on the Eve of the Revolution.* New York, 1986.

Baker, J. H. "Personal Liberty Under the Common Law of England, 1200–1600." In *The Origin of Modern Freedom in the West,* ed. Richard W. Davis. Stanford, 1995.

Bakewell, Peter J. *Silver Mining and Society in Colonial Mexico, Zacatecas 1546–1700.* Cambridge, 1971.

Bakewell, Peter J. *Miners of the Red Mountain: Indian Labor in Potosi, 1545–1650.* Albuquerque, N.M., 1984.

Bamford, Paul W. *Fighting Ships and Prisons: The Mediterranean Galleys of France in the Age of Louis XIV.* Minneapolis, Minn., 1973.

Barbour, Violet. "Marine Risks and Insurance in the Seventeenth Century." *Journal of Economic and Business History* 1(1929):561–96.

Barbour, Violet. "Dutch and English Merchant Shipping in the Seventeenth Century." *Economic History Review* 2(1930).

Barrett, J. Ward. "Caribbean Sugar-Production in the Seventeenth and Eighteenth Centuries." In *Merchants and Scholars: Essays in the History of Exploration and Trade,* ed. John Parker. Minneapolis, Minn., 1965.

Barrowman, James. "Slavery in the Coal-Mines of Scotland." *Transactions of the Mining Institute of Scotland* 19(1897–8, part 2):117–29.

Barry, Boubacar. *La Sénégambie du XVe au XIX Siècle: Traite Négrière, Islam et Conquête Coloniale.* Paris, 1988.

Baugh, Daniel A. *British Naval Administration in the Age of Walpole.* Princeton, N.J., 1965.

Bean, Richard. "A Note on the Relative Importance of Slaves and Gold in West African Exports." *Journal of African History* 15(1974):351–6.

Bean, Richard Nelson. *The British Trans-Atlantic Slave Trade, 1650–1775.* New York, 1975.

Beattie, John M. *Crime and the Courts in England, 1660–1800.* Princeton, 1986.

Beckles, Hilary McD. *Natural Rebels: A Social History of Enslaved Black Women in Barbados.* New Brunswick, N.J., 1989.

Beckles, Hilary McD. *White Servitude and Black Slavery in Barbados.* Knoxville, Tenn., 1989.

Beckles, Hilary McD. "A 'riotous and unruly lot': Irish Indentured Servants and Freemen in the English West Indies, 1644–1713." *William and Mary Quarterly* 47(1990):503–22.

Beckles, Hilary McD. "The 'Hub of Empire': The Caribbean and Britain in the Seventeenth Century." In *The Oxford History of the British Empire,* ed. Nicholas P. Canny, 4 vols. Oxford, 1998.

Beckles, Hilary McD. and Andrew Downes. "The Economics of Transition to the Black Labor System in Barbados, 1630–1680." *Journal of Interdisciplinary History* 18(1987):225–47.

Beer, George Louis. *The Old Colonial System, 1660–1754.* Vol. 1. 2 vols. New York, 1912.

Behrendt, Stephen D., David Eltis, and David Richardson. "The Structure of the Transatlantic Slave Trade, 1595–1867." A paper delivered at the Social Science History Meetings, Chicago, 1995 (November).

Behrendt, Stephen D. "The British Slave Trade, 1785–1807: Volume, Profitability and Mortality" (Unpublished PhD thesis, University of Wisconsin, 1993).

Beinart, Haim. "The Conversos and Their Fate." In *Spain and the Jews,* ed. Elie Kedourie. London, 1992.

Berkin, Carol. *First Generations: Women in Colonial America.* New York, 1996.

Blackburn, Robin. *The Overthrow of Colonial Slavery, 1776–1848.* London, 1988.

Blackburn, Robin. *The Making of New World Slavery: From the Baroque to the Modern 1492–1800.* London, 1997.

Blaut, James M. *The Colonizer's Model of the World: Geographic Diffusionism and Eurocentric History.* New York, 1993.

Boulle, Pierre. "Marchandises de traite et développement industriel dans la France et L'Angleterre du XVIIIe siècle." *Revue francaise d'histoire d'outre-mer* 42(1975):309–30.

Bouwsma, William. "Liberty in the Renaissance and Reformation." In *The Origins of Modern Freedom in the West*, ed. Richard W. Davis, 203–34. Stanford, Ca., 1995.

Bowden, Peter J. *The Wool Trade in Tudor and Stuart England*. London, 1962.

Boxer, Charles R. *The Golden Age of Brazil, 1695–1750*. Berkeley, 1962.

Boxer, Charles R. *Portuguese Society in the Tropics*. Madison, Wis., 1965.

Boyd-Bowman, Peter. "Patterns of Spanish Emigration to the Indies until 1600." *Hispanic American Historical Review* 56(1976):580–604.

Braudel, Fernand. *The Identity of France*. Vol. 1. London, 1988.

Breen, T. H. *Puritans and Adventurers: Change and Persistence in Early America*. New York, 1980.

Brenner, Robert. "Agrarian Class Structure and Economic Development in Pre-Industrial Society." *Past and Present* 70(1976).

Brenner, Robert. *Merchants and Revolution: Commercial Change, Political Conflict, and London Overseas Traders, 1550–1653*. Cambridge, 1993.

Brewer, John and Roy Porter, eds. *Consumption and the World of Goods*. London, 1993.

Bridenbaugh, Carl. *Vexed and Troubled Englishmen*. Oxford, 1968.

Bridenbaugh, Carl. *No Peace Beyond the Line; the English in the Caribbean, 1624–1690*. New York, 1972.

Britnell, R. H. *The Commercialisation of English Society, 1000–1500*. Cambridge, 1993.

Bucher, Henry. "The Atlantic Slave Trade and the Gabon Estuary: The Mpongwe to 1860." In *Africans in Bondage: Studies in Slavery and the Slave Trade*, ed. Paul E. Lovejoy. Madison, Wis., 1986.

Buhofer, Heinz, and Bruno S. Frey. "A Market for Men, or There is no such Thing as a Free Lynch." *Journal of Institutional and Theoretical Economics* 142(1986).

Burnard, Trevor. "'The Grand Mart of the Island': Kingston, Jamaica in the mid-Eighteenth Century and the Question of Urbanisation in Plantation Societies." In *Aspects of Jamaican History from the Eighteenth to the Twentieth Century*, eds. Kathleen Monteith and Glenn Richards. Kingston, Jamaica, forthcoming.

Burnard, Trevor. "Inheritance and Independence: Women's Status in Early Colonial Jamaica." *William and Mary Quarterly* 48(1991):93–114.

Burnard, Trevor. "The Composition of Jamaica's White Population, 1655–1780 (Unpublished, 1996).

Burnard, Trevor. "European Migration to Jamaica, 1655–1780." *William and Mary Quarterly* 53(1996):769–96.

Burnard, Trevor. "Who Bought Slaves in America?: Purchasers of Slaves from the Royal African Company in Jamaica, 1674–1708." *Slavery and Abolition* 17(1996):68–92.

Burnard, Trevor. "Prodigious Mine: The Wealth of Jamaica Once Again" (Unpublished paper, 1998).

Campbell, Alan B. *The Lanarkshire Miners: A Social History of their Trade Unions, 1775–1874*. Edinburgh, 1979.

Campbell, Mildred. "Social Origins of Some Early Americans." In *Seventeenth Century America*, ed. James Morton Smith. Chapel Hill, N.C., 1959.

Campion, Emile. *Etude sur la colonisation par les transportés anglais, russes et français*. Rennes, 1901.

Canny, Nicholas and Anthony Pagden, ed. *Colonial Identity in the Atlantic World, 1500–1800*. Princeton, N.J., 1992.

Caron, Peter. "'Of a nation which others do not understand:'Bambara Slaves and African Ethnicity in Colonial Louisiana, 1718–60." *Slavery & Abolition: A Journal of Slavery and Post-Slave Studies* 18(1997):98–121.

Carr, Cecil T. *Select Charters of the Trading Companies, 1530–1707*. London, 1913.

Carr, Lois Green and Russell R. Menard. "Immigration and Opportunity: The Freedman in Early Colonial Maryland." In *The Chesapeake in the Seventeenth Century: Essays on*

Anglo-American Society, eds. Thad W. Tate and David L. Ammerman. Chapel Hill, N.C., 1979.

Carr, Lois Green and Lorena S. Walsh. "The Planter's Wife: The Experience of White Women in Seventeenth-Century Maryland." *William & Mary Quarterly* 34(1977):542–71.

Chaunu, Pierre. *European Expansion in the Later Middle Ages*. Amsterdam, 1979.

Choquette, Leslie. *Frenchmen into Peasants: Modernity and Tradition in the Peopling of French Canada*. Cambridge, Ma., 1997.

Clark, Alice. *Working Life of Women in the Seventeenth Century*. London, 1919.

Clark, Gregory. "Yields per Acre in English Agriculture, 1250–1860: Evidence from Labour Inputs." *Economic History Review* 44(1991):445–60.

Clignet, Remi. *Many Wives, Many Powers: Authority and Power in Polygynous Marriages*. Evanston, Ill., 1970.

Clissold, Stephen. *The Barbary Slaves*. London, 1977.

Coates, Timothy Joel. "Exiles and Orphans: Forced and State Sponsored Colonizers in the Portuguese Empire, 1550–1720." Unpublished PhD thesis, University of Minnesota, 1993.

Coats, A. W. "Changing Attitudes to Labour in the mid Eighteenth Century." *Economic History Review* 11(1958–9):35–51.

Cohen, David Steven. *The Dutch-American Farm*. New York, 1992.

Cohen, William B. *The French Encounter with Africans: White Response to Blacks, 1530–1880*. Bloomington, Ind., 1980.

Cohn, Raymond L. "Maritime Mortality in the Eighteenth and Nineteenth Centuries: A Survey." *International Journal of Maritime History* 1(1989):159–91.

Coldham, Peter Wilson. *The Complete Book of Emigrants, 1607–1660*. Baltimore, Md., 1988.

Coldham, Peter Wilson. *The Complete Book of Emigrants, 1661–1699*. Baltimore, Md., 1990.

Coldham, Peter Wilson. *Emigrants in Chains: A Social History of Forced Emigration to the Americas of Felons, Destitute Children, Political and Religious Non-Conformists, Vagabonds and Other Undesirables, 1606–1776*. Baltimore, Md., 1992.

Cole, Jeffrey A. *The Potosi Mita, 1573–1700: Compulsory Indian Labor in the Andes*. Stanford, 1985.

Coleman, D. C. *The British Paper Industry, 1495–1860: A Study in Industrial Growth*. Oxford, 1958.

Coombs, Douglas. *The Gold Coast, Britain and the Netherlands, 1850–1874*. London, 1963.

Cooper, J. P. and Joan Thirsk, eds. *Seventeenth Century Economic Documents*. Oxford, 1972.

Crafts, N. F. R. *British Economic Growth During the Industrial Revolution*. Oxford, 1985.

Craton, Michael. *Testing the Chains: Resistance to Slavery in the British West Indies*. Ithaca, N.Y., 1982.

Crosby, Alfred W. *Ecological Imperialism: The Biological Expansion of Europe, 900–1900*. Cambridge, 1986.

Cundall, Frank. *The Mico College, Jamaica*. Kingston, 1914.

Cunningham, Hugh. "The Employment and Unemployment of Children in England c. 1680–1851." *Past and Present* 126(1990):115–50.

Curtin, Philip D. "Epidemiology and the Slave Trade." *Political Science Quarterly* 83(1967):190–216.

Curtin, Philip D. *The Atlantic Slave Trade: A Census*. Madison, Wis., 1969.

Curtin, Philip D. *Economic Change in Precolonial Africa: Senegambia in the Era of the Slave Trade*. Vol. 1, 2. 2 vols. Madison, Wis., 1975.

Curtin, Philip D. *Economic Change in Pre-Colonial Africa: Supplementary Evidence*. Madison, Wis., 1975.

Curtin, Philip D. "The Abolition of the Slave Trade from Senegambia." In *The Abolition of the Atlantic Slave Trade*, eds. David Eltis and James Walvin. Madison, Wis., 1981.

Curtin, Philip D. "Africa and the Wider Monetary World, 1250–1850." In *Precious Metals in the Later Medieval and Early Modern Worlds*, ed. J. F. Richards. Durham, N.C., 1983.

Curtin, Philip D. *Cross-Cultural Trade in World History*. Cambridge, 1984.

Curtin, Philip D. *The Rise and Fall of the Plantation Complex: Essays in Atlantic History*. Cambridge, 1990.

Curtin, Philip, Steven Feierman, Leonard Thompson, and Jan Vansina. *African History*. Boston, 1978.

Curto, Jose C. "A Quantitative Reassessment of the Legal Portuguese Slave Trade from Luanda, Angola, 1710–1830." *African Economic History* 20 (1992):1–25.

Daaku, Kwame Yeboa. *Trade and Politics on the Gold Coast, 1600–1720*. Oxford, 1970.

Darby, Henry C. *Draining the Fens*. Second ed. Cambridge, 1956.

Darity, William A. "British Industry and the West Indies Plantations." In *The Atlantic Slave Trade: Effects on Economies, Societies, and Peoples in Africa, the Americas, and Europe*, eds. Joseph E. Inikori and Stanley L. Engerman. Durham, N.C., 1992.

Davies, C.S.L. "Slavery and Protector Somerset: The Vagrancy Act of 1547." *Economic History Review* 19(1966):533–49.

Davies, Kenneth G. *The Royal African Company*. London, 1957.

Davies, Kenneth G. "Joint-Stock Investment in the late Seventeenth Century." *Economic History Review* 4(1952).

Davis, David Brion. *The Problem of Slavery in Western Culture*. Ithaca, N.Y., 1966.

Davis, David Brion. *Slavery and Human Progress*. New York, 1984.

Davis, Ralph. "English Foreign Trade, 1600–1700." *Economic History Review* 7(1954):150–66.

Davis, Ralph. *The Rise of the English Shipping Industry*. London, 1962.

Davis, Ralph. *The Industrial Revolution and British Overseas Trade*. Leicester, 1979.

Deane, Phyllis, and W. A. Cole. *British Economic Growth, 1688–1959*. Cambridge, 1969.

Debien, Gabriel. "Les engagés pour les Antilles (1634–1715)." *Revue d'histoire des colonies* 38(1951):5–274.

Degler, Carl N. *Neither Black nor White: Slavery and Race Relations in Brazil and the United States*. New York, 1971.

Dickson, T. *Scottish Capitalism: State and Nation from Before the Union to the Present*. London, 1980.

Dixon, Ruth B. "The Roles of Rural Women, Female Seclusion, Economic Production, and Reproductive Choice." In *Population and Development: the Search for Selective Intervention*, ed. Ronald Ridker. Baltimore, Md., 1976.

Domar, Evsey. "The Causes of Slavery and Serfdom: A Hypothesis." *Journal of Economic History* (1970):18–32.

Donagan, Barbara. "Codes and Conduct in the English Civil War." *Past and Present* 118(1988): 65–95.

Donnan, Elizabeth. *Documents Illustrative of the Slave Trade to America*. 4 vols. Washington, 1930–33.

Drescher, Seymour. "Capitalism and Abolition: Values and Forces in Britain, 1783–1814." In *Liverpool, the African Slave Trade, and Abolition*, eds. Roger Anstey and P. E. H. Hair. Liverpool, 1976.

Drescher, Seymour. *Capitalism and Antislavery: British Mobilization in Comparative Perspective*. London, 1986.

Drescher, Seymour. *Econocide: British Slavery in the Era of Abolition*. Pittsburgh, Pa., 1976.

Drescher, Seymour. "The Ending of the Slave Trade and the Evolution of European Scientific Racism." *Social Science History* 14(1990):415–50.

Drescher, Seymour. "The Long Goodbye: The Dutch Case in the Capitalism and Anti-Slavery Debate." In *The Lesser Antilles in the Age of European Expansion*, eds. Robert L. Paquette and Stanley L. Engerman. Gainesville, Fla., 1995.

Dumas, Silvio. *Les filles du roi en Nouvelle France*. Quebec, 1972.

Dunn, Richard S. *Sugar and Slaves: The Rise of the Planter Class in the English West Indies, 1624–1713*. New York, 1972.

Dunn, Richard S. "Sugar Production and Slave Women in Jamaica." In *Cultivation and Culture: Labor and the Shaping of Slave Life in the Americas*, eds. Ira Berlin and Philip D. Morgan. Charlottesville, Va., 1993.

Edel, Matthew. "The Brazilian Sugar Cycle of the Seventeenth Century and the Rise of West Indian Competition." *Caribbean Studies* 9(1969):24–44.

Ekirch, A. Roger. *Bound for America: The Transportation of British Convicts to the Colonies, 1718–1775*. Oxford, 1987.

Elbl, Ivana. "The Volume of the Early Atlantic Slave Trade, 1450–1521." *Journal of African History* 38(1997):31–75.

Eltis, David. "The British Contribution to the Transatlantic Slave Trade." *Economic History Review* 32(1979):211–27.

Eltis, David. "Nutritional Trends in Africa and the Americas, 1819–1839." *Journal of Interdisciplinary History* 12(1982):453–75.

Eltis, David. *Economic Growth and the Ending of the Transatlantic Slave Trade*. New York, 1987.

Eltis, David. "Trade Between Western Africa and the Atlantic World before 1870: Estimates of Trends in Value, Composition and Direction." *Research in Economic History* 12(1989):197–239.

Eltis, David. "Europeans and the Rise and Fall of African Slavery in the Americas." *American Historical Review* 98(1993):1399–423.

Eltis, David. "New Estimates of Exports from Barbados and Jamaica, 1665–1701." *William and Mary Quarterly* 53(1995):631–48.

Eltis, David. "Labour and Coercion in the English Atlantic World from the Seventeenth Century to the Early Twentieth Centuries." *Slavery & Abolition* 14(1993):207–26.

Eltis, David. "The Relative Importance of Slaves in the Atlantic Trade of Seventeenth Century Africa." *Journal of African History* 35(1994):237–49.

Eltis, David. "The Total Product of Barbados, 1664–1701." *Journal of Economic History* 55(1995):321–36.

Eltis, David. "The Volume and African Origins of the Seventeenth Century English Transatlantic Slave Trade: A Comparative Assessment." *Cahiers d'Etudes d'Africaines* 138(1995): 620.

Eltis, David. "The British Transatlantic Slave Trade Before 1714: Annual Estimates of Volume and Direction." In *The Lesser Antilles in the Age of European Expansion*, eds. Robert L. Paquette and Stanley L. Engerman. Gainesville, Fla., 1996.

Eltis, David. "The Slave Economies of the Caribbean: Structure, Performance, Evolution and Significance." In *The UNESCO General History of the Caribbean*, ed. Franklin W. Knight, 3, 1997.

Eltis, David and Stanley L. Engerman. "Fluctuations in Sex and Age Ratios in the Transatlantic Slave Trade, 1663–1864." *Economic History Review* 46(1993):308–23.

Eltis, David and Stanley L. Engerman. "Was the Slave Trade Dominated by Men?" *Journal of Interdisciplinary History* (1993).

Eltis, David and Lawrence C. Jennings. "Trade Between Western Africa and the Atlantic World in the Pre-Colonial Era." *American Historical Review* 93(1988):936–59.

Eltis, David and David Richardson. "Productivity in the Slave Trade." *Explorations in Economic History* 32(1995):465–84.

Eltis, David and James Walvin, eds. *The Abolition of the Atlantic Slave Trade: Origins and Effects in Europe, Africa and the Americas*. Madison, Wis., 1981.

Eltis, David, Stephen D. Behrendt, and David Richardson. "The Volume of the Transatlantic Slave Trade: A Reassessment with Particular Reference to the Portuguese Contribution." (Unpublished paper, 1998).

Engerman, Stanley L. "The Slave Trade and British Capital Formation in the Eighteenth Century: A Comment on the Williams Thesis." *Business History Review* 46(1972):430–43.

Engerman, Stanley L. "Some Considerations Relating to Property Rights in Man." *Journal of Economic History* 33(1973):49–51.

Engerman, Stanley L. "Notes on the Pattern of Economic Growth in the British North American Colonies in the Seventeenth, Eighteenth and Nineteenth Centuries." In *Disparities in Economic Development since the Industrial Revolution*, eds. Paul Bairoch and Maurice Levy-Leboyer. New York, 1981.

Engerman, Stanley L. "Economic Change and Contract Labor in the British Caribbean: The End of Slavery and the Adjustment to Emancipation." *Explorations in Economic History* 21(1984):133–50.

Engerman, Stanley L. "Coerced and Free Labor: Property Rights and the Development of the Labor Force." *Explorations in Entrepreneurial History* 29(1992):1–29.

Engerman, Stanley L. "The Atlantic Economy of the Eighteenth Century: Some Speculations on Economic Development in Britain, America, Africa and Elsewhere." *Journal of European Economic History* 24(1995):145–75.

Engerman, Stanley L. "Europe, the Lesser Antilles, and Economic Expansion, 1600–1800." In *The Lesser Antilles in the Age of European Expansion*, eds. Robert L. Paquette and Stanley L. Engerman, 1996.

Engerman, Stanley L. "British Imperialism in a Mercantilist Age, 1492–1849: Conceptual Issues and Empirical Problems," *Revista de História Econômica* 15(1998):195–234.

Engerman, Stanley L. "Cultural Values, Ideological Beliefs, and Changing Labor Institutions: Notes on Their Interactions." *The Frontiers of New Institutional Economics*, eds. John N. Drobak and John Nye. San Diego, Ca., 1997.

Engerman, Stanley L. "Introduction." In *The Terms of Labour*, ed. Stanley L. Engerman. Stanford, 1999.

Engerman, Stanley L., Fraginals, Manuel Moreno, and Herbert S. Klein. "The Level and Structure of Slave Prices on Cuban Plantations in the Mid-Nineteenth Century: Some Comparative Perspectives." *American Historical Review* 88(1983):1201–18.

Engerman, Stanley L., and Herbert S. Klein. "Long-Term Trends in African Mortality in the Transatlantic Slave Trade." *Slavery & Abolition* 18(1997): 36–48.

Engerman, Stanley L., and R. W. Fogel. "A Model for the Explanation of Industrial Expansion during the Nineteenth Century." In *The Reinterpretation of American Economic History*, eds. R. W. Fogel and S. L. Engerman. New York, 1971.

Evans, William McKee. "From the Land of Canaan to the Land of Guinea: The Strange Odyssey of the 'Sons of Ham.'" *American Historical Review* 85(1980):15–43.

Farrar, P. A. "The Jews in Barbados." *Journal of Barbados Museum and Historical Society* 9(1942):130–4.

Fenoaltea, Stefano. "Europe in the African Mirror: The Slave Trade and the Rise of Feudalism" (Unpublished paper, 1991).

Fernández-Armesto, Felipe. *The Canary Islands After the Conquest, The Making of a Colonial Society in the Early Sixteenth Century*. Oxford, 1982.

Fick, Carolyn E. *The Making of Haiti: The Saint Domingue Revolution from Below*. Knoxville, Tenn., 1990.

Fields, Barbara Jeanne. "Slavery, Race and Ideology in the United States of America." *New Left Review* 181(1990 (May–June)):95–118.

Finley, M. I. *The Ancient Economy*. Berkeley, 1973.

Finley, Moses. "A Peculiar Institution." *Times Literary Supplement* (July 2, 1976).

Fischer, David Hackett. *Albion's Seed: Four British Folkways in America*. New York, 1989.

Fisher, F.J. "London's Export Trade in the Early Seventeenth Century." *Economic History Review* 3(1950):151–61.

Fisher, Humphrey John. "A Muslim William Wilberforce? The Sokoto *Jihad* as Anti-Slavery Crusade: An Enquiry into Historical Causes." In *De la Traite a l'esclavage du Ve au XIXème siècle: Actes du Colloque International sur la traite des Noirs, 1985*, ed. Serge Daget. Nantes, 1988.

Flinn, Michael W. *History of the British Coal Industry. Vol. 2: 1700–1830: The Industrial Revolution.* Oxford, 1984.

Floud, Roderick and Donald McCloskey. eds. *An Economic History of Modern Britain.* Cambridge, 1994.

Fogel, Robert W. *Railroads and American Economic Growth: Essays in Econometric History.* Baltimore, Md., 1964.

Fogel, Robert W. *Without Consent or Contract: The Rise and Fall of American Slavery.* New York, 1989.

Foner, Eric. *Free Soil, Free Labor, Free Men: The Ideology of the Republican Party Before the Civil War.* New York, 1970.

Fortune, Stephen A. *Merchants and Jews: The Struggle for British West Indian Commerce, 1650–1750.* Gainesville, Fla., 1984.

Fox, J. "For Good and Sufficient Reasons: An Examination of Early Dutch East India Company Ordinances on Slaves and Slavery." In *Slavery, Bondage, and Dependency in South-East Asia,* ed. Anthony Reid. St. Lucia, Queensland, 1983.

Fox-Genovese, Elizabeth and Eugene D. Genovese. *The Fruits of Merchant Capital: Slavery and Bourgeois Property in the Rise of and Expansion of Capitalism.* New York, 1983.

François, Michel, and Nathalie Picard-Tortorici. *La Traite des Esclaves au Gabon du XVIIe au XIXe Siècle: Essai de Quantification pour le XVIII siècle.* Paris: CEPED, 1993.

Frederickson, George M. *White Supremacy: A Comparative Study in American and South African History.* New York, 1981.

Frederickson, George M. *The Arrogance of Race: Historical Perspectives on Slavery, Racism and Social Inequality.* Middletown, Conn., 1988.

Friedman, Ellen G. *Spanish Captives in North Africa in the Early Modern Age.* Madison, Wis., 1983.

Furniss, Edgar. *The Position of the Laborer in a System of Nationalism.* New York, 1921.

Galenson, David. "Middling People or Common Sort? The Social Origins of Early Americans Reexamined." *William and Mary Quarterly* 39(1978):499–540.

Galenson, David. "The Social Origins of Some Early Americans: A Rejoinder." *William and Mary Quarterly* 36(1979):264–86.

Galenson, David. *White Servitude in Colonial America: An Economic Analysis.* Cambridge, 1981.

Galenson, David. *Traders, Planters and Slaves: Market Behaviour in Early English America.* Cambridge, 1986.

Galloway, J. H. *The Sugar Cane Industry: An Historical Geography from its Origins to 1914.* Cambridge, 1989.

Gaspar, David Barry. "Sugar Cultivation and Slave Life in Antigua Before 1800." In *Cultivation and Culture: Labor and the Shaping of Slave Life in the Americas,* eds. Ira Berlin and Phillip D. Morgan. Charlottesville, Va., 1993.

Geggus, David. "Sex Ratio, Age and Ethnicity in the Atlantic Slave Trade: Data from the French Shipping and Plantation Records." *Journal of African History* 30(1989):23–44.

Gemery, Henry A. "Emigration from the British Isles to the New World, 1630–1700: Inferences from Colonial Populations." *Research in Economic History* 5(1980):179–232.

Gemery, Henry A., and Jan S. Hogendorn. "The Atlantic Slave Trade: A Tentative Economic Model." *Journal of African History* 15(1974):223–46.

Gemery, Henry A., and Jan S. Hogendorn. "Comparative Disadvantage: The Case of Sugar Cultivation in West Africa." *Journal of Interdisciplinary History* 9(1979):429–49.

Gemery, Henry A., and Jan S. Hogendorn. "Assessing Productivity in Precolonial African Agriculture and Industry, 1500–1800." *African Economic History* 19(1990–1991):31–5.

Gemery, Henry A., and James Horn. "British and French Indentured Servant Migration to the Caribbean: A Comparative Study of Seventeenth Century Emigration and Labor Markets." In *The Peopling of the Americas: Proceedings of an IUSSP Conference at Vera Cruz,* Liège, 1992.

George, Dorothy. *London Life in the Eighteenth Century.* London, 1925.

Glamann, Kristoff. *Dutch-Asiatic Trade, 1620–1740.* The Hague, 1958.

Glennie, P. "Measuring Crop Yields in Early Modern England." In *Land, Labour, and Livestock: Historical Studies in European Agricultural Productivity*, eds. B. M. S. Campbell and M. Overton. Manchester, 1991.

Godfrey, Sheldon J., and Judith C. Godfrey. *Search Out the Land: The Jews and the Growth of Equality in British Colonial America, 1740–1867.* Montreal, 1995.

Godinho, Magalhaes. "Le Portugal, les flottes du sucre et les flottes de l'or, 1670–1770." *Annales: économies, sociéties, civilisations* 5(1950).

Goldsmith's-Kress Library of Economic Literature: A Consolidated Guide. 4 vols. Woodbridge, Conn., 1976–77.

Gomez, Michael. *Exchanging Our Country Marks: The Transformation of African Identities in the Colonial and Antebellum South.* Chapel Hill, N.C., 1998.

Goody, Jack. *Technology, Tradition and the State in Africa.* Cambridge, 1971.

Goody, Jack. *Cooking, Cuisine and Class.* Cambridge, 1982.

Goslinga, Cornelis Ch. *The Dutch in the Caribbean and the Guianas, 1680–1791.* Assan, 1985.

Gragg, Larry. "'To Procure Negroes': The English Slave Trade to Barbados, 1627–60." *Slavery and Abolition* 16(1995):65–84.

Green, William A. "Race and Slavery: Consideration of the Williams Thesis." In *British Capitalism and Caribbean Slavery: The Legacy of Eric Williams*, eds. Barbara L. Solow and Stanley L. Engerman. Cambridge, 1987.

Green-Pedersen, Sv. E. "The Scope and Structure of the Danish Negro Slave Trade." *Scandinavian Economic History Review* 19(1971):149–95.

Greene, Jack P. "Changing Identity in the British Caribbean: Barbados as a Case Study." In *Colonial Identity in the Atlantic World, 1500–1800*, eds. Nicholas Canny and Anthony Pagden. Princeton, N.J., 1987.

Greene, Jack P. *Pursuits of Happiness: The Social Development of Early Modern British Colonies and the Formation of American Culture.* Chapel Hill, N.C., 1988.

Greene, Sandra. *Gender, Ethnicity and Social Change on the Upper Slave Coast.* Portsmouth, N.H., 1996.

Griffiths, Trevor, Philip Hunt, and Patrick O'Brien. "Political Components of the Industrial Revolution: Parliament and the English Cotton Textile Industry, 1660–1774." *Economic History Review* 44(1991):395–423.

Grubb, Farley. "Redemptioner Immigration to Pennsylvania: Evidence on Contract Choice and Profitability." *Journal of Economic History* 46(1986): 407–18.

Grubb, Farley. "Servant Auction Records and Immigration into the Delaware Valley, 1745–1831: The Proportion of Females Among Immigrant Servants." *Proceedings of the American Philosophical Society* 133(1989):154–69.

Grubb, Farley. "German Immigration to Pennsylvania, 1709–1820." *Journal of Interdisciplinary History* 20(1990):417–36.

Grubb, Farley. "The Long-run Trend in the Value of European Immigrant Servants, 1654–1831: New Measurements and Interpretations." *Research in Economic History* 14(1992):167–240.

Grubb, Farley and Tony Stitt. "The Liverpool Emigrant Servant Trade and the Transition to Slave Labor in the Chesapeake, 1697–1707." *Explorations in Economic History* 31(1994): 376–405.

Gwyn, Aubrey. "Documents Relating to the Irish in the West Indies." *Analecta Hibernica* no 4(1932):139–286.

Hajnal, J. "European Marriage Patterns in Perspective." In *Population in History: Essays in Historical Demography*, eds. D. V. Glass and D. E. C. Eversley. Chicago, 1965.

Hakluyt, Richard. *The Principal Navigations, Voyages, Traffiques and Discoveries of the English Nation.* 10 vols. London, 1927.

Hall, Gwendlyn Midlo. *Africans in Colonial Louisiana: the Development of Afro-Creole Culture in the Eighteenth Century.* Baton Rouge, La., 1992.

Handler, Jerome S. "Small-Scale Sugar Cane Farming in Barbados." *Ethnology* 5(1966):264–83.

Handler, Jerome S. "An African-Type Healer/Diviner and His Grave Goods: A Burial from a Plantation Slave Cemetery in Barbados, West Indies." *International Journal of Historical Archaeology* 1(1997):91–130.

Handler, Jerome S. and Frederick W. Lange. *Plantation Slavery in Barbados: An Archaeological and Historical Investigation*. Cambridge, Mass., 1978.

Hane, Mikiso. *Peasants, Rebels and Outcasts: The Underside of Modern Japan*. New York, 1982.

Harley, C. Knick. "Ocean Freight Rates and Productivity, 1740–1913: The Primacy of Mechanical Invention Reaffirmed." *Journal of Economic History* 48(1988):851–76.

Harlow, Vincent T. *History of Barbados, 1625–1685*. Oxford, 1926.

Harper, Lawrence A. *The English Navigation Laws: A Seventeenth Century Experiment in Social Engineering*. New York, 1939.

Harrison, William. *The Description of England*. Ithaca, 1968.

Haskell, Thomas L. "Capitalism and the Origins of the Humanitarian Sensibility, Part 1 and Capitalism and the Origins of the Humanitarian Sensibility, Part 2." In *The Antislavery Debate: Capitalism and Abolitionism as a Problem in Historical Interpretation*, ed. Thomas Bender. Berkeley, Calif., 1992.

Hellie, Richard. *Slavery in Russia, 1450–1725*. Chicago, 1982.

Herskovits, Melville J. "A Preliminary Consideration of the Culture Areas of Africa." *American Anthropologist* 26(1924):50–63.

Herskovits, Melville J. *The Myth of the Negro Past*. New York, 1941.

Higham, C. S. S. *Development of the Leeward Islands under the Restoration*. Cambridge, 1921.

Higman, Barry. *Slave Populations of the British Caribbean*. Baltimore, Md., 1984.

Hill, Bridget. *Women, Work and Sexual Politics in Eighteenth Century England*. London, 1989.

Hill, Christopher. "Pottage for Freeborn Englishmen: Attitudes to Wage Labour in the Sixteenth and Seventeenth Centuries." In *Socialism, Capitalism and Economic Growth: Essays Presented to Maurice Dobb*, ed. H. Feinstein. Cambridge, 1967.

Hogendorn, Jan S. and Marion Johnson. *The Shell Money of the Slave Trade*. Cambridge, 1986.

Holderness, B. A. "Prices, Productivity and Output." In *The Agrarian History of England and Wales, 1750–1850*, ed. G.E. Mingay, 6. Cambridge, 1989.

Horn, James. "Servant Emigration to the Chesapeake in the Seventeenth Century." *In The Chesapeake in the Seventeenth Century: Essays on Anglo-American Society*, eds. Thad W. Tate and David L. Ammerman. Chapel Hill, N.C., 1979.

Horn, James. "Adapting to a New World: A Comparative Study of Local Society in England and Maryland." In *Colonial Chesapeake Society*, eds. Philip D. Morgan, Lois Green Carr, and Jean B. Russo. Chapel Hill, N.C., 1985.

Hosmer, James Kendall. *Winthrop's Journal 'History of New England, 1630–1649.'*. 2 vols. New York, 1908.

Hotten, John Camden, ed. *The Original Lists of Persons of Quality; Emigrants; Political Rebels; Serving Men Sold for a Term of Years; Apprentices; Children Stolen; Maidens Pressed; and Others who Went from Great Britain to the American Plantations, 1600–1700*. London, 1874.

Hoyle, R. W. "Tenure and the Land Market in Early Modern England: Or a Late Contribution to the Brenner Debate." *Economic History Review* 43(1990):1–20.

Huggins, Nathan Irvin. *Black Odyssey: The Afro-American Ordeal in Slavery*. New York, 1977.

Hughes, Paul L. and James F. Larkin, eds. *Tudor Royal Proclamations*. Vol. 3: *The Later Tudors* (1588–1603). New Haven, Conn., 1969.

Hunwick, John. "Islamic Law and Polemics over Black Slavery in Morocco and West Africa." *Princeton Papers* 7(1998):43–68.

Iliffe, John. *The African Poor: A History*. Cambridge, 1987.

Inikori, Joseph. "Slavery and the Development of Industrial Capitalism in England." In *British Capitalism and Caribbean Slavery: The Legacy of Eric Williams*, eds. Barbara Solow and Stanley L. Engerman. Cambridge, 1987.

Inikori, Joseph. "Export Versus Domestic Demand: the Determinants of Sex Ratios in the Transatlantic Slave Trade." *Research in Economic History* 14(1992):117–66.

Inikori, Joseph. "Measuring the Unmeasured Hazards of the Atlantic Slave Trade: Documents Relating to the British Trade." *Revue Française d'Histoire d'Outre* 83 (1996):53–92.

Isichei, Elizabeth. *A History of the Igbo People*. London, 1976.

Jacobs, Auke Pieter. "Legal and Illegal Emigration from Seville, 1550–1650." In *"To Make America": European Emigration in the Early Modern Period*, eds. Ida Altman and James Horn. Berkeley, Calif., 1991.

Jenkinson, Hilary. "The Records of the English African Companies." *Transactions of the Royal Historical Society* 6(1912):185–220.

Jensen, Richard A., and Richard H. Steckel. "New Evidence on the Causes of Slave and Crew Mortality in the Transatlantic Slave Trade." *Journal of Economic History* 46(1986): 57–78.

Johnson, Marion. "The Ounce in Eighteenth Century West African Trade." *Journal of African History* 7(1966):197–217.

Johnson, R. C. "The Transportation of Vagrant Children from London to Virginia, 1618–22." In *Early Stuart Studies in Honor of D.G. Willson*, ed. H. S. Reinmuth. Minneapolis, Minn., 1970.

Jones, Alice Hanson. *Wealth of a Nation to Be: The American Colonies on the Eve of the Revolution*. New York, 1980.

Jones, E. L. *The European Miracle: Environments, Economies and Geopolitics in History of Europe and Asia*. Cambridge, 1981.

Jones, Howard. *Mutiny in the Amistad*. New York, 1986.

Jones, Richard and Colin McEvedy. *Atlas of World Population History*. Harmondsworth, 1978.

Jordan, Winthrop. *White Over Black: American Attitudes Toward the Negro, 1550–1812*. Chapel Hill, N.C., 1968.

Jordan, Winthrop. "On the Bracketing of Blacks and Women in the Same Agenda." In *The American Revolution: Its Character and Limits*, ed. Jack P. Greene. New York, 1987.

Kea, Ray A. "Firearms and Warfare on the Gold and Slave Coasts from the Sixteenth to the Nineteenth Centuries." *Journal of African History* 12(1971):185–213.

Kea, Ray A. *Settlements, Trade and Politics in the Seventeenth Century Gold Coast*. Baltimore, Md., 1982.

King, Gregory. "Natural and Political Observations and Conclusions upon the State and Condition of England, 1696." In *The Earliest Classics: John Graunt and Gregory King*. Farnborough, 1973.

Klein, Herbert S. *Slavery in the Americas: A Comparative Study of Virginia and Cuba*. Chicago, 1967.

Klein, Herbert S. *The Middle Passage: Comparative Studies in the Atlantic Slave Trade*. Princeton, N.J., 1978.

Klein, Herbert S. "African Women in the Atlantic Slave Trade." In *Woman and Slavery in Africa*, eds. Claire Robertson and Klein Martin A., Madison, Wis., 1983.

Klein, Martin A. "Introduction: Modern European Expansion and Traditional Servitude in Africa and Asia." In *Breaking the Chains: Slavery, Bondage and Emancipation in Modern Africa and Asia*, ed. Martin A. Klein. Madison, Wis., 1993.

Klein, Martin A., and Claire C. Robertson, eds. *Women and Slavery in Africa*. Madison, Wis., 1983.

Klooster, Wim. "Dutch Trade, Capital and Technology in the Atlantic World, 1595–1667." A paper delivered at the American Historical Association Annual Meeting, 1998.

Klooster, Wim. *Illicit Riches: Dutch Trade in the Caribbean, 1648–1795*. Leiden, 1998.

Knittle, Walter A. *Early Eighteenth Century Palatine Emigration*. Philadelphia, Pa., 1937.

Koehler, Lyle. *A Search for Power: The 'Weaker Sex' in Seventeenth Century New England*. Chicago, 1980.

Kopytoff, Igor, and Suzanne Miers, eds. *Slavery in Africa: Historical and Anthropological Perspectives*. Madison, Wis., 1977.

Kopytoff, Igor, and Suzanne Miers. "African Slavery as an Institution in Marginality." In *Slavery in Africa: Historical and Anthropological Perspectives*, eds. Igor Kopytoff and Suzanne Miers. Madison, Wis., 1977.

Kossmann, E.H. "Freedom in Seventeenth-Century Dutch Thought and Practice." In *The Anglo-Dutch Moment: Essays on the Glorious Revolution and its World Impact*, ed. Jonathan Israel. Cambridge, 1991.

Kritz, Mary M. "The British and Spanish Migration Systems in the Colonial Era: A Policy Framework." A paper delivered at The Peopling of the Americas: Proceedings, Vera Cruz, 1992.

Kuethe, Allen J. "Los Llorones Cubanos: The Socio-Military Basis of Commercial Privilege in the American Trade Under Charles IV." In *The North American Role in the Spanish Imperial Economy, 1760–1819*, eds. Jacques A. Barbier and Allan J. Kuethe. Manchester, 1984.

Kulikoff, Allan. *Tobacco and Slaves: The Development of Southern Cultures in the Chesapeake, 1680–1800*. Chapel Hill, N.C., 1986.

Kupperman, Karen Ordahl. *Providence Island, 1630–1641: The Other Puritan Colony*. Cambridge, 1993.

Kussmaul, Ann. *Servants in Husbandry in Early Modern England*. Cambridge, 1981.

Kussmaul, Ann. *A General View of the Rural Economy of England*. Cambridge, 1990.

Lambert, Shiela, ed. *House of Commons Sessional Papers* 145 vols. Wilmington, Del, 1975.

Landes, David S. *The Wealth and Poverty of Nations: Why Some are so Rich and Some are so Poor*. New York, 1998.

Langbein, John H. *Torture and the Law of Proof: Europe and England in the Ancien Regime*. Chicago, 1977.

Law, Robin. "'Here is No Resisting the Country': The Realities of Power in Afro-European Relations on the West African 'Slave Coast.'" *Itinerario: European Journal of Overseas History* 18(1994):50–64.

Law, Robin. *The Slave Coast of West Africa, 1550–1750*. Oxford, 1991.

Law, Robin. *The Kingdom of Allada*. Leiden, 1997.

Law, Robin. "Ethnicity and the Slave Trade: 'Lucumi' and 'Nago' as ethonyms in West Africa." *History in Africa* 24(1997):205–19.

Law, Robin. "The Royal African Company of England in West Africa, 1681–99." In *Source Material for Studying the Slave Trade and the African Diaspora: Papers from a Conference of the Centre of Commonwealth Studies, University of Stirling, April 1996*, ed. Robin Law. Stirling, 1997.

Leadham, I.S. "The Last Days of Bondage in England." *Law Quarterly Review* 9(1983):348–65.

Lebsock, Suzanne. *"A Share of Honour" Virginia Women, 1600–1945*. Richmond, Va., 1987.

Lemps, Christian Huetz de. "Indentured Servants Bound for the French Antilles and Canada in the Seventeenth and Eighteenth Centuries." In *'To Make America': European Emigration in the Early Modern Period*, eds. Ida Altman and James Horn. Berkeley, 1991.

LeVeen, E. Phillip. *British Slave Trade Suppression Policies*. New York, 1977.

Lewis, Bernard. *Race and Slavery in the Middle East: An Historical Inquiry*. New York, 1990.

Lindert, Peter H., and Jeffrey G. Williamson. "Revising England's Social Tables, 1688–1812." *Explorations in Economic History* 19(1982):385–408.

Linebaugh, Peter. *The London Hanged: Crime and Civil Society in the Eighteenth Century*. London, 1992.

Linebaugh, Peter, and Marcus Rediker. "The Many-Headed Hydra: Sailors, Slaves and the Atlantic Working Class in the Eighteenth Century." *Journal of Historical Sociology* 3(1990): 225–51.

Locke, Mary Stoughton. *Anti-Slavery in America*. Boston, 1901, reprinted 1968.

Louis, William Roger, *The Oxford History of the British Empire*, 4 vols. Oxford, 1998–.

Lovejoy, Paul. *Transformations in Slavery: A History of Slavery in Africa*. Cambridge, 1983.

Lovejoy, Paul. "Partial Perspectives and Abolition: The Sokoto *Jihad* and the Transatlantic Slave Trade, 1804–37 (Unpublished paper, 1998).

Lovejoy, Paul E. "The Identification of Enslaved Africans in the African Diaspora." In *Constructions of Identity: African Communities in the Shadow of Slavery*, ed. Paul E. Lovejoy. London (forthcoming).

Lucassen, Jan. *Dutch Long Distance Migration: A Concise History, 1600–1900*. Amsterdam: IISG, 1991.

Lucassen, Jan. "The Netherlands, the Dutch and Long-Distance Migration in the late Sixteenth to early Nineteenth Centuries." In *Europeans on the Move: Studies in European Migration*, ed. Nicholas Canny, 153–91. Oxford, 1994.

Lucassen, Jan, and Leo Lucassen, eds. *Migration, Migration History, History: Old Paradigms and New Perspectives*. Bern, 1997.

Ly, Abdoulaye. *La Compagnie du Sénégal*. Paris, 1993.

MacCleod, Duncan J. *Slavery, Race and the American Revolution*. Cambridge, 1974.

Macfarlane, Alan. *Origins of English Individualism*. London, 1978.

Macpherson, C. B. *The Political Theory of Possessive Individualism: Hobbes to Locke*. Oxford, 1962.

Magalhaes-Godinho, Vitorino. "L'émigration portuguaise du XVe siécle à nos jours: Histoire d'une constante structurale." In *Conjoncture économique-structures sociale: Hommage à Ernest Labrousse*. Paris, 1974.

Mann, Julia de Lacy and Alfred P. Wadsworth. *The Cotton Trade and Industrial Lancashire*. New York, 1968.

Manning, Patrick. "The Slave Trade in the Bight of Benin, 1640–1890." In *The Uncommon Market: Essays in the Economic History of the Transatlantic Slave Trade*, eds. Henry A. Gemery and Jan S. Hogendorn. New York, 1979.

Manning, Patrick. *Slavery and African Life: Occidental, Oriental and African Slave Trades*. Cambridge, 1990.

Marshall, Dorothy. "The Old Poor Law, 1662–1795." *Economic History Review* 1(1937).

McCaa, Robert. "Paradise, Hells, and Purgatories: Population, Health and Nutrition in Mexican History and Prehistory." A paper delivered at the Conference on History and Physical Anthropology, Ohio State University, 1993.

McClelland, Peter D. "The Cost to America of British Imperial Policy." *American Economic Review* 59(1969):370–81.

McCusker, John J. *Money and Exchange Rates in Europe and America, 1600–1775: A Handbook*. Chapel Hill, N.C., 1978.

McCusker, John J. *Rum and the American Revolution: The Rum Trade and the Balance of Payments of the Thirteen Continental Colonies, 1650–1775*. New York, 1989.

McCusker, John J., and Russell R. Menard. *The Economy of British North America, 1607–1789*. Chapel Hill, N.C., 1985.

McDaniel, Antonio. *Swing Low Sweet Chariot: The Mortality Cost of Colonizing Liberia in the Nineteenth Century*. Chicago, 1995.

McDonald, John, and Ralph, Shlomowitz. "Mortality on Convict Voyages to Australia, 1788–1868." *Social Science History* 13(1989):285–313.

McDonald, John, and Graeme D. Snooks. *Domesday Economy: A New Approach to Anglo-Norman History*. Oxford, 1986.

McGowan, Winston. "African Resistance to the Atlantic Slave Trade in West Africa." *Slavery and Abolition: A Journal of Comparative Studies* 11(1990):5–29.

Mechner, Emily. "Paupers and Planters: The Transition to Sugar in Barbados, 1638–1674." A paper delivered at the Cliometric Conference, Toronto, May, 1997.

Menard, Russell. "From Servants to Slaves: The Transformation of the Chesapeake Labor System." *Southern Studies* 16(1977):355–90.

Menard, Russell R. "The Tobacco Industry in the Chesapeake Colonies, 1617–1730: An Interpretation." *Research in Economic History* 5(1980): 109–77.

Menard, Russell R. "British Migration to the Chesapeake Colonies in the Seventeenth Century." In *Colonial Chesapeake Society*, eds. Philip D. Morgan, Jean B. Russo, and Lois Green Carr. Chapel Hill, N.C., 1988.

Menard, Russell R. "'The Sweet Negotiation of Sugar': 1640–1660" (Unpublished paper, January 1995).

Mettas, Jean. *Rèpertoire des Expèditions Négrièrs Françaises au XVIIIe Siècle*. 2 vols. Paris, 1978–84.

Meyers, Allan D. "Ethnic Distinctions and Wealth among Colonial Jamaican Merchants, 1685–1716." *Social Science History* 22(1998):47–81.

Mill, John Stuart. *Principles of Political Economy with Some of Their Applications to Social Philosophy*. 2 vols. London, 1895.

Miller, Joseph C. "The Significance of Drought, Disease and Famine in the Agriculturally Marginal Zones of West-Central Africa." *Journal of African History* 23(1982):17–61.

Miller, Joseph C. "Capitalism and Slaving: The Financial and Commercial Organization of the Angolan Slave Trade, According to the Accounts of Antonio Coelho Guerreiro (1684–1692)." *International Journal of African Historical Studies* 17(1984):1–52.

Miller, Joseph C. "Slave Prices in the Portuguese Southern Atlantic, 1600–1830." In *Africans in Bondage: Studies in Slavery and the Slave Trade*, ed. Paul E. Lovejoy. Madison, Wis., 1986.

Miller, Joseph C. *Way of Death: Merchant Capitalism and the Angolan Slave Trade, 1730–1830*. Madison, Wis., 1988.

Minchinton, Walter E. *Naval Office Shipping Lists for Jamaica, 1683–1818*. Wakefield, 1977.

Minchinton, Walter, Celia King, and Peter Waite, eds. *Virginia Slave Trade Statistics, 1698–1775*. Richmond, Va., 1984.

Mintz, Sidney. *Sweetness and Power. The Place of Sugar in Modern History*. New York, 1985.

Mintz, Sidney, and Richard Price. *An Anthropological Approach to Afro-American Past: A Caribbean Perspective*. Philadelphia, Pa., 1976.

Mitchell, Brian R. *British Historical Statistics*. Second edition, Cambridge, 1988.

Moitt, Bernard. "Behind the Sugar Fortunes: Women, Labour and the Development of Caribbean Plantations During Slavery." In *African Continuities*, eds. Simeon Waliaula and Sada Niang Chilungu. Toronto, 1989.

Moller, Herbert, "Sex Composition and Correlated Culture Patterns of Colonial America," *William and Mary Quarterly*, 2(1945):113–51.

Moody, Robert, ed. *Saltonstall Papers, 1607–1815*. 3 vols., Boston, 1972–4.

Morgan, Edmund S. "The Labor Problem at Jamestown, 1607–18." *American Historical Review* 76(1971).

Morgan, Edmund S. "Slavery and Freedom: The American Paradox." *Journal of American History* 59(1972):26–7.

Morgan, Edmund S. *American Slavery American Freedom*. New York, 1975.

Morgan, Kenneth. *Bristol and the Atlantic Trade in the Eighteenth Century*. Cambridge, 1993.

Morgan, Philip D. "British Encounters with Africans and African-Americans, circa 1600–1780." In *Strangers within the Realm; Cultural Margins of the First British Empire*, eds. Bernard Bailyn and Philip D. Morgan. Chapel Hill, N.C., 1991.

Morgan, Philip D. "Cultural Implications of the Atlantic Slave Trade: African Regional Origins, American Destinations and New World Developments." *Slavery and Abolition* 18(1997): 122–45.

Morner, Magnus. "Spanish Migration to the New World prior to 1810: A Report on the State of Research." In *First Images in America: The Impact of the New World on the Old*, ed. Fredi Chiappelli et al., 2. Berkeley, Calif., 1976.

Morner, Magnus. *Adventurers and Proletarians: The Story of Migrants in Latin America*. Pittsburgh, Pa., 1985.

Mullin, Gerald W. *Flight and Rebellion: Slave Resistance in Eighteenth Century Virgina*. New York, 1972.

Munford, Clarence J. *The Black Ordeal of Slavery and Slave Trading in the French West Indies, 1625–1715*. 3 vols. Lewiston, N.Y., 1991.

Munford, Clarence J. *Race and reparations: A Black perspective for the twenty-first century*. Trenton, N.J., 1996.

Nash, Robert. "English Transatlantic Commerce, 1680–1750: A Quantitative Study." Unpublished DPhil thesis, Cambridge University, 1982.

Nath, Dwaka. *A History of Indians in Guyana*. London, 1970.

Nef, J.U. *The Conquest of the Material World*. Chicago, 1964.

North, Douglass. "Sources of Productivity Change in Ocean Shipping, 1600–1850." *Journal of Political Economy* 76(1968):953–70.

North, Douglass C., and Robert Paul Thomas. *The Rise of the Western World: A New Economic History*. Cambridge, 1973.

Northrup, David. *Trade Without Rulers: Pre-Colonial Economic Development in South-Eastern Nigeria*. Oxford, 1978.

Nwokeji, G. Ugo. "Household and Market Persons: Servitude and Banishment in the Making of the Biafran Diasporas, c. 1750–c. 1890." A paper delivered at the "Black Atlantic: Race, Nation and Gender Seminar," Rutgers University, 1997 (October).

Onody, Oliver. "Quelques traits caracteristiques de l'evolution historiques de la population de Brazil." A paper delivered at the Population and Economics: Proceedings of the Fourth Congress of the International Economic History Association, Winnipeg, 1968.

Oostindie, Gert (ed.), *Fifty Years Later: Anti-Slavery, Capitalism and Modernity in the Dutch Orbit*. Pittsburgh, 1996.

Overton, Mark. *Agricultural Revolution in England: The Transformation of the Agrarian Economy, 1500–1850*. Cambridge, 1996.

Paley, Ruth. "After Somerset: Mansfield, Slavery and the Law of England." In *Crime, Law and Society*, eds. Norma Landau and Donna Andrews. Cambridge, forthcoming.

Palmer, Colin. *Slaves of the White God: Blacks in Mexico, 1579–1650*. Cambridge, Mass., 1976.

Palmer, Colin. *Human Cargoes: The British Slave Trade to Spanish America*. Urbana, 1981.

Pares, Richard. "Merchants and Planters." *Economic History Review, Supplement* 4(1960): 1–91.

Pateman, Carole. *The Sexual Contract*. Stanford, 1988.

Patterson, Orlando. *The Sociology of Slavery: An Analysis of the Origins, Development and Structure of Negro Slave Society in Jamaica*. London, 1967.

Patterson, Orlando. "Slavery and Slave Revolts: A Sociohistorical Analysis of the First Maroon War." In *Maroon Societies: Rebel Slave Communities in the Americas*, ed. Richard Price. Baltimore, Md., 1979.

Patterson, Orlando. *Slavery and Social Death: A Comparative Study*. Cambridge, Mass., 1982.

Patterson, Orlando. *Freedom in the Making of Western Culture*. 3 vols. New York, 1991– .

Peabody, Sue. '*There are no slaves in France*': *The Political Culture of Race and Slavery in the Ancien Regime*. New York, 1996.

Perdue, Theda. *Slavery and the Evolution of Cherokee Society, 1540–1866*. Knoxville, Tenn., 1979.

Pétré-Grenoiulleau, Olivier. *Les Traites des Noirs*. Paris, 1997.

Phillips, William D. *Slavery from Roman Times to the Early Atlantic Slave Trade*. Minneapolis, Minn., 1984.

Piersen, W.W. "White Cannibals, Black Martyrs: Fear, Depression and Religious Faith as Causes of Suicide Among Slaves." *Journal of Negro History* 62(1977):147–59.

Pike, Ruth. *Penal Servitude in Early Modern Spain*. Madison, Wis., 1983.

Pitman, Frank Wesley. *The Development of the British West Indies, 1700–1763*. New Haven, Conn., 1917.

Pollard, Sidney. *The Genesis of Modern Management*. London, 1965.

Post, John D. "Famine, Mortality, and Epidemic Disease in the Process of Modernization." *Economic History Review* 29(1976).

Posthumus, N.W. *Inquiry into the History of Prices in Holland*. Vol. 1. 2 vols. Leiden, 1946–64.

Postma, Johannes. "West African Exports and the Dutch West India Company, 1675–1731." *Economisch en Sociaal-Historisch Jaarboek* 36(1973): 53–74.

Postma, Johannes. "Mortality in the Dutch Slave Trade, 1675–1795." In *The Uncommon Market: Essays in the Economic History of the Atlantic Slave Trade*, eds. Jan S. Hogendorn and Henry A. Gemery. New York, 1979.

Postma, Johannes Menne. *The Dutch in the Atlantic Slave Trade, 1600–1815*. Cambridge, 1990.

Price, Jacob M. "Economic Function and Growth of American Port Towns in the Eighteenth Century." *Perspectives in American History* 8(1974):123–86.

Price, Jacob M. *Joshua Johnson's Letterbook, 1771–1774: Letters from a Merchant in London to his Partners in Maryland*. London, 1979.

Price, Jacob M. *Capital and Credit in British Overseas Trade: The View from the Chesapeake, 1700–1776*. Cambridge, Ma., 1980.

Price, Jacob, and Paul Clemens. "A Revolution of Scale in Overseas Trade: British Firms in the Chesapeake Trade, 1675–1775." *Journal of Economic History* 47(1987):1–43.

Priestley, Margaret. "Anglo-French Trade and the 'Unfavorable Balance' Controversy, 1660–1685." *Economic History Review* 4(1951).

Puckrein, Gary. *Little England: Plantation Society and Anglo-Barbadian Politics, 1627–1700*. New York, 1984.

Rabb, Theodore K. *Enterprise & Empire: Merchant and Gentry Investment in the Expansion of England, 1575–1630*. Cambridge, Mass., 1967.

Rathbone, Richard. "Some Thoughts on Resistance to Enslavement in West Africa." *Slavery and Abolition: A Journal of Comparative Studies* 6(1986):5–22.

Renault, François. *Liberation d'Esclaves et Nouvelles Servitude*. Abidjan, 1976.

Reynolds, Edward. *Trade and Economic Change on the Gold Coast, 1807–1874*. London, 1974.

Richards, Eric. "Women in the British Economy Since About 1700: An Interpretation." *History* 59(1974):337–57.

Richardson, David. *The Mediterranean Passes*. Wakefield, 1981.

Richardson, David. "The Slave Trade, Sugar, and British Economic Growth, 1748–1776." In *British Capitalism and Caribbean Slavery: The Legacy of Eric Williams*, eds. Barbara Solow and Stanley L. Engerman, 103–33. Cambridge, 1987.

Richardson, David. "Slave Exports from West and West-Central Africa 1700–1810: New Estimates of Volume and Distribution." *Journal of African History* 30(1989):1–22.

Richardson, David. "Prices of Slaves in West and West-Central Africa: Toward an Annual Series, 1698–1807." *Bulletin of Economic Research* 43 (1991):21–56.

Rodney, Walter. "African Slavery and Other Forms of Social Oppression on the Upper Guinea Coast in the Context of the Atlantic Slave Trade." *Journal of African History* 7(1966): 431–43.

Rodney, Walter. "Gold and Slaves on the Gold Coast." *Transactions of the Historical Society of Ghana*, 10(1969).

Roediger, David R. "Frederick Douglass Meets the Slavery Metaphor: Race, Labor and Gender in the Languages of Antebellum Social Protest." In *Terms of Labor*, ed. Stanley L. Engerman. Stanford, Calif., 1999.

Rogers, J., ed. *Family Building and Family Planning in Pre-Industrial Society*. Uppsala, 1980.

Rogers, James Thorold. *A History of Agriculture and Prices in England*. Vol. 5. Oxford, 1887.

Rogers, Nicholas. "Vagrancy, Impressment and the Regulation of Labour in Eighteenth Century England." *Slavery and Abolition* 15(1994):10–13.

Ronciere, Charles de la. *Négres et Négrières*. Paris, 1933.

Rosenblat, Angel. *La Poblacion Indigena y el Mestizaje en America*. 2 vols. Buenos Aires, 1950.

Rowen, Herbert H. "The Dutch Republic and the Idea of Freedom." In *Republicanism, Liberty and Commercial Society, 1649–1776*, ed. David Wootton. Stanford, Calif., 1994.

Russo, Jean B. "Self Sufficiency and Local Exchange: Free Craftsmen in the Rural Chesapeake Economy." In *Colonial Chesapeake Society*, eds. Philip D. Morgan, Jean B. Russo, and Lois Green Carr. Chapel Hill, N.C., 1988.

Ryden, David Beck. "Does Decline Make Sense?" Paper presented to the Social Science History Association, Washington, D.C., 1997.

Salinger, Sharon. "'Send No More Women': Female Servants in Eighteenth-Century Philadelphia." *Pennsylvania Magazine of History and Biography* 107(1983):29–48.

Saunders, A. C. de C. M. *A Social History of Black Slaves and Freedmen in Portugal, 1441–1555*. Cambridge, 1982.

Schama, Simon. *The Embarrassment of Riches: An Interpretation of Dutch Culture in the Golden Age*. New York, 1987.

Schlegel, Alice (ed.), *Sexual Stratification: A Cross–Cultural View*. New York, 1977.

Schnakenbourg, Christian. "Statistiques pour l'histoire de l'économie de plantation en Guadeloupe et Martinique (1635–1835)." *Bulletin de la Société de la Guadaloupe* 31(1977): 1–126.

Schofield, R. S., and E. A. Wrigley. *The Population History of England, 1541–1871: A Reconstruction*. London, 1981.

Schwartz, Stuart B. "Free Labor in a Slave Economy: The Lavradores de Cana of Colonial Brazil." In *Colonial Roots of Modern Brazil*, ed. Dauril Alden. Berkeley, Calif., 1973.

Schwartz, Stuart B. "Comparación entre dos Economías Azucareras Coloniales: Morelos, México y Bahía, Brasil." In *Haciendas, Latifundios y Plantaciones en América Latina*, ed. Enrico Florescano. Mexico, 1975.

Schwartz, Stuart B. "Patterns of Slaveholding in the Americas: New Evidence from Brazil." *American Historical Review* 87(1982):55–86.

Schwartz, Stuart B. "Colonial Brazil, c. 1580–c. 1750: Plantations and Peripheries." In *The Cambridge History of Latin America*, ed. Leslie Bethell, 8 vols. Vol. 2, *Colonial Latin America* Cambridge, 1985.

Schwartz, Stuart B. *Sugar Plantations in the Formation of Brazilian Society*. Cambridge, 1985.

Schwartz, Stuart B. "The Formation of a Colonial Identity in Brazil." In *Colonial Identity in the Atlantic World, 1500–1800*, eds. Nicholas Canny and Anthony Pagden. Princeton, N.J., 1988.

Schwarz, Suzanne. *Slave Captain: The Career of James Irvine in the Liverpool Slave Trade*. Wrexham, 1995.

Scott, Rebecca. "Comparing Emancipations: A Review Essay." *Journal of Social History* 20 (1987):565–83.

Scott, W.R. *The Constitution and Finance of English, Scottish and Irish Joint-Stock Companies to 1720*. 3 vols. Cambridge, 1910.

Searing, James F. *West African Slavery and Atlantic Commerce: The Senegal River Valley, 1700–1860*. Cambridge, 1993.

Selling, J. Thorsten. *Slavery and the Penal System*. New York, 1976.

Sen, Amartya. "More than 100 Million Women are Missing." *New York Review of Books* 36, no. 20(1991):61–6.

Sen, Indrani. "Trends in Slave Shipments from the Gold Coast: New Evidence on Slave Prices, 1710–1792" (Unpublished paper, 1996).

Shammas, Carole. "English-Born and Creole Elites in Turn of the Century Virginia." In *The Chesapeake in the Seventeenth Century: Essays on Anglo-American Society*, eds. Thad W. Tate and David Ammerman. Chapel Hill, N.C., 1979.

Shell, Robert. Carl–Heinz. *Children of Bondage: A Social History of the Slave Society at the Cape of Good Hope, 1652–1838*. Hanover, N.H., 1994.

Shepherd, James F., and Gary M. Walton. "Economic Change after the American Revolution: Pre- and Post-War Comparisons of Maritime Shipping and Trade." *Explorations in Economic History* 13(1976):397–422.

Shepherd, Jill. *The "Redlegs" of Barbados. Their Origins and History.* Millwood, 1981.

Shurtleff, Nathaniell B. *Records of the Governor and Company of the Massachusetts Bay in New England.* 2 vols. New York, 1968.

Shyllon, F.O. *Black Slaves in Britain.* London, 1974.

Simonsen, Roberto C. *Historia Económica do Brasil*(1500/1820). Sixth ed. São Paolo, 1969.

Slack, Paul A. "Vagrants and Vagrancy in England, 1598–1664." *Economic History Review* 27(1974):360–79.

Smith, Abbot Emerson. "The Transportation of Convicts to the American Colonies in the Seventeenth Century." *American Historical Review* 39 (1933–4):233–6.

Smith, Abbott Emerson. *Colonists in Bondage: White Servitude and Convict Labour in America, 1607–1776.* Chapel Hill, N.C., 1947.

Smith, Adam. *Wealth of Nations.* New York, 1937.

Snell, K. D. M. *Annals of the Labouring Poor: Social Change and Agrarian England, 1660–1900.* Cambridge, 1985.

Solow, Barbara. "Caribbean Slavery and British Growth: The Eric Williams Hypothesis." *Journal of Developmental Economics* 17(1985):99–115.

Sosin, Jack M. *English America and the Restoration Monarchy of Charles II: Transatlantic Politics, Commerce and Kinship.* Lincoln, 1980.

Sowell, Thomas. *Ethnic America: A History.* New York, 1981.

Spierenberg, Pieter. "The Sociogenesis of Confinement and its Development in Early Modern Europe." *Centrum voor Maatschappij Geschiedenis* 12 (1984):9–77.

Spierenburg, Pieter. *The Prison Experience: Disciplinary Institutions and Their Inmates in Early Modern Europe.* New Brunswick, 1991.

Starna, William A., and Ralph Watkins. "Northern Iroquoian Slavery." *Ethnohistory* 38(1991): 34–57.

Steele, Ian K. *The English Atlantic, 1675–1740: An Exploration of Communication and Community.* Oxford, 1986.

Steengard, Niels. "The Growth and Composition of the Long-Distance Trade of England and the Dutch Republic Before 1750." In *The Rise of Merchant Empires: Long-Distance Trade in the Early Modern World, 1350–1750,* ed. James D. Tracy. Cambridge, 1990.

Stein, Robert Louis. *The French Slave Trade in the Eighteenth Century: An Old Regime Business.* Madison, Wis., 1979.

Stein, Robert Louis. "The Free Men of Colour and the Revolution in Saint Domingue, 1789–1792." *Histoire Sociale* 14(1981):7–28.

Steinfeld, Robert J. *The Invention of Free Labor: The Employment Relation in English and American Law and Culture, 1350–1870.* Chapel Hill, N.C., 1991.

Steinfeld, Robert J. "Changing Legal Conceptions of Free Labor." In *The Terms of Labor,* ed. Stanley L. Engerman. Stanford, Calif., 1998.

Stinchcombe, Arthur L. *Sugar Island Slavery in the Age of Emancipation: The Political Economy of the Caribbean World.* Princeton, N.J., 1995.

Stone, Thora G. "The Journey of Cornelius Hodges in Senegambia, 1689–90." *English Historical Review* 39(1924):89–95.

Stott, Ingrid. "Emigration from England, 1640–1680." Unpublished Master's thesis, Queen's University, 1993.

Strickland, Matthew. *War and Chivalry: The Conduct and Perception of War in England and Normandy, 1066–1217.* Cambridge, 1996.

Tannenbaum, Frank. *Slave and Citizen, the Negro in the America.* New York, 1947.

Tattersfield, Nigel. *The Forgotten Trade: Comprising the Log of the Daniel and Henry of 1700 and Accounts of the Slave Trade from the Minor Ports of England, 1698–1725.* London, 1991.

Tawney, R. H. *Religion and the Rise of Capitalism.* London, 1961.

Temperley, Howard. "Capitalism, Slavery and Ideology." *Past and Present* 75(1977):94–118.

Temperley, Howard. "Anti-Slavery as a Form of Cultural Imperialism." In *Anti-Slavery, Religion and Reform: Essays in Memory of Roger Anstey,* eds. Christine Bolt and Seymour Drescher. Folkeston, Kent, 1980.

Thompson, Edward P. "The Moral Economy of the English Crowd in the Eighteenth Century." *Past and Present* 50(1971):76–123.

Thompson, I. A. A. "A Map of Crime in Sixteenth Century Spain." *Economic History Review* 21(1968):244–67.

Thornton, A. P. "Spanish Slave Ships in the West Indies, 1660–1685." *Hispanic American Historical Review* 25(1955):374–85.

Thornton, A. P. *West India Policy Under the Restoration.* Oxford, 1956.

Thornton, John. "The Slave Trade in Eighteenth Century Angola: Effects on Demographic Structures." *Canadian Journal of African Studies* 14(1980): 417–27.

Thornton, John. *The Kingdom of the Kongo: Civil War and Transition, 1641–1718.* Madison, Wis., 1983.

Thornton, John. "Sexual Demography: The Impact of the Slave Trade on Family Structure." In *Women and Slavery in Africa,* eds. Martin A. Klein and Claire C. Robertson. Chapel Hill, N.C., 1983.

Thornton, John. *Africa and Africans in the Making of the Atlantic World.* Cambridge, 1992.

Tinker, Hugh. *A New System of Slavery: The Export of Indian Labour Overseas, 1830–1920.* London, 1974.

Toledano, Ehud R. "Ottoman Concepts of Slavery in the Period of Reform, 1830s–1880s." In *Breaking the Chains: Slavery, Bondage and Emancipation in Modern Africa and Asia,* ed. Martin A. Klein. Madison, Wis., 1993.

Turley, David. *The Culture of English Anti-Slavery, 1780–1860.* London, 1991.

Turner, Mary, ed. *From Chattel Slaves to Wage Slaves: The Dynamics of Labour Bargaining in the Americas.* London, 1995.

Unger, W. S. "Bijdragen tot de geschiedenis van de Nederlandse slavenhandel." *Economisch-Historisch Jaarboek* 26(1956).

Vagts, Alfred. *A History of Militarism: Civilian and Military.* New York, 1959.

Valdés, Dennis Nodin. "The Decline of the Sociedad de Castas in Mexico City." Unpublished PhD thesis, University of Michigan, 1978.

Van den Boogart, Ernst. "The Trade Between Western Africa and the Atlantic World, 1600–90." *Journal of African History* 33(1992):369–85.

Van Dantzig, A. "The Ankobra Gold Interest." *Transactions of the Historical Society of Ghana* 14(1973):169–85.

Van Dantzig, A., ed. *The Dutch and the Guinea Coast, 1674–1742: A Collection of Documents from the General State Archive at the Hague.* Accra, 1978.

Vaughan, Alden T., and Vaughan, Virginia Mason. "Before Othello: Elizabethan Representations of Sub-Saharan Africans." *William and Mary Quarterly* 54(1997):19–44.

Verger, Pierre. *Trade Relations Between the Bight of Benin and Bahia 17th–19th Century.* Ibadan, 1976.

Verlinden, Charles. *The Beginnings of Modern Colonization: Eleven Essays with an Introduction.* Ithaca, N.Y., 1970.

Vilar, Enriqueta Vila. *Hispanoamerica y el Comercio de Esclavos.* Seville, 1977.

Villamarin, Juan A., and Judith E. Villamarin. *Indian Labour in Mainland Colonial Spanish America.* Newark, N.J., 1975.

Vries, Jan de. *European Urbanization, 1500–1800.* Cambridge, Mass., 1984.

Vries, Jan de. "Between Purchasing Power and the World of Goods: Understanding the Household Economy in Early Modern Europe." In *Consumption and the World of Goods,* eds. John Brewer and Roy Porter. London, 1993.

Vries, Jan de. *The First Modern Economy: Success, Failure and Perseverance of Dutch Economy, 1500–1815*. Cambridge, 1997.

Wallerstein, Immanuel. *The Modern World System III: The Second Era of the Capitalist World-Economy 1730–1840s*. New York, 1989.

Walsh, Lorena S. "Slave Life, Slave Society, and Tobacco Production in the Tidewater Chesapeake, 1620–1820." In *Cultivation and Culture: Labor and the Shaping of Slave Life in the Americas*, eds. Ira Berlin and Philip D. Morgan. Charlottesville, Va., 1993.

Walton, Gary M. "Trade Routes, Ownership Proportions and American Colonial Shipping Characteristics." In *Las rutas del Atlantico: trabajos del Noveno Coloquio Internacional de Historia Maritima*. Seville, 1969.

Walton, Gary M. "The New Economic History and the Burdens of the Navigation Acts." *Economic History Review* 24(1971):533–42.

Ward, J. R. "The Profitability of Sugar Planting in the British West Indies, 1650–1834." *Economic History Review* 31(1978):203.

Ward, J. R. *British West Indian Slavery, 1750–1834*. Oxford, 1988.

Watson, James L. "Slavery as an Institution, Open and Closed Systems." In *Asian and African Systems of Slavery*, ed. James L. Watson. Berkeley, Calif., 1980.

Watts, David. *The West Indies: Patterns of Development, Culture and Environmental Change since 1492*. Cambridge, 1987.

Westergaard, W. *The Danish West Indies Under Company Rule*. New York, 1917.

Whistler, Henry. "Extracts from Henry Whistler's Journal of the West India Expedition." In *The Narrative of General Venables, with an Appendix of Papers Relating to the Expedition to the West Indies and the Conquest of Jamaica, 1654–1655*, ed. Charles H. Firth. London, 1900.

White, Richard. *The Middle Ground: Indians Empires and Republics in the Great Lakes Region, 1651–1815*. Cambridge, 1991.

Wiedmann, T. E. J. *Slavery*. Oxford, 1987.

Wiles, Richard C. "The Theory of Wages in Later English Mercantilism." *Economic History Review* 21(1968):113–26.

Wilks, Ivor. "Land, Labour, Capital, and the Forest Kingdom of Asante: A Model of Early Change." In *The Evolution of Social Systems*, eds. J. Friedman and M. J. Rowlands. London, 1977.

Williams, Eric. *Capitalism and Slavery*. Chapel Hill, N.Y., 1944.

Williams, Gomer. *History of the Liverpool Privateers*. London, 1897.

Wilson, E. M. Carus. "Trends in the Export of English Woollens in the Fourteenth Century." *Economic History Review* 3(1950):162–79.

Winks, Robin. *Blacks in Canada: A History*. New Haven, Conn., 1971.

Winston, Sanford. "Indian Slavery in the Carolina Region." *Journal of Negro History* 19(1934): 431–40.

Wokeck, Marianne. "The Flow and the Composition of German Immigration to Philadelphia, 1727–1775." *Pennsylvania Magazine of History and Biography* 105(1981):249–78.

Wolf, Eric. *Europe and the People without History*. Berkeley, Calif., 1982.

Wood, Alan. "Siberian Exile in the Eighteenth Century." *Siberica* 1(1990): 39–63.

Wood, Peter H. "Indian Servitude in the Southeast." In *Handbook of North American Indians*. 20 vols., Washington 1978–. vol 4. *History of Indian White Relations*, ed. Wilcomb E. Washburn. Washington, 1988.

Woodward, Donald. *Men at Work: Labourers and Building Craftsmen in the Towns of Northern England*. Cambridge, 1995.

Wootton, David. "The Dutch Republic and the Idea of Freedom." In *Republicanism, Liberty and Commercial Society, 1649–1776*. Stanford, Calif., 1994.

Worden, Nigel. *Slavery in South Africa*. Cambridge, 1985.

Wright, Sue. "'Churmaids, Huswyfes and Hucksters': The Employment of Women in Tudor and Stuart Salisbury." In *Women and Work in Pre-Industrial England*, eds. Lindsey Charles and Lorna Duffin. London, 1985.

Wrightson, Keith. *English Society, 1580–1680*. London, 1982.

Wrigley, E. A. *People, Cities and Wealth: The Transformation of Traditional Society*. Oxford, 1987.

Zahedieh, Nuala. "Trade, Plunder, and Economic Development in Early English Jamaica." *Economic History Review* 39(1986):205–22.

Zook, George F. *The Company of Royal Adventurers Trading into Africa*. New York, 1919.

Zysberg, André. "La société des galériens au milieu de XVIIIe siècle." *Annales: économies, sociéties, civilisations* 30(1975 (January-February)):43–65.

Zysberg, André. "Galley and Hard Labor Convicts in France (1550–1850) from the Galleys to Hard Labor Camps: Essay on a Long Lasting Penal Institution." *Centrum voor Maatschappij Geschiedenis* 12(1984):78–110.

Index

abolition, 3, 12, 58, 77, 257, 259, 263, 272, 273, 273n35, 276, 278, 279, 281-4; in Americas, 82; beginnings of, 7; British, 266; capitalism and, 81; uniquely western concept, 4, 279

abolitionism, 274, 275n35, 283

Abora, 59

Accra, 174, 249-50, (map) 309

acquits de Guinée, 120

Adangme (language), 254

Adja (language), 254

Africa/Africans, 2-3, 8, 15, 19, 21; agency in shaping Atlantic World, 146; as consumers, 262-3; Dutch-English interaction with, 27-8; effect of European contact on, 23; and Europe in early modern era, 137-63; famine in, 20; impact on transatlantic slave trade, 164-92; insider status, 79, 282; kinship structures, 18, 21; plantation complex in, 139, 140-1, 144-6, 148, 149; the poor in, 20n43; population loss, 67; productive potential of, 140-5, 149; relations with Europeans, 137-9; self-perception, 3, 227; sex and age characteristics of, 285-92; shaping slave trade, 153-4, 169, 192; slave departures from, 165-7, 166t; in slave trade, 59, 131-6, 146-7, 150, 159-60, 161, 163, 178-9; slave status of, 57, 59-61, 64, 72, 73; slavery reserved for, 223, 262, 273, 279; social structures, 23; trading relations with, 13, 137, 148-9; women in slave trade from, 105-10, 112-13; women's roles in 91-4, 100

African arrivals in British Americas: coastal origins of, 244-56, 245t

African coast: slave trading on, 120, 121, 122, 125-6, 132, 135

African peoples: relations with Europeans in Americas, 63-4

African slavery in Americas, see slavery

Africanness, 226; conceptions of, 257

Africans-as-victims paradigm, 145

Afro-European relations, 160-3, 192; regional diversity in, 164-76, 184-5, 187, 189-90, 192

Afro-Portuguese, 138-9

age (slaves), 250, 252, 253, 284-97

Agga, 249

agriculture, 30, 31-2, 89, 269; and migration, 31-2; women and children in, 88, 92

Akan/Adja culture, 255-6, 257

Akwamu, 138, 182

Alampo (Alampi), 249, (map) 309

Allada, 182

Americas, 2, 3, 8, 15, 16, 19, 28; African slaves transported to, 11-12; English migration to, 38; European expansion into, 139-40, 161-2; Europeans and African slavery in, 57-84; exploitation of labor in, 26; exports from, 12-13; migration in, 13; non-European exclusivity of slavery in, 18; percentages of African males, children, women, men, girls, and boys carried to (1663-1713), 105t; sex ratio, 87; slave resistance in, 172; social structure, 23; status and rights in, 21;

339